WORLD
FOLKLORE
FOR STORYTELLERS

WORLD FOLKLORE FOR STORYTELLERS

Tales of Wonder, Wisdom, Fools, and Heroes

Josepha Sherman

SHARPE REFERENCE

an imprint of M.E. Sharpe, Inc.

SHARPE REFERENCE

Sharpe Reference is an imprint of M.E. Sharpe, Inc.

M.E. Sharpe, Inc.
80 Business Park Drive
Armonk, NY 10504

Library of Congress Cataloging-in-Publication Data

World folklore for storytellers: tales of wonder, wisdom, fools, and heroes / Josepha Sherman,
editor.
   p. cm.
Includes bibliographical references and index.
ISBN 978-0-7656-8174-4 (hardcover: alk. paper)
1. Folklore—Classification. 2. Folk literature—History and criticism. 3. Storytelling.
4. Oral tradition. I. Sherman, Josepha.

GR72.56.W67 2010
398.09—dc22   2009010525

Cover image: Rumpelstiltskin spinning, illustration from "Once Upon a Time" published by
Ernest Mister, c.1900 (color litho) by G.H. Thompson (twentieth century). Private Collection/
The Bridgeman Art Library.

Printed and bound in the United States of America

The paper used in this publication meets the minimum requirements of
American National Standard for Information Sciences
Permanence of Paper for Printed Library Materials,
ANSI Z 39.48.1984.

(c) 10 9 8 7 6 5 4 3 2 1

Publisher: Myron E. Sharpe
Vice President and Director of New Product Development: Donna Sanzone
Vice President and Production Director: Carmen Chetti
Executive Development Editor: Jeff Hacker
Project Manager: Laura Brengelman
Program Coordinator: Cathleen Prisco
Assistant Editor: Alison Morretta
Text Design: Carmen Chetti and Jesse Sanchez
Cover Design: Jesse Sanchez

Contents

v

HERO TALES

TALES OF FOOLS AND WISE PEOPLE

Introduction

What is folklore? Literally, it is the collected lore—the stories, jokes, customs and related beliefs, folk arts and music, and more—of the folk, in this case, of people everywhere. This book narrows the subject to concentrate only on folktales, the stories of the people.

The actual English words *folklore* and *folktale* are not very old. The first use of the term *folklore* was by an English antiquarian, William Thoms, in 1846. For about 100 years after that, no one could agree on the proper spelling. Was it "folklore," "folk-lore," or even "Folk Lore"? And were the tales to be called "folktales" or "folk tales"? Variant spellings still are to be found.

But regardless of written semantics, folklore itself goes back as far as human history. The earliest folktales we know come from ancient Sumer and Egypt. These folktales were written down by scribes in the third and second millennia B.C.E., but the stories may be far older. Obviously, folktale research can go back only as far as written records exist.

There are tantalizing hints, though, that the original versions of folktales we know may date back to preliterate times. For instance, in a folktale from England in which a hero slays a giant, the giant's last wish is to be buried in a mound. Does this date the folktale, or at least that segment of it, to the first millennium B.C.E. or even earlier? Or did some more recent storyteller see the mounds and think they would make a fine burial place for a giant? After all, folktales often accrete to what is not thoroughly understood.

A case in point is the Long Barrow in Wiltshire, England. It is a first millennium B.C.E. "family" burial site, and it is literally a long burial mound. But newcomers to the region, such as the Celts, were not sure what the mound was. A nineteenth-century folktale claims that a man in flowing white robes walked on top of the mound in the company of a red-eared white dog. The red-eared white dog is a traditional Celtic image of a fairy dog, and the man in those robes is probably someone's passed-down image of a Celtic druid.

However old folktales may be, it is fascinating that parallels can be drawn between them. We are all human, after all, and we experience the same human emotions. Carl Jung, a pioneering psychiatrist who was fascinated with folklore, coined the term *collective unconscious* to reference the archetypical images all human beings have in common. These include such figures as the Wise Old Man or Woman, the Trickster, the Shadow, and many others.

Thus, the concept of the collective unconscious helps explain why cultures separated by continents have similar folktales. Another explanation might be simply that people, even in the days before the wheel was discovered, traveled widely. And they took their stories with them.

Hearing a new folktale, a storyteller might not remember it perfectly or might not be familiar with a cultural reference. In such a case, the storyteller might "plug in" an episode of his or her own, which would explain different versions and cultural variations in the tales.

An example is the "Cinderella" tale type, or category of folktale—at least 920 variants of this tale have been collected by folklorists around the world. Those Cinderella tales from cultures without a concept of a "fairy godmother" might feature a helpful animal, the ghost of the heroine's mother, or even, in Jewish Cinderella stories, the Prophet Elijah. But regardless of such variations, these still are recognizable as Cinderella stories.

Whatever scholars wish to make of them, folktales are our stories—we, the people of this world. Folktales belong to us all, and it is up to us, this modern generation, to keep these treasured tales alive through reading and telling them.

Josepha Sherman

Wonder Tales

Wonder tales are what people usually imagine when they hear the word *folktale*. These are the most familiar folktales, including tales of magic, strange beings, and enchanted transformations. "Cinderella" is a wonder tale, as is "Beauty and the Beast," as are tales of dragon-slayers and lands that lie "east o' the sun and west o' the moon."

In wonder tales, there are magical beasts and fairy folk, witches good or bad, and incredible magicians. There are swords with wills of their own and quests that last for magical lengths—three days, seven months, even seven years. There are marvelous places with evocative names, such as the above-mentioned East o' the Sun and West o' the Moon, and realms above the sky or beneath the sea.

The natural laws do not apply in wonder tales, in which rocks may talk or heroes turn into animals without explanation, but some constants exist. The third son or daughter often is the one to succeed. While scholars argue the reasons (some claim ancient laws of inheritance, now forgotten), the idea of the third child succeeding is ingrained in wonder stories from around the world.

In these stories, a good heart, kindness, loyalty, and courage often are keys to happiness. Perhaps the most important constant in a wonder tale is the triumph of good over evil.

BEAUTY AND THE BEAST

"Beauty and the Beast" is one of the most popular of archetype folktales—that is, a folktale that appears in every culture in some form or another, and is always greeted with delight. Variants on the tale include monster husbands, snake husbands, crocodile husbands, dog husbands, and indeed almost every animal imaginable—all under a spell, all ultimately transformed by the love and steadfastness of the heroine. Sometimes, her love is enough. Sometimes, she must undergo an ordeal or a quest to win her love. In some versions, the animal man is a supernatural being who can take either shape. He may be human, or he may be a nature spirit, such as in North American tribal tales of women marrying fish deities or bear spirits.

Another popular worldwide variant on the major folktale type is the animal bride, the theme of the transformed female and the human male. The forms the female "animal" takes vary widely. She may be a fox, a swan, a frog, even a snake. She may be a human under a spell, a nonhuman being such as a *kitsune,* a Japanese fox being, changing to human on a whim or for love of a human man, a seal-being whose skin has been captured by the man, or a spirit such as the Chinese White Snake, who falls so deeply in love with her husband that she goes on a quest to save his life.

Falling into this latter category are fairy brides, who sometimes are won by a human groom without disguise but who often are captured. The human hero often will catch his bride when she is in human form and steal her magic skin or other object so that she must remain human. In such cases, the marriage ends with her recovering her magic and returning to animal form. In other stories, the marriage may be happy so long as the human husband does not criticize his nonhuman bride. Once he does, the marriage is over, and she returns to her own kind.

In still other animal bride stories, the hero is forced to marry an animal, only to learn that she really is an enchanted human. These stories tend to end happily for bride and groom. However, other animal bride tales do not end happily for the human man. His wife may return to her people, or she may abandon him. But some of these tales do show a nice compromise: In a Japanese fox bride tale, the fox wife returns every night to her human husband as his wife.

Because the transformed beast can be male or female, this section has been divided into two main categories: "The Transformed Female" and "The Transformed Male."

The Transformed Female

The transformed female, unlike the transformed male, usually is a free shapeshifter, often a magical animal who can transform into a human female. Sometimes, this is a voluntary shift on her part, although in certain cases, such as the tales of swan maidens, it is the theft by a human man of her magical garb that holds her in human form.

Fox Brides

The idea of a fox being able to turn into a woman or, more rarely, a man, turns up mostly in Asia, although the folk motif also can be found in other cultures, such as the Inuit tale told below. The basic story line tends to follow that of all animal-human matings, with the animal wife being unintentionally (or intentionally) insulted by her human husband and fleeing back to the wild. For similar endings, see the section on seal people.

The Fox Wife: A Folktale from Japan

Stories of fox spirits, known in Japanese as *kitsune,* have been popular throughout Japan for literally centuries. This tale, which may date as far back as the eighth century C.E., claims to give the origin of *kitsune,* the word for fox spirit, since the word can mean *kitsu-ne* ("come and sleep") or *ki-tsune* ("always comes").

There was a female fox who fell in love with a human man. To be with him, she turned herself into a woman and wooed him. They fell in love, and even though she admitted to him that she actually was a fox, they married and were very happy together. Years passed, and they had several children together.

But, sadly, the fox wife's secret could not stay hidden forever. Even as a woman, she remained terrified of dogs. And when a dog threatened her in front of everyone in the village, she instinctively returned to her fox shape.

Now that her secret was known, she knew that she must leave her happy home. But her loving husband begged her to stay with him at least part of the time.

"We have spent so many happy years together," he told her. "We have had several children together. My dear wife, I cannot simply forget you. Please come to me every night."

The fox could not deny her love for him. So she agreed. From that night on, she returned to her husband in the shape of a woman, leaving again each morning in the shape of a fox.

Sources
Mayer, Fanny Hagin, trans. *Ancient Tales in Modern Japan: An Anthology of Japanese Folk Tales.* Bloomington: Indiana University Press, 1984.

Nozaki, Kiyoshi. *Kitsune: Japan's Fox of Mystery, Romance and Humor.* Tokyo, Japan: Hokuseido, 1961.

The Fox Woman: A Folktale from the Inuit of Labrador, Canada

This folktale has an element common to many tales of nonhuman brides, the taboo against complaining about any aspect of the bride. Here, the husband's complaint is about the fox bride's foxy scent.

Once, there was a hunter who lived by himself. But one day when he came home, he saw that someone had taken care of everything, just as a nice wife would do. There was even a hot meal waiting for him.

Who could this mysterious person be?

The hunter left the next day as though going on a hunt, but instead he hid and watched and waited. He saw a fox slip into the house. Aha, it must be looking for food! The hunter followed it inside—and found himself facing the most beautiful woman he had ever seen. A fox skin hung on a peg on one wall of the house.

"Are you the one who has been keeping my house?" the hunter asked.

"I have become your wife," the woman said demurely. "I trust that you are satisfied?"

Oh, he was very satisfied! They lived together happily for a time.

But one day, the hunter noticed a musky smell, a wild-thing smell. Once he had noticed it, the smell seemed to grow stronger and wilder. At last, he asked his wife what it was.

"That is my fox smell," she said. "Don't you like it?"

"It is not the smell of a normal woman."

"If you are going to find fault with me, then I am gone!" the fox woman cried. She snatched up her fox skin, changed back into a fox, and raced away.

The hunter was left alone.

Sources
Thompson, Stith. *Folk Tales of the North American Indians.* 1929. North Dighton, MA: J.G., 1995.
Turner, Lucien M. "Ethnology of the Ungava District, Hudson Bay Territory." In *Report of the Bureau of American Ethnology.* Vol. 11. Washington, DC: Smithsonian Institution, 1894.

The Fox Wife: A Folktale from Korea

Folktales often are attached to historic figures. This fox-wife tale is the only one to give such a figure a fox for a mother. Whether or not Kang Kamch'an (948–1031 C.E.), a famous general of the early Koryo period, was aware of this story or whether it started up after his death is unknown.

Once, when a man was walking alone along a lonely mountain road, the storm winds began to blow. Looking for shelter, he saw the lights of a house, and ran to it. He was made welcome by a beautiful young woman, the only resident there. For three days the storm raged, and for three days, the man and woman stayed together and became lovers.

When the storm ended, the man set out for his home, promising to return to his lover. But when he tried to find her house again, he never could.

Years passed. Then one day, the woman appeared at his home, leading a boy child by the hand. She said to the man, "The house you entered that stormy night was not a human's home. It was the shelter of a fox. I am that fox, and I was in woman form when we loved. This is your child. I have foreseen great things for him, so I wish him to be raised as a human, as your son."

As soon as the man took the child in his arms, the woman vanished. She had, indeed, been a fox.

She also was right about her prophesy for their son. He grew up to be Kang Kamch'an, who became a great general for Korea's king.

Source

Grayson, James H. *Myths and Legends from Korea. An Annotated Compendium of Ancient and Modern Materials.* London: Routledge, 2000; Richmond, United Kingdom: Curzon, 2001. Reprint of story recorded in 1923 by Son Chint'ae in Koesan County, North Ch'ungch'ong Province from a local man, An Chusang.

Frog Brides

Although these amphibians may seem less romantic than fox brides, almost as many world tales feature a frog-into-woman transformation as fox brides. One reason for the popularity of such tales may be the idea of the small and seemingly helpless actually having power, even over the high and mighty. Another reason may be the seemingly magical nature of the transformation of pollywog into frog.

The Frog Maiden: A Folktale from Burma

This folktale features a theme common to world folktales: the longed-for child who turns out to be an animal in shape but is otherwise a normal human child. In these tales, the animal shape is only a shell, and the human appears seemingly at will, with no major spell to be broken.

Once, there lived an aging couple whose one sorrow was that they had no children. Then, when the wife found that she was with child, they were filled with joy. But the wife did not give birth to a human child. She gave birth to a little female frog.

However, they soon learned that the little frog behaved and even spoke like a human child. Her parents came to love her and called her "Little Miss Frog."

Sadly, the mother died. The father was married again, this time to a widow with two ugly daughters. They took an instant dislike to Little Miss Frog and did their best to be cruel to her.

One day, the youngest of the king's four sons announced that he would perform the hair-washing ceremony, a coming of age ritual, and he invited all young ladies to join in the ceremony. At the end of it, he would choose one of them to be his princess.

On the morning of the ceremony, the two ugly sisters put on their finest clothing and started for the palace, each of them full of hope that she would be the chosen one. Little Miss Frog ran after them, even though they ignored her.

Upon reaching the palace, Little Miss Frog spoke so politely to the guards that they let her go in. There, she found crowds of maidens waiting for the prince, standing in a circle around a lovely pool of clear blue water.

Suddenly, the ladies all fell silent as the prince appeared. He was so handsome! He washed his hair in the pool, and the maidens all let down their hair and washed it as well, joining in the ritual of cleaning. But at the end of the ceremony, the prince looked around and sighed.

"You are all so beautiful that I do not know which of you to chose. And so I will throw a strand of jasmine into the air, and she on whom it lands shall be my bride."

The jasmine landed right on Little Miss Frog. The prince was surprised and alarmed, but knew he had to keep his word. So he and the frog were wed, making her Little Princess Frog.

Not long after, the old king called his four sons together and said, "My sons, I feel I am now grown too old to rule, and wish to retire. I shall give you a task to perform, and he who can perform it shall be king in my place. You are to bring me a golden deer at dawn seven days from now."

The youngest prince went home to Little Princess Frog and told her about the task.

"Is that all?" Princess Frog exclaimed. "Have no worry, my prince. On the seventh day you will have your golden deer."

So the youngest prince stayed at home, while the three elder princes went into the forest in search of the deer. And sure enough, on the seventh day, the youngest prince arrived at the palace with a pure gold deer. The other three sons had found only ordinary deer. To their disappointment, the youngest son was declared the royal heir.

"Give us a second chance!" they pleaded with their father.

"Very well," he said. "On the seventh day from now, bring me rice that never grows stale and meat that never spoils."

The youngest prince went home and told Princess Frog about the new task. "Do not worry, my sweet prince," she said. "On the appointed day, I will have the rice and meat."

Sure enough, on the appointed day, Princess Frog handed the youngest prince the rice and meat. And the rice would not grow stale, nor would the meat spoil. The youngest son was again declared the royal heir.

But the three elder princes again pleaded for one more chance, and the king said, "This is positively the last task. On the seventh day from now at sunrise, bring me the most beautiful woman in the world."

The three elder princes were delighted. "Our wives are very beautiful, and we will bring them. One of us is sure to be named heir, and our weak little young brother will be nowhere!"

What could the youngest prince do? His wife was a frog!

"Do not worry, my dear," said Princess Frog. "Take me to the palace on the appointed day. Surely I shall be named the most beautiful woman."

The young prince was astonished, but she had, after all, helped him win the first two tests. "Very well," he said. "I shall take you to the palace."

On the appointed day, when the prince entered the audience chamber with his frog princess, the three elder princes with their wives already were there.

The king looked at the prince in surprise and asked, "Where is your beautiful maiden?"

"I will answer for the prince, my king," said the frog princess. "I am his beautiful maiden."

She then took off her frog skin and stood there, a beautiful maiden dressed in silk and satin. The king declared her to be the most beautiful maiden in the world, and selected the prince as his successor on the throne. The prince asked his princess never to put on the ugly frog skin again, and the former frog princess said, "I will never need it again."

With that, she threw the skin on the fire.

Sources
Aung, Maung Htin. *Burmese Folk-Tales.* Calcutta, India: Oxford University Press, 1948.
Hla, Ludu U. *Folktales of Burma.* Mandalay, Burma: Letsaigan, Gondanwin, 1972.

The Frog Tzarina: A Folktale from Russia

At least three Russian versions of this folktale are known, though in almost all, the youngest son has the traditional name of Ivan. Sometimes, the bride is Vasilisa the Beautiful, sometimes Elena the Fair. Sometimes, the story ends right after Ivan's bride wins the contest. Sometimes, it continues on, and Baba Yaga—or three sister Baba Yagas—becomes involved. Sometimes, the new bridegroom is nameless, and sometimes, he is Koschei the Deathless. The only elements that remain the same throughout the versions are the frog skin, the test of the hero, and the three tests of the brides.

Once, there was, and once, there was not a tzar with three sons. The tzar decided that it was time for his three sons to get married, and he called them together.

"Each of you is to shoot an arrow, and whatever maiden is nearest where your arrow lands will be your bride."

The eldest son drew back his bow and shot his arrow. It hit next to a nobleman's daughter.

The middle son then drew his bow, and shot his arrow. It landed by a merchant's daughter.

Then, it was the turn of the youngest son, Ivan. He shot his arrow—but it flew off into a swamp and landed next to a frog. His bride was to be a frog!

"Never fear," said the frog. "All may still be well for us both."

Soon after his sons were married, the tzar called them together once more.

"I have decided to give your wives certain tasks to see who can achieve the best results. The first task is to see who can bake the finest loaf of bread."

Ivan went home and told his frog bride about baking the bread.

"Do not worry," the frog replied. "Now, my dear, go to bed and sleep."

After Ivan was sound asleep, the frog removed her skin and turned into Vasilisa the Beautiful. She clapped her hands, and mysterious servants came running to her aid.

When Ivan awoke the next morning, the frog said, "See?" There on the table was a beautiful loaf of perfectly baked white bread.

The tzar tasted the loaf of the first wife. Bah! He spat out a pebble. He tasted the loaf of the second wife. Bah! He spat out unbaked grains. Then, he tasted the loaf of the frog bride.

"Delicious!" the tzar said. "I declare Ivan's wife the winner."

The second task, the tzar declared, was to weave a beautiful carpet. Once again, the frog sent Ivan to bed, shed her skin, summoned her servants, and created a magnificent carpet.

The tzar looked at the carpet of the first wife. No! There were great patches of missing thread. He looked at the carpet of the second wife. No! There were smears all over where the dye had run. He looked at the carpet of the frog wife.

"Wonderful!" the tzar said. "I declare Ivan's wife the winner."

The third task, the tzar declared, was to see which wife could dance the best at the royal ball. Now Ivan was worried. He went home and told the frog the story.

"Do not worry," the frog said. "Just be sure to arrive at the ball alone, and I will follow an hour later."

And so Ivan arrived alone, and an hour later his wife, Vasilisa the Beautiful, arrived. Everyone gasped to see her. She began to dance, and as she danced, she took up a bone from the table and slipped it into her right sleeve. She took up a goblet and shook the last drops into her left sleeve. Now as she danced, she waved her right hand, and a lake and a woodland appeared. She waved her left hand, and a flock of singing birds appeared. She stopped dancing, and all that disappeared. Smiling, she took her seat beside Ivan.

The other two wives tried to copy her. But when they waved their right hands, the bones flew out of their sleeves and hit the guests. When they waved their left hands, the guests were sprinkled with wine.

"Enough of this!" cried the tzar. "Ivan's wife has won!"

When Ivan got home, the first thing he did was to cast the frog skin into the fire.

"No!" cried Vasilisa. "If only you had waited a year, I would have been yours forever. Now I must leave! Seek me beyond the thrice ninth kingdom, in the thrice tenth kingdom."

With that, she vanished.

Ivan set out on a quest to find her again. He came at last to an odd hut on chicken legs, which were turning the hut around and around. Ivan, wise in some strange ways, knew what to say. "Little hut, little hut, stand the old way, thy back to the forest, thy front to me."

The hut stopped. Within the hut sat Baba Yaga, an eerie, mysterious, and magical old hag. Ivan knew that she ate the occasional traveler, but that he must show her courtesy and bravery.

Baba Yaga commented that Russian bones made not a sound, but here came Russian bones to her of their own free will. "Whither go you, Prince Ivan?"

"First, good old mother, give me food and drink, and then I will answer your questions."

Baba Yaga fed him, and heard his story. "I fear that your wife already has forgotten you. But there is still hope. I will send you on to my older sister. She knows more about this than I."

So off Ivan went to the next Baba Yaga, who Ivan thought looked just like the first one. But she greeted him with, "It took you long enough to get here! Your wife has forgotten you and is about to marry someone else. She is staying with my eldest sister. When you get there, you will see that she is disguised as a golden spindle, and her golden dress as the thread. My sister will wind up the thread and put the spindle and thread into a box. You must find the key, open the box, break the spindle and cast the top before you, the bottom behind you, and then shall you find your wife again."

So off Ivan went to the eldest Baba Yaga, who Ivan thought looked just like the other two. He hid and waited until she had finished winding the golden thread on the golden spindle, then put the thread and spindle into a box. He watched her lock it, then watched to see where she hid the key.

Aha! Ivan seized the key, opened the box, and broke the spindle as he had been told, throwing the top in front of him, the bottom behind him. And there was his wife!

"Ivan!" she cried. "You have been so long in coming for me. I almost married someone else—but now I remember you and all about you. Let us go home."

The other bridegroom was coming for Vasilisa the Beautiful. But the eldest Baba Yaga gave Ivan and his wife a magic carpet, and they flew home.

Sources
Afanas'ev, Aleksander. *Russian Fairy Tales*. New York: Pantheon, 1945.
Ralston, W.R.S. *Russian Folk-Tales*. London: Smith, Elder and Son, 1873.
Thompson, Stith. *One Hundred Favorite Folktales*. Bloomington and Indianapolis: Indiana University Press, 1968.

The Little Singing Frog: A Folktale from the Czech Republic

An unusual feature in this tale is the prince's ability to see that beauty is only skin deep: He loves the frog's voice and is willing to marry her even when he learns that she is in frog shape. The shape does not matter to him because he likes her so much. This goes against the usual reluctance of a prince in this tale type to wed a frog, or for that matter, an ugly person.

Once, there was a poor man and his wife who had no children. Every day they would sigh for a child, a little daughter. One day, they went to a shrine and prayed for a child. The wife said, "I would be glad for any child of our own, even if it were a frog!"

Their prayers were answered. They had a child, a daughter—a little frog daughter. They loved their little frog child dearly. But when they heard the neighbors whisper about their child being a frog, they grew ashamed. They decided that when people were around, they would keep the frog girl hidden.

So the frog girl grew up without playmates of her own age, seeing only her father and mother. She sometimes would hop up into the branches of a tree and sing. And she sang so very sweetly that even the birds grew still to listen, and so she became known as the Little Singing Frog.

One day, the Tzar's youngest son rode by and heard the frog girl singing. He heard the sweet song, but could not find the singer.

"She must be a truly lovely girl with so sweet a voice. If only I could find her, I would marry her and take her home to my father's palace."

"I hear you," said the Little Singing Frog, as she hopped down from the branches.

"I do not care that you are a frog," the prince told her. "I love your singing, and so I love you. And I mean to marry you if you will marry me."

"I will!" said the Little Singing Frog.

"I nearly forgot!" cried the prince. "My father, the Tzar, bids me and my brothers bring our brides to him tomorrow. Each bride must bring him a flower. He will give the kingdom to the prince whose bride brings the finest flower."

"I can do that," said the Little Singing Frog. "But I cannot come hopping to the royal court. I must ride. You shall send me a snow white rooster."

"I will," the prince promised. And before night, the snow white rooster was there.

Early the next morning, the Little Singing Frog prayed to the Sun. "Oh golden Sun, give me a gown woven of your golden rays so that I do not shame my prince when I go to the royal court."

The Sun heard her prayer and gave her a gown of cloth of gold. Instead of a flower, the Little Singing Frog took a spear of wheat in her hand. Then, she mounted the white rooster and rode to the palace. At first, the palace guards did not want to admit a mere frog. But when she told them she was the youngest prince's bride, they were afraid to drive her away and let her enter.

The Little Singing Frog dropped the golden gown over her head, and suddenly she became a lovely maiden on a snow-white horse. She entered the palace with the two other promised brides and outshone them both.

The first bride carried a rose. The Tzar looked at it and her and then shook his head.

The second bride carried a carnation. The Tzar looked at it and her and then shook his head.

Then the third bride, she who had been Little Singing Frog, approached with her stalk of wheat. The Tzar looked at it and her, and nodded. He took the stalk of wheat from her, and said to all the court, "This, the bride of my youngest son, is my choice! See how beautiful she is! But she is clever as well, for she has not brought me some quickly fading blossom, but a stalk of wheat, and wheat is the most beautiful for it feeds us all. My youngest son shall be the Tzar after me, and she shall be the Tzarina, his bride."

So it was. And every day the prince listened in delight as his wife sang to him in her sweet voice.

Sources

Baudis, Josef. *The Key of Gold: 23 Czech Folk Tales.* London: Allen and Unwin, 1917; Iowa City, IA: Penfield, 1992.

Fillmore, Parker. *The Laughing Prince: Jugoslav Folk and Fairy Tales.* New York: Harcourt, Brace, 1921.

The Frog Wife: A Folktale from the Cochiti of New Mexico

This folktale from the Cochiti people is different from the usual type in that the frog wife comes to realize that she liked her amphibian life better than her human one, especially with her froggy choice of many lovers. As a result, she simply leaves her chosen human without any prohibitions being broken.

There was a frog girl who decided to turn into a human woman. Soon after that, she saw a handsome young man and made a second decision to marry him. He liked the look of her, too, never guessing what she really was, and he married her.

They set out together for his home. It was a long walk for a human, and longer still for a frog girl not used to walking. "Is your home very far away?" she asked. "I am very tired."

"We are almost there," he told her. "See? There is the village. And there is the house. I live on the east side of it, on the second story."

They went up. "Grandmother," the man called, "here is a daughter-in-law."

"With all my heart, I welcome her," the old woman said.

They all ate together, and then the man and his new wife went to bed. The old woman said to herself, "I will help the new wife. I will shell some corn for her so she will be able to grind it in the morning."

When the daughter-in-law was awake, she began to grind the corn. Her husband went out hunting as she prepared the corn meal. The husband came back with rabbits, and they all had a fine meal.

But the next morning, the new wife had to do the shelling and grinding herself. She found it very difficult. She could not seem to break even one kernel of the corn. And she began to sing:

> Wa! Wa! (It was the sound a frog makes.)
> Wa! Wa!
> Down at the river are many lovers.
> For that I am homesick.
> Wa! Wa!

She remembered how nice it had been to be a frog with no corn to grind. She remembered the cool river and the many frog lovers.

That night, the grandmother woke up. She called for the new wife, but there was no answer. She got up to look, but there was no one there.

The frog girl went back to the river, dropped back into frog form, and lived there forever.

Source
Benedict, Ruth. *Tales of the Cochiti Indians.* Bureau of American Ethnology Bulletin no. 98.
    Washington, DC: Smithsonian, 1931.

Silkies/Selchies and Seal Brides

Selchie is the Gaelic word for seal, and is pronounced Sel-key. This often is heard and written as Silky. There are many stories about seal brides, mostly from Celtic lands such as Scotland and Ireland, which are surrounded by water. A seal's melting brown eyes probably looked human to early Celtic folk, and this may have inspired the idea that some seals could shed their skins and take human form—and human lovers. Some families in Ireland and Scotland even claim selchie ancestry, and anyone born with heavier than normal webbing between his or her fingers is said to have selchie blood.

Tom Moore and the Seal Woman: A Folktale from Kerry, Ireland

Seal bride stories always involve the stealing of the sealskin or sealskin hood by the human male. They always end with the seal bride recovering her stolen property. She may or may not be reluctant to leave, but she always returns to her seal people.

At one time, there lived a fine young man named Tom Moore. He was all alone in the world, but tending his farm gave him no time to be lonely. He did, though, begin to long for a wife.

One day, walking on the sea strand, Tom saw the loveliest of women lying asleep on a rock in the sun. The tide was coming in, and he called to her in alarm, "Wake up! When the tide rises, you will be drowned!"

She woke but only laughed at his warning. She slipped easily into the water and was gone.

Tom did no more work that day, thinking of her. He got no sleep that night, thinking of her. In the morning, he returned to the sea strand, and there she was.

"Good morning to you," Tom called.

She gave him no answer.

"Will you come with me?" he asked.

Again, she said nothing. But this time, Tom saw the sealskin hood she wore, and knew what he had only suspected until then. This was a seal woman. He rushed forward and snatched the hood from her.

"Give me my hood!" she cried.

"I will not," he answered. "The Good Lord brought us together, and I'm thinking my wife you will be."

She made no argument. He took her before the priest, and they were wed.

The woman made the finest wife, and Tom and she lived in harmony for seven years. In that time, they had three sons and two daughters. The only strangeness about her was that she would not tolerate the killing of a seal, calling it murder. The villagers were well aware of what she was, but for Tom's sake, they stopped killing seals.

Then one day, the woman was cleaning the house and found the sealskin hood. At that moment, a great seal began roaring from the sea. "That is my brother looking for me," she said.

She set everything in the house in order. She kissed her children, each in turn. And then she returned to the sea.

They say that even to this day, the descendants of Tom Moore and his seal wife have the seal webbing between their fingers and toes.

Sources

Curtin, Jeremiah. *Irish Folk-Tales.* Dublin: Educational Company of Ireland, 1943.
———. *Tales of the Fairies and of the Ghost World Collected from Oral Tradition in South-West Munster.* Boston: Little, Brown, 1895; New York: B. Blom, 1971.
Glassie, Henry. *Irish Folk Tales.* New York: Pantheon, 1985.

MacCodrum and His Seal Wife: A Folktale from Scotland

In this seal bride tale, once the seal woman has recovered her sealskin she again returns to the sea. But in this version, there is a slight difference: She retains an interest in her half-human offspring and keeps a guardian eye on them.

Though his full name has not been recorded, he was a young man of the Mac-Codrum clan. It was the day after a storm, and he was down beachcombing, looking to see what valuables and edible seaweeds might have been washed ashore. All at once, he heard people laughing and singing.

Curious, the young man stole forward, not wanting to intrude where he had not been invited, but wondering who might be having a party on the beach.

What he saw made him stare in wonder. Seals were making for the beach, then slipping out of their skins and becoming fair men and women joining the dance. And oh, there was one young woman who seemed to him fairer than all the rest.

He watched to see what would happen. The other seals, one by one, grew weary of the dance and put on their sealskins, leaving human form and diving into the waves.

He could not lose her like that, the young man thought. And so he stole down to where the lovely young woman had left her skin. He hid it away.

When the lovely one came to look for her skin, she could not find it, and began to wail and weep. The other seals, frightened, swam off and left her, but the young man was ready and took her in his arms, gentling her terror with soothing words.

She knew he had her skin, and begged him for it, but he ignored that, and brought the lovely one home. When she was not watching, he hid the skin away in the rafters in the barn.

Time passed, and the lovely one went from weeping and pining away to smiling and, at last, seeming fully human. She and the young man now loved each other, and they wed.

The years passed. They had several lovely children, and the woman seemed quite content.

Then, it happened that one of the children, playing in the barn up in the rafters, found the sealskin. "Oh, Mother," he said that night as she was putting him to bed, "I found such a lovely thing in the barn today."

"And what was it?"

"A sealskin, all soft and beautiful."

She knew then what she was and what she must become. "I am going away, my loves. But I shall always watch over you, and you will never want for fish."

She was never again seen in human form. But now and again, a seal would come to shore and call, and leave fish for the children. And they knew it must be their seal mother watching over them as she had promised.

Sources

Bruford, Alan, and Donald A. MacDonald. *Scottish Traditional Tales*. Edinburgh, United Kingdom: Polygon, 1994. Tale recorded from Donald MacDougall, North Uist, by Angus John MacDonald, 1968, for the Sound Archive of the School of Scottish Studies, University of Edinburgh.

Pottinger, J.A. "The Selkie Wife." In *Old-Lore Miscellany of Orkney, Shetland, Caithness and Sutherland*. Vol. 1. 1908. Leicester, United Kingdom: The Viking Society for Northern Research, 1992.

Mermaid Brides

Folktales featuring mermaids as brides most often follow the shape of the seal bride folktales: The bride is captured when the human male steals her skin (or other magical item), forcing her to stay in human form. She often escapes when she steals back the missing magic item.

But there are exceptions. Not all mermaids make human brides. Some steal human men and pull them undersea—where the men generally drown. Other mermaids refuse to be brides at all.

The Lady of Gollerus: A Folktale from Ireland

In this version of the captured transformed bride story, the merrow, or mermaid, uses a magic cap to make her transformation.

On the shore of Smerwick harbor, near the town of Gollerus, one fine summer's morning, Dick Fitzgerald was astonished to find a beautiful young woman combing her yellow-green hair.

What else could this lovely woman be but a merrow, a mermaid? There it was, the *cohuleen druith*, or little enchanted cap, which the sea people used for diving down into the ocean, lying near her. He knew that if he took the cap, she would be trapped in mortal form, and so he snatched it away. The merrow cried out in despair and burst into tears that tore at Dick's heart. But he would not give up the cap.

"Don't cry, my darling," he begged, and took her hand. "What's your name, darling?"

But either she failed to understand him or else she could not speak. Then, without warning, she asked, "Do you mean to eat me?"

"I'd sooner eat myself!" Dick cried.

"Man," said the merrow, "what will you do with me, if you will not eat me?"

"Why, I'll marry you," he said.

She agreed. But first she whispered to the water, then added, "I am just sending word to my father not to worry."

Away they went across the strand to Father Fitzgibbon and were wed. Like any other newlyweds, they returned to Dick's home well pleased with each other. The merrow made the best of wives, and they lived together in the greatest contentment. At the end of three years, they had two boys and a girl.

One day, Dick went off to market, leaving the wife minding the children at home.

Dick was no sooner gone than Mrs. Fitzgerald set about cleaning up the house, and what should she find in a hole in the wall but her own cohuleen druith? She took it out and looked at it, and then she remembered her family and the freedom of the open sea, and felt a great longing to return to them and it.

It must be. She kissed her children, and then went down to the strand. In that instant, seeing the open sea, family and husband were forgotten. Truly a merrow again, she placed the cohuleen druith on her head and plunged into the sea.

When Dick came home in the evening, he found his wife gone—and with her, the cohuleen druith.

Year after year, did Dick Fitzgerald wait, expecting the return of his wife, but he never saw her again. To this day, she is still remembered as the Lady of Gollerus.

Sources

Croker, Thomas Crofton. *Fairy Legends and Traditions of the South of Ireland*. Vol. 2. London: Murray, 1828.

O'Sullivan, Sean, ed. and trans. *Folktales of Ireland*. Chicago and London: University of Chicago Press, 1966.

Ne Hwas, the Mermaids: A Folktale from the Passamaquoddy of New England

Here is a variant on the theme: Two sisters who become mermaids avoid being snared by a human. Even though he seizes the hair that should make one of the mermaids his bride, the other sister threatens him with drowning until he gives up, and no marriage is made.

Once, there was a husband and wife and their two daughters.

The two daughters were wild young things. Most of all, they loved swimming in the forbidden lake (some say the sea). One day, they failed to return. When their parents went looking for them, all they found were the girls' clothing on the shore.

Then, the father saw them swimming far out in the water. He called to them. They came up to the shore, but would not leave the water.

When he saw them up close, he realized why. They had changed in the forbidden water. From the waist down, they were water snakes. They also had become very beautiful, with long black hair floating in the water and large, dark eyes. Their father tried to offer them their clothes, but they sang sweetly:

> Leave them there.
> Do not touch them.
> Leave them there.

Now their mother began to weep. But the girls sang sweetly to her:

> It is not your fault.
> It is all our fault.
> But do not blame us.
> We are happy.
> You shall not want.
> When you go in your canoe,
> Just relax.
> We shall carry it along.

So it was that whenever their parents wished to travel by canoe, the girls would pull it for them.

Time passed, and the girls forgot they had ever been human. One day, a man saw them sporting in the water and wished them for wives. He had heard that if one cut off a mermaid's long black hair, she would become his captive.

So he set out in his canoe, caught one mermaid by her long black hair, and cut it off.

But the other mermaid began to rock his canoe so savagely, demanding back her sister's hair, that he became terrified that they were going to drown him. At last, he tossed the hair back.

And that was the last time anyone tried to catch a mermaid.

Sources
Leland, Charles G. *The Algonquin Legends of New England, or, Myths and Folk Lore of the Micmac, Passamaquoddy, and Penobscot Tribes.* Boston: Houghton Mifflin, 1884.
Parsons, Elsie Clews. *Micmac Folklore.* Whitefish, MT: Kessinger, 2007.

Swan Brides and Other Bird Maidens

Though swans are, in reality, rather foul-tempered birds, they are lovely and graceful to see, and it is not difficult to see a connection between their grace and the idealized grace of a folktale heroine. The same is true of other graceful birds, such as the crane, a bird that is a favorite image in Japanese folklore.

The Swan Maiden: A Folktale from Sweden

This is the most typical form of the swan maiden folktale: The bride stays with her husband until she can get back her feathered garb, and then, unlike the seal wife, who often shows some regret, leaves him without a backward glance.

Once, a young hunter saw three swans flying toward him and land nearby. Stalking them, he was amazed to see the swans leave off their feathers and become three beautiful maidens. They played in the water for a time, then put on their feathery garb once more, turned back into swans, and flew away.

One of them, the youngest and fairest, had so captured the young man's heart that he knew he must win her. His mother was wise in such matters. She told him, "Go back to where you saw them last. Wait until the chosen one has left her feathery garb and take it."

He did just that. Two of the swans took wing, but the third one, unable to find her feathery garb, soon found the young hunter instead. She begged him to return her swan garb to her, but the hunter could not give her up, and instead he took her to his home.

Preparations were soon made for a wedding. After that, the young couple dwelt lovingly and contentedly together for seven years.

Then, one fateful evening, the hunter showed his wife her swan garb. It was a foolish move.

No sooner had he revealed the feathery garb than she seized it, became a swan once more, and took flight. The hunter saw his wife no more, and he perished soon after from sheer loneliness and loss.

Sources
Booss, Claire, ed. *Scandinavian Folk and Fairy Tales: Tales from Norway, Sweden, Denmark, Finland, Iceland*. New York: Avenel, 1984.

Hofberg, Herman. *Swedish Fairy Tales*. Trans. W.H. Myers. Chicago: W.B. Conkey, 1893.

The Swan Princess: A Folktale from Finland

This folktale has echoes of *Swan Lake*, the 1875–1876 ballet by Russian composer Pyotr Ilyich Tchaikovsky. As in the ballet, the swan maidens here are not supernatural beings but human women who have fallen under a spell.

Once, long ago, there lived a young man called Vaino. Vaino lived alone in the forest, near a small lake. One morning, he heard the flapping of great wings and hurried to the lakeside just in time to see nine swans landing.

He hid behind a bush. To his wonder, the nine swans shed their feathers and became nine lovely maidens. But one was more beautiful than all the rest, and Vaino fell instantly in love with her.

Then, the maidens became swans again and flew away. Vaino raced off to the hut of an old Lapp wisewoman. "Please, how can I break the spell so that the maiden is no longer a swan?"

The old woman thought a bit, and then said, "Tomorrow, when the swans return, you must seize the maiden's feathery garb and burn it. Then recite this charm:

> Pala tuli, pala mieli
> Kaunis neitosen.
> (Burn fire, burn heart
> of beautiful maiden.)

Vaino thanked her. The next day, he hid himself again and waited. Sure enough, the nine swans came swooping down and transformed into the nine lovely maidens. Vaino watched carefully, then he seized the feathery garb of the maiden he loved and burned it. Eight maidens turned to swans and flew away. The ninth remained.

"You who have stolen my robe, hear me," she cried. "If you are older than I, my father you shall be. If you are younger than I, my brother you shall be. If you are as old and no older, my husband you shall be."

Vaino answered her:

> Pala tuli, pala mieli
> Kaunis neitosen.
> (Burn fire, burn heart
> of beautiful maiden.)

He stepped out of hiding, and she, glad to see how handsome and kind he looked, fell into his arms.

"I am a human," she said, "but a wicked spell turned me into a swan. My father is the king, and it was an enemy who bespelled me and my sisters. But come to my father's palace with me."

Though the king was overjoyed to see his daughter, there were still eight princesses in swan form. "Vaino, if you wish my daughter's hand, you must free them all, and that cannot be done by destroying their feathered garb. Go into the heavens and fetch me the golden chains that hang from the clouds."

Vaino hurried to the hut of the old Lapp wisewoman. "Please, can you tell me how to find the golden chains that hang from the clouds?"

The old wisewoman thought for a while. Then she said, "Take the horse I give you. Keep your eyes shut! You will feel the horse slip out from under you. Still keep your eyes shut! Stretch out your hands and you will feel the golden chains. Take them. And only then may you open your eyes."

So Vaino followed her words. He kept his eyes shut, and he grabbed the golden chains.

Then at last, he opened his eyes. Where was he? This was a vast plain, with nowhere to go. But he started forward at random, and soon came to the eerie sight of two skeletons fighting.

"Brothers," Vaino asked, "why do you fight?"

"At last!" one skeleton cried. "Here is someone to settle our quarrel! My neighbor here claims I owe him money. But I claim I paid it!"

"Brothers, there is no need to fight," Vaino said. "You are both dead, and all debts are settled."

"We are both dead!" the skeletons cried. "There is no reason to fight." They hugged each other. Then one skeleton said, "Wise one, here is a reward. Take this stone with you, for you will have a use for it."

Vaino walked on. He came to two more fighting skeletons. This time, the quarrel was over land they both claimed.

"Brothers, there is no need to fight," Vaino said. "You are both dead, and neither owns the land now."

The skeletons ceased fighting and gave Vaino another stone as a reward.

Vaino walked on. He came to a third pair of fighting skeletons. This time, the quarrel was over which of them was the wisest.

"Brothers, there is no need to fight," Vaino said. "You are both dead and equally wise now."

The skeletons ceased fighting and gave Vaino a third stone as reward.

"But how am I to get back to my bride?" he wondered.

He shook the golden chains. Every type of sea creature appeared before him. Vaino said to them, "Carry me from this dead land to the land of the living."

"We cannot," said the sea creatures, and vanished.

Vaino shook the chains again. This time, every type of animal appeared. Vaino said to them, "Carry me from this dead land to the land of the living."

"We cannot," said the animals, and vanished.

Vaino shook the chains a third time. This time, all the birds of the air appeared. Vaino said to them, "Carry me from this dead land to the land of the living."

A great eagle asked, "Do you have the chains?"

"Yes."

"Do you have the three stones?"

"I do."

"Then, I will take you back to the land of the living."

Vaino climbed onto the eagle's back and they flew, and still they flew. The eagle said, "I grow weary. Drop one of the three stones."

Vaino did, and a mountain surged up. The eagle landed on it, and they rested.

When the eagle was ready, they flew, and still they flew. When the eagle grew weary, Vaino dropped the second of the three stones. A second mountain surged up. The eagle landed on it, and they rested.

When the eagle was ready, they flew, and still they flew. When the eagle grew weary, Vaino dropped the third of the three stones. A third mountain surged up. The eagle landed on it, and they rested.

On the fourth day of their flight, the eagle brought Vaino back to the land of the living, straight to the palace of the king. There was the princess waiting for him.

Vaino gave the chains to the king. The king shook them, and instantly the eight remaining swans appeared and turned back into his other daughters. The evil spell was broken.

Vaino and his princess were married, and they lived well and happily.

Sources

Booss, Claire, ed. *Scandinavian Folk and Fairy Tales: Tales from Norway, Sweden, Denmark, Finland, Iceland.* New York: Avenel, 1984.

Bowman, James Cloyd, and Margery Bianco, eds. *Tales from a Finnish Tupa.* Trans. Aili Kolehmainen. Chicago: A. Whitman, 1936.

The Crane Maiden: A Folktale from Japan

> Versions of this folktale can be found across Japan, where the crane is a symbol of long life and prosperity. Origami paper cranes are commonly made, and millions of paper cranes were used in the second half of the twentieth century as part of protests against nuclear weapons.

Once, long ago, there lived a man named Karoku with his elderly mother. They were not wealthy, and one day, Karoku took some of his precious money to buy a new futon.

On the way to market, Karoku saw a lovely crane entangled in a net. The poor thing was struggling so fiercely that he wanted to help it get free. But as soon as he started trying to free it, the men who had set the net came running.

"Leave our net alone!"

"I am just trying to free the frightened crane."

"We caught it. It's ours."

Karoku saw the crane struggle and said, "All right, I will buy the crane from you."

He gave them the money he had saved up for the futon. They took the money and let him free the crane. Karoku watched it take flight, and felt its joy warm his heart.

Then he went home. "Where is the futon?" his mother asked.

"I spent the money to free a poor, frightened crane from a net," Karoku admitted.

"Ah well, kindness is never wrong," his mother said with a small sigh.

That night, a lovely young woman came to their house. "Please let me spend the night here," she said.

"Our house is so poor!" Karoku told her.

"Oh, I do not mind. Please, let me spend the night here."

She was a charming guest, and Karoku felt his heart warm to her. Was he falling in love with her?

Then the maiden said to his mother, "Will you let me become Karoku's wife?"

Karoku cut in, "I am a poor man. I never know where our next meal will come from."

"Please, will you give your permission?" the maiden asked his mother. "I truly wish to be your son's wife."

She won over both Karoku and his mother. And soon Karoku and the lovely young woman were wed.

Not long after that, the new bride said, "I wish you to shut me in that cabinet. Leave me there for three days, and do not look inside. I will come out at the end of the three days."

It seemed a strange thing to do, but she was determined. And at the end of three days, she came out with a beautiful length of woven fabric. "Take this to market, Karoku, and sell it for not less than 2,000 *ryo*." A ryo was a very valuable coin.

A lord saw the cloth and paid Karoku 3,000 ryo for it. "Who wove such lovely fabric?" the lord asked.

"My wife."

"Can she weave me another bolt like it?"

"I will have to ask her."

"Here, I will even give you the money for it in advance."

So Karoku went home, dazed, and told his wife what had happened.

"I can do it," she said. "I simply must have more time. This time, shut me in the cabinet for a full week. Do not worry about me. And above all, do not look inside!"

Karoku promised not to look inside. But the days passed slowly, and he became more and more worried about his wife. What was she doing in there? Was she all right? What if she was dying in there?

At last, on the very last day of the week, Karoku could stand it no longer. He opened the cabinet door—and found not a woman, but a crane. She was pulling out her feathers and using them to weave the beautiful fabric.

The crane said sadly, "The cloth is finished. But since you have seen me as I really am, our marriage is over. I am the crane you saved from the net."

With that, she flew off, and was joined by a huge flock of cranes.

Karoku was now a wealthy man, but a lonely one.

Sources

Dorson, Richard M. *Folk Legends of Japan*. Rutland, VT, and Tokyo, Japan: Charles E. Tuttle, 1962.

Seki, Keigo, ed. *Folktales of Japan*. Trans. Robert J. Adams. Chicago: University of Chicago Press, 1969.

The Geese Maidens: A Folktale from the Smith Sound Inuit of Greenland

This is one of the few transformed bride tales with a grim ending. Unlike most folktales of this type, it is a sparse, chilling story of retribution and accidental homicide.

Once, a man who had been walking came to a pond. There were many geese in that pond. But as the man watched, he saw the geese take off their feathered garments and become women.

The man hurried to grab the feathered garments. He gave back all but one. That one, he kept, and he took the woman who could not change back to a goose as his wife. They lived together, but she was always a wild thing, even after she had two children.

One day, when her husband had gone hunting, the goose woman found her feathered garb. She put this on herself and parts onto her two children. The three of them turned into geese and flew away.

When the man came home, he found them gone, and set out to follow them. He walked a long way down the beach. At last, he came to a large man. The man was chopping bits of wood with an axe. He would throw each chip into the water, saying, "Be a *quajuvaq*," and it would become a hooded seal, or "Be an *uxxsung*," and it would become a ground seal.

The man asked the large man if he could be taken to his wife. The large man agreed. He took the man into his boat, warning him to keep his eyes closed, and they started off for the distant shore.

Meanwhile, the two geese children saw their father and flew home to tell their mother that he was coming for her. She refused to believe them. She thought the distance was too great. But her husband landed on that distant shore.

When the goose woman heard her husband enter her house, she pretended to be dead. He buried her and went into mourning. But she dug her way up.

He thought she was now an evil spirit, and he slew her. But his two children flew away, and he never saw them again.

Sources

Kroeber, Alfred L. "Tales of the Smith Sound Eskimo," *Journal of American Folk-lore*, 12:7 (1899): 166–182.

Thompson, Stith. *Folk Tales of the North American Indians*. 1929. North Dighton, MA: J.G., 1995.

Other Animal Brides

Some animal-into-woman brides do not fall into easy folkloric categories. These are within the animal bride category, but feature animals generally not found in world folklore, such as the French tale of the White Cat.

The White Cat: A Folktale from France

This is a folktale that was popular during the time of Louis XIV (1638–1715), the "Sun King," when folktales often were told at court. Some of the more elegant details of the white cat's palace probably date from the day of that glittering court. However, the triple theme (three castles, three sons, three foals) is much older, and turns up in tales across Europe—although it is not used very much in the rest of this folktale. Possibly an older tale was overlaid by a more sophisticated one in later tellings.

Once, there was a king who owned three castles. Then, oh wondrous thing, his wife gave birth to triplets, three fine sons. But the wonders were not over yet. That same night, the king's prize mare gave birth to not one, not even two, but three healthy foals.

"This is amazing," the king said. "But now I can give one castle and one foal to each of my sons. But who shall have the kingdom and the crown? I vow, they will go to the wisest of the three."

The years passed. The babies grew into boys. The boys grew into young men. They soon gained nicknames that clung to them: Grand-Jean (Big-John), Non-Jean (Not-John), and Bon-Jean (Good-John). All three were brave and good to see. But while Grand-Jean loved military things and Non-Jean loved dancing, Bon-Jean was a wise, clever young man. He never spoke much, which made people think he was nothing but a dreamer.

The king called his three sons to him. "I have a test for you. You must go out there into the world and in three weeks come back with a way to thread twelve ells (a common measurement of cloth) of cloth through the eye of a needle."

"If there exists such finely woven cloth, I shall find it," Grand-Jean proclaimed, and set out.

"If there is some crafty way to get that cloth, I shall bring it back," Non-Jean said.

But Bon-Jean said nothing. He was thinking, but everyone, including his brothers, thought he was just daydreaming.

Grand-Jean set out to the border to find some merchants. Non-Jean set out for town, looking for clever seamstresses.

Bon-Jean took a path through a lovely, flower-filled meadow, and he smiled at the beauty around him as he rode. But as he rode through the day, night began to fall. Ahead of him, he saw lights blazing, and he urged his horse toward them.

He had found a castle lit by hundreds of candles. But when Bon-John entered, the castle seemed oddly empty. He knocked on the door—and it was opened by a large, gray cat.

"I have never seen a cat as doorman," Bon-Jean said.

"Please enter," said the cat. "The lady of this castle awaits you and trusts you will take supper with her."

The gray cat led Bon-Jean down a beautiful corridor, past elegant rooms with wooden paneling and fine paintings. There was no one around at all, though.

The gray cat showed Bon-Jean into a lovely dining room with a fine oak table set for two. Bon-Jean politely stood waiting to see his hostess. And who should enter but the most beautiful white cat he had ever seen. Behind her trailed a whole procession of gray cats.

"Please be seated," said the white cat, curling up on one of the chairs.

Bon-Jean would have loved to pet that beautiful cat, but instead, he bowed politely and took his seat. The gray cats served him a wonderful meal fit for a prince. The white cat, he could not help but notice, was eating mice, so neatly and cleanly she could have been a fine lady.

"I seldom have guests for dinner," she said, "and I would be delighted if you would tell me why you have come here."

So Bon-Jean told her everything, down to the fact that everyone thought him only a dreamer.

"A cloth so fine that twelve ells of it will pass through the eye of a needle," the white cat murmured. "That is possible. For now, will you kindly stay here and keep me company?"

"The honor would be mine," said Bon-Jean.

He stayed there for three weeks, and enjoyed the white cat's company very much. She was wise and witty, and as charming as a fine lady.

At the end of the three weeks, the white cat gave him a small box.

"When you are ready, pull on this golden thread," she told him.

So Bon-Jean said his goodbyes to her, and returned home. Grand-Jean had a bale of cloth in his arms. Non-Jean did, too.

"Father," Grand-Jean said, "this is the finest of cloth. But as for getting it through the eye of a needle—that is impossible."

"My cloth is even finer," said Non-Jean. "But it still will not fit through the eye of a needle."

Bon-Jean pulled on the golden thread. Then he took out a large needle with a big eye. The cloth billowed out from the box, fine as light, white as snow, and it slipped easily through the big-eyed needle.

"That's not fair!" cried Grand-Jean.

"We need another test," agreed Non-Jean.

"Very well," said the king. "You three must go your separate ways. In three weeks, you must bring me back a horse with its head where its tail should be."

Off the three brothers went. But Bon-Jean went straight to the palace of the white cat. She was overjoyed to see him again, and he was overjoyed to be with her again. This time, they both knew the answer to the riddle right away, but he stayed with her for three weeks, laughing and talking.

When the three weeks were up, Bon-Jean went home. Grand-Jean and Non-Jean were already there, arguing with their father that no such horse existed. Bon-Jean merely smiled. "If you will follow me to the stables," he said, "I will show you the solution."

Sure enough, there in the stable was a horse with its head where its tail should be: Bon-Jean had tied it backwards in its stall, so that its tail was in the manger and its head faced the back of the stall.

"That's a trick!" Grand-Jean shouted.

"We need another test," Non-Jean agreed.

"Very well," the king said. "In three weeks each of you must return with a bride. The kingdom will belong to whichever one of you brings back the finest princess to be queen."

Off the three brothers went. But Bon-Jean, as before, rode straight to the palace of the white cat.

"My lovely white cat," he said, "it is with you I would like to spend my days."

"Do you promise to do whatever I ask?"

"Of course I do."

They spent three happy weeks together. Then, the white cat led Bon-Jean to a great axe. "You must now keep your promise, my dear," she said. "You must take up that axe and with one blow cut off my tail."

"I couldn't hurt you like that!" Bon-Jean protested.

"You gave your word."

That was true. So Bon-Jean, trembling, picked up the axe. With one great blow, he cut off the tail of the white cat.

Oh, what a wonder! All the cats disappeared. In their place were courtiers and nobles. And where the white cat had stood was the most beautiful princess ever. Bon-Jean stared in wonder as she told him how a jealous fairy had placed the cat enchantment on her and her people. And then he took her in his arms and kissed her.

The beautiful princess and Bon-Jean returned to his father together, and there could be no finer couple. And so they were wed and inherited the kingdom.

Sources

Pourrat, Henri. *French Folktales from the Collection of Henri Pourrat.* Trans. Royall Tyler. New York: Pantheon, 1989.
———. *Le tresor de contes.* 7 vols. Paris: Gallimard, 1977–1986.

The Snail Lady: A Folktale from Korea

In the West, we usually think of snails as being slow and slimy, and so there are almost no Western tales of transforming snails. But the shells of some snails actually are quite lovely, and in Asia, snails often are seen as pretty things with those multicolored shells.

Once, there lived a young farmer all alone. He worked very hard to keep himself from thinking how lonely he was.

One day, though, he said aloud, "I do not know why I bother with this rice field when there is no one to eat with me."

"You can eat with me," a woman's voice said.

He looked around, but saw no one. He sighed, sure he was hearing things.

On he went with the hoeing. Soon, he had to complain again, "From morning to night I work this field, but there is no one to eat the rice with me."

"I can eat it with you," said the woman's voice. "Take me to live with you."

The voice had come from the ground. He looked down and saw a large, pretty snail in its shell. Well, it was better than no company at all, the young man thought, and put it in his pocket. He probably had imagined the woman's voice.

That night, he put the pretty snail in a water jar, then went to sleep.

In the morning, he woke to the pleasant smell of food cooking. He hastily dressed and found dishes of hot food on his table. But no one was around. Who could have prepared this?

"Whoever you are," he called, "thank you!"

That night, when he came home from the fields, he found another tableful of hot food. "Thank you!" he called out. But he was thinking, "I have to find out who this mysterious cook might be!"

The next morning, he pretended to go off to the fields as usual. But he hid instead, and peeked into his house.

Oh, amazing! A beautiful young woman had climbed out of the water jar, stretching and growing to human size. She straightened her clothing, then set about cleaning the kitchen and mending the young man's clothes. Then, at night, she prepared his dinner, then slipped back into the water jar as the pretty snail once more.

The young man ate his dinner, and called out, "Thank you!" But he was thinking only of the lovely young woman.

The next day, he hid until she took woman shape, then came out of hiding. "Will you marry me?" he said.

Blushing, she agreed.

And for some time, they lived happily as man and wife. The young farmer was no longer lonely, and neither was the snail maiden.

But then, the king of that land happened to ride by. He saw the lovely wife and thought she was too good for a mere farmer. "I want her as *my* wife!"

So the king had the young farmer brought before him. "I have a test for you," the king said, "a contest between us. Do you see that heavily forested mountain? Let us see who can be the fastest to cut down the most trees. If you lose, you must give up your wife. But if I lose, you get half my kingdom."

"Do not worry," the snail bride said to her husband. She wrote a message on a scrap of paper, and then tied it to a ring she took off her finger. "Take this and throw it into the sea. My father is the Dragon King, and he will help you."

The young man went to the sea and threw the ring and the message into the sea. Suddenly the sea parted, revealing a road leading down under the sea. He followed it to the Dragon King's palace.

"I see that you love my daughter, and I know that she loves you," said the Dragon King in his booming voice. "Take this gourd. Cut it open when you need aid, and it will help you."

So the young farmer returned to the land. On the day of the contest, he saw that the king had brought hundreds of his soldiers to cut down the trees. The young farmer cut open the gourd, and an endless stream of tiny men with axes poured out, cutting down trees here, there, faster than the eye could see.

At the end of the contest, it was clear to all that the young farmer had won.

But the king was not ready to give up. "We must have two more challenges," he declared. "We shall cross that mighty river on horseback. He who reaches the other side first, wins."

The king had a powerful war horse. The Dragon King sent the young farmer a skinny little horse. But it was a sea horse, and it ran over the river like the wind. The king had lost.

"There is one more challenge!" the king shouted. "We shall have a boat race!"

The king's boat was large and glittering with gold. The Dragon King sent the young farmer a small boat barely big enough to hold one man. But it was a seaboat, and it sped lightly over the water. The king jumped up and down on his boat in fury. The boat turned over, and a great wave surged up and swallowed boat and king.

The young man was now the ruler. He gave away all the king's riches to the poor, and he and his snail wife lived happily and wisely ever after.

Sources

Grayson, James H. *Myths and Legends from Korea: An Annotated Compendium of Ancient and Modern Materials*. London: Routledge, 2000; Richmond, United Kingdom: Curzon, 2001.

Han, Suzanne Crowder. *Korean Folk and Fairy Tales*. Elizabeth, NJ: Hollym, 1991.

White Snake: A Folktale from Zhejiang Province, China

This folktale contains more than one important folk motif. There is, of course, the animal bride, who in this case is a supernatural animal, but there is also the magical plant that returns life, the awakening of a dead man, who thinks his death was only a dream, and the guardian of the magical plant/Tree of Life. This is also one of the few tales of this type with a happy ending.

This folktale is particularly popular in China, and is even the subject of a Chinese opera, *Lady White Snake*. It may date to the Song dynasty (960–1279 C.E.), or at least that is the era of the earliest written versions.

In long ago days, there lived a kindhearted boy named Xuxian (Shu-shian). One day, he saw a merchant selling animals and snakes. Xuxian saw a tiny white snake that no one wanted, and that the merchant was about to kill. The boy felt so sorry for the tiny white snake that he asked the merchant to give it to him. The merchant did, since that saved him the trouble of killing it, and the boy set the snake free in a field.

Years passed, and Xuxian grew up. He had forgotten all about the tiny white snake—but the snake had not forgotten about Xuxian. The white snake actually was a supernatural being who could take on snake or human woman form. Now that Xuxian was grown, White Snake decided to go looking for him to thank him for sparing her life. With her, she took a friend, another supernatural being, named Blue Snake.

White Snake and Blue Snake searched and soon found where Xuxian was living. White Snake and Xuxian came face to face—and they both fell fast in love. Blue Snake politely left, and White Snake and Xuxian talked together and walked together for a long time.

"Will you marry me?" Xuxian asked.

"Happily," answered White Snake.

And for some time after that, they were as blissful as any other newly married couple. But trouble was to come, since the one thing White Snake as a human could not do was drink wine. If she took even a sip, she would forget what she was and become a great white serpent.

But it was festival time, and Xuxian urged his wife to take a sip, only a sip of the wine. White Snake foolishly did. She turned into a great white serpent. Xuxian died from the shock.

White Snake was horrified. Then, she remembered the magic linzhi plant that grew on Quenlun Mountain, where it was guarded by another supernatural being, Xiantong. White Snake instantly flew to Quenlun Mountain and picked the linzhi plant.

But Xiantong, in the form of a dragon, attacked White Snake. Fortunately for White Snake, a magician was on the mountain. When she gasped out her story to him, he took pity on her and ordered Xiantong to leave her alone.

White Snake flew back to Xuxian and forced some of the magic plant into his mouth. Suddenly he swallowed, and then began to breathe again. He opened his eyes.

"What a terrible dream I had," he said. "I dreamed you were a great white serpent!"

"It was only a dream," White Snake soothed.

And once again they took up their happy life as loving man and wife.

But now there was new trouble, from someone who only meant well. His name was Faha, and he was a priest. He was sure there was something supernatural about White Snake. And he tricked Xuxian into the temple, where he locked the young man in and began to lecture him about supernatural beings and how Xuxian would suffer if he stayed with one.

Meanwhile, White Snake was worried when her husband failed to return, and she went looking for him. She learned that he was locked up in the temple. She urged the sea to flood the temple, but Faha was too strong and resisted the flood.

White Snake was forced to give up. Sorrowing, she started away, sure that her happy marriage was over.

But suddenly Xuxian was with her. He said to her, "The priest was so busy trying to keep out the flood that he never noticed I had escaped the temple. White Snake, I learned from him what you are, but I also learned how you risked your life to save me. I do not care what you are, my love, supernatural being, snake, or woman. I love you. And I will always love you."

"And I will always love you," White Snake said.

Once again, they had a happy marriage. And this time no one disturbed them.

Sources

Chin, Yin-lien. *Traditional Chinese Folktales.* Armonk, NY: M.E. Sharpe, 1989.

Giskin, Howard. *Chinese Folktales.* Lincolnwood, IL: NTC, 1997. Version collected in 1993 and 1994 from Zhao Dinghua, Zhejiang Province, China.

Sanders, Tao Tao Liu. *Dragons, Gods and Spirits from Chinese Mythology.* New York: Schocken, 1983.

Fairy Brides

In a folk motif related to that of the animal bride, the "otherly" bride in the fairy bride tales is not an animal but a being out of the fairy realms. She may be an undersea being or one from a hollow hill, but, in all cases, she is clearly described, almost from the start of the tale, as being a fairy woman.

In many cases, the ending is the same as in tales with an animal bride, with the fairy bride's human husband breaking some prohibition and with her returning to her own people. Sometimes, though, she continues to live happily with her human husband and brings him and their descendents good fortune.

The Farmer's Son and His Fairy Bride: A Folktale from Wales

This folktale of a fairy bride features charming elements of everyday life: The couple meets like ordinary humans, and the young man goes to the fairy bride's father for permission to wed her. Violating the prohibition set by her father, however, breaks up the couple—but the girl and her mother work out a solution.

Once, there was a farmer's son who was out tending the family sheep on a foggy morning. Who should he find but a lovely young woman, her hair like gold, her eyes bright blue.

He was smitten with love at first glance. "May I speak with you?" he asked.

"You are the hope of my heart," she replied.

From that day on, they met on the same spot. They walked and talked, and maybe exchanged a kiss or two, but no more than that, for the farmer's son wanted so much to marry her. That she was a fairy maiden, he soon learned, but that did not lessen his love for her, or hers for him.

"Will you marry me?" he asked.

"You must first gain my father's permission," she said.

Her father came to them at midnight, under the light of the full moon. And if the girl was fair, her father was as handsome as no words could speak.

"I give my permission for this marriage," he said, "for I see you love each other. But there is but one thing you must never do, man. You must never strike my daughter with iron."

"I would never strike her at all," said the farmer's son.

So the farmer's son and the fairy maiden were wed, and they lived together happily. The fairy folk brought them wealth, and they had a fine farm and lovely children.

But after nine years had passed, she and he went riding, and her horse was stuck in the mire. As they got the horse free again, the stirrup of iron struck the fairy woman on the knee.

Instantly, she was gone, back to her own people. From that day on, the farmer's son and the fairy woman could not be husband and wife.

But women, fairy or human, can puzzle things out. Between the fairy woman and her mother, they got a small island of turf to float in a lake. And there, every day, the lovers could still meet.

Sources

Davis, Jonathan Ceredig. *Folk-lore of West and Mid-Wales*. Norwood, PA: Norwood Editions, 1974.

Ross, Anne. *Folklore of Wales*. Stroud, United Kingdom, and Charleston, SC: Tempus, 2001.

Sikes, Wirt. *British Goblins: Welsh Folk-lore, Fairy Mythology, Legends, and Traditions*. Boston: Osgood, 1881.

The Huldre Bride: A Folktale from Norway

The *huldre* are the fairy folk of Scandinavia, said to inhabit the hollow hills or the deep forest. This tale is different from the standard fairy bride type in that there are no prohibitions. The huldre wife reforms her grumpy human husband with a very neat threat, and they stay together.

Once, there was a young man who witnessed a *huldre* celebration. He meant no harm by it: He had been overcome by the night and taken shelter in an old barn that they seemed to fancy, too.

But then he saw one of the huldre women, and his heart stood still. He took out his knife and threw it into a wall, scaring off all the huldre folk but the one woman.

"I'll be yours," she said, "if you'll be mine."

So they were wed. And for some time, they got along well. But soon, the wife found that her man was given to complaining and sulking, and that did not suit her at all.

One day, she found him trying to shoe a horse and complaining because he could not get the horseshoe to fit correctly.

"What's the matter?" she asked.

"It's too tight," he snapped.

"Can't you widen it?"

"No, I can't widen it," he said. "If I could, I would!"

"Let me have it," the huldre wife said.

He handed the horseshoe to her. She calmly pulled it apart with her hands. Now, the horseshoe was too wide. So she just as calmly bent it back again, until it was just the right size. Handing the horseshoe back to her open-mouthed spouse, the huldre wife said:

"If you are ever mean to me again, I'll do the same thing to you."

Well, they got along much better after that.

Source

Kvideland, Reimund, and Henning K. Sehmsdorf, eds. *Scandinavian Folk Belief and Legend*. Minneapolis: University of Minnesota Press, 1988. Collected in 1924 from an unnamed informant by Peter Lund in Byeland, Norway.

The Fairy Woman of Takitimu Mountain: A Folktale from the Maori of New Zealand

The fairy woman in this folktale is more independent than the norm, and she seems closer to a nature spirit or even a nature goddess. Unlike most fairy women of this tale type, this fairy woman is very determined not to wed a human.

Once, a young man named Hautapu was out hunting on the mountainside. There was no one around him but the birds.

Then suddenly, Hautapu heard an odd sound, as if someone's jewelry had clanked together. Who else was up here?

Hautapu rushed forward. He found himself staring at the most beautiful woman he had ever seen. She was half-crouching in surprise at being caught watching him. When he drew her to her feet, cascades of wonderful reddish hair gave her a natural cloak.

"My beautiful new wife!" Hautapu cried in wonder.

She said nothing.

"What is your name?" he asked. "Who are your people?"

"I am Kai-heraki," she said. "I have no people, I come of no race, I know no one. My home is up there." She pointed up the steep mountain.

"You speak my language," Hautapu said.

"I know many tongues, even the language of the birds. Takitimu the mountain is my mother."

Now Hautapu knew he faced a fairy woman. There was great danger for a mortal in wedding one of her kind unless the proper rites were performed. Hautapu knew those rites: They would turn her from a fairy to a mortal woman.

As the fairy woman watched in confusion, Hautapu kindled a small fire. But a spark landed on her foot. Fire was alien to the fairy folk, and its touch drew blood.

Kai-heraki darted off in terror. Hautapu raced after her, but a great fog rolled down the mountain and hid everything from his sight.

Hautapu never saw the beautiful fairy woman again. But some tales do say that Kai-heraki still roams free on her mountain, never to wed a mortal man.

Sources

Cowan, James. *Fairy Folk Tales of the Maori.* Wellington, New Zealand: n.p., 1930.
Orbell, Margaret. *The Illustrated Encyclopedia of Maori Myth and Legend.* Christchurch, New Zealand: Canterbury University Press, 1995.

The Feather Robe: A Folktale from Japan

This is a variant on the fairy bride theme. Here, the story begins with the stealing of magic clothing, but the man who steals it does not want a bride. He just wants a chance to see something literally heavenly.

Once, there was a fisherman named Hakurioo. One day, while he was walking on the coast, he saw something gleam ahead of him, and he hurried to see what it might be.

There lying on the sand, he found a marvelous white robe, delicate as air and woven all from white feathers. From where the shoulders would fit, there hung two gleaming white wings.

Hakurioo picked up the marvelous robe, suspecting what would happen if he took it away. Sure enough, a stunningly beautiful maiden appeared before him, sobbing and demanding he give her the robe. He refused, wanting to find out more about her.

At last, the maiden admitted that she was a celestial goddess who had come to mortal lands on a whim. Without the robe, she could never return to heaven, but would be forever trapped on Earth.

Moved by a surge of pity, the fisherman told her, "I will return the robe if in return you will let me see the heavenly dance with which you daughters of heaven soar through the clouds."

"Give me my robe," the maiden said, "and you will see the most beautiful dance that I am able to dance."

"Dance first," the fisherman countered. "Then, I will give you the robe."

"Shame on you!" the maiden cried. "Would you doubt the word of a goddess?"

No, Hakurioo would not. He handed her the feather robe. She quickly put it on and soared up into the air.

Then, true to her words, the maiden performed the most exquisite of dances, singing in the most wonderfully clear voice the most exquisite of melodies. The fisherman fell to the sand without knowing it, staring up at her in awe.

With each loop of the dance, the maiden rose higher. But it was a long time before she finally vanished, with the last strains of her heavenly song drifting down to him.

Sources

Dorson, Richard M. *Folk Legends of Japan*. Rutland, VT, and Tokyo, Japan: Charles E. Tuttle, 1962.

Seki, Keigo, ed. *Folktales of Japan*. Trans. Robert J. Adams. Chicago: University of Chicago Press, 1969.

Undead and Demon Brides

The Tim Burton movie *The Corpse Bride* made many people at least somewhat familiar with this folktale type. The bride in this rarer type of folktale may be one of the undead, rescued by her human husband's love, or she may be a demon bride who is wed by the human man by mistake.

The Undead Princess: A Folktale from Germany

In this folktale, the undead, vicious princess is under a curse, thanks to her parents' foolishness. She can be brought into the world of the living when the curse is broken.

Once, there lived a royal couple who had no children. So desperate were they for a child that they made the foolish mistake of swearing that they wanted a child, even if it was with the devil's help.

The devil must have been listening. The couple did have a lovely daughter, but she died at fourteen. She was laid out with royal honors in the chapel, her coffin guarded by soldiers.

The horror began with the first midnight, when the princess rose as an undead demon who slew the guards and tore off their heads. At dawn, she was back in her coffin.

This terrible series of events happened for several nights. The other guards finally were too afraid to stand guard—all but the youngest of the guards, who had secretly loved the girl when she was alive and could not fear her even now.

"I will gladly guard the princess," he told the king. "But first, I must be given a few hours of leave."

The king gladly granted him leave. The young guard hurried off into the forest where he knew a wise man dwelt. The wise man already knew what the young guard wanted, and he told him, "Wear these blessed clothes and take this blessed chalk. Draw a circle around yourself with it. Then, when the princess rises at midnight, she will be unable to see you. At dawn, she will return to sleep. Come to me tomorrow."

The young man agreed. He went to the chapel alone, then changed into the blessed clothes and drew a circle around himself with the blessed chalk. At midnight, the princess rose from her coffin and prowled about like a beast seeking its prey.

"I know you are here," she cried, "but I cannot see you!"

She prowled about all night, then at dawn returned to her coffin.

The king was overjoyed to find the young guard still alive in the morning. "I will guard her again tonight," the young guard said. "But I must have a few hours of leave first."

The king gladly granted him leave, and the young guard returned to the wise man.

This time, the wise man told him, "There will be three nights in which you must guard her. For the second night, hide behind the chapel organ, and use the blessed chalk to draw a circle around you. Then, return to me tomorrow."

So the young guard hid behind the chapel's organ and drew a magic circle around himself. Once again, at midnight, the princess rose from her coffin and prowled about.

"I know you are here," she cried, "but I cannot see you!"

She prowled about all night, then at dawn returned to her coffin.

Once more, the king was thrilled to see that the young guard was still alive. "I will guard her again tonight," the young guard said. "But once again, I must have a few hours of leave first."

The king gladly granted him leave, and the young man returned to the wise man.

The wise man said, "Tonight will be the third and most dangerous of the nights. You must hide behind the altar. She will be enraged, but she will not be able to reach you. Then, while she is trying to find a way, you must run for her coffin and jump into it. The princess will try to pull you out of it, but you must bite her finger hard enough to draw blood. And then, we shall see what we shall see."

So the young guard hid behind the chapel altar. Sure enough, at midnight, the princess rose from her coffin. She knew there was someone behind the altar, but she could not approach it. Furiously, she began to prowl about, hunting a way to get to her prey.

As soon as the princess's back was turned, the young guard dashed to the coffin and leaped into it.

"Get out of there!" the princess screamed.

"I will not."

"Get out!"

The princess grabbed at him. But the young guard bit her on the forefinger, hard enough to draw blood.

And that, the shedding of her blood, broke the curse on the princess. She swayed and nearly fainted, and was now truly human.

In the morning, the king found the young couple kneeling side by side at the altar. "You have saved my daughter," the king cried. "And you make such a charming couple. Let it be so! You shall be husband and wife."

So they were wed. And if they have not died, they are still alive today.

Source

Ranke, Kurt. *Folktales of Germany.* Trans. Lotte Baumann. Chicago: University of Chicago Press, 1966. Recorded in 1935 by Hedwig Surmann from a storyteller named Paschka in Rossberg, Silesia.

The Demon Bride: A Jewish Folktale

Demons in Jewish folklore are closer to nature spirits or forces of chaos than to forces of evil. The idea of demons as definitely evil comes from Christianity.

Rabbi Isaac Luria (1524–1572), the wise resolver of this story, was an historic figure. This is an example of a folktale becoming attached, through the folk process, to an actual person. This also is the folktale type that inspired Tim Burton's *The Corpse Bride.*

A group of young men were walking along jesting merrily, when they saw what looked very much like a finger sticking up out of the ground.

Being in a frivolous mood, one of the young men jokingly placed his ring on the finger as a wedding token. The finger disappeared into the ground. The young men went their way, and they eventually forgot what had happened.

The day came for the wedding of the young man who had given away his ring. But before he could exchange vows with his bride, a woman shouted, "He cannot marry another! He already is wed to me! See, here is his ring on my hand!"

The wedding party was in an uproar. The furious father of the bride took his daughter home, leaving the young man alone with the stranger. Rabbi Isaac Luria, alone of all those there, recognized the woman for what she truly was: a demon.

The rabbi took the young man aside and asked, "Do you truly wish to be wed to this she-demon?"

"No!" the young man cried. "Who would be fool enough to *want* to marry a demon?"

The rabbi called the she-demon to him. "Why do you want to wed this young man? He is a human. Go and wed one of your own people."

The she-demon shook an impatient head. "How can I marry anyone else after he wedded me with his ring?"

"That was an error," the rabbi told her. "He never saw your face. He did not even know you were a demon! It was only a joke that his ring was placed on your finger."

The she-demon was stubborn. Maybe she did not want to be a mere human's wife, but the young man had given her his ring. She was married to him, and that was that.

Rabbi Luria found a solution: He summoned a scribe and had the young man give the she-demon a legal divorce. After making sure that the she-demon swore not to bring any demonic vengeance on the young man or his family, the rabbi nodded his approval.

The she-demon was satisfied, the young man was relieved, and Rabbi Luria sent the she-demon on her way. The subdued young man married a second time—this time to a human bride.

Source
Sherman, Josepha. *A Sampler of Jewish-American Folklore.* Little Rock, AR: August House, 1992.

A Nonliving Bride

This folktale type takes the lack of life in the bride one step further. The bride is not dead, she simply is not living. And, depending on the tale, she might come to life as a human wife—or not.

The Man Who Married a Branch: A Folktale from the Salish of British Columbia, Canada

Although the following folktale begins as a variant of the ancient Greek myth of the sculptor Pygmalion who creates so lovely an image that it comes to life, it is actually a trickster tale with a happy ending.

Once, there was a man who lived all alone. There was no one near him, and he had no family.

The man grew very lonely. He longed for a wife. At last, he grew so lonely that he made himself an image of a woman out of tree branches. He pretended it was real, and talked to it, gave it food and water, and did his best to believe it was real.

A woman who lived in a distant country was just as lonely. She heard about the man with the tree-branch wife, and she knew he was not crazy, just very lonely. She decided to go to see him. She waited until he went off to hunt. Then, she ate the food and drank the water he had left for the tree-branch wife. Then, she tidied up the house and lit the fire.

The man came home. He did not see the woman hiding. Who, then, had done all this for him? Could the tree-branch wife actually be coming alive? Such things were said to happen, at least in tales.

The next day, the woman again ate the food and drank the water, then tidied up the house. This time, though, she threw the tree-branch wife onto the fire.

When the man came home, the tree-branch wife was gone. He was so stunned he nearly burst into tears. It had left him, it had come to life and left him.

The woman laughed, and stepped out from hiding. "The tree branch never came alive," she said gently. "It was me doing all that work for you. You are not crazy, just lonely. I was lonely, too. I will be your wife."

And so the two lonely people were lonely no longer. They lived together joyfully, and had many children.

Sources

Coffin, Tristram Potter. *Indian Tales of North America: An Anthology for the Adult Reader.*
    Philadelphia: American Folklore Society, 1961.

Teit, James A. "The Man Who Married a Branch." *Journal of American Folklore* (1912): 309.

The Transformed Male

The transformed male, unlike the transformed female, is generally a human man who has been turned into a beast through a spell that the heroine has to break, or for whom she must undertake a lengthy quest. However, in some tales, such as those from the Pacific Northwest, the transformed males are deities or spirits who can voluntarily shift shape.

Beauty and the Beast: A Basque Folktale

This Basque folktale follows the pattern of the "classic" Western European folktale, although the hero has been cursed with snake form rather than monster form. It makes a nice change for storytellers looking for a familiar yet somewhat exotic version of the folktale type.

Once in the long ago days, there was a king with three daughters. He pampered his two oldest daughters and was forever bringing them gifts. But he ignored his youngest daughter, Fifine, even though she was sweet, pretty, and kind.

Then one day, he remembered her. "I never bring anything home for you," the king said. "Tell me, then, what you want, and you shall have it."

Fifine told her father, "I do not want anything."

"Yes, I insist, I am going to bring you something."

"Very well then, bring me a flower."

The king went off on his journey. He bought an elegant hat for his oldest daughter and a beautiful gown for his second daughter. But he nearly forgot his youngest daughter, until he happened to pass a lovely garden full of flowers. Being a king, he thought nothing of taking the prettiest of the flowers.

But a voice from out of nowhere said, "Who gave you permission to take that flower? As you have three daughters, if you do not bring me one of them before the year be finished, you shall be burnt wherever you are—you, and your whole kingdom."

The king went home. He gave his three daughters their presents and tried not to think about the mysterious voice. But he grew sadder and sadder yet.

His oldest daughter asked, "What is wrong?"

"If one of my daughters will not go to a certain garden before the end of the year, I shall be burned."

But his eldest daughter said, "I shall not go. I have no wish at all to go there. Settle it with the others."

The second daughter also said, "I do not wish to go."

Now, the youngest daughter, Fifine, asked, "Why are you so sad, my father?"

"When I went to get your flower, a voice said to me, 'I must have one of your daughters before the year is up, or you will be burned,' and now I do not know what I must do."

"Do not be troubled, father. I will go."

Princess Fifine immediately set out in a carriage. She arrived at the garden and saw a castle behind it. She entered, and heard music and sounds of rejoicing everywhere, and yet she did not see anyone. Food was ready for her, as was a pretty bedchamber. She went to bed. The next day, she found her chocolate ready (in the morning) and her dinner the same. She went to bed, but still she saw no one.

The next morning, a voice said to her, "Shut your eyes; I wish to place my head on your knees for a moment."

"Come in. I am not afraid."

What entered was not a man, but an enormous serpent. When the princess felt the serpent's head on her knees, she could not help but give a little shudder. The serpent went away.

For days after that, Princess Fifine lived very happily, without lacking anything—except for human company. Every day, the serpent came to her. His name was Azor, he said, and he was always very kind and gentle with her. Soon, the princess forgot to be afraid of him.

One day, Azor asked her if she did not wish to go home.

She answered politely, "I am very happy here."

"You are lonely. You may go home for three days. Take the ring that lies on that table. If its stone changes color, that means that I am ill, and if it turns to blood, I shall be in great misery."

The princess went back to her father's house, where her father was very glad to see her.

Her sisters wanted to know, "With whom do you live there?"

Fifine told them, "With a great serpent. He may be a snake, but he has been very kind to me."

They would not believe her. The three days flew by like a dream. On the fourth day, she looked at her ring, and saw that the stone was now dark red. She rubbed it with her finger, and it began to bleed.

"Oh no! The poor serpent trusted me!"

Fifine quickly told her father that she was leaving and raced back to the serpent's castle. There, she found everything sad. There was no music, there was no light. "Azor!" she called. "Azor, where are you?"

She searched the whole castle, then went out to the garden, still calling, "Azor! Azor! Where are you?"

A corner of the garden was frozen and chill, and the princess made a fire there to warm it. Azor appeared out of the thawed earth. "You had forgotten me. If you had not made this fire, it would have been all up with me."

"Yes," Fifine said guiltily, "I had forgotten you, but the ring made me remember."

"That is why I gave you the ring. Now, Princess Fifine, will you marry me?"

"I must think."

"Will you marry me?"

"I do not know."

"Will you marry me?"

Could she really marry a serpent? Azor had been so very kind to her, and he had nearly died without her. The princess said, "Yes. I will marry you."

As soon as she had said that, the music began once more, and the castle lights all blazed. "Go home," Azor said, "and get all things ready that are necessary, and we will be married the next day."

Fifine went home and told her father that she was going to be married to the serpent on the morrow. Would he prepare everything for that?

Her puzzled, unhappy father finally agreed. Her sisters were astounded to hear that she meant to wed a serpent.

A beautiful carriage came to the door. Within it was the serpent, and Fifine climbed in beside him.

"Leave the curtain shut," Azor said. "Let no one see me until we reach the church."

When they reached the church, servants opened the carriage door. And everyone cried out in surprise. There was no serpent with Fifine, but a charming young man, and he and Fifine went into the church.

But when they came out of the church newly married, Azor said to his new wife, "We must not have a wedding feast tonight. There is something that must be done first. We will have the feast tomorrow instead."

That night, Azor brought Fifine a large basket holding a coiled up serpent skin. "You must make a great fire. At the first stroke of midnight, you must throw this serpent skin into the fire. It must be burned to ash, and the ashes thrown out the window before the last stroke of twelve has ceased striking. If you do not do that, we shall both be wretched for ever."

Fifine said, "Do not be afraid. I will do it."

She built the great fire. As soon as she heard the first stroke of midnight, Fifine threw the serpent skin onto the fire. Taking two spits, one in each hand, she stirred the fire and burned the skin. Ten strokes of midnight had sounded. Eleven.

Fifine grabbed a shovel, and threw the ashes outside just as the twelfth stroke was ending. A terrible voice roared, "I curse your cleverness, and what you have just done!"

Azor ran into the room and kissed and hugged his wife joyfully. "If you had not done as I told you, I should have been enchanted for twenty-one years more. Now, it is all over, and we will go at our ease tomorrow to your father's house for the wedding feast."

They did, and all were joyful.

Sources

Barbier, Jean. *Legendes Basques*. Baiona, France: Elkar, 1991.
Webster, Wentworth. *Basque Legends*. London: Griffith and Farran, 1877.

Snake and Crocodile Husbands

Few folktales feature a crocodile or alligator as hero, but there are many from around the world about snake husbands who are transformed into human husbands. Whether or not the Freudians are right about the symbolism of the snake, it does seem to be a popular folkloric figure.

The Crocodile Husband: A Folktale from Botswana, Africa

A crocodile may seem like an unlikely husband, but it could well be that the original storyteller or tellers deliberately picked such a dangerous animal to play up the heroine's goodness of heart.

Once, there lived a lovely young girl named Madila, or Sweet Cream, since she was the darling of her parents. They did not spoil her, though, and she grew up as sweet as her name.

Madila had a brother, Masilo. Their parents were old, and when they died, there also was a terrible drought, so that the farmland was no longer able to grow crops. A magic bird told Masilo and Madila, "This land will not recover. Follow me and I will find you a happier place to live."

Madila and Masilo followed the magic bird to find a place to live. The bird took them to a great rock. "Rock, open!" the bird cried. And the rock opened, revealing a clean, pretty cave for the brother and sister to call home.

Madila and Masilo were happy there. He went hunting, and always brought back game. She found that the nearby riverbank had perfect clay for making pots.

But whenever Madila went to the river, for clay or for water, she saw a great crocodile watching her. It never tried to hurt her, but Madila grew very nervous.

"Go away, crocodile," she said, "or I will have Masilo shoot you with his arrows."

"Do not hurt me," the crocodile replied. "I wish to be your friend."

How human it sounded! "Very well," Madila said. "We will be your friends."

After that, the crocodile brought Madila bags of seed for planting. She set to work, and she soon had a nice crop growing. The crocodile brought Masilo a herd of cattle, and he soon had a good farm.

Then, the crocodile came up to Madila and seemed almost afraid. "What is wrong?" she asked.

"I wish to marry you."

Madila thought about it. Yes, he was a crocodile, but he had been so very kind to her and to her brother. Kinder, in fact, than many a man might have been. "Very well," she said.

To her surprise, the crocodile led her to a handsome mansion. "This is our new home," he said.

That night, they lay down side by side. The crocodile sighed. "How can you ever love me? I am all ugly scales."

"You are kind of heart," Madila said. "That is more important." And she kissed him.

Ah, what a wonder! No more crocodile was there, but a handsome prince. Madila had broken the spell binding him, and all the rocks in the river came to life as his subjects.

And they lived happily after that.

Sources

Knappert, Jan. *Myths and Legends of Botswana, Lesotho and Swaziland*. Leiden, The Netherlands: E.J. Brill, 1985.

McCall Smith, Alexander. *The Girl Who Married a Lion and Other Tales*. New York: Random House, 2005.

The Fairy Serpent: A Folktale from China

Here is an example of a folktale showing influences of both Western and Eastern cultures. This version follows the familiar beauty and the beast form, but it has Eastern touches, such as the heroine agreeing to keep a neat house and the three sisters' talent in embroidery.

Once, there was a man who had three daughters he loved very much. They were talented in embroidery, and every day on his way home from work, he would gather some flowers for them to use as patterns.

One day when he found no flowers, the man went into the woods to look for them. Doing so, he accidentally trespassed on the domain of a fairy serpent that coiled around him and held him tightly.

"How dare you trespass upon my garden?" the serpent cried.

"Please forgive me. I merely came into the forest to find a few flowers for my daughters. They will be sadly disappointed if I cannot bring them any."

"I will only let you go if you promise me one of your daughters in marriage."

The man tried every argument he could imagine, but the serpent would not listen. At last, the man thought that at least if he was freed, he could still protect two of his daughters. So he reluctantly agreed to the serpent's demand.

That night, the man was sad and would not eat. For days, his sadness lingered. His worried daughters tried to puzzle out the reason for it. Had they somehow displeased him? At last, they decided that each of them in turn would go to him and try to see what was wrong.

The eldest daughter went first. "Father, I am worried about you. What is wrong?"

"Will you, for my sake, marry a serpent?"

"No!" she cried, and left.

The second daughter then went to him. But she, too, refused to wed a serpent.

Then, the youngest daughter went to her father. When she heard the whole story, she at once announced, "If you will be happy again, I will become the bride of the serpent."

For a time after that, all seemed well. Perhaps the serpent had forgotten about them. But one morning as the girls were sitting at their embroidery, a wasp flew into the room and sang:

> Buzz! I buzz and come the faster.
> Who will wed the snake, my master?

They chased the wasp away. But the next morning two wasps came, singing:

> Buzz! We buzz and come the faster.
> Who will wed the snake, our master?

They chased the two wasps away. But there were three the next morning, all singing:

> Buzz! We buzz and come the faster.
> Who will wed the snake, our master?

The youngest daughter sighed. "I will go to meet my bridegroom."

The wasps guided her into the woods, where the fairy serpent awaited her in an elegant palace. There were rooms filled with furniture inlaid with precious stones, chests full of silken fabrics, caskets of jade, and jewels of gold.

The girl saw right away that the serpent had beautiful eyes, deep and brown. His voice when he greeted her was musical. But his skin was the scaly skin of a snake, and that made her shudder.

After the wedding supper, at which the two sat alone, the girl told her spouse, "I wish to thank you for all that you have provided for me. I promise to perform my domestic duties perfectly."

For many days, she kept the palace neat, cooked delicious meals, and made all things pleasant for the serpent. He was so kind and so gentle that, little by little, she forgot to be afraid. Soon, she truly liked him.

One day, the girl found that the palace well had mysteriously dried up. She went off into the forest to hunt for a clear stream, and carried water back in buckets. On her return, the girl was horrified to find the serpent lying all but lifeless on the ground.

"Oh, you are dying of thirst!" she cried.

To save his life, she poured the water into a large basin, and plunged the serpent into the water—and he arose from it transformed into a handsome young man.

"I was caught by a wicked enchantment," he told her. "But your kindness and pity set me free."

From that day on, the happy couple visited her family and brought gifts to those who were less happy than them.

Sources
Fielde, A.M. *Chinese Fairy Stories*. New York: G.P. Putnam Sons, 1893.
Sanders, Tao Tao Liu. *Dragons, Gods and Spirits from Chinese Mythology*. New York: Schocken, 1983.

Yu Duo and the Snake Husband: A Folktale from the Dai of China

The Dai people, who may be related to the people of Thailand, are one of the many ethnic minorities in China. This beauty and the beast variant is unusual in that the quest theme of the seven mountains—which also turns up in Scandinavian and Slavic variants—is here undertaken by husband and wife together. Some versions of this tale, incidentally, end with the cruel daughter getting eaten by a nonmagical snake.

Once, long ago indeed, there lived a poor girl named Yu Duo. Since both her parents had died when she was very young, she was forced to live as a slave in the household of Xi Ti.

Now, Yu Duo never saw Xi Ti. Unfortunately, Yu Duo did see far too much of his wife, who was cruel to her. The wife had a daughter, Xiang Han, as lazy as could be and cruel as her mother. Poor Yu Duo worked hard for them, but whatever she did, it was never good enough.

One day, Yu Duo came back from a long day of gathering firewood. She was tired and weak from hunger. When she saw a mango tree, she almost burst into tears.

"If a kindhearted man picked a mango for me, I swear I would marry him."

"Do you mean what you say?" asked a voice from up in the tree. "Dear girl, would you marry me?"

It was a huge snake, but a handsome one, its scales glinting with the reflections of the ripe mangoes. Yu Duo gasped and turned to leave. But she heard the snake say sadly, "I knew you did not mean it."

That made Yu Duo turn back to study the snake. "Please do not be afraid," it pleaded. "I am not like any other snakes in all the world. And I swear by my life that I would never harm you. Wait, and I will shake mangoes down to you."

He did, and she happily ate the sweet, sweet fruit. "Oh snake, kind snake, what can I say? You have treated me more gently than any human ever has. Yes, I will marry you."

Xi Ti's family was united in their horror. What, Yu Duo had married a *snake*? She and the snake were forbidden to enter the house.

Yu Duo could not help but weep. Now, she had no money, no home. But the snake rested his head ever so gently on her shoulder, comforting her.

"Do not weep, dear wife. You are far better off out of that terrible place. From now on, we shall live a free life."

Together, they built a neat straw hut, and lived happily for a time. The snake, for all that he had no arms or legs, could use his jaws and muscular body to handle many farm tasks, and Yu Duo helped him. Gradually, she realized that she did, indeed, love him as he loved her.

One night, the snake said, "Dear wife, I used to be She Lang, the Prince of Magic Snake. But three years ago, a witch placed a curse on me, as you see. If you want to help me break the curse—"

"Oh, I do!" Yu Duo cried.

"Then, we must cross seven mountains together to reach a magic river. There, we must fast for five days and nights. At the end of that time, we must bathe separately. You must remember this, my dear, or we will be lost forever: Whatever you see floating down the river, do not touch it. Should there be an accident, though, and you need me, you have only to call me."

"I will go with you," Yu Duo said.

So they began the long journey over the seven mountains. At last, they reached the magic river, sparkling in the sunlight. Together, they fasted for five days and nights.

"Now, we must bathe separately," the snake said. "Remember, do not touch anything you see floating in the river."

They parted, he going upstream, she going downstream. Carefully, Yu Duo stepped into the clear waters. As soon as the water touched her, she became more beautiful than a princess.

Just then, a magnificent silver belt floated downstream. Oh, what a wonder! But Yu Duo remembered her husband's words, and even though she wanted to pick it up, she did not touch it. Following the silver belt came small, exquisite silver and gold bowls, one after another. Yu Duo refused to touch these as well. But when the last bowl was passing, her foot slipped and her hand brushed the bowl. Her arm vanished!

Terrified, Yu Duo called, "She Lang! Oh please, She Lang!"

A radiantly handsome young man appeared before her. "I am he, your husband. The belt was my snake skin, and the bowls were my scales."

"My arm . . ."

"Darling, do not be afraid. Yours was only a minor transgression, not something meriting punishment." He sucked lightly on her shoulder, and suddenly her arm returned.

Yu Duo and She Lang returned home, not to a straw hut, but to his golden palace. There, they lived a wonderful life.

Sources

Fielde, A.M. *Chinese Fairy Stories*. New York: G.P. Putnam Sons, 1893.
Hoskin, John, and Geoffrey Walton. *Folk Tales and Legends of the Dai People: The Thai Lue in Yunnan, China*. Trans. Ying Yi. Bangkok, Thailand: D.D., 1992.

The Woman and the Snake: A Folktale from Kerala Province, India

This folktale has two versions. Following is the more "PG" version, but there also is a more bluntly honest one in which the wife wishes her husband were human so she could have sex with him. This tale comes from the Kadar people, an ethnic minority within Kerala Province in southern India.

Once, a snake went to a father and mother who had a daughter old enough to marry. "I wish to wed her," the snake said. He gave them a good deal of money as a bride price, which is the price a man traditionally gave to a family for the right to marry their daughter.

The parents could not refuse so large a sum. So they sent their daughter off to live with the snake. He was kind to her, but she yearned for a human husband. She was terrified that the snake would kill her, despite his kindness.

"If only he was a man!" she wept.

The snake overheard this. And with that, he shed his snake skin and became a handsome man. But his wife never saw him in man shape by day, and she wondered who this strange nighttime man might be.

One morning, she overheard the birds speaking to each other, since that was in the days when people and animals could understand each other.

"It was a man," said one bird.

"It was a snake," insisted a second bird.

"You are both wrong," cried a third bird. "It is a man with a magic snakeskin. I saw him change."

Oh, wonderful! The woman wrote down all that the birds had said, and showed it to the snake.

He laughed. "So be it! You have decided what shape I will wear." And he removed the snakeskin.

The woman looked at her handsome husband with delight. "I do like you far better like this," she said.

Sources
Menon, T. Madhava, Deepak Tyagi, and B. Francis Kulirani, eds. *People of India: Kerala*. Vol. 27. New Delhi, India: Affiliated East-West Press for Anthropological Survey of India, 2002.
Thundy, Zacharias P. *South Indian Folktales of Kadar*. Sadar, India: Archana, 1994.

Frog Husbands

Frog husbands are very common in the world's folklore, again possibly because of the frog's seemingly magical metamorphosis from tadpole to adult. Also, a frog, cool and clammy, is the very antithesis of the folktale hero, so that the change to human is that much more dramatic.

The Frog Prince: A Folktale from Germany

This folktale is a variant on the best-known version, that of the princess who is so ungracious that she throws the frog against the wall and accidentally disenchants him. In this version, the frog has the magical power of clouding or clearing water, as well as a lovely singing voice. The youngest of the three daughters is, of course, the heroine, and although she does not throw out the frog, she does begin to regret the lost sleep he causes her—until he becomes a disenchanted prince.

Once upon a time, there was a king with three daughters. In his courtyard, there was a well with wonderfully clear, clear water.

One hot summer day, the oldest daughter drew herself a glass of the cool well water. But it looked oddly cloudy to her, too cloudy for drinking. This was strange!

She was about to pour the water back into the well, when a frog jumped up onto the well's edge. It said:

> If you will be my darling dear,
> I will give you water clear.

The eldest daughter made a face of disgust. "Who wants to be the darling of a frog?" she cried, and ran away.

She told the middle sister what had happened. The middle sister went to the well and drew up a glass full of water. It looked cloudy to her, too.

Once again, the frog appeared. It said:

> If you will be my darling dear,
> I will give you water clear.

"Ugh, no! Not me!" And the second daughter ran away.

Now, it was the turn of the third and youngest daughter. She, too, drew up a glass full of water. She, too, found it too cloudy to drink.

Once again, the frog appeared. It said:

> If you will be my darling dear,
> I will give you water clear.

"Very well, I will be your darling if you will give me clear water." But the youngest princess was thinking, A silly frog, even if he *can* talk, can never be my darling!

The frog leaped back into the well. The youngest princess drew up a glass—and ah, yes, it was clear and cool and wonderful water. "You see, my sisters, it was foolish to be afraid of a frog."

She did not think anything else about it, until late that night when she woke with a start. Someone was singing in a pleasant voice:

> Open up, open up.
> Youngest daughter of the king,
> Remember that you promised me
> To be my darling dear.

It was the frog. A promise was a promise, the princess thought, so she opened the door. The frog hopped in and landed on her bed. It settled down at her feet and did not bother her. The princess, after a time, went back to sleep. In the morning, the frog was gone.

The same thing happened on the second night.

The same thing happened on the third night. "This is the third and last time," the princess said with a yawn, tired of not getting a full night's rest.

She went back to sleep, sure that the frog would be gone in the morning.

There was no frog in the morning. Instead, there was a handsome prince. "You broke the spell on me by agreeing to be my sweetheart, and by letting me sleep on your bed for three nights."

They spoke together and suddenly realized they loved each other. Soon after, they married. The former frog often sang sweetly to his bride.

And the two older princesses were sorry they had not been kinder to frogs.

Sources

Grimm, Brothers. *The Complete Fairy Tales of the Brothers Grimm.* Trans. Jack Zipes. New York: Bantam, 1987.

Ranke, Kurt. *Folktales of Germany.* Trans. Lotte Baumann. Chicago: University of Chicago Press, 1966.

The Frog and the Starry Girl: A Folktale from the Mishmi of Lohit Valley, India

This frog hero seems to have many aspects of a culture hero, a hero who protects and defends his people and often has supernatural attributes. In this case, these include his warrior abilities and his determination—which seems almost a culture hero need—to marry a girl from the sky. This tale comes from the Mishmi, an ethnic minority living in the mountainous region of northeastern India.

Once, there was a couple in a certain village who had only one child—a frog. They had both been horrified when the woman had given birth to him. But the frog soon picked up speech and all the ways of human beings, and he became truly their son despite his shape.

One day, when he was as old as a young man, the frog said, "Mother, I wish to go hunting. Please give me a bow and arrows."

"My dear son, how can you hunt? You are a frog. You must understand that you have limitations."

"I will prove myself. Please give me that bow and arrows."

With a sigh, the mother did so. And the frog did go hunting, and he proved to his parents that he was a fine shot, able to bring down good game, even deer.

"Now that I have proved myself as a hunter," the frog said, "I wish to take a bride. I would like a starry girl to marry." This meant, a girl of the upper realms of the sky.

"Very well," said his mother, and made the trip up there—the realms were not yet quite separate. She found a lovely starry girl, Kadingya, and brought her back. Kadingya was excited about living among humans and having a handsome husband.

When she found that her husband was to be a frog, she was angry and disappointed. But the frog was kind to her day after day, and slowly he won her over. So they were wed.

After a while, Kadingya noticed that her husband was making some beautiful baskets. How could a frog do that? She snuck up on him in the night, and saw that he had shed his frog's skin and turned into a handsome young man.

Quickly, Kadingya hunted for the frog's skin. She found it, and cast it into the fire.

At first, the frog man was terrified and furious, sure he was going to die. But the skin burned to ashes and he lived.

Kadingya and her handsome husband lived happily after that.

Sources
Negi, Dev Singh. *A Tryst with the Mishmi Hills.* New Delhi, India: Tushar, 1997.
Tayeng, Obang. *Mishmi Folk Tales of Lohit Valley.* New Delhi, India: Mittal, 2007.

The Two Orphans: A Folktale from Kerala Province, India

This is perhaps the simplest of the frog husband stories, with a princess who is not afraid of the frog. She shows the frog kindness, and thus breaks the spell and gains a human husband. This tale comes from the Kadar people, an ethnic minority within Kerala Province in southern India.

Once, there lived a lonely woman. She had neither father nor mother. She had no husband.

One day, as she was going down to the river for water, she almost stepped on a frog. It croaked at her in alarm. Feeling sorry for the little thing, she picked it up and placed it gently in the water. But the frog hopped out again. And to her surprise, it spoke.

"I am an orphan like you, and I am lonely. Please take me with you. I promise I will not be any trouble." So the woman took the frog home and raised it as her son.

When the frog had grown old enough to be married, it said, "Mother, I am ready to be wed. I will marry the daughter of the chief of the village to the east. But if I go there, they will never give her to a frog."

"I will go there for you," said the woman.

So she went, and told everyone in the village to the east about her handsome son. She persuaded the daughter of the chief to come with her and wed her son.

When the daughter came to the woman's home, she saw the frog. She realized that this was to be her husband. It was a very nice-looking frog, she thought, but it was a frog. The girl picked it up and stroked it gently—

And the frog instantly changed into a handsome young man.

"You have broken the spell!" he cried. "The gentle touch of a kindhearted girl was all it took."

They were married. And the couple, as well as the former frog's mother, all lived happily after that.

Plate 1.
Beauty sits prim and proper upon her chair. The beast has not yet won her heart.

Illustration by William Heath Robinson (1872–1944). Courtesy of The Granger Collection, New York.

Plate 2.
The Little Singing Frog sits high up in her tree hideout, singing her sweet song.

Illustration by Nadir Quinto (1918–1994). Courtesy of Private Collection/ © Look and Learn/
The Bridgeman Art Library.

Plate 3.
In this painting, the artist has given the Swan Princess a coy, almost mischievous expression.

Illustration, dated 1900, by Mikhail Aleksandrovich Vrubel (1856–1910). Courtesy of The Bridgeman Art Library/Getty Images.

Plate 4.
Upon entering the castle, the hero discovers—much to his amazement—
that the court is made up entirely of cats.

Illustration by Ambrose Dudley (fl. 1920s). Courtesy of Private Collection/The Bridgeman Art Library.

Plate 5.
Popular in China, the tale of the White Snake is the subject of a folk opera, *Lady White Snake*.

Courtesy of Marie Mathelin/Roger Viollet/Getty Images.

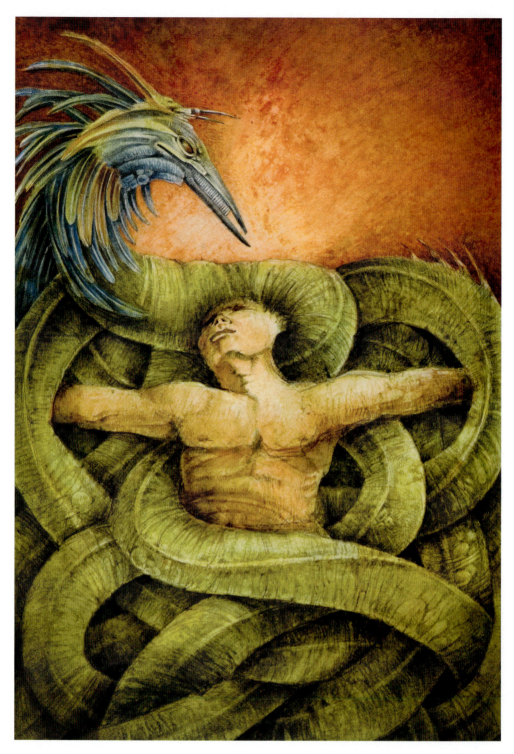

Plate 6.
Like Yu Duo's snake husband in the story, this serpent or dragon is transforming into a man.

Courtesy of Rodex/Artbox Images/Getty Images.

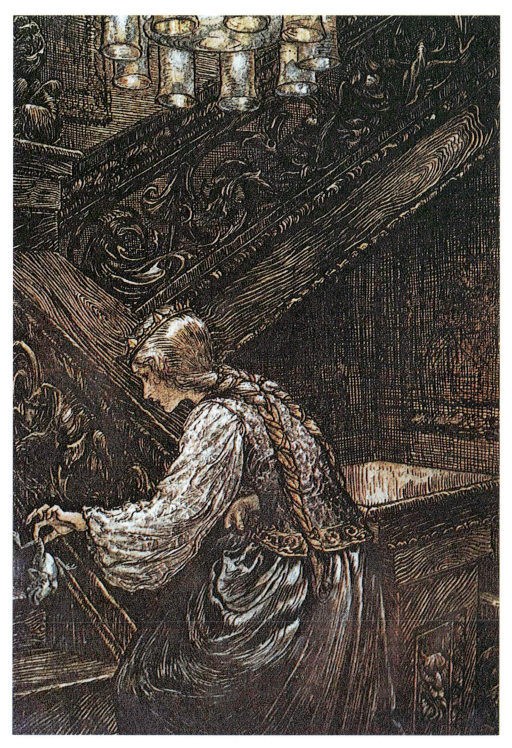

Plate 7.
The princess is not exactly overjoyed at her froggy companion. In fact,
she does not like holding him at all.

Illustration by Arthur Rackham (1867–1939). From Once Upon a Time: The Fairy Tale World of
Arthur Rackham. *Edited by Margery Darrell. New York: Viking Press, 1972.*

Plate 8.
Cinderella dreams of going to the ball.

Illustration by Arthur Rackham (1867–1939). From Cinderella. *Retold by C.S. Evans and illustrated by Arthur Rackham. 1919. New York: Viking, 1972.*

Sources

Menon, T. Madhava, Deepak Tyagi, and B. Francis Kulirani, eds. *People of India: Kerala*. Vol. 27. New Delhi, India: Affiliated East-West Press for Anthropological Survey of India, 2002.

Thundy, Zacharias P. *South Indian Folktales of Kadar*. Sadar, India: Archana, 1994.

The Toad Husband: A Folktale from the Hmong of Laos

The Hmong traditionally dislike toads, thinking of them as ugly and lazy. They even dislike touching toads, although boys may dare each other to do so.

The *qeng* is the main Hmong musical instrument. This wind instrument is made up of six bamboo tubes, each containing a metal reed and holes to produce the different notes. The lowest and highest tubes contribute a drone to the music, which is played on the four other tubes.

Long ago, there lived a young man in the form of a toad. He lived with his older brother and the brother's wife.

Every market-festival day, the sister-in-law would go into town. The toad would wait until she was gone, then bathe and turn into a handsome young man. He would head off to the market, playing his *qeng* (a wind instrument of the Hmong) as he went.

While he was in the market, playing and dancing to his music, Nzeu, the youngest daughter of the village headman, noticed the handsome young man and began watching him with fascination.

But somehow she lost sight of him. He hurried home, and then turned back into a toad.

This went on for several days. Each time Nzeu saw the handsome young man, she grew more fascinated. But each time, the mysterious man got away.

Back in toad form, he told his sister-in-law, "I am going to marry the headman's daughter, Nzeu."

"Are you sure?" the woman asked carefully.

"Quite sure," the toad said, and off he hopped to the headman's home. The dogs began barking at him, and Nzeu was sent out to see why. Hah, nothing but a toad! She threw a stone at him to chase him away, but he would not move.

"Mother, there is a toad outside. I threw a stone at him, but he will not go away."

So the mother went out and asked, "Why are you here, Toad?"

"I have come to marry Nzeu."

"No!" shouted Nzeu. "I will not marry an ugly old toad! Never!"

But the toad refused to leave. The headman came home and asked, "Why are you here, Toad?"

"I have come to marry Nzeu."

"No, no, and no!" shouted Nzeu. "Never!"

So the headman said to the toad, "If you really want to marry Nzeu, you must first bring me that huge boulder that lies at the edge of the village. Place it by my front door. Then, I will let you marry Nzeu."

The toad hopped off. "That will take care of him," the headman said. "Either he will give up or the boulder will crush him."

But it was not long before the toad came back with the huge boulder on his back. "Where would you like this?" he asked.

"Oh—ah—right here," the headman stammered.

"I win!" the toad cried. "I get to marry Nzeu!"

"No, no, no, and no!" Nzeu cried.

But the headman took her aside. "Just go to bed with the toad. Once he is asleep, your mother and I will come to kill him and throw him away."

Nzeu finally agreed. That night, the headman and his wife tiptoed into her room carrying a knife and a basket. They were planning to kill the toad with the knife, scoop the body into the basket, and toss the whole thing away.

But when they neared the bed, there was not a toad. There was a handsome young man, and he and Nzeu were smiling in their sleep.

"Well, there's a nice surprise," the wife whispered to the husband. "Let's go back to bed."

The next day, the handsome young man was a toad again. "I am going to break this spell now," he told Nzeu. "Come to the river with me."

When they got to the river, he said, "I must go on alone. You wait here. If you see a foam of red bubbles, do not touch it. But if you see a foam of white ones, touch as many bubbles as you wish."

Nzeu waited, all alone. First there came a foam of red bubbles, and she did not touch it. Then there came a foam of white bubbles, and she touched the white bubbles. The foam became lovely rings, one for each finger.

And here came her husband, a toad no longer, but the handsome young man. So the two young people started their happy lives together.

Source
Johnson, Charles, and Se Yang, eds. *Myths, Legends and Folk Tales from the Hmong of Laos.* St. Paul, MN: Linguistics Department, Macalester College, 1985. Story collected from Lou Lee (Mrs. Chia Pao Yang) by Se Yang, who also provided the translation into English.

Fish Husbands

Although fish may seem as unlikely as frogs or crocodiles to be the hero of this variant on the beauty and the beast theme, this rare form of the theme generally features a fish man who is a powerful spirit being and not truly human, even while in man form.

The Fish Man: A Folktale from the Salish of British Columbia, Canada

In several folktales from the cultures of the Pacific Northwest, a young woman who refuses all suitors winds up with a spirit or animal spouse. These tales often end unhappily, with the woman escaping or being rescued from her spirit or animal spouse. In this folktale, though, she is happy with her choice.

Somewhere near the mouth of the Fraser River lived a young woman who had refused all suitors. But then a stranger, a handsome man, came to her at night, and pleased her, and they slept together as man and wife. But by day, he would swim away as a fish man.

The young woman said to him, "You must stay until daylight, and show yourself to my parents."

He answered, "No. Your people would not like me."

But, of course, the young woman told her parents, and they were very angry that she had wed an unknown. All the people agreed on this fact, and they refused to meet him.

Then, the fish man, insulted, caused the sea to recede many miles from the village. He made all the freshwater streams dry up and let no rain fall. The animals became thirsty and left the country. The people could get no fish, no game, and no water to drink.

The young woman told the people, "My husband has done this, because you were angry with him and refused to meet him."

Then, the people realized the truth: She had not married a nobody, she had married a fish man, a powerful water spirit. They decided to honor him and this odd marriage.

So they made a long walk of planks over the mud to the edge of the sea. At the end of this, they built a large platform of planks, which they covered with mats, then heaped many woolen blankets on it. They dressed the young woman in a fine robe, combed and oiled her hair, painted her face, and put soft down on her head. They placed her on the top of the blankets and left her there.

At once, the sky became overcast, rain fell, the springs burst out, the streams ran, and the sea came in. The people watched until the sea rose, and floated the platform with the blankets. They saw a man shed fish form and climb up beside the young woman.

The couple stood up together, arm in arm, and the young woman called, "Now all is well. I shall visit you soon."

Night came on, and the people saw them no more. In two days, though, the young woman came back, and told the people, "I live below the sea, in the fish country. The houses there are just the same as here, and the people live in the same way."

She returned a second time with her husband, bringing presents of fish. She said, "From now on, people here shall always be able to catch plenty of fish."

Once more, she came to show them her newly born child. After that, she returned to the sea, and was never seen again.

Source

Boas, Franz. *Folk-Tales of Salishan and Sahaptin Tribes.* Memoirs of the American Folk-Lore Society. Vol. 11. Lancaster, PA, and New York: American Folk-Lore Society, 1917. Collected by Jame A. Teit, ca. 1915, from an unnamed old man; Teit noted that similar versions were told by neighboring tribes.

Seal and Sea Lion Husbands

As with the female seal and mermaid folktales, a number of male seal and sea lion folktales feature the beauty and the beast theme as well. Most of these do not end happily for the groom. But in some, the human woman does like being the wife of her nonhuman husband.

Ahewauwen and the Woman: A Folktale from the Selknam of Tierra del Fuego

> The Selknam live on some of the most barren stretches of land, the southern edge of South America. They depend on the sea for much of their livelihood. Their folklore includes tales about sea beings who can take human or animal form at will.

A hewauwen was a sea lion and a man, either shape, depending on his mood. One day, the sea lion fell in love with a human woman. The woman, however, thought him only an animal, and took no interest in him at all. He followed her all along the coast as she gathered food, but she ignored him.

Then one day, Ahewauwen saw the women of the village coming down to the beach to hunt for fish. The woman he loved was among them, and he waited.

When she threw out her fishing line, he bit off a piece of the bait, a chunk of meat, without letting himself be seen. Shaking her head, she fastened a larger piece of meat, but the sea lion bit that off too. Finally, she stepped into the water with the largest bait yet—and the sea lion rushed forward and carried her off.

"You will drown me!" she cried.

No, he would not. He carried her very carefully to be sure she did not drown.

He swam with her to an island and came ashore. There, the woman learned that this was Ahewauwen, sea lion and man, and that he loved her. They spent time together, learning each other's ways, and they fell in love.

Meanwhile, the men of the village knew only that a sea lion had stolen a woman. They went hunting for them, but Ahewauwen and the woman hid from them every time, since the sea lion knew every rock and cave.

They lived together happily for a time. But the woman still could not swim as easily as he did. So Ahewauwen turned her into a sea lioness. And the two swam joyfully together ever after.

Source
Wilbert, Johannes, ed. *Folk Literature of the Selknam Indians: Martin Guisinde's Collection of Selknam Narratives.* Los Angeles: UCLA Latin American Center Publications, 1975. Collected from Tenenesik by Martin Guisinde, ca. 1931.

The Woman Who Married a Seal: A Folktale from the Coos of Oregon

This folktale from the Coos people is of a happy marriage between a human woman and a seal man. This tale is unusual in that it changes the viewpoint from husband and wife to the woman's family.

A woman went in a canoe down the river, keeping close to the shore. Suddenly, she saw a good-looking man.

"Halloo, my wife!" he called. "What are you always looking for?"

"I am looking for some food all the time."

"We two will go home," he said to her.

Indeed, she was so inclined.

"You will have much food, all kinds of food," he said to the woman.

Indeed, the two went.

"Won't people be looking for me?" the woman asked.

"You will always be seen," he told her. "You will, at any rate, leave your canoe here, and your father will find your canoe. We two will go down into the water. Hold me by my belt." He added, "You must close your eyes when we two go down."

"Won't I lose my breath?"

"No. You will be in no danger. We two will go through to a house. When I tell you so, then you shall look."

They went down into the water. The woman closed her eyes.

They came to a house, and she was told to open her eyes. The people she saw living there looked like normal persons.

On the land, the woman was lost. Just her canoe was found.

"Where may she have gone?" they wondered.

The tracks led down into the water. Everywhere, they looked for her. She was not found.

The woman was lost.

One morning, many seals were on the sand beach at the mouth of the river. One seal seemed to be marked with red paint. Then, it was not a seal but the woman. People went after her. The seals ran into the water, and the woman ran with them into the water. Now, there were only seals diving into the water.

The people decided, "We will head them off."

Many people started down the stream. There were, indeed, many seals on the sand beach, and there among them was the woman. But even before the seals moved, the woman was back in the water.

Then, her father went alone to the shore, and there he saw her walking along the shore.

"Halloo, my child! I am traveling here," he said.

"I have two children now," she told her father. "I cannot come back. You will not see me again. But I am happy with my husband and children."

Wading, she went down into the river. There, she dove.

Thus, the story ends.

Sources

Frachtenberg, Leo J. *Coos Texts. Columbia University Contributions to Anthropology.* Vol. 1. New York: Columbia University Press, 1913.

Frachtenberg, Leo J., and Henry H. St. Clair. "Traditions of the Coos Indians of Oregon." *Journal of American Folklore* 22 (1909).

The Great Silkie of Sule Skerry: A Folktale from Scotland

Although many of the folktales about seals feature seal women or women becoming seals, one famous Scottish and Orkney ballad features a tragic male *selchie*, or silkie. The text of the ballad in its most common version is given below.

> I heard a mother lull her bairn,
> and aye she rocked, and aye she sang.
> She took so hard upon the verse
> that the heart within her body rang.
>
> "O, cradle row, and cradle go,
> and aye sleep well, my bairn within.
> I ken not who thy father is,
> nor yet the land that he dwells in."
>
> And up then spake a gray selchie,
> as aye he woke her from her sleep,
> "I'll tell where thy bairn's father is:
> He's sittin' close by thy bed feet."
>
> "I am a man upon the land,
> I am a selchie on the sea,
> and when I'm far frae ev'ry strand,
> my dwelling is in Sule Skerry."
>
> "And foster well my wee young son,
> aye for a twal'month and a day,
> and when that twal'month's fairly done,
> I'll come and pay the nourice fee."
>
> And when that weary twal'month gaed,
> he's come tae pay the nourice fee.
> He had ae coffer fu' o' gowd,
> and anither fu' o' the white money.
>
> "Upon the skerry is thy son,
> upon the skerry lieth he.

Sin thou would see thine ain young son,
now is the time tae speak wi' he."

"But how shall I my young son know,
when thou ha' ta'en him far frae me?"
"The one who wears the chain o' gowd,
'mang a' the selchies shall be he."

"And thou will get a hunter good,
and a richt fine hunter I'm sure he'll be,
and the first ae shot that e'er he shoots
will kill baith my young son and me."

Sources

Child, Francis J. *The English and Scottish Ballads.* Vol. 2. Mineola, NY: Dover, 1962.
Orkneyjar: The Heritage of the Orkney Islands. http://www.orkneyjar.com.

Other Animal Husbands

The two heroes of these tales take less than heroic animal forms. One is a dog, and the other is part hedgehog. But, in both stories, the heroes are transformed into human beings.

The Small-Tooth Dog: A Folktale from England

Dogs are rarely featured as heroes of the beauty and the beast stories. They tend to turn up more as helpers and friends, or in the more sinister role of Black Dogs haunting British back roads.

Once upon a time, there was a merchant who traveled a great deal. On one of his journeys, he was attacked by thieves. They surely would have robbed and killed him if a large dog had not come to his rescue and driven the thieves away.

The dog then led the merchant to a handsome mansion, where the merchant's wounds were dressed. As soon as the merchant could travel again, he thanked the dog for his kindness. "What reward can I offer in return?"

The dog said, "I will not refuse the most precious thing you have."

The merchant asked, "Will you accept a fish that can speak twelve languages?"

"No," said the dog, "I will not."

"Will you accept a goose that lays golden eggs?"

"No," said the dog, "I will not."

"Will you accept a mirror in which you can see what anybody is thinking?"

"No," said the dog, "I will not."

"Then what will you have?" said the merchant.

"Let me fetch your daughter, and bring her to my house."

When the merchant heard this, he was sorely grieved, but what he had promised had to be done. Sadly, he said, "You can come and fetch my daughter after I have been home for a week."

At the end of the week, sure enough, there was the dog at the merchant's house to fetch his daughter. She was waiting for him.

The dog said, "Jump on my back, and I will take you away to my house."

So she mounted on the dog's back, and away they went at a great pace, until they reached the dog's house. For a month, she was happy and wanted for nothing. But there were no other people in the house, only the dog. And after a month, the girl began to cry.

"Why are you crying?" asked the dog.

"I miss my father," she said.

"Very well," said the dog. "If you will promise not to stay there for more than three days, I will take you there. But first of all," said he, "what do you call me?"

She thought he was a great, foul, small-tooth dog. But he was being kind to her, so she said, "I call you Sweet-as-a-Honeycomb."

"Jump on my back," said he, "and I will take you home."

So off he sped with her on his back, when they came to a fence.

"And what do you call me?" he asked.

Without thinking, the girl said, "A great, foul, small-tooth dog."

When she said this, the dog's ears and tail went down. He turned and raced back with her to his own home.

After another week had gone by, the girl said, "I am sorry. You are Sweet-as-a-Honeycomb."

So they headed off again, and the dog leaped over the first fence.

"And what do you call me?" asked the dog with a wag of his tail.

She was thinking more of her father and her own house than of the dog, so she answered foolishly, "A great, foul, small-tooth dog."

Then, the dog was in a great rage. Again, he turned right round about, and raced back with her to his own house.

After another week had passed, the girl said, "I am sorry. You are Sweet-as-a-Honeycomb."

So away they went, with the girl careful to say only kind things to the dog until they reached her father's house.

When they got to the door of the merchant's house, the dog said, "And what do you call me?"

At that moment, with her hand on the door latch, the girl forgot the loving things she meant to say and began, "A great—," but then she saw how grieved the dog looked and remembered how good and patient he had been with her, so she said, "Sweeter-than-a-Honeycomb."

When she had said this, the dog suddenly stood upon his hind legs, and with his forelegs he pulled off his dog's head and tossed it high in the air. His hairy coat dropped off. And there stood the handsomest young man in the world, with the finest and smallest teeth you ever saw.

Of course, they were married, and lived together happily.

Sources

Addy, Sidney Oldall. *Household Tales with Other Traditional Remains*. London: David Nutt, 1895.

Briggs, Katherine M., and Ruth L. Tongue. *Folktales of England*. Chicago and London: University of Chicago Press, 1965.

Hans My Hedgehog: A Folktale from Germany

This is perhaps the only folktale featuring a half-hedgehog hero in a beauty and the beast role. Hedgehogs are cute little animals, but hardly to be thought of as heroic. Nor does the easygoing protagonist act like a typical folklore hero until well into the folktale.

There was once a farmer who was well off, but one thing was lacking to complete his happiness: He had no children.

Many a time, when he met other farmers at market, they would tease him about being childless. At length, he grew so angry that he exclaimed, "I must and will have a child of some sort or kind, even should it only be a hedgehog!"

Soon after, his wife gave birth to a child, but though the lower half of the little creature was a fine boy, from the waist upwards it was a hedgehog. When the new mother first saw the baby, she was quite frightened.

"You did it," she accused her husband. "You cursed the child yourself."

"Well, there is no use making a fuss now," the farmer said. "What can we possibly call the child?"

"There is nothing we can call him but Hans My Hedgehog," the wife replied.

Hans My Hedgehog lived and grew for eight years. One day, there was a big fair at the market town, so the farmer asked his wife what she wanted, and then said, "Well, Hans My Hedgehog, what shall I bring you?"

Hans My Hedgehog replied, "Do bring me bagpipes."

When Hans had got his bagpipes, he said, "Daddy, do go to the smithy and have the house rooster shod for me. Then, I will ride off and trouble you no more."

His father, who was delighted at the prospect of getting rid of such a weird son, had the rooster shod. When the rooster was ready, Hans My Hedgehog mounted it and rode off to the forest, followed by all the pigs and donkeys that he had promised to look after for his father.

Having reached the forest, Hans My Hedgehog made the rooster fly up to the top of a very tall tree with him, and there he sat looking after his pigs and donkeys. He found a favorite tree in which to sit and play his pipes, drawing lovely music from them, and was quite content. Hans My Hedgehog stayed there for several years, until he had quite a big herd, but all this time, his father knew nothing about him.

As he sat up in his tree playing one day, a king who had lost his way heard the music and sent one of his servants to find out where it came from.

The man returned and said, "I found nothing but a little creature, which looked like a rooster with a hedgehog sitting on it, perched up in a tree."

"Was it the piper?"

"Yes."

"Then ask it why it sits there, and if it knows the shortest way to my kingdom."

Hans My Hedgehog jumped lightly down from his tree and said, "I will happily show you the way, Your Majesty, if you will in turn give me your written promise that I may have whatever first meets you on your return home."

The king thought, "That is easy enough to promise. The creature will not understand a word about it, so I can just write what I choose."

So he took pen and ink and wrote something, and when he had finished, Hans My Hedgehog pointed out the way, and the king got safely home.

Now, when the king's daughter saw her father returning after so long an absence, she ran to meet him and threw herself into his arms.

Then, the king remembered Hans My Hedgehog. He told his daughter, "An extraordinary creature showed me the way home, but in exchange, I was obliged to give him a written promise to bestow whatever I first met when he got home. The creature," said he, "rode on a rooster as though it had been a horse, and it made lovely music, but as it certainly could not read I just wrote that I would not give it anything at all."

"Thank heavens!" cried the princess. Nothing would have induced her to have gone off with Hans My Hedgehog.

Meantime, Hans My Hedgehog minded his donkeys and pigs, sat in his tree, played his bagpipes, and was always cheerful.

After a time, another king who had lost his way heard the lovely pipe music and sent a servant to locate the musician. Down came Hans My Hedgehog. He told the king he would show him the right way if the king would promise to give him the first thing he met in front of his royal castle.

This king was more honorable than the last. He said "Yes." And he also gave Hans a written promise.

Then, Hans pointed out the way, and the king reached his own country in safety. Now, this king had a beautiful daughter who ran to meet him, threw her arms round his neck, and kissed him heartily.

Then, she drew back and asked, "Father, what is wrong?"

He told her how he had lost his way and how he had met a strange creature, half-man, half-hedgehog, which rode a rooster and sat up in a tree making lovely music. And that the creature had shown him the right way.

"I pledged my word to give him the first thing that met me outside my castle gate," the king said. "I never guessed it would be you!"

"Never mind," the princess said. "I will be quite willing to go with him, because he brought you home safely."

Meanwhile, Hans My Hedgehog continued to herd his pigs and donkeys. The herds had grown so large that he decided he was not going to live there any more. He sent a message to his father, "Please have all the stables and outhouses in the village cleared, as I am going to bring home an enormous herd."

His father was not happy at this news, for he had thought Hans My Hedgehog had died long ago.

Hans My Hedgehog drove his pigs and donkeys before him into the village, and let every one there kill as many pigs as they chose, and such a hacking and hewing of pork went on as you might have heard for miles off.

Then Hans said to his father, "Daddy, let the blacksmith shoe my rooster once more. Then I will ride off, and I promise you I will never come back again as long as I live."

So the father had the rooster shod, and rejoiced at the idea of getting rid of his son.

Hans My Hedgehog set off for the first kingdom, and found that the king had given strict orders that anyone riding a rooster and carrying a bagpipe was on no account to be allowed to enter the palace. So when Hans My Hedgehog rode up, the guards charged him with their bayonets. But he put spurs to his rooster, flew up over the gate right to the king's windows, and called out that if he was not given what had been promised him, both the king and his daughter should pay for it with their lives. Then, the king coaxed his daughter to go with Hans My Hedgehog and so save both their lives.

The princess dressed herself all in white, and her father gave her a coach with six horses and servants in gorgeous liveries, as well as great quantities of money. She stepped into the coach, and Hans My Hedgehog with his pipes took his place beside her. When they had got a certain distance from the town, Hans My Hedgehog tore all the princess's smart clothes off her, and pricked her all over with his bristles, saying, "That is what you get for treachery. Now go back. I have no more to say to you."

Then Hans My Hedgehog rode on with his rooster and bagpipes to the country of the second king to whom he had shown the way. This king had given orders that if Hans came there, the guards were to present arms, the people to cheer, and he was to be conducted in triumph to the royal palace.

When the king's daughter saw Hans My Hedgehog, she was startled, for he certainly was very peculiar looking. But she told herself that she had given her word. So she made Hans My Hedgehog welcome. They were betrothed to each other, and at dinner he sat next her at the royal table, and they ate and drank together.

When the dinner ended, the princess was afraid that Hans My Hedgehog might kiss her and hurt her with his prickles.

"Do not be afraid," he told her. "No harm will befall you."

Then, he said to the king, "Please place a watch of four men just outside my bedroom door. Have them make a big fire. When I am about to lie down in bed, I will creep out of my hedgehog skin and leave it lying at the bedside. Then, the men must rush in, throw the skin into the fire, and stand by until it is entirely burnt up."

And so it was. As soon as the skin was burned to ash, Hans was released from his enchantment. He lay in bed a man from head to foot, but one who looked as though he had been scorched all over. The king's physicians treated him, and there he was, healed and handsome. When the king's daughter saw him, she was delighted.

On the next day, the marriage ceremony was performed. And the king bestowed his kingdom on Hans My Hedgehog.

Sources

Grimm, Brothers. *The Complete Fairy Tales of the Brothers Grimm*. Trans. Jack Zipes. New York: Bantam, 1987.

Ranke, Kurt. *Folktales of Germany.* Trans. Lotte Baumann. Chicago: University of Chicago Press, 1966.

Other Odd Husbands

Some transformed or transforming husbands defy easy categorizing. They may be dragons who become human or invisible beings who become husbands.

The Dragon Prince: A Folktale from Turkey

This may indeed be the only beauty and the beast folktale featuring a dragon-to-human protagonist and an older wife.

Once, there lived a Padishah and his wife who had only one sorrow: They were childless. One day, the Padishah and his wife saw a dragon with five young ones.

"Dear Allah!" he complained. "Thou hast blessed this creature with so many offspring. Would that this dragon had one less, and that Thou hadst given me one child!"

Time passed. Then one night, the Padishah's wife fell seriously ill. But the first nurse who arrived fell mysteriously dead. So did the second. And the third.

As it happened, in the royal palace was a servant with a stepdaughter she hated. Here, she thought, was a way to finally be rid of the girl. So the servant said to the Padishah, "My Lord and Shah, my daughter is skilled in nursing. Surely she can cure your poor wife."

But the girl knew nothing of nursing. She stopped at her mother's grave and said a prayer for aid, remembering that Allah always helped those in need. And sure enough, as soon as she had finished her prayer, a voice told her, "Bring a kettle of milk to the sick one."

So the girl did bring a kettle of milk into the sickroom. She came out very soon after with news that a prince had been born—but the prince was in the form of a dragon. The Padishah may have remembered his rash words about having a child. At any rate, he contented himself with the thought that he now had an heir, no matter how odd.

The young dragon grew swiftly, and soon it was time for him to be educated. But every teacher was killed before he or she could begin to teach. Hearing this, the stepmother went again to the Padishah and said: "My Lord and Shah, the maiden who assisted at the birth of the dragon also can teach him the desired instruction."

The Padishah ordered that the maiden be fetched. Before coming to the royal palace, however, she visited her mother's grave. While she was praying for divine protection and deliverance, a staff appeared, and her mother's voice said, "Take this staff, my daughter, and should the dragon attack, show him this staff, and he will retreat."

So the maiden took the staff and went to the dragon. When he attempted to bite her, she raised the staff, and he backed down and let her teach him. The Padishah was so pleased that he rewarded the maiden with a pile of gold and let her go home.

Years passed, and the Dragon Prince was now old enough to wed. But he slew the first and second brides brought to him. So the stepmother went to the Padishah and said, "My Lord and Shah, the maiden who assisted at the birth of the Prince, and who has taught him also would make him a good wife."

The Padishah immediately sent for the maiden. Before obeying the royal summons, the maiden poured out her sorrow at her mother's grave. The voice of the dead was heard from the tomb once more. "My daughter, take the skin of a hedgehog and make a mask thereof. When thou goest to the dragon, he will seek to harm thee, but the prickles will wound him. He will then say, 'Take off the mask,' and you are to answer, 'I will take off the mask if thou wilt take off thy clothing.' When he has taken off his clothes, seize them and cast them in the fire."

So the maiden and the Dragon Prince were wed. As soon as they were alone, he tried to attack his bride, but the prickly hedgehog mask stopped him.

"Take off that mask," he snapped.

"I will only take off the mask if thou wilt take off thy clothes," she answered.

Without hesitation the dragon undressed. As soon as the last piece of clothing was discarded, the maiden threw all of his clothes in the fire.

And—oh, wonder of wonders, instead of a dragon, a handsome youth stood before her. They fell into each other's arms and embraced and kissed in utter joy.

The stepmother was put to death. But all else lived in happiness and delight.

Sources
Kunos, Ignácz. *Forty-four Turkish Fairy Tales*. London: George G. Harrap, 1913.
Walker, Barbara. *The Art of the Turkish Tale*. Vol. 1. Lubbock: Texas Tech University Press, 1990.

Princess Kemang and Her Tree Husband: A Folktale from Bengkulu, Indonesia

Here is another odd husband—a transformed tree. In the original folktale, there are hints that the heroine may be gay (she cares nothing about men), although the traditional wedding does take place at the end. This tale comes from Bengkulu, an Indonesian province that lies in southern Sumatra.

Once, there lived a princess who was as fierce and clever as a prince. So her father let her hunt and fight as she would, and she grew up both brave and honorable. Her name was Princess Kemang.

One day, Princess Kemang was hunting in an unfamiliar forest. She stopped for a moment by a beautiful old mango tree. "You are a beautiful tree," she said.

But then she saw a deer and drew her bow. "Be careful!" the tree called. "That deer is a tiger in disguise."

She shot the deer, which did, indeed, transform into a tiger as it died. Princess Kemang turned back to the tree in amazement—then stared even more. It had become a handsome young man.

"Who are you?" she asked.

"I am the guardian of the forest," he told her.

"Oh, come hunt with me!" the princess cried.

"I cannot. I cannot leave this forest until everything in it has changed form into a kingdom."

"I will go home," she said, "and ask the wise men how that may be done."

So she headed off. But there was a river to cross, and her way was blocked by crocodiles.

"Ah, our meal approaches," they said.

Princess Kemang never flinched. "I understand that you are the biggest and strongest of animals. But I must warn you that I can fight a thousand crocodiles."

"Is that so?" said the head crocodile. "Let me call my friends."

"Line up," Princess Kemang told them. "I want to be able to count you to be sure there really are a thousand of you."

She jumped onto the back of the first crocodile. "One." From there, she jumped to the second. "Two." This went on until she had used the line of crocodiles as a bridge across the river.

"Thank you, my stupid friends," she said to them as she hurried on. "You made a fine bridge."

On she went to the royal palace. Once there, she went straight to the wise men. "Go back to the forest," they said. "You will see a wonder."

Back she went. But there was no forest! Instead, there was a wondrous kingdom.

Princess Kemang met an old man and asked, "What is the name of this kingdom, and who is its ruler?"

"This is known as Kemang Kingdom," he said. "And Prince Kemang is the ruler. He and his people were cursed one day, and they became a forest. Only a princess speaking to the tree he became would break the spell."

The handsome young man approached. "So you did break the spell," he said.

"I am Princess Kemang."

"I am Prince Kemang."

After five days and nights of two kingdoms feasting and rejoicing, they were wed, and their two lands became one.

Sources

Bunanta, Murti, and Margaret Read MacDonald. *Indonesian Folktales*. Westport, CT: Libraries Unlimited, 2003.

Soebiantoro, Afwani, and Manel Ratnatunga. *Folk Tales of Indonesia*. New Delhi, India: Sterling, 1983.

Habogi: A Folktale from Iceland

Here, the transformation is from rough and ugly to young and handsome. It has a distant relationship to the Grimm Brothers' "King Thrushbeard," though, in that tale, the ugly disguise is to teach a stubborn woman a lesson, while here, the woman is quite willing to go along with her Habogi.

Once upon a time, there lived two peasants who had three daughters. Although the older two were vain and self-centered, the youngest was as beautiful as she was kind and gentle, even when it meant doing most of the work.

The time came when all three girls were grown up and thinking of marriage.

The eldest daughter decided, "I will never wed any man who is not called Sigmund."

"There are a great many Sigmunds in this part of the world," replied her father, "so you can take your choice."

The second daughter spoke up. "I think that there is no name so fine as Sigurd."

"Very good. There are almost as many Sigurds in this part of the world. And what about you, my youngest child? What name do you wish for your husband?"

The youngest daughter was about to say she had no name in mind. But then a voice whispered in her ear, "Marry no one who is not named Habogi."

So, though she had no idea why, the girl found herself saying, "If I do marry, it will be to no one except Habogi."

"Who is Habogi?"

Her sisters cried, "We have never heard of such a person!"

"All I can tell you," the youngest said helplessly, "is that he will be my husband, if ever I have one." And that was all she would say.

Before very long, the young men in the region who were named Sigmund or Sigurd came in crowds to visit the two older sisters. But never was there one called Habogi.

The two elder sisters made their choice from out of the Sigurds and the Sigmunds, and it was decided that both weddings should take place at the same time. Invitations were sent out to the friends and relations.

Then, on the wedding day, when all the guests were assembled, a rough, coarse old peasant came up to the brides' father.

"My name is Habogi, and that young lady shall be my wife."

The youngest daughter stood still in shock.

"I cannot talk of such things just now," answered the father, who hated the thought of giving one of his daughters to such a horrible creature. Her two sisters, though, were delighted that their bridegrooms outshone hers.

When the wedding feast was over, Habogi led up a beautiful white horse bearing a splendid golden saddle. "Come, my dear, mount. You shall return here, but I wish you to see the house in which you shall live."

The old man helped her mount, then sprang up before her as gracefully as a young man. The horse broke into an easy lope, and off they went.

After some time of traveling, they rode through a meadow with lush green grass. Feeding on it were herds of sheep with curly white wool.

"What lovely sheep!" the youngest daughter cried. "Whose are they?"

"They belong to your Habogi. Indeed, all that you see belongs to him. But the finest sheep in the whole herd, with little golden bells hanging between its horns, you shall have for yourself."

Since the youngest daughter had never had anything all her own, she thanked Habogi with true joy.

They left the sheep and came to a new meadow with a herd of beautiful cows graceful as deer.

"How lovely they are!" the youngest daughter said. "I imagine their milk must be sweeter than any other. Do they, too, belong to you?"

"They do, indeed. And the finest of the herd shall be yours, and you shall taste her sweet, pure milk."

"Thank you!" she cried in joy.

Next, they came upon a herd of horses kicking up their heels and galloping about in play.

"Oh, the beautiful things!" the youngest daughter cried. "Do they, too, belong to you?"

"They do, indeed. And the one you like the best shall be yours to ride and pet."

"Thank you, oh, thank you!" she exclaimed.

But then Habogi drew rein before a small house, very ugly and mean-looking, one that seemed on the point of tumbling to pieces. "This is my house, and it is to be yours," he said.

The youngest daughter's heart sank. If Habogi owned such marvelous sheep, cows, and horses, how could he live in such a hovel? But what could she do? Habogi led her inside.

The youngest daughter stared in wonder. Inside was nothing but beauty, with silken curtains, golden walls, richness everywhere. How could this be?

"I must begin the preparations for our wedding at once," Habogi said. "But my foster brother will take you home, as I promised. In three days, he will bring you back here, with your parents and sisters, and any guests you wish to invite."

The youngest daughter's parents were happy to see her. They wanted to know all that she had seen and done. But all she told them was that they must come and see for themselves in three days, when she would be wed.

In three days, the wedding party set out. The two older sisters were full of envy when they saw the sheep, cows, and horses. But then, they stared at the sight of the hovel.

"We would be ashamed of living in such a place!"

But then they went inside and were struck dumb at the splendor they saw. They grew even more envious than before when they saw the wedding gown, which looked like hundreds of glittering crystals.

That night, the older sisters stole the wedding dress and buried it in the ash pit. But the ashes changed into roses. And the sisters found themselves stuck where they were for a whole day.

On the morning of the wedding, the hovel was gone, and in its place was a mansion. Instead of a rough, ugly old man, there stood a handsome young man in rich clothing.

"Who is that?" everyone asked.

Only the youngest sister knew who it was, and that by agreeing to wed him, she had broken a dark spell.

"That is my Habogi," she said.

Sources
Lang, Andrew. *The Brown Fairy Book*. London and New York: Longmans, Green, 1904.
Simpson, Jacqueline. *Icelandic Folk Tales and Legends*. Berkeley: University of California Press, 1979.

The Invisible Man: A Folktale from the Micmac of Nova Scotia, Canada

It is never explained how or why the hero is invisible, but the beauty and the beast test here is to actually see him so that he will become visible. That he is a spirit being is an unusual part of this folktale.

It is and is not true. One day, a young woman and her brother gained permission from a village chief to camp on his territory. There was nothing strange about that—but her brother was invisible.

The invisible brother built a fine lodge and provided himself and his sister with much meat, since he was a good hunter. Then, his sister went out among the villagers and announced that her brother would marry the first woman to see him.

First came the chief's daughter. But she could not see him.

Now, all the women tried. No one could see him.

At the far end of the village lived an old man with three daughters. The older two were lazy and made their younger sister do all the work. They also were cruel to her and beat her so often she was known as Oojeegwee-esgay, or She-who-is-covered-with-scars.

The two older sisters decided to try their luck. Dressed in their finery, they went to the invisible man's lodge. But they had no luck at all. They even heard the invisible brother laughing at them.

That night, Oojeegwee-esgay dreamed of a handsome young man who said, "Come to me. I am waiting for you. You are the one I wish."

So, even though she had only rags to wear and was ashamed of her scars, she went to take the test.

And she saw him. "Oh, he is the man in my dream! And his tumpline is like the rainbow!" (The tumpline is a strap worn across the forehead to help support a pack.)

"You do see him!" cried the sister in delight.

"But . . . no one will want me, since I have all these scars."

"What scars?" the sister asked. "Look in the pool."

Oojeegwee-esgay stared in wonder. The scars were gone, and she was beautiful. She was given lovely clothes to wear.

Then, the young man appeared, no longer invisible.

"I am Little Thunder," he said, "and this is Sister Rain. Will you be my wife?"

"Oh yes!"

"Then we shall leave right now."

Sister Rain caused a downpour. When it was over, she, her brother, and her brother's new wife were gone. And they lived happily together.

Sources

Melancon, Claude. *Indian Legends of Canada*. Trans. David Ellis. Toronto, Ontario, Canada: Gage, 1974.

Parsons, Elsie Clews. *Micmac Folklore*. Whitefish, MT: Kessinger, 2007.

The Lord of the Winds: A Folktale from the Nenets of Siberia

This folktale comes from the Nenets, a nomadic people who survive on their reindeer herds and the meager hunting to be done in northern Siberia. The transformation in this tale is not from beast to human, but from demonic force to near-human man. The traditional themes here are of the youngest of three children being the victor and the girl properly performing the tasks laid out before her.

Once, in the cold, hard northern lands, there lived a nomad herder with his three daughters.

One winter was worse than any other, with a wind that never seemed to stop screaming and blowing the snow around. The herder said, "This is the doing of Kotura, Lord of the Winds. He must be very angry with us, though I know not why. But I do know that he can only be calmed by a young woman."

So he sent his eldest daughter out in a sled. He warned her, "Turn to the north, push the sled forward, and follow where it leads. Do not stop to shake the snow from you. At last, a small bird will perch on your shoulder. Pet him kindly. Then, jump onto your sled. It will take you straight to Kotura's home. Do exactly as he tells you."

Off she went. She did not heed her father's warnings. She shook the snow from her. She pushed the bird away. When she arrived at Kotura's home, she found roast venison cooking. She ate it all.

Then, Kotura entered. He was a tall, handsome fellow, nearly a giant. "Why are you here?" he asked.

"My father sent me to you."

"I have a mission for you. Take the meat in this bowl to the old woman who is my neighbor. Do not enter her house. Simply offer her the meat and wait for her to return the bowl."

But it was cold out there. The eldest daughter tossed the meat into the snow and claimed she had given it to the neighbor. An old Snow Woman asked for help: Something had gotten into her eye. But the eldest daughter refused to help. When Kotura asked her to mend his torn tunic, she did a hasty, sloppy job.

Kotura was furious. He threw the eldest daughter away into the frozen waste.

Now, it was the turn of the second daughter. She, too, ignored her father's warnings, she, too, was rude and unkind. And she, too, was thrown away by Kotura into the frozen waste.

Now, only the youngest daughter was left. She set out behind the sled, and did not stop to shake off the snow, even when it crept into her boots. When the bird perched on her shoulder, she said, "Hello, pretty bird," and petted it gently. She followed the sled to Kotura's home, and entered. She saw the roast venison, but no one had invited her to eat, so the girl simply sat and waited.

Kotura entered. He saw the girl and smiled, and she could not help but smile back at him. "Why are you here?" he asked.

"My father has sent me to ask you to be kinder to the people."

"Has he, indeed? There, I have brought meat. Cook it, and we shall eat, for you must be hungry."

The youngest daughter cooked the meat, and they ate together. Then, Kotura put some meat in a bowl and told the girl to take it to the old woman who was his neighbor. She set out into the cold and dark, following the dimly seen sign of smoke rising from a chimney. But it was not the home of a mortal woman she found, but the snow mound of a Snow Woman.

"Who are you?" asked a rough voice.

"I have come from Kotura with some meat for you," the girl said politely.

"Very well." The Snow Woman's ancient face appeared out of the snow mound. "Wait here."

Soon, she returned the empty bowl to the girl, who fought her way back through the cold and dark to Kotura's home. "Let me see the bowl," he said.

It was not empty after all. In it were the finest bone needles and knives the girl had ever seen.

"Perfect for you," said Kotura. "My best tunic is ripped. Please mend it for me. And then take that smooth deerskin and make mittens and a new coat, as well."

How could she ever finish all that? The girl set to work, sewing carefully, enjoying the smoothness of the needles. But as she worked, another ancient Snow Woman poked her head into the home.

"Help me, my child," she said. "Something is in my eye."

"Let me see . . . there. It was only a piece of dirt. It is gone now."

"That is much better. Now, child, look in my right ear. What do you see?"

"There is a maiden sitting in there!"

"Call, and she will help you."

So the girl called, and the maid jumped out and began to sew faster than any mortal could sew. In no time at all, the work was done. The maid jumped back into the Snow Woman's ear, and the Snow Woman left.

Kotura returned. "Have you finished?" he asked the girl.

"Yes, I have. Here is your tunic and your new coat and mittens, too."

"Excellent! I like you, and my mother and sister do, too. Yes, that was they you met. Do you like me?"

"Yes," she admitted meekly.

"Then you shall be my wife. And I proclaim the storm over. From now on, let there be peace between me and your people."

Sources

Golovnev, Andrei V., and Gail Osherenko. *Siberian Survival: The Nenets and Their Story.* Ithaca, NY: Cornell University Press, 1999.

Riordan, James. *The Sun Maiden and the Cresent Moon: Siberian Folk Tales.* Edinburgh, United Kingdom: Cannongate, 1989.

The Heroine's Quest

In this subsection of the basic beauty and the beast folklore theme, the heroine—sometimes through breaking a prohibition, sometimes through no fault of her own—loses her beast lover and must go on a quest to find him again. In almost all tales of this type, she must undergo several ritual tests to save him from danger and win him once again.

The Black Bull o' Norroway: A Folktale from Scotland

This folktale begins with a reversal on the idea of the three brothers setting off to find their fortune. Here, it is the three daughters setting out. The first two find traditional destinies and marriage, bringing the folktale back to the beauty and the beast tale type, with the youngest daughter helping the black bull regain his humanity. The heroine's quest theme begins when the girl accidentally breaks a taboo. She then must undergo a ritual seven years of questing until she can find her lover again and free him.

In Norroway, long ago, there lived a lady with three daughters.

The eldest daughter told her mother, "Bake me a bannock [of bread], and roast me a collop [of meat], for I am going away to seek my fortune."

Her mother did so, and the eldest daughter went away to an old witch and told her purpose. The old witch told her to stay that day, and look out the back door, and see what she could see. She saw nothing on the first day. The second day, she saw nothing. On the third day, she looked again, and saw a coach-and-six coming along the road.

"Yon's for you," said the witch.

So they took her into the coach and galloped off.

The second daughter said to her mother, "Bake me a bannock, and roast me a collop, for I am going away to seek my fortune."

Her mother did so, and away the second daughter went to the old witch, as her sister had done. On the first day, she saw nothing. On the second day, she saw nothing. On the third day, she looked out of the back door, and saw a coach-and-four coming along the road.

"Yon's for you," the old witch said.

So they took her in, and off they set.

Now, it was the third daughter's turn. "Mother, bake me a bannock, and roast me a collop, for I am going away to seek my fortune."

Her mother did so, and away the third daughter went to the old witch. The witch bade her look out of the back door, and see what she could see. She did so, and when she came back, said she saw naught. The second day, she did the same, and saw naught. The third day, she looked and saw nothing but a great black bull coming along the road.

"Yon's for you," said the old witch.

On hearing this, the girl was terrified. But she was lifted up and set on his back, and away they went.

On they traveled, and on they traveled, until she grew faint with hunger.

"Eat out of my right ear," said the black bull, "and drink out of my left ear."

So she did as he said, and found a fine meal in his right ear and fine drink in his left ear.

Long they rode, and hard they rode, until they came in sight of a handsome castle. "My eldest brother lives there," the black bull said. "There shall we spend the night."

The castle folk lifted her off the black bull's back, and took her in, and they sent the black bull away to a park for the night. In the morning, when they brought the black bull home, the castle folk gave the girl a beautiful golden apple, telling her not to break it until she was in the greatest trouble in the world, and that would bring her out of it.

She thanked them. Again, she was lifted on the black bull's back. After she had ridden far, and far again, they came in sight of a far finer castle, far farther away than the last.

The black bull said, "My second brother lives there, and there shall we spend the night."

The castle folk lifted her down and took her in, and they sent the black bull to a field for the night. In the morning, when they brought the black bull back, they gave the girl the finest silver pear she had ever seen, bidding her not to break it until she was in the greatest trouble anyone could be in, and that would get her out of it.

Again, she was lifted and set on the black bull's back, and away they went. And long they rode, and hard they rode, until they came in sight of the far biggest castle they had yet seen.

The black bull said, "My younger brother lives there, and there shall we spend the night."

The castle folk lifted her down, took her in, and they sent the black bull to a field for the night. In the morning, when he returned, they gave the girl a glittering diamond plum, telling her not to break it until she was in the greatest trouble of all, and that would get her out of it.

The castle folk set her on the black bull's back, and away they went. And on they rode, and on they rode, until they came to a dark and ugly glen, where they stopped. The black bull said, "Here you must stay while I go and fight the Old One, the devil. You must sit on that stone, and move neither hand nor foot until I come back, or else I will never find you again. If everything around about you turns blue, I have beaten the Old One. But should all things turn red, he will have conquered me."

She set herself down on the stone and waited, and by and by, all around her turned blue. So glad was she that her companion was victorious, she was overcome with joy and moved a foot. The black bull returned and sought her, but never could find her.

Long, the girl sat and wept, until she wearied of mourning. At last, she rose and wandered on, until she came to a great hill of glass. She tried and tried to climb it, but could not, and hunted for a way across. At last, she came to a smith's house. The smith promised that if she would serve him for seven years, he would make her iron shoes with which she could climb over the glassy hill.

At seven years' end, the girl got her iron shoes, climbed the glassy hill, and came to an old washerwife's home. There, she was told of a gallant young knight who had given in some bloodstained clothes to wash. Whoever washed out the stains was to be his wife.

The old wife had washed the clothes until she was tired, and then she had set her daughter at it. Both washed, and they washed, and they washed, in hopes of getting the young knight. But for all they could do, they could not wash out so much as a single stain.

"Let me try," the girl said.

As soon as she began, the stains vanished, leaving the shirt pure and clean. When the young knight returned, the old wife made him believe it was her daughter who had washed the stains out of the clothes. So the young knight and the old wife's daughter were to be married.

The girl wept at the thought of it, for she had fallen deeply in love with the young knight. This was her black bull in his true form!

She remembered the golden apple. Breaking it open, she found it filled with gold and precious jewelry.

"All these are yours," she said to the old wife's daughter, "if only you will put off your wedding for one day and let me stay at his bedside at night."

The woman agreed. But the old wife had given the young knight a sleeping potion, and he slept all night, even as the girl sang over him in vain:

> Seven long years I served for thee,
> The glassy hill I climbed for thee,
> Thy bloody clothes I cleaned for thee,
> And wilt thou not waken and turn to me?

But he never stirred. And the next day, the girl knew not what to do for her grief.

Then, she broke the pear, and found it filled with jewelry far richer than the contents of the apple. With these jewels, she bargained with the old wife for permission to stay a second night in the young knight's bedchamber.

But once again, the old wife gave the young knight a sleeping drink, and again he slept until morning. All night, the girl kept sighing and singing as before:

> Seven long years I served for thee,
> The glassy hill I climbed for thee,
> Thy bloody clothes I cleaned for thee,
> And wilt thou not waken and turn to me?

Still he slept. And the girl nearly lost hope altogether.

But that day, when the young knight was out hunting, one of his servants asked him who had been singing at night in his bedchamber.

He said, "I have heard no singing."

But all the servants assured him that they had, and so he resolved to keep awake that night to hear what he could hear.

Despairing, not knowing the young knight's plan, the girl broke open the third and last magic fruit, the plum. It held by far the richest jewelry of the three. She bargained as before.

The old wife, as before, took in the sleeping drink to the young knight's chamber. But this time, he told her he could not drink it without sweetening. When she went to get some honey to sweeten it, he poured out the drink, and made the old wife think he drank it.

Sitting by his bedside as before, the girl sang:

> Seven long years I served for thee,
> The glassy hill I climbed for thee,
> Thy bloody clothes I cleaned for thee,
> And wilt thou not waken and turn to me?

At last, the young knight heard, and turned to her. Joyfully, they fell into each other's arms. She told him all that had happened to her, and he told her all that had happened to him.

The treacherous old washerwife and her daughter were put to death.

The young knight and his faithful love were married. And he and she are living happily to this day, for all I know.

Sources

Campbell, J.F. *Popular Tales of the West Highlands*. Vol. 2. Edinburgh, United Kingdom: Edmonton and Douglas, 1860.

Douglas, George. *Scottish Fairy and Folk Tales*. London: Walter Scott, 1901.

East o' the Sun and West o' the Moon: A Folktale from Norway

Here is another quest folktale. This time, the heroine quests for a man who has been transformed into a white bear. The scope in this folktale is larger than in the previous tale, with the winds themselves helping the heroine to find her lost love and free him.

Once upon a time, there was a poor man with a wife and many children. The prettiest and kindest was his youngest daughter.

One wild, stormy evening, there came three taps on the window. The father went out to see who was there, and what he found was a huge white bear.

"Good evening to you," said the white bear as courteously as though he were a man.

"The same to you," said the man.

"Will you give me your youngest daughter? If you will, I will make you as rich as you are now poor," said the bear.

The man hardly would mind being rich. But he wanted to talk about it with his youngest daughter first.

At first, the girl was afraid. She wanted to say no. But then she thought better of it. Her family would be rich and want for nothing. So she packed what few things she owned, cleaned herself up, and was ready to go. She got upon the great wide back of the white bear with her bundle, and off they went.

After they had traveled a bit, the white bear asked, "Are you afraid?"

"No," the girl answered.

"Very good. Hold fast to my shaggy coat, and there will be nothing to fear."

They went on a long, long way, until they came to a steep hill. The white bear knocked, a door opened, and they entered a castle as grand as could be. The girl climbed down from the white bear, and he gave her a silver bell.

"Whatever you need, just ring the bell and it will be there."

She rang for food and she rang for drink. That night, she rang for a bed. There it was, a grand bedchamber with a fair, white bed with silken curtains. Once she had gone to bed and blown out the light, a man came to join her.

She had no idea what he looked like, but she knew in her heart that this was the white bear in human form. He was kind and loving. But she never saw him, for he always came after she had put out the light, and before the day dawned he was up and off again.

So things went on happily for a while. But at last, she began to get silent and sorrowful, being all alone all day. And she began to miss her father, mother, brothers, and sisters. When the white bear asked what was wrong, she told him how she missed her family.

"Well, well!" said the bear, "perhaps there is a cure for all this. But you must promise me one thing."

"Anything."

"Do not talk alone with your mother, only when the rest are near. I fear she will try to lead you into a room alone to talk. You must not do that or you will bring bad luck on both of us."

She agreed. And off they went, she riding on his back, far and long to where her family now lived. There was a grand house, and her family was happy and full of joy.

"You kept your promise!" she said to the bear.

"I did. But do not forget what I told you, else you will make us both unlucky."

"No, I will not forget," she promised.

When she had jumped down, the white bear turned right about and left her. She went in to her father and mother, and all were overjoyed. Everyone wanted to thank her for all the good she had done for them. Now, they were no longer poor or starving.

"But what about you?" they asked. "How is it where you live?"

"It is very good where I live, and I have all I wish." But more than that, she did not say. Then, her mother wanted to talk with her alone, but she remembered what the white bear had said, and would not do it.

But finally, her mother got the better of her. The girl told her mother the whole story, how she had a lovely man but never got to see him, and how all day she was lonely for him.

"He could be a troll!" her mother cried. "Here is how to see him: Take a bit of candle and light that while he is asleep—but be careful not to drop any of the candle tallow on him."

So the girl went away with the white bear. He warned her, "If you have listened to your mother's advice, you have brought bad luck on us both, and then, all that has passed between us will be as nothing."

That night, when she heard he slept, she lit the candle and let the light shine on him. Oh, he was so handsome! She fell so deeply in love with him on the spot, that she thought she could not live if she did not give him a kiss there and then. But as she kissed him, she dropped three hot drops of tallow on his shirt, and he woke up.

"What have you done?" he cried. "If only you had held out for this one year, I would have been freed from this spell. I have a stepmother who bewitched me so that I am a white bear by day, a man by night. But now, all ties between us are broken. Now, I must set off from you to her. She lives in a castle, which stands east o' the sun and west o' the moon, and there, too, is a long-nosed princess, and she is the wife I must have now."

The girl burst into tears. "I am sorry, so very sorry. May I at least go with you?"

"No. It cannot be."

"Tell me the way, then," she said, "and I will search you out. Surely, I may do that!"

"Yes, you might. But I know no clear way to that place that you could follow."

The next morning, when she woke up, both prince and castle were gone. The girl lay on a patch of grass in the middle of a thick forest, and with her was the same bundle of ragged clothes she had first brought with her from her father's house.

Once she had wept a bit, the girl set out on her way. She walked many, many days, until she came to the foot of a mountain. There sat an old hag, playing with a golden apple.

"Good day to you, old mother," the girl said politely. "Do you know the way to the castle that lies east o' the sun and west o' the moon, and to the prince who is to marry the long-nosed princess?"

"Ah, and are you the lassie who ought to have had him?"

"Yes, I am."

"So, so, it's you, is it?" exclaimed the old hag. "Well, all I know about him is that he lives in the castle that lies east o' the sun and west o' the moon, and thither you'll come, late or never. But you may have the loan of my horse, and on him you can ride to my next neighbor. Maybe she'll be able to tell you."

"What of your horse?"

"Oh, when you get there, just give the horse a switch under the left ear, and beg him to be off home. Ah, wait, this golden apple you may take with you. You may find a use for it."

So the girl got onto the horse, and rode a long, long time, until she came to another mountain. Under the mountain sat another old hag, this one playing with a golden comb. The hag answered as the first, saying she knew nothing of the castle except that it was east o' the sun and west o' the moon.

"And thither you'll come, late or never. But you shall have the loan of my horse to my next neighbor. Maybe she'll tell you all about it. Oh, and when you get there, just switch the horse under the left ear, and beg him to be off home. Yes, and take this golden comb with you. You may find a use for it."

So the girl got up on the horse, and rode a far, far way, and a weary time. At last, she came to another mountain, under which sat another old hag, spinning with a golden spinning wheel. But this one did not know any more than had the other two hags, save that the castle lay east o' the sun and west o' the moon.

"And thither you'll come, late or never," the old hag said. "But I'll lend you my horse, and then I think you had best ride to the East Wind and ask him. Maybe he knows those parts, and can blow you thither. When you get to him, you need only give the horse a switch under the left ear, and he'll trot home of himself. Ah, and take this golden spinning wheel. Maybe you'll find a use for it," said the old hag.

Then on she rode many, many days, a weary time, before she got to the East Wind's house. But at last she did reach it. So the girl asked the East Wind, "Can you tell me the way to the prince who lives east o' the sun and west o' the moon?"

"I have often heard tell of it," the East Wind said, "but I cannot tell you the way. I have never blown so far. But I will take you to my brother the West Wind. Maybe he knows the way."

She rode on his back, and they went briskly along to the West Wind's house. Again, the girl asked if he knew the way to the castle.

But the West Wind did not. Still, he offered to take her to the South Wind, who was stronger than either the East Wind or the West Wind.

She rode on his back, and they went briskly along to the South Wind. But the South Wind did not know the way to the castle that lay east o' the sun and west o' the moon.

But he said, "I can take you to our brother the North Wind, who is the oldest and strongest of us all."

So she rode on his back and off they flew to the North Wind.

"Yes, I know well enough where the castle is," said the North Wind. "Once I blew an aspen leaf thither, but I was so tired I could not blow a puff for many days after. But if you really wish to go there, I will take you on my back and see if I can blow you thither."

"Yes!" the girl cried. "Yes, with all my heart."

"Very well, then," said the North Wind, "but you must sleep here tonight, for we must have the whole day before us, if we are to get that far at all."

Early the next morning, the North Wind puffed himself up and made himself as stout and big as was possible. And off they went through the air. They tore on and on over the sea as if they would never stop until they got to the world's end.

But the North Wind grew more and more weary, and so out of breath he could scarce bring out a puff. His wings drooped and drooped, until at last he sunk so low that the crests of the waves dashed over his heels.

It was a fortunate thing that they were not very far from land. The North Wind managed to throw the girl onto the shore under the windows of the castle that lay east o' the sun and west o' the moon. Then, he went off to sleep and rest for several days.

The next morning, the lassie sat down under the castle window, and began to play with the golden apple. The first person she saw was the long-nosed princess who was to have the prince.

"What do you want for your golden apple?" asked the long-nosed princess.

"It is not for sale for gold or money," said the girl.

"If it is not for sale for gold or money, you may name your own price," said the princess.

"I would like to sit beside the prince's bedside tonight. If you grant me that, the apple is yours."

"Done!" cried the princess.

So she got the golden apple. But when the girl came to the prince's bedroom, she found him so heavily asleep that she could not wake him.

The next morning, she sat down under the castle windows and began to comb her hair with her golden comb, and the same thing happened. The long-nosed princess asked what she wanted for the golden comb. She said it was not for sale for gold or money, but if she might get leave to go up to the prince and be with him that night, the princess should have it.

But when the girl went up, she found the prince fast asleep again. For all she called, and all she shook, and wept, and prayed, she could not wake him.

The next morning, the girl sat down outside, under the castle window, and began to spin with her golden spinning wheel. That, too, the long-nosed princess wanted to have. So she said that, yes, if she could have the golden spinning wheel, the girl might spend the night in the prince's bedroom once more.

Some of the servants in that castle were good of heart, and they told the prince that there had been a young woman in his room sorely trying to wake him. That evening, when the long-nosed princess came with a drink for him, the prince pretended to drink. But he threw it over his shoulder, for he could guess it was a sleepy drink.

This time, when the girl came in, she found the prince wide awake. After much embracing and kissing, she told him the whole story of how she had come thither.

"Ah," said the prince, "you have just come in the very nick of time, for tomorrow is to be our wedding day. But now I will not have the long-nosed princess, and you are the only woman in the world who can set me free. I will say I want to see what my wife is fit for, and beg her to wash the shirt that has the three spots of tallow on it. She will say yes, for she does not know it was you who put them there. But she is a troll, not someone who can do this task. So I will say that I will not have any other for my bride than the woman who can wash the spots out, and ask you to do it."

That next day, the prince said, "Before I wed, I would like to see what my bride is fit for. I have a fine shirt that I would like for my wedding shirt, but somehow or other it has three spots of tallow on it, which I must have washed out. And I have sworn never to take any other bride than the woman who is able to do that. If she cannot wash out the spots, she is not worth having."

"That is no great thing," said the long-nosed princess, and she began to wash away as hard as she could. But the more she rubbed and scrubbed, the bigger the spots grew.

"Ah!" said the stepmother, "you cannot wash. Let me try."

But with all her rubbing, and wringing, and scrubbing, the spots grew bigger and blacker, and the darker and uglier was the shirt.

Then all the other troll women began to wash. But the longer they washed, the blacker and uglier the shirt grew.

"Ah!" said the prince, "you are none of you worth a straw if you cannot wash. Why there, outside, sits a beggar lass, and I will be bound she knows how to wash better than the whole lot of you. Come in, lassie!" he shouted.

In the girl came.

"Can you wash this shirt clean?" the prince asked.

"I do not know," she said, "but I think I can."

And almost before she had taken it and dipped it in the water, the shirt was as white as driven snow, and whiter still.

"Yes, you are the wife for me," said the prince.

At that, the stepmother flew into such a rage, she burst on the spot, and the long-nosed princess after her, and the whole pack of trolls after that.

As for the prince and princess, they set free all the poor human prisoners who had been carried off and shut up there by the trolls. Then, they took with them all the silver and gold, and flitted as far away as they could from the castle that lay east o' the sun and west o' the moon.

Sources
Asbjornsen, Peter Christen, and Jorgen Engebretsen Moe. *East o' the Sun and West o' the Moon.* Trans. George Webbe Dasent. New York: Dover, 1970.
Kvideland, Reimund, and Henning K. Sehmsdorf, eds. *Scandinavian Folk Belief and Legend.* Minneapolis: University of Minnesota Press, 1988.

CINDERELLA AND CINDERLAD

The story of Cinderella is, at least for now, the most widespread and common folktale type, with more than 920 versions collected by folklorists in almost every country of the world. Why this, of all folktale types, should be so popular around the world in so many cultures is a mystery.

Some stories contain the magic slipper, others do not. Some versions replace the fairy godmother with a magical animal, a talking doll, or other magical being. Others, known as the Donkey Skin variation, feature the heroine setting out into the world to find her own fortune.

The "Cinderlad" variant is not as common. In it, the main character is male. He hides his heroism behind a kitchen scullery disguise until he is revealed, usually by the princess he is to marry.

Cinderella

The most familiar version of "Cinderella," at least to the modern Western reader, has the basic elements of the fairy godmother (or other magical helper) and a slipper or similar object. It also features a heroine who comes from a noble or wealthy background and has fallen on hard times.

Ashey Pelt: A Folktale from England

This is one of the basic forms of the Cinderella folktale, but with the difference of a black ewe and a magic rod replacing the fairy godmother. The motif of the slipper is here, although it is a silk slipper, not the "traditional" glass slipper. (In fact, the motif of the glass slipper is the result of a typographical error.)

Now, in the old days, it was thought to be lucky for a farm to own a black ewe. And so it proved.

There was a wealthy farmer who was a widower with one daughter. He married again, this time, to a woman with two daughters.

The stepmother and two stepdaughters did not like the farmer's daughter, and they made fun of her. They called her Ashey Pelt, because she often had kitchen ashes all over herself from working so hard.

One day, there was to be a great party held by the prince of the land. Poor Ashey Pelt! Her stepmother and stepsisters dressed themselves in all their gaudy finery. But she knew she could not go. She had no fine clothes, and she never could get all the ashes out of her hair.

So Ashey Pelt went out into the field by an old standing stone so that she could cry alone. But a black ewe stepped out from the stone and said, "Don't you cry. Go look under the stone, and you will find a rod. Strike the stone three times with it, and whatever you wish will appear. Just be certain to be home by midnight, for the enchantment will only last until then."

Ashey Pelt found the rod, and she struck the stone three times with it. Instantly, she was dressed as finely as any princess, and not an ash clung to her hair. A carriage appeared and took her to the party.

There, the prince saw her. They danced together, and they fell in love. But when the clock began to strike midnight, Ashey Pelt ran away. So fast did she run that she ran right out of one of her silk slippers.

The prince found Ashey Pelt's silk slipper. He took it all over the country, trying to find the foot that it would fit.

When the stepsisters heard the prince's procession approaching, they threw Ashey Pelt out to take care of the cows. The stepsisters pared down their big feet as much as possible, and one of them did manage to squeeze into the slipper, even though it hurt her so much she nearly yelled. But fit into it she did, and off she rode with the prince.

But the black ewe called to the prince:

> Nippet foot and clippet foot
> With the king's son rides.
> But bonny foot and pretty foot
> In with the cows, she hides.

So the prince rode back. He took the slipper from the stepsister, and he went and found Ashey Pelt.

They loved each other all over again and were wed. And if they live happy, so may we.

Sources
Briggs, Katherine M. *British Folk-Tales*. New York: Pantheon, 1970.
Damant, M. "Ashey Pelt," *Folk-Lore* 6 (1895): 305–306.

Aschenzuttel: A Folktale from Serbia

This Cinderella variant has the odd beginning of an ancient superstition coming true: The heroine's mother does, indeed, become a cow. (Is this a leftover motif from some earlier transformation tale that got attached to a Cinderella tale? There is no evidence one way or the other.) Then, after the cow is slain and buried, another Cinderella motif occurs, with the fairy godmother replaced by the mother's ghost.

Once, a group of young women were tending their families' cattle and keeping themselves busy by chatting as they sat spinning near a pit. An old man passing by saw them and warned, "Do not drop your spindle into that pit! If you do, your mother will be transformed into a cow."

One girl, Mara, was so startled that she accidentally did drop her spindle. When she got home—oh, horror—her mother had, indeed, become a cow!

There was worse to come. Her father, thinking that his wife was dead or at the very least had abandoned him, married again, choosing a widow with one daughter.

The new stepmother promptly hated Mara for being more beautiful than her own ugly daughter. She decided to spoil Mara's beauty by turning her into a servant and giving her impossible tasks to do. One morning, she gave Mara a whole sackful of flax.

"You must spin this flax and wind it into a ball by evening, or do not even think of coming home," she said.

Poor Mara! She took the cows out to pasture and sat and spun and spun and spun, but by the afternoon she wept to see how much was left to spin.

"Do not sorrow, my dear daughter," said the cow that had been her mother. "I will chew the flax. Then, a thread will come out at my right ear, which you can then wind into a ball."

So it was. Delighted, Mara hugged the cow, and then she hurried home with the large ball of thread.

The stepmother was astonished and furious, and she gave Mara even more flax to be spun the next day. But again, Mara was helped by the cow and brought home a large ball of thread.

"That girl cannot be doing all this on her own," the stepmother muttered. "Daughter, spy on her tomorrow. See who is helping her."

So it happened that the stepdaughter saw Mara being helped by the cow, and she rushed home to tell her mother.

"Husband," the stepmother said, "that old cow is past her usefulness. She gives no milk. She bears no calves. Let us slay her for the meat."

Poor Mara! She wept bitterly. But the cow comforted her, saying, "Do not be afraid, my dear. You must eat none of my flesh when I am slain, but be sure to collect all of my bones and bury them under the great stone behind the house. Then, whenever you are in trouble, come to my grave for help."

Now, Mara soon had another name, a nickname her stepmother gave her because she had to do all the dirty work of the house and hearth. She was now called Aschenzuttel, or Ashyhead.

One Sunday, Mara would have loved to go to church, but her stepmother only laughed. "You? What would you do, go in your kitchen rags? Here, if you have nothing else to do, let me give you a task."

The stepmother scattered a large bowl of millet all over the house.

"There! If you have not collected it all, and cooked dinner as well, expect a night out in the wilderness."

Mara tried, but knew she would never find all the millet seeds. She went out to the grave of her mother.

There, she found a large chest. Opening it, Mara found that it was full of lovely dresses. Two white doves perched on the chest's lid and sang, "Choose a dress. Choose a dress. Go to church, and we will do the tasks."

So Mara put on a lovely dress and hurried off to church. Everyone there remarked on her beauty—but it was the emperor's son who noticed her the most.

At the end of the service, Mara hurried home and returned the lovely dress to the chest, which vanished. She put on her kitchen rags once more. Going into the house, she was relieved to find all the millet sorted and the dinner ready.

On the next Sunday, the stepmother scattered still more millet. This time, Mara did not hesitate. She went right to her mother's grave, and there was the chest and there were the two white doves.

Mara put on one of the lovely dresses and went to church. This time, the emperor's son looked long and long again at her.

But Mara hurried home at the end of the service and changed back into her kitchen rags. Going into the house, she found all the millet sorted and the dinner ready.

By now, the emperor's son had fallen madly in love with the mysterious maiden. When she appeared in church on the third Sunday, he started toward her after the service.

But Mara ran off, accidentally losing a shoe as she ran.

The emperor's son picked up the shoe. From that day on, he went from house to house across the whole of the empire. In each case, he tried to see who the shoe would fit, but it would fit none.

At last, the emperor's son came to Mara's house. The stepmother hastily hid Mara under a heavy trough when she heard the prince coming. She pushed her own daughter forward to try on the shoe, but no matter how the girl struggled to get her foot into it, she failed. The angry stepmother told the emperor's son, "That is it. I have no other daughter."

But the rooster flew to the trough and perched on it. "Kickeriki!" it crowed. "Kickeriki, kickeriki, the maiden is under this trough."

"The devil take you!" the stepmother snarled at the rooster.

But the emperor's son and his servants lifted the trough. Sure enough, there was Mara, a little breathless but still in her lovely clothes—and with no shoe on her right foot.

The emperor's son recognized Mara at once. Smiling, he held out the shoe, and sure enough, it fit perfectly.

"Will you marry me?" asked the emperor's son.

"I will," Mara said.

And the spirit of her mother rose to heaven, content.

Sources
Cox, Marian Roalfe. *Cinderella: Three Hundred and Forty-five Variants of Cinderella, Catskin, and Cap O' Rushes, Abstracted and Tabulated, with a Discussion of Mediaeval Analogues, and Notes.* London: David Nutt for the Folk-lore Society, 1893.
Karajich, Vuk. *Serbian Folk-Tales.* Trans. Wilhelmine Karajich. Berlin, Germany, 1854.

Burenushka, the Little Red Cow: A Folktale from Russia

Here is another folktale with a cow for helper, but in this case, the Little Red Cow is a magical animal, not a transformed human. The idea of girls with more than two eyes turns up in other folktales as well, and they usually are seen as evil or at least nasty people.

This folktale, unlike many of the Cinderella variants, does not end with the wedding. Instead, it continues on as a transformation tale in which the heroine must be returned to human form before there can be the happy ending.

In a certain kingdom in a certain land, there lived a king and queen and their daughter, Maria. Now, this princess was as kind as she was beautiful, and for a time their lives were happy.

But then, sorrow of sorrows, the queen died, and the king married again, this time to a woman named Yagishna. Yagishna bore the king two daughters, one with two eyes, the other with three eyes, and Yagishna and her daughters were as mean as they were ugly.

Yagishna hated poor Maria and sent her out to be the cowherd for Burenushka, the Little Red Cow, with nothing but a dry crust of bread to eat and nothing but rags to wear.

But Maria knew Burenushka was a magic cow. She bowed to the cow's right leg, and food and drink appeared. She bowed to the cow's left leg, and a gown suitable for a lady appeared.

Maria spent a pleasant day out there in the green fields with Burenushka. At the end of it, she bowed to the cow's right leg and the food and drink disappeared. She bowed to the cow's left leg, and the gown disappeared. Dressed in rags again, she led the Little Red Cow home.

This went on for several days. Yagishna began to wonder how Maria was surviving on only one dry crust of bread. So she sent her two-eyed daughter out to spy on Maria and Burenushka. But Maria knew this was a trick.

"Let me pick the lice from your head," she said to her stepsister. The stepsister lay down, and Maria began to pick the lice from her head. But as she did, she sang softly, "Sleep, sleep, little sister, sleep, sleep one eye, sleep, sleep second eye."

The stepsister fell asleep. When she got home that night, she had to tell her mother, "I saw nothing."

Furious, Yagishna scolded her. She then told her three-eyed daughter to go out with Maria and Burenushka in the morning. But Maria knew this was a trick.

"Let me pick the lice from your head," she said to her stepsister. The stepsister lay down, and Maria began to pick the lice from her head. But as she did, she sang softly, "Sleep, sleep, little sister, sleep, sleep one eye, sleep, sleep second eye." But she forgot to sing the third eye to sleep. And the third eye spied on her.

That night, the three-eyed daughter told her mother all that she had seen, of the magic food and drink and of the fine gown. Yagishna had the Little Red Cow slaughtered that same night.

But Maria begged for at least a bone or some entrails to bury, saying she had been very fond of the poor cow. So she was given some scraps of meat. She buried it, and from it sprang up a great green bush with the sweetest of berries. And every kind of singing bird perched on this bush and sang of heroes and their deeds.

Prince Ivan, son of the ruler of a neighboring land, heard about Maria. He knew magic was involved. So he went to Yagishna with a bowl and said, "Whoever can fill this bowl with those sweet berries shall be my wife."

Yagishna sent her two-eyed daughter. But the birds swarmed around her and threatened to pick out her eyes. She ran away. Yagishna sent her three-eyed daughter. But the same thing happened.

"Let Princess Maria try," said the prince.

Maria took the bowl and went to pick the berries, and the birds all sang sweetly around her. She returned with a full bowl of berries.

Maria and the prince smiled at each other. They were wed soon after and lived happily for a time.

After a time, Maria gave birth to a fine son. She wished to show her father his grandson—but Yagishna turned Maria into a gray goose and transformed her two-eyed daughter into a copy of Maria.

The old tutor of the prince was a wise man. He washed himself in the purest water, then took the baby out to an open field. When a flock of gray geese flew by, he cried, "Gray geese, gray geese, where is this baby's mother?"

"In the next flock," cried the geese.

The next flock of gray geese flew by. The old tutor called, "Gray geese, gray geese, where is this baby's mother?"

Princess Maria's gray goose skin slid from her. She turned back into a woman, and she nursed her baby tenderly. But she told the old tutor, "Today, I nurse my child. Tomorrow, I will nurse my child. But the day after tomorrow, I must fly beyond the forest, beyond the mountains high."

The old tutor and the prince went out together to the field the next day with the baby. When a flock of gray geese flew by, the tutor cried, "Gray geese, gray geese, where is this baby's mother?"

"In the next flock," cried the geese.

The next flock of gray geese flew by. The old tutor called, "Gray geese, gray geese, where is this baby's mother?"

Princess Maria landed, the gray goose skin slid from her, and she nursed her baby tenderly. But she warned, "Tomorrow, I must fly beyond the forest, beyond the mountains high."

But the prince was wise in magic, too. He quickly built a fire, seized the gray goose skin, and threw it into the flames. He grabbed Princess Maria. She turned to a frog, she turned to a lizard, she turned to a dragon, but he held her fast. At last, she turned into a spindle.

Prince Ivan broke the spindle, threw the top half behind him and the bottom half before him—and Princess Maria appeared. The spell was broken, and they went home.

The false Maria, Yagishka's daughter, was put to death.

But Princess Maria, her prince, and their baby lived happily after that.

Sources

Afanas'ev, Aleksander. *Russian Fairy Tales.* New York: Pantheon, 1945.
Rooth, Anna Birgitta. *The Cinderella Cycle.* Lund, Norway: Skanska Centraltryckeriet, 1911.

The Story of Tam and Cam: A Folktale from Vietnam

This Cinderella folktale differs from the majority of the Cinderella tales in three elements. The first is the replacement of the fairy godmother with the Buddha; that, in itself, is not so strange, since there is no tradition of fairy godmothers in Vietnamese folklore. But a non-Buddhist element appears again in the magic fish and its bones. A third unusual element is the transmutation of souls, from woman to nightingale to tree to fruit to woman again; this is definitely a Buddhist element, the rebirth of souls.

Once, there lived a man and wife and their daughter, little Tam. Sadly, the wife died, and the man married a second time. But this time, the new wife was a wicked woman. She told lies about Tam that turned her father away from the girl, and treated her more like a servant than a stepdaughter.

Things grew worse when the second wife gave birth to a daughter, Cam. Now, Tam really was treated like a servant, kept in the kitchen to work there, with only a few rags on which to sleep.

One day, the stepmother sent Tam and Cam out to do some fishing. Tam was diligent, and soon caught many fish. Cam just daydreamed. But just before they were ready to go home, Cam cried, "Oh Tam, your hair is all full of mud! Go wash it, or Mother will never want you back."

As Tam washed her hair, Cam stole her fish and ran home with them.

Tam sank down to the ground and began to cry. She realized that this had all been a trick, an excuse for the stepmother to beat her.

Suddenly, a sweet breeze swept across her face. Tam looked up to see the Buddha smiling at her.

"What is wrong, sweet child?" the pure, kind voice asked.

"Oh, great Buddha, my stepsister stole all my fish so that my stepmother will beat me."

"Have confidence in me, child. Your misfortunes will soon end. Now, look in your fishing basket."

Tam looked, and found a lovely fish with ruby red fins and golden eyes.

"Take the fish home," the Buddha said, "and keep it in the well behind the house. Feed it with whatever you can save from your own meals."

Tam thanked the Buddha and did exactly what he had said. But the stepmother was always spying on Tam, and finally she caught the girl going out to the well and feeding the fish with ruby fins and golden eyes. The stepmother killed the fish and ate it.

When Tam went to feed the fish with ruby fins and golden eyes, she saw nothing but blood on the water. She knew what had happened and began to weep.

Then, she heard the Buddha's kind, compassionate voice. "Do not weep. Find the bones from the fish and bury them in the ground under your sleeping mat. Ask them for whatever you need."

Tam found the bones and buried them in the ground under her mat. She asked once for a nice dress, and it appeared. But she did not dare ask for too much in case the stepmother got suspicious.

There was to be the great autumn festival. Tam wanted so much to go! But the stepmother and Cam, all dressed up in their finery, laughed at her. And the stepmother spilled out two big baskets of green beans and black beans.

"Have those sorted and in the right baskets when we get home, or it shall go badly for you!" the stepmother warned. And she and Cam went off to the festival.

Tam asked the bones for help. Instantly, a flock of sparrows appeared and quickly sorted out the beans into the right baskets. Tam asked for a gown, and a beautiful blue and silver gown with lovely embroidered slippers appeared. She bathed, put on the gown and slippers, and set out for the festival.

Tam had a fine time at the festival, and everyone wondered who the lovely girl might be. But then, Tam saw her stepmother and Cam, and she was afraid that they would recognize her. She ran home, but in her haste, lost one of her slippers.

A courtier picked up the slipper and brought it to the king. The king looked at its fine embroidery, and he was moved to know what lady had lost it. That lady, he vowed, would be his queen.

So messengers went out over the land, and girl after girl tried on the slipper. But it would fit only Tam.

Tam left her stepmother and Cam, and went to the king. They were wed, and they lived happily for a time.

But the stepmother and Cam were so jealous that they could not bear it. One day when Tam was in the royal garden, the stepmother chopped down a tree and killed Tam by making it fall on her.

Now, Cam became the king's wife.

But Tam's soul was pure and innocent, and it could not find rest. In the form of a nightingale, she sang to a palace maid, "Be careful with my husband's robe. Do not let the thorns tear it."

The maid rushed to tell the king. "Oh, nightingale," the king said, tears in his eyes, "if you are my beloved wife's soul, come into my wide sleeves."

The nightingale flew into one sleeve, and she rubbed her head lovingly against the king's hand. He had a beautiful big golden cage made for the nightingale in his bedroom, and the two did their best to communicate through songs.

Cam was furious. She stole into the room one day and killed the nightingale. She told the king, "She must have been bored and flew off."

But once again, Tam's pure and innocent soul was transformed, this time into a tree with golden fruit. A good-hearted old woman passed underneath, and a golden fruit fell right into her basket.

When the old woman got home, she saw a lovely lady come out of the golden fruit. They lived together as mother and daughter for a time.

Then one day, the king went hunting, and he came upon the old woman's house. She served him a meal, and he cried, "This is the way my wife prepared it!"

"There is only my adopted daughter here," said the old woman.

"Let her come to me."

It was Tam. Husband and wife were joyously reunited, and Tam was restored to her rightful rank as queen.

The old woman was given a place at court. But Cam was put to death, and the stepmother, with no one left, died of a broken heart.

Queen Tam and her king lived in peace and happiness the rest of their lives.

Sources

Quang, Mai Ly. *Vietnamese Legends and Folk Tales*. Hanoi, Vietnam: Thé Gioi, 2001.

Schultz, George F. *Vietnamese Legends*. Rutland, VT, and Tokyo, Japan: Charles E. Tuttle, 1965.

An American Cinderella: A Folktale from New Hampshire

A phenomenon in American folklore that came over with the British colonists is the loss of magical elements from both stories and ballads. This tale from eighteenth-century New Hampshire is an example. Here, there is no fairy godmother or magic slipper, but only the bare bones of the Cinderella tale: The abused but hopeful girl marries the prince (or in this case, the governor) and lives happily ever after. Perhaps the only element of magic left to this American Cinderella is her constant prophetic refrain about riding in the golden carriage with the four white horses.

In the Colonial days, there lived a poor girl named Martha, in Portsmouth, who worked at the Inn of the Earl of Halifax.

The inn was owned by Mistress Stavers, and she never gave poor Martha a chance to rest. The girl was busy all day long with washing the dishes, cleaning the rooms, and bringing pail after heavy pail of water from the well. But she never complained. Indeed, she grew prettier every day, and nothing Mistress Stavers could do could stop Martha from smiling.

"Scold all you wish, Mistress Stavers. Dress me in rags and feed me but scraps. But someday, I will ride in a carriage of gold drawn by four white horses."

Now, the other young people of Portsmouth who knew Martha liked her, and they would help her when the work was just too heavy for one young woman to bear. Unfortunately, Mistress Stavers saw them, and she berated Martha the worse for it.

"From now on," she shrieked, "you will sleep not in the inn but out with the pigs!"

"There is no harm sleeping with pigs," said Martha. "But the day will come when I ride in a golden carriage drawn by four white horses."

That only made Mistress Stavers scream even louder.

Now, it happened that the governor of New Hampshire Colony was passing by. He heard the shrieking, and asked, "Why Mistress Stavers, what is wrong?"

"It is this girl! She is lazy, she never works, she is useless—and above all, she claims that she will someday ride in a golden carriage drawn by four white horses!"

"Is this true, Martha?" the governor asked.

"No, sir. Not all of it. I am not lazy, and I work hard from day to night, and if you do not believe me, you can ask the other young people of Portsmouth. It is true that I say that someday I will ride in a golden carriage drawn by four white horses."

"You will be riding nowhere," snapped Mistress Stavers, "for I am casting you out right this day."

Before Martha could be afraid, the governor said, "My mansion needs a new maid. You are hired, Martha."

Martha's life was far better from that day on. She made beds and slept in a cozy one herself. She set the table and had nice meals herself. And she grew prettier each day.

The governor, who was still a young man, noticed. He saw what a good worker she was, and how kind she was to everyone.

At last, he said to her, "Martha, my dear, will you marry me?"

So they were wed. And they rode together in the bridal coach—a golden carriage drawn by four white horses.

Sources

Hansen, Harry. *New England Legends and Folklore.* New York: Hastings House, 1967.

Jagendorf, M. *New England Bean Pot: American Folk Stories to Read and to Tell.* New York: Vanguard, 1948.

The Donkey Skin Tale Type

In the Donkey Skin versions of the Cinderella tale type, the heroine either is cast out by her father for loving him "as meat loves salt"—a motif familiar to those who know Shakespeare's play King Lear—or escapes an unwanted marriage to him. It is she who seeks her destiny, but must, for safety's sake, hide her beauty under a disguise and serve as a kitchen maid until her fortunes turn for the better. These versions generally end with the father being invited to the wedding feast, tasting unsalted meat, and then realizing just how much his daughter did love him. A joyous reunion often follows.

Peu d'Ane (Donkey Skin): A Folktale from France

The French variants of "Cinderella" often do feature a fairy godmother, as does this one. She often is quite elegant and stylish. The tale *Peu d'Ane* was made into a 1970 movie by French director Jacques Demy. In it, the fairy godmother is the very height of fashion; she even uses a helicopter to get around.

Once upon a time, there was a good king with a wife who was both charming and beautiful, and they had a lovely little daughter.

Alas, the queen was struck mortally ill. At last, dying, she told her husband, "Promise me that when I am gone, if you find a woman wiser and more beautiful than I, you will marry her and so provide an heir for the throne."

The king so promised, and his wife died in his arms. For a time, the king was inconsolable in his grief, both day and night.

Some months later, however, on the urging of his courtiers, the king agreed to marry again, but because of his promise to his wife, he could not find a new wife with all the attractions he sought. Only his daughter had a charm and beauty that not even the queen had possessed.

So the king proposed marriage to his daughter. She tried to show him the mistake he was making, but he would not listen. So she fled to her fairy godmother, who lived in a grotto of pearls and coral.

"I know why you are here," the fairy said. "Nothing will harm you if you follow my advice. Tell your father that before you can marry, you must have a dress the color of the sky."

So she told him that. But his tailors did make such a dress in only a few days. When the princess saw it, she fled back to the fairy godmother. "Now, my dear," the fairy said, "Ask for a dress the color of the moon."

So the princess told him that. But in only a few days, the dress was ready. Once more, she fled to the fairy godmother. "Now," the fairy said, "you must ask for a dress as bright as the sun."

So she told her father that. But his tailors did make such a dress in only a few days. The princess heard the fairy godmother whisper, "Now, ask him for the skin of the donkey in the royal stable."

It was a bizarre request. But so besotted was the king that he granted it. He even had the donkey skin cured and softened for the princess.

"Now what shall I do?" the frightened princess asked the fairy godmother.

"You must prepare to escape to some far country. Here is a small chest into which you are to put the three dresses, your mirror, and your jewels. Take this magic wand. The chest will not be seen until you touch the wand to the ground. Hide yourself in the folds of the donkey skin, for when you are inside it, no one will believe that anyone so beautiful could be hidden in anything so frightful."

So the princess fled. On and on she traveled and on again, avoiding her pursuers until they gave up. Wherever she went, the princess hunted for some place where she might find work, but most people, seeing only a beggar in an ugly donkey skin, turned her away.

At last, she found a farm where they needed a kitchen worker to do all the hard jobs. There, the princess stayed, exposed to ridicule from the other workers who called her Donkey Skin, and she slept in a tiny cupboard of a room.

Only on Sundays did she have a little rest. Then, she bathed and tried on one of the three dresses, and enjoyed being pretty again—if only for a day.

Now, on this farm was an aviary that belonged to the king. The king's son often stopped to visit the many unusual birds and have a cool drink. Donkey Skin saw him once and again, and she fell in love with him.

One day, the prince happened to catch the barest glimpse of the princess in her golden gown. She was so lovely, and she seemed so kind that he, too, was smitten. But when he tried to find her again, he could not.

Back in his father's palace, the prince lost his appetite and was sad all day. When he asked who he had seen, he was told that it must have been Donkey Skin, the ugliest creature one could find, and a certain cure for love. This, he would not believe, and he refused to forget what he had seen.

Finally, the prince said that he wished Donkey Skin to make him a cake with her own hands. Everyone was horrified at the thought, but the prince insisted.

So Donkey Skin bathed and found a clean apron, then she began to make the cake. But into the cake, more by purpose than mere chance, she happened to drop a golden ring from her hand.

The prince all but devoured the cake—then found the ring in it just in time. He knew, oh, he knew he had not been deceived. He told his parents, "I will marry only the young woman this ring fits."

A search began for whoever might be able to fit the ring on her finger, no matter what her station in life. The trials began with the princesses, the marquesses, and the duchesses, but their fingers, although delicate, were too big for the ring. Then the countesses, the baronesses, and all the noble ladies presented their hands, but all in vain.

Next came the working girls, but the ring would not fit them, either. Finally, it was the turn of the servants, the kitchen help, and the poultry keepers. Putting the tiny ring on their clumsy fingers was like trying to thread a big rope through the eye of a needle.

At last, there remained only Donkey Skin. "Let her try," said the prince.

At that, some started to laugh. Others cried out against bringing that frightful creature anywhere near the prince. But when she drew out from under the donkey skin a delicate little hand and the ring vas placed on her finger and fitted perfectly, everyone was astounded.

"Before I appear before the court," Donkey Skin said, "pray allow me to change my clothes."

There were some snickers at that, but they gave her leave. And the young woman who appeared before the court was the princess with her golden hair combed and her golden dress gleaming. The prince cried out with delight, "I knew it was you!"

The king and queen were completely delighted with her. Preparations for the wedding were begun at once, and the kings of all the surrounding countries were invited.

But none appeared in such splendor as the bride's father, who now recognized his daughter and begged her forgiveness. His madness had passed, and now he was overjoyed to see her again. The fairy godmother was at his side, and perhaps she had helped his madness pass, too.

And, of course, they all lived happily from then on.

Sources

Massignon, Genevieve. *Folktales of France*. Chicago: University of Chicago Press, 1968.
Perrault, Charles. *Old-Time Stories Told by Master Charles Perrault*. Trans. A.E. Johnson. New York: Dodd Mead, 1921.

La Sendraoeula (Cinderella): A Folktale from Italy

Unique motifs turn up in this Cinderella folktale. First are the three thrones that the father uses to show his mood. Are they a storyteller's fancy, or do they refer to some ancient, now lost custom?

As does the evil stepmother in the traditional "Snow White," the father wishes his daughter's heart, and there is the same sympathetic guard who substitutes an animal heart. Perhaps the most unusual motif is the replacement of the fairy godmother with three witches, who decide to help the heroine and give her a magic wand.

There once lived a king with three daughters. The two older daughters were haughty and selfish. They hated their younger sister, who was as kind as they were haughty and as lovely as they were selfish.

Now that king had three thrones, one red, one white, and one black. When he was feeling happy and at peace, he sat on the white throne. When he felt neither good nor bad, he sat on the red throne. But when he was angry, he sat on the black throne. And it was on the black throne that the three daughters found him one day.

"Why are you angry, Father?" asked the eldest daughter. "Are you angry at us?"

"I am! You do not love me."

"I do love you!" proclaimed the eldest. "I love you as much as eating the finest meat."

"You do love me," the king said. "Off with you."

"I love you, too," said the middle daughter. "I love you as much as eating the finest of freshly baked bread."

"You do love me," the king said. "Off with you."

The youngest daughter told her father, "I love you very much. I love you as much as grains of salt."

"What nonsense! You do not love me!"

Spurred on by the two older sisters, the king ordered a servant to take the youngest daughter into the wood and kill her. "Bring back her heart and clothing as proof!"

The servant had no choice but to take the youngest daughter into the woods. But once they were alone, he said to her, "I will not kill an innocent girl. Let me see what I can do to save you."

He found an old donkey and skinned it, then dried it out. "Here. I am afraid that this will have to serve you as clothing."

The girl took off her fine gown and wrapped herself in the donkey skin.

Then, the servant killed a sheep and cut out its heart. "This will do," he said.

He showed the girl a hollow tree in which she could shelter from the cold. "I can do no more for you," the servant said, and he left her there.

When the servant returned to the king and showed him the heart and clothing, the king fell into the deepest of sorrows. But the two older sisters were merry as two birds.

Meanwhile, the poor girl in the donkey skin slept a bit. She woke at midnight when a voice said, "Who is this?"

Some witches were passing through the wood. But they were not evil witches, and they felt sorry for her. One of them gave her a wooden wand and a little nut.

"Whenever you need anything, my child, just tap the nut with the wand and see what you get."

Now, her father the king often went hunting. His dogs recognized the youngest daughter, even in her disguise, and wagged their tails happily. The king did not recognize her in that donkey skin, but since the dogs liked her so much, he decided to take her back to the castle. Even a beggar girl, or so he thought, could serve in the kitchen.

So the girl returned. Soon she was called La Sendraeula, or Cinderella, because she would sit in the warm ashes by the fireplace. The kitchen staff treated her well. And, of course, her two sisters were too proud and haughty to ever go down to the kitchen.

Soon, it was announced that there was to be a grand three-day ball at the palace of a neighboring prince. The two older sisters went off to the ball in all their gaudy finery.

La Sendraeula watched them go. When everyone was gone, she tapped the little nut with the wand, and a lovely dress and shoes appeared. She tapped it again, and there was a coach and four horses. Now dressed as a princess, she rode off to the ball.

Everyone wondered who this beautiful lady might be. The prince even danced with her. But at midnight, she knew that the spell would wear off, as it was at midnight that she had gotten the magic wand and nut. So she hurried home.

La Sendraeula was back in the kitchen when the sisters returned. She heard them wonder who the mysterious lady had been. "Me," she whispered, but too softly for any to hear. "It was me."

On the second night, La Sendraeula again tapped the wand on the little nut. A second dress and shoes appeared, more dazzling than the first. She got into the magical coach and rode to the ball.

Again, everyone wondered who the beautiful lady was. And again, the prince danced with her. But at midnight, she ran away once more.

La Sendraeula was back in the kitchen when the sisters returned. She heard them wonder who the mysterious lady had been. "Me," she whispered, but too softly for any to hear. "It was me."

On the third and final night of the ball, La Sendraeula once more tapped the little nut with the wand. A third dress and shoes appeared, and if the first two had been beautiful, this one outshone them both. She got into the magic coach and rode to the ball.

This time, the prince danced only with her. He had fallen in love with her, and she, looking up into his tender eyes, fell in love with him, too. She almost forgot to listen for midnight. The clock was striking the last few chimes when she gasped and ran. The prince ran after her, but all he caught was one of her golden shoes.

La Sendraeula just barely got home in time. She completely forgot to take off her golden stockings. But no one noticed.

The next morning, the prince issued an edict. He would marry only she whose foot fit the golden shoe. All over the prince's city, then all over the king's land went the royal procession. But the shoe would not fit any of the women they found.

At last, they reached the king's palace. The two older sisters struggled and wept, but they could not get the shoe to fit. Angrily, they snapped, "You might as well try it on La Sendraeula down in the kitchen."

Down went the prince, and the king, and the two older daughters. La Sendraeula did not want her father to see who she was, but the prince recognized her even without her finery, seized her foot, and slipped it into the shoe. Everyone saw the golden stockings.

"You are alive!" the king cried. "Oh, my dear daughter, how can you ever forgive me?"

"By letting me marry your daughter," said the prince. "If she will have me."

"I will," she said.

What about the two older sisters? They were furious as mad dogs. But there was not a thing they could do to spoil their sister's happiness.

Sources
Pigorini-Beri, Caterina. *"La Cenerentola a Parma e a Camerino"* (Cinderella in Parma and in Camerio). *Archivio per la Studio delle Tadizioni Popolari* (Archive for the Study of Popular Culture), Palermo, Italy, 1883.

Zipes, Jack, trans. and ed. *Beautiful Angiola: The Great Treasury of Sicilian Folk and Fairy Tales Collected by Laura Gonzenbach.* London and New York: Routledge, 2004.

Love Like Salt: A Folktale from the Hottentot of South Africa

In this shorter version of the tale type, which comes from the Hottentot people, there again are the motifs of the youngest daughter saying she loves her father "like salt" and her being carried off to be killed. Again, she is helped by kind servants. There is no magic in this tale, however, only a happy ending with a wedding, when the father realizes what a fool he was.

Once, a group of girls were talking about how much they loved their fathers. One girl, Katje Leiro, said that she loved her father like salt. When her father heard that, he was outraged.

"You do not really love me at all!" he cried.

He ordered his servants to carry Katje Leiro off into the wilderness and kill her, bringing back her hair and blood as proof of the deed.

But the servants took pity on her. They had to cut off her hair, but that did not hurt her. Then, they pricked their own arms with porcupine quills and rubbed the blood on the heads of their clubs. When they returned to her father, they claimed that the blood was hers.

Meanwhile Katje Leiro disguised herself in rags and fled. She came to a farm where she hid in the stables, pretending to be a beggar. Only when no one was around would she take off the rags and put on her finery.

The servants would have thrown the "dirty beggar girl" out, but the son of the farm's owner stopped them. He took pity on her.

Then one day, the farmer's son saw Katje Leiro dressed in her finery, and he realized she was not a beggar at all. He took her to his mother and insisted that Katje Leiro was a guest. Soon after that, Katje Leiro and he fell in love and were married.

Then one day, Katje Leiro's father came to visit. Katje Leiro disguised herself and served him food without salt, which was tasteless. He started to add some salt, but Katje Leiro stopped him. "So you see," she said, "I loved my father very much."

Her father was overjoyed to see her. He kept saying over and over how sorry he was.

Katje Leiro and her husband lived happily after that. And the servants who had spared her life were given gold and high honors, and they lived happily after that, too!

Sources

Klipple, May Augusta. *African Folktales with Foreign Analogues*. The Garland Folklore Library. New York and London: Garland, 1992.

Savory, Phyllis. *Bantu Folk Tales from Southern Africa*. Cape Town, South Africa: Howard Timmins, 1974.

Cap o' Rushes: A Folktale from England

The heroine of this story is a spunky young woman. She is not afraid to throw the ring into the gruel to show her chosen husband who she is.

Once, there was a wealthy gentleman with three daughters, and he thought he would test them to see how well they loved him.

So he asked the eldest daughter, "How much do you love me, my dear?"

"Why," she answered, "as I love my life."

"Very good," he said.

Now he asked the second daughter, "How much do *you* love me, my dear?"

"Why," she answered, "better than all the world."

"Very good," he said.

Now he asked his youngest daughter, "How much do *you* love me, my dear?"

She answered, "I love you as fresh meat loves salt."

Oh, that angered him! "You do not love me at all, then, and in my house you shall stay no longer!"

Thrown out, the youngest daughter went on and away until she came to a marsh. There, she gathered a load of rushes and wove them into a hooded cloak to hide her and her fine gown from head to foot.

Then, she went on and away again until she came to a great house.

"Do you need a maid?" she asked.

"No, we do not."

"Please, listen. I have nowhere to go and will do any sort of work in exchange for food and shelter."

"Well, then, if you wish to wash pots and scrape saucepans, you may stay."

So she stayed there, and she did all the dirty kitchen work without complaint. And since she would give them no name, they took to calling her Cap o' Rushes.

One day, there was to be a grand dance a little way off, and the servants were allowed to go and see all the great people. Cap o' Rushes said she was too tired to go. But when everyone else was gone, she took off her rushy disguise, cleaned herself up, and off she went to the dance.

Who was there but the master's son himself. He fell in love with her the moment he saw her. And he refused to dance with anyone else.

But before the night was done, she slipped away and hurried home. When the other servants returned, there was Cap o' Rushes, seemingly sound asleep.

The next morning, the servants were full of gossip about the beautiful lady and how the master's son never took his eyes off her.

"I should have liked to have seen her," Cap o' Rushes said.

"There is to be another dance tonight, and maybe she will be there."

But that evening, Cap o' Rushes again said she was too tired to go with them. Once everyone was away, though, off came her rushy disguise, and away she went to the dance.

The master's son had been hoping to see her again. He danced with no one else, and he never took his eyes off her.

But, before the dance was over, she slipped away, and home she went. When the servants came back, she pretended to be asleep with her cap o' rushes on.

The next morning, the servants were even more full of gossip about the beautiful lady and the master's son.

"I should have liked to have seen her," Cap o' Rushes said.

"There is to be another dance tonight, and maybe she will be there."

But that evening, Cap o' Rushes again said she was too tired to go with them. Once everyone was away, though, off came her rushy disguise, and away she went to the dance.

The master's son was overjoyed to see her. He danced with no one but her and never took his eyes off her. When she would not tell him her name, or where she came from, he gave her a ring. He told her if he did not see her again he should die.

Once again, before the dance was over, off she slipped, and home she went. When the servants came home, she was pretending to be asleep with her cap o' rushes on.

The master's son tried every way to find out where the lady had gone. But go where he might and ask whom he might, he never heard anything about her. And he got worse and worse for the love of her until he had to take to his bed.

The cook was told, "Make some gruel for the master's son. The poor thing is dying for love of the lady."

"Let me make it," said Cap o' Rushes.

So she made it. And as she made it, she slipped the ring into it. No one saw her do this, and the cook took the gruel upstairs.

The young man drank the gruel, and then he saw the ring at the bottom of the bowl.

"Who made this gruel?" he asked.

The cook was frightened. "I did," she said.

He stared at her. "No, you didn't. Say who did it, and I promise you will not be punished for lying."

"It was Cap o' Rushes," the cook admitted.

"Send Cap o' Rushes here," he said.

So, Cap o' Rushes came.

"Did you make my gruel?" he asked.

"Yes, I did."

"Where did you get this ring?"

"From him who gave it to me," she said.

"Who are you, then?" he asked.

"I will show you," she said. And she cast off her cap o' rushes, and there she was in her beautiful clothes.

Well, the master's son got well very soon, and the happy couple was to be married in a little time. It was to be a very grand wedding, and everyone was asked far and near. Cap o' Rushes' father was asked. But she never told anybody who she was.

Before the wedding, she went to the cook, and said, "I want you to prepare every dish without a grain of salt."

"That will be nasty," the cook said.

"That does not matter."

The cook shrugged. "Very well."

The wedding day came, and the happy couple was married.

After they were married, all the company sat down to the dinner. When they began to eat the meat, it was so tasteless they could not eat it. Cap o' Rushes' father tried first one dish and then another, and then he burst out crying.

"What is the matter?" asked the master's son.

"I had a daughter," he said. "I asked her how much she loved me. And she said. 'As much as fresh meat loves salt.' And I turned her from my door, for I thought she did not love me. And now I see that she loved me best of all. And she may be dead for aught I know."

"No, father, here she is!" said Cap o' Rushes. She threw her arms around him.

And so they were all happy ever after.

Sources
Jacobs, Joseph. *English Fairy Tales*. London: David Nutt, 1890.
Steel, Flora Annie. *English Fairy Tales*. London: Macmillan, 1918.

All-Kinds-of-Fur: A Folktale from Germany

This is one of the Donkey Skin folktales, clearly featuring a father's thoughts of incest. The king here has no excuse of insanity: He is determined to marry his daughter, because she alone has her mother's beauty and golden hair. The heroine is more sensible, and she needs no fairy godmother to help her.

Messengers were sent about far and wide, but none of them could find any woman who was the late queen's equal. But the king's daughter had grown up as beautiful as her mother, with the same golden hair.

The king suddenly saw this, and he felt a violent love for her. He told his councilors, "I will marry my daughter, for she is the counterpart of my late wife."

When the councilors heard that, they were shocked, and said, "God has forbidden a father to marry his daughter! No good can come from such a crime, and the kingdom will be involved in the ruin."

The daughter was even more shocked than they. But she decided to trick her father into giving up his decision.

The princess told him, "Before I marry you, I must have three dresses, one as golden as the sun, one as silvery as the moon, and one as bright as the stars. I also wish for a mantle of a thousand different kinds of fur and hair joined together."

But she thought, "To get that will be quite impossible. By the time my father realizes this, I shall have distracted him from his wicked intentions."

The king, however, did not give up. The cleverest maidens in his kingdom had to weave the three dresses, one as golden as the sun, one as silvery as the moon, and one as bright as the stars. And the king's huntsmen had to catch one of every kind of animal in the whole of his kingdom, and take from it a piece of its skin, and out of these was made a mantle of a thousand different kinds of fur.

At length, when all was ready, the king had the mantle spread out before the princess, and he said, "The wedding shall be tomorrow."

The princess realized that the king could not be moved. Her only hope was to run away from him.

That night, she took three things from her treasures: a golden ring, a golden spinning wheel, and a golden reel. The three dresses of the sun, moon, and stars she put into a nutshell. She put on her mantle of all kinds of fur, and she blackened her face and hands with soot.

Then, she commended herself to God, and left, walking the entire night until she came to a great forest. Tired, she found a hollow tree and curled up in it, and was soon fast asleep. She slept all the way into full daylight.

The king to whom this forest belonged went hunting in it. When his dogs came to the hollow tree, they sniffed, and ran barking round about it. The king said to his huntsmen, "See what kind of wild beast has hidden itself in there."

The huntsmen said, "A wondrous beast is lying in the hollow tree. We have never before seen one like it. Its skin looks like a patchwork of fur of a thousand different kinds. But it is lying asleep."

The king said, "See if you can catch it alive, and we will take it with us."

When the huntsmen seized the princess, she awoke full of terror and cried to them, "I am a poor child, deserted by father and mother. Have pity on me, and take me with you."

Not knowing what to call her and thinking her some poor near-witless thing, they said, "All-Kinds-of-Fur, you can work in the kitchen. Come with us, and you can sweep up the ashes."

So they took the princess to the royal palace. There, they pointed out to her a closet under the stairs and said, "You can live and sleep there."

Then, she was sent into the kitchen, and there she carried wood and water, swept the hearth, plucked the fowls, picked the vegetables, raked the ashes, and did all the dirty work. She was miserable, but she did her best to do whatever needed to be done.

But one day, a feast was held in the palace. All-Kinds-of-Fur asked the cook, "May I go upstairs for a while and look on?"

The cook answered, "Yes, go. But you must be back here in half an hour to sweep the hearth."

All-Kinds-of-Fur went into her little closet, took off her fur dress, and washed the soot off her face and hands. She opened the nut and took out the dress that shone like the sun.

Then, she went up to the feast. No one knew her, and everyone thought she must surely be a king's daughter.

The king came to meet her and danced with her, thinking that surely he had never seen anyone so beautiful. But when the dance was over, she curtsied, then ran off, straight to her little closet. There, she became All-Kinds-of-Fur again.

She went into the kitchen, and was about to get to work and sweep up the ashes when the cook said, "Leave that alone until morning, and make me the soup for the king. I, too, will go upstairs awhile, and take a look. Eh, but do not let any hairs fall in, or in future you will get nothing to eat."

So the cook went away, and All-Kinds-of-Fur made the soup for the king, the best she could. When it was ready, she fetched her golden ring from her little closet and put it in the bowl in which the soup was served.

When the dancing was over, the king ate his soup, and it seemed to him he had never tasted better. But when he came to the bottom of the bowl, he found the golden ring. How did it get there?

The king ordered the cook to come before him. The cook was terrified and sent All-Kinds-of-Fur instead. When All-Kinds-of-Fur came, the king asked, "Who are you?"

"I am a poor girl who no longer has any father or mother."

"Where did you get the ring that was in the soup?"

She answered, "I know nothing about the ring."

So the king could learn nothing. And he sent her away.

After a while, there was another feast. Then, as before, All-Kinds-of-Fur begged the cook for leave to go and look on. The cook answered, "Yes, but come back again in half an hour, and make the king that soup he likes so much."

Then, All-Kinds-of-Fur ran to her closet and put on the dress as silvery as the moon.

As the princess entered the feast, the king rejoiced to see her once more, and they danced together. But when that dance was ended, she again disappeared so quickly that the king could not observe where she went.

She, however, had run back to her little closet, transformed herself into All-Kinds-of-Fur, and went into the kitchen to prepare the soup. This time, she slipped the little golden spinning wheel into the soup.

The king enjoyed his soup once again, then found the little golden spinning wheel. All-Kinds-of-Fur again was sent before the king, but she answered that she knew nothing at all about the little golden spinning wheel.

When, for the third time, the king held a feast, all happened just as it had done before. This time, though, the princess wore the dress that shone like the stars. Once again, the king danced with her. And while he did, he managed to slip a golden ring onto her finger.

When the dance ended, the king wanted to hold the princess, but she tore free and ran away. But this time, she had stayed too long, and, in her haste, could only throw her fur mantle over the dress, and one finger did not get covered by soot. Then, All-Kinds-of-Fur ran into the kitchen. She cooked the soup for the king, then slipped her golden reel into it.

When the king found the reel at the bottom of the soup, he called All-Kinds-of-Fur to him. Ah, and now he saw that white finger, and on it the ring he had slipped onto it. So he caught her, and the fur mantle swung open, revealing the star dress.

The king tore off the mantle, and there was the lovely princess.

"I thought it was you," he cried. "You are my dear bride, and we will never more part from each other."

She agreed. They were wed, and lived happily until their death.

Sources

Grimm, Jacob, and Wilhelm Grimm. *Household Tales.* Trans. Margaret Hunt. London: George Bell, 1884; Detroit, MI: Singing Tree, 1968.

Ranke, Kurt. *Folktales of Germany.* Trans. Lotte Baumann. Chicago: University of Chicago Press, 1966.

Rashin-Coatie: A Folktale from Scotland

Here is a Donkey Skin folktale with a little red calf as helper and a heroine without a stepmother but with a mean older sister who is the favorite of her parents. Like many of this type of folktale, this one features the motif of the heroine's slipper that will fit only her.

Once, a long time ago, there was a gentleman with two daughters. The older of the two was mean-spirited and ugly, but the younger was sweet-natured and pretty. Yet the older daughter was their parents' favorite, and they ill-used the younger one.

The younger daughter was sent off into the woods to herd the cattle, and all the food she had to take with her was some porridge.

Among the cattle was a little red calf. It said to the girl, "Give that mess to the dogs and come with me."

So she followed the calf to a pretty little house, where there was a nice dinner ready for them. After a good meal, they went back to the herding.

Every day, the calf took the girl away, and they dined nicely. And every day, the girl grew prettier.

Her parents and the older daughter knew something was up, and they spied on her until they saw her with the calf. So they decided to kill the calf. No, no, they decided, it would be the girl who had to kill him.

When the girl heard this, she could do nothing but weep. But the calf told her not to weep, but to do as he told her.

Sure enough, the day came when she was to kill the calf. So she raised the axe—and brought the flat of it down on her sister's head. In the confusion, she leaped onto the calf's back, and they were away.

At last, they stopped in a meadow full of rushes, and the girl made a coat for herself out of it as a disguise.

They traveled on until they came to the king's home. The kitchen needed a girl, and so Rashin-Coatie (Rush-Coat) was hired. So the girl and the calf stayed there, and everybody was well pleased with her.

When Yule came, Rashin-Coatie was to stay at home and make the dinner, while all the rest went to church.

After they were gone, the calf asked, "Would you like to go?"

"I would, but I have no clothes, and I cannot leave the dinner."

"Wait," said the calf. He went out, and came back with a grand dress, all silk and satin, and a nice pair of slippers. The girl put on the dress, and before she left she said:

> Ilka peat gar anither burn,
> An' ilka spit gar anither turn,
> An' ilka pot gar anither play,
> Till I come frae the kirk on gude Yule day.
> (Every [piece of] peat give another burn,
> And every spit give another turn,
> And every pot give another boiling,
> Till I come from the church on good Yule day.)

So the girl went to the church, and nobody knew who she was. As soon as the young prince saw her, he fell in love with her, and resolved he would find out who she was.

But Rashin-Coatie hurried off before the rest, so that she might get home in time to take off her dress, and look after the dinner.

When the prince saw her leaving, he raced after her, but she got away. In her hurry, she lost one of her shoes. The prince kept the shoe.

Rashin-Coatie got home all right. And the folk said the dinner was very nice.

Now, the prince was resolved to find out who the lovely lady was, and he sent a servant through all the land with the shoe. Every lady was to try it on, and the prince promised to marry the one it would fit.

That servant went to a great many houses, but he could not find a lady that the shoe would go on, it was so little and neat. At last, he came to a henwife's house, and her daughter had little feet. At first, the shoe would not go on, but she pared her feet, and clipped her toes, until the shoes went on.

Now, the prince was very angry. He knew it was not the lady that he wanted, but, because he had promised to marry whomever the shoe fit, he had to keep his promise.

The marriage day came. As they were all riding to the church, a little bird flew through the air, and sang:

> Clippit feet an' paret taes is on the saidle set,
> But bonnie feet an' braw feet sits in the kitchen neuk.
> (Clipped feet and pared toes is on the saddle seat,
> But pretty feet and brave feet sits in the kitchen nook.)

The prince turned his horse and rode home. He went straight to his father's kitchen, and there sat Rashin-Coatie. He knew her at once, and when she tried on the shoe it fit her.

And so the prince married Rashin-Coatie, and they lived happily. And they built a house for the red calf who had been so kind to her.

Sources
Bruford, Alan, and Donald A. MacDonald. *Scottish Traditional Tales*. Edinburgh, United
    Kingdom: Polygon, 1994.
Douglas, George. *Scottish Fairy and Folk Tales*. London: Walter Scott, 1901.

The Princess Who Would Not Marry Her Father:
A Folktale from Portugal

Here is another Donkey Skin folktale featuring the incest theme. The helper here is a mysterious old woman. The princess is a strong-willed person who does not hesitate at such deeds as killing the ducks she has been set to tend so that she may move closer to her goal of winning the prince.

There once were a king and a queen. But a few years after their marriage, the queen died. At her death, she placed a ring on a table, and bade the king marry whomsoever that ring should fit.

It happened that their daughter, the princess, approached the table by chance, saw the ring, and tried it on. She then ran to the king her father, and said, "Sire, do you know that a ring, which I found on the table, fits me as though it had been made expressly for me!"

The king, on hearing this, replied, "Oh, my daughter, you will have to marry me, because your mother, before she died, expressed a wish that I should marry whoever this ring would fit."

The princess, greatly distressed, ran off and shut herself up in a room that had a window looking out over the palace garden. There, she burst into sobs.

Suddenly, a little old woman appeared in the room and asked her, "Why do you weep, royal lady?"

Too miserable to be surprised at the woman's sudden appearance, the princess sobbed, "What can I do? My father says that I must marry him."

The little old woman shook her head. "Listen to me, royal lady. Go and tell your father that you will only marry him if he buys you a dress the color of the stars in the heavens." With that, she disappeared.

The princess then went up to the king, who asked her, "Well, my daughter, are we to be married?"

She replied, "I shall marry you when you bring me a dress the color of the stars in the heavens."

The father bought the dress, and gave it to her. The princess went to her room to cry.

The little old woman again appeared to her, and asked her, "What ails you, royal lady?"

She replied, "My father has bought me the dress I asked him for, and he wishes to marry me."

The old woman said, "Never mind. You must now ask him to bring you a dress of all the colors of the flowers that grow in the fields."

The princess again went to her father and told him that she could marry him only if he bought her a gown of all the colors of wildflowers. The king bought the dress and gave it to her. The princess, once more in trouble, went to her room to weep.

The little old woman again appeared and demanded, "What ails you, royal lady?"

The princess replied, "My father has bought me the second gown, and he is determined to marry me."

"Never mind. Now, ask your father for a robe of all the colors."

The princess asked for a robe of all the colors, and the king bought her the robe. The princess returned to her room to weep over her new trouble. Again, the little old woman came to her and asked what troubled her.

"My father has bought me the third robe and is determined we shall wed. What can I do now to prevent it?"

The little old woman replied, "Royal lady, you must now send for a carpenter and order him to make you a dress of wood. Get inside it and go to the palace of the king who lives yonder, who requires a servant to tend the ducks."

The princess did as she was told. She had a dress made of wood, put all her jewels, and everything else she would require, inside, and getting inside it herself; she ran away.

She walked on and on until she arrived at the other palace, then asked if their king needed a maid to tend the ducks. He did.

When she was asked for her name, the princess said that she was Maria do Pau (Maria of Wood). That was fine. She was sent to tend the ducks, which were in a field next to the palace gardens.

The moment the princess reached the field, she gladly removed the wooden dress, cleaned herself up, and put on the dress that was the color of the stars. The king happened to be taking a walk in the garden. He noticed a lovely maiden in the field driving the ducks, and he heard her sing:

> Ducks here, ducks there,
> A king's daughter tends the ducks,
> A thing never seen before!

When she had finished singing this, she killed one of the ducks. Then, she took off her dress that was the color of the stars and got back into her wooden dress.

At night, she went before the king and said, "Alas, I killed one of the ducks."

The king asked her, "Maria do Pau, who was that beautiful maiden so splendidly clothed that minded the ducks?"

"Indeed, there was no one else there but myself in disguise."

The next day, the king again sent Maria do Pau to tend the ducks. And when she was in the field she did the same thing as the day before, save that this time she wore the dress that was all the colors of wildflowers, then went about driving the ducks, singing as before:

> Ducks here, ducks there,
> A king's daughter tends the ducks,
> A thing never seen before!

After that, she killed another duck. Then, she took off her robe that was all the colors of wildflowers and got back into her wooden dress.

The next day, Maria do Pau did as the day before, but, this time, she put on the robe of all the colors. She went about driving the ducks, singing, and then killed another duck.

In the evening, the king said to her, "I do not wish you to take care of the ducks any longer. For every day, we find a duck has been killed! Now, you shall remain indoors instead. We are to have a feast that will last three days, but I shall not allow you to go to it."

"Oh my king, do let me go!" Maria do Pau begged.

"No, indeed. You shall not go."

On the first day of the feast, she again begged of the king to allow her to go to it, and the king threw his boots at her and left.

Maria do Pau hurried to her little room and put on the gown the color of the stars, then went to the feast. The king, who had his eyes continually fixed upon her, asked where she was from.

She answered, "I come from the land of the boot."

Then she hurried off.

The next day, the king again attended the feast. But before leaving, he said to Maria do Pau, "You shall not be allowed to go there."

When she insisted, he threw a towel at her.

The princess hurried to her little room, put on the gown that was all the colors of wildflowers, and hurried off to the feast. The king, who had been charmed with her on the first day of the feast, now admired her all the more. Where was she from?

"From the land of the towel," she said.

Then, she hurried off.

The next day, as the king was on the point of going to the feast, Maria do Pau once again begged to go. He struck her with his walking stick.

The king went to the feast, and there, the princess presented herself before him in the robe of all the colors. If on the previous days she had appeared most beautiful, on this day of the feast, she looked absolutely dazzling. Where was she from?

"From the land of the walking stick," she said.

Then she hurried out.

The king returned to the palace, thinking, "Today, I again saw the same princess who is so beautiful. But can this be the same woman? At one time, she says that she comes from the land of the boot, the next time that she is from the land of the towel, and lastly she says she is from the land of the walking stick."

And then, for he was not really a foolish king, the likeness of the beautiful princess to Maria do Pau struck him. He went straight to her little chamber, and there she was, still in her dress of all the colors.

The princess was startled, but the king said to her: "Do not be frightened. First, you must forgive me for throwing the boots at you, then for throwing the towel at you, and then for hitting you with my walking stick."

"I do."

"And now I wish you to marry me. But first, will you tell me your history?"

So she did, and they were wed. And, at the feast, was the little old woman who had helped her—and who turned out to be a fairy.

Sources

Fyleman, Rose. *Folk-Tales from Many Lands*. Toronto, Ontario, Canada: Methuen, 1954.

Pedroso, Consiglieri. *Portuguese Folk-Tales. Folk Lore Society Publications*. Vol. 9. Trans. Henriqueta Monteiro. New York: Folk Lore Society Publications, 1882.

The Woman with Two Skins: A Folktale from Nigeria

> This folktale from southern Nigeria must be one of the most unusual of the Donkey Skin variants. The heroine is not human at all, but she wears a human disguise. The helper of both the heroine and her son is a water shaman or Ju Ju man.

Eyamba I of Calabar was a very powerful king. But none of his wives had borne him a son.

Because an heir was needed, his councilors begged him to marry one of the spider woman's daughters, since spiders have many children. When the king saw the spider's daughter, he did not like her because she was ugly. But to please his people, he married her, and built her a separate house so that his other wives would not constantly jeer at her.

What no one knew was that the new wife, Adiaha, had two skins. The outer one was ugly, but the second skin was beautiful. Her mother had made her promise not to remove the ugly skin save at night and to put it on again at dawn.

Now, the king's head wife chanced to find this out, and she was afraid that the king might actually fall in love with the spider's daughter. So the head wife went to a Ju Ju man, a man with magical powers, and she had him make up a potion to make the king forget the new wife. It worked, and after four months, the new wife grew weary of being ignored and went back to her parents.

Her father, the spider man, took his daughter to another Ju Ju man. He by making spells and casting lots, very soon discovered that it was the king's head wife who had made the Ju Ju and had enchanted the king so that he would not look at Adiaha. He gave Adiaha a potion that would break the prior spell.

That very day, Adiaha made a small dish of food, into which she had placed the potion, and presented it to the king. As soon as the king tasted the dish, he remembered Adiaha, and he sent for her that evening. As soon as it was dark, Adiaha removed her ugly skin, and the king was overjoyed to see how beautiful she was. But when the cock crowed, Adiaha pulled on her ugly skin again, and she went back to her own house.

In due course, Adiaha gave birth to a son. This made the head wife even more jealous than before. Back she went to the Ju Ju man for a potion that would make the king sick and believe that only throwing his son in the river would save him. So it was done.

But the Ju Ju man who had helped Adiaha was a water Ju Ju. And when the king threw the boy into the river, the Ju Ju man saved him, took him home, and kept him alive. And the boy grew up very strong.

After a time, Adiaha gave birth to a daughter, and the jealous wife also persuaded the king to throw her away. But the water Ju Ju was ready again, and when he had saved the little girl, he thought the time had come to punish the jealous wife.

So the water Ju Ju persuaded the young men to hold a grand wrestling match, to which all the strongest men in the country were invited. And the king promised to attend with his head wife.

All the people of the country came to see the great contest. To the winner, the king had promised to present prizes of cloth and money, and all the strongest men came. When they saw the king's son, they laughed and said, "Who is this small boy? He can have no chance against us."

But when they came to wrestle, they very soon found that they were no match for him. The boy was very strong, indeed, beautifully made, and good to look upon. And all the people were surprised to see how like this boy was to the king.

After the match was over, the king's son was declared the winner, having thrown every one who had stood up against him. The king presented him with cloth and money, and he invited the boy to dine with him in the evening.

The boy gladly accepted his father's invitation. When they sat down to their meal, the king's own son, though he did not know it, was sitting next to him.

On the other side of the boy sat the jealous wife, who had been the cause of all the trouble. All through the dinner, this woman did her best to make friends with the boy, with whom she had fallen violently in love. The boy, however, was quite aware of everything the jealous woman had done. And although he pretended to be flattered at the advances of the king's head wife, he went home as soon as he could.

The boy told the water Ju Ju everything that had happened. The water Ju Ju told him, "Now that you are in the king's favor, ask him for a boon. Let all the country be called together, and a certain case shall be tried. And when the case is finished, the man or woman who is found to be in the wrong shall be killed."

So the following morning, the boy went to the king, who readily granted his request. Then, the water Ju Ju told the boy to go to his mother and tell her who he was. And he would tell her as well that, on the day of the trial, she could take off the ugly skin and appear in all her beauty, since the time had come when she no longer needed to seem ugly.

When the day of trial arrived, Adiaha sat in a corner of the square. Nobody recognized the beautiful stranger as the spider's daughter. Her son sat down next to her, and he brought his sister with him. Adiaha joyfully embraced both of her children.

The king and his head wife arrived. They sat on their stones in the middle of the square while all the people saluted them. The king said that he had called them together to hear a case at the request of the boy who had won the wrestling. He had promised that if the case went against him, he would offer up his life—but if the case was decided in the boy's favor, then the other party would be killed, even though it were himself or one of his wives. To this, all the people agreed and said they would like to hear what the boy had to say.

The boy then walked round the square, and bowed to the king and the people. He asked, "Am I not worthy to be the son of any chief in the country?" And all the people answered "Yes!"

The boy then led forth his sister. She was a beautiful girl and well made. When everyone had looked at her, he said, "Is not my sister worthy to be any chief's daughter?" And the people replied that she was worthy of being anyone's daughter, even the king's.

Then, he called his mother Adiaha. She came out, looking very beautiful. And all the people cheered, as they had never seen a finer woman. The boy then asked them, "Is this woman worthy of being the king's wife?" And a shout went up from everyone present that she would be a proper wife for the king and that she looked as if she would be the mother of plenty of fine, healthy sons.

Then, the boy pointed out the jealous woman who was sitting next to the king, and told the people his story: How that his mother, who had two skins, was the spider's daughter and had married the king; how the jealous head wife had made a bad Ju Ju for the king, which made him forget his wife; how she had persuaded the king to throw himself and his sister into the river, which they all knew had been done; and how the water Ju Ju had saved both of them and brought them up.

Then, the boy said, "I leave the king and all of you people to judge my case. If I have done wrong, let me be killed. If, on the other hand, the woman has done evil, then let her meet her fate."

When the king knew that the wrestler was his son, he was overjoyed. The jealous wife was put to death.

The king then embraced Adiaha and their children, and he proclaimed Adiaha his proper wife and queen. They all lived together quite happily for some years. When the king died, his son came to the throne and ruled wisely.

Sources

Dayrell, Elphinstone. *Folk Stories from Southern Nigeria, West Africa.* London: Longmans, Green, 1910; New York: Negro Universities Press, 1969.
Klipple, May Augusta. *African Folktales with Foreign Analogues.* The Garland Folklore Library. New York and London: Garland, 1992.

Sir Gawain and Dame Ragnell: A Folktale from Medieval England

Although this folktale is part of the greater Arthurian cycle, it is a Donkey Skin variant as well. The heroine changes shape from hideous to lovely after Sir Gawain proves he is a wise as well as a brave knight.

Once, it came to pass that King Arthur went hunting in the forest of Inglewood. But even as he chased a deer, he became separated from his companions.

Soon, he was in an unfamiliar part of the forest. While the king was alone with the deer, there suddenly came to him a menacing figure, a knight strong and mighty. He said these grim words to the king:

"Well met, King Arthur! You have done me wrong many a year, and woefully I shall repay you now. Indeed, you have wrongfully given my lands to Sir Gawain. What say you, king, alone as you are?"

"Sir knight, what is your honored name?" said Arthur.

"Sir king," he answered, "Gromer Somer Joure (Summer Day Man), I tell you now the truth."

"Ah, Sir Gromer Somer, think you well that slaying me here will get you no honor," said Arthur.

"Abide, king, and hear me awhile. First, you shall swear upon your sword that you will tell me when next we meet what women love best. And you shall meet me here at the end of twelve months, with no knights with you. If you fail to bring an answer, you shall lose your head. What do you say, king?"

"Sir, I swear to you as a true king to come again at the end of twelve months and bring you your answer."

Home rode King Arthur. There, he sat a time in silent sorrow. Finally, Sir Gawain said to the king, "Sir, I am much amazed and wonder at what makes you sorrowful."

King Arthur related the tale of his humiliation in the forest. Sir Gawain then proposed that they ride forth and ask every woman they found what she most desires and collect the answers in a book.

The two knights set out and asked women what they desired. Soon, they had a huge book of answers. But as many answers as they had found, they were still uneasy that any of the answers they had was the true one.

The next day, King Arthur rode out his gate back into Inglewood, and there he met with a lady. She was the ugliest creature that a man ever saw, and King Arthur stared at her in wonder. Her face was red, her eyes were bleary, her nose was running, her mouth was wide, her teeth, all yellow, hung out of her lips. Her neck was thick, her hair tangled, and her back was curved as a lute. In short, she had ugliness to spare. Yet she sat upon a gaily outfitted horse. Odd, the king thought, to see so foul a creature ride so well.

"God speed, sir king," she said. "I am well pleased to meet with you. Listen to me, for your life is in my hand. Only I can save you from death."

"What do you want with me, lady?"

"All the answers you have now will do you no good. What, did you think I do not know your secret? I know it all. And without my help, you are dead."

"What is your name, I pray you tell me."

"Sir King, I am called Dame Ragnell, who never yet lied to a man. Grant me only one thing, sir king, and I will save you. Grant me a knight to wed. His name is Sir Gawain."

Home rode the king. The first man he met was Sir Gawain, who asked, "Sire, how have you done?"

"Never so badly," said the king. "Gawain, I met the foulest lady today, certainly the worst I have ever seen. She told me she would save my life. But first she wants to have a husband—you."

"Is that all?" said Gawain. "I shall wed her and wed her again, even if she be a fiend, even were she as foul as Beelzebub. Otherwise, I would not be your friend. You are my honored king and have done me good many times. Therefore, I hesitate not to save your life, my lord. It is my duty."

So the king rode out again, no more than a mile, when he met Dame Ragnell.

"Sir king, you are welcome here!"

"Sir Gawain will marry you," the king said. "He has promised to save my life. Now, since it is the only way, tell me your answer."

"Some men say we desire to be beautiful, or that we desire sex with as many men as we can find. Others say we want many husbands. You men just do not understand. We want an entirely different thing. Yes, we like to be seen as young and fresh, yes, we like to be flattered cleverly. But what we desire most from men both rich and poor is to have our own will without lies."

The king rode on a long time as fast as he could go to the appointed place to meet Sir Gromer.

"Come now, sir king," the knight said sternly, "what is your answer?"

The king pulled out the two books of comments he and Sir Gawain had gathered.

"Sir, here is my answer."

Sir Gromer looked at each answer. "No, no, sir king. You are a dead man."

"Wait, Sir Gromer," said King Arthur, "I have one answer that cannot miss."

"Let us see it," said Sir Gromer. "Or else, so help me God, you shall have a violent death."

The king was unafraid. "Here is the answer, the true one. What women desire most from rich men and poor is simply this: Their own will. And you, Sir Gromer, are beaten."

Gromer roared in frustration! "Only my sister could have told you that! May she burn in the fires of hell for her treachery! Go where you will, King Arthur, I will bother you no more."

So Arthur returned to Ragnell and brought her back with him to court.

Then, Sir Gawain came forth. "Sire, I am ready to do what I promised, ready to fulfill my vows."

"God-a-mercy!" shouted Dame Ragnell. "For your sake, I wish I were a good-looking woman, since you are such a good man."

Then Sir Gawain wed her. And Dame Ragnell was happy.

All the ladies at court wept for Sir Gawain.

At last, the wedding feast was over, and the couple was led to their chamber. There, Gawain gazed at the fire, reluctant to touch his bride, until she requested a kiss.

"Ah, Sir Gawain, since I have married you, show me a little courtesy in bed. You cannot rightfully deny me that. Indeed, Sir Gawain," the lady said, "if I were beautiful, you would act a bit differently. But you take no heed of marriage. Still, for Arthur's sake, at least kiss me."

Sir Gawain said, "I will do more than kiss, I swear to God!"

So he turned . . . and saw she was the fairest creature alive.

"Dear Lord!" he said. "What are you?"

"Sir, I am certainly your wife. Why are you unkind to me?"

"Ah, lady, I am to blame. I ask your mercy, fair madam. I had not realized. You are so beautiful, and yet earlier you were the ugliest woman I have ever seen. I am happy, lady, to see you thus."

So he embraced her, and together they made great joy, certainly.

"Sir," she said, "thus shall you have me. Choose one—for my beauty will not hold. Choose whether you will have me beautiful in the nights and as ugly in the days, when men see me, or else have me beautiful in the day and the ugliest woman in the nights. One or the other you must have. Choose."

"Alas!" said Gawain, "Choosing the best is difficult. Instead, you choose what you think best, my lady. Do as you wish, as you choose."

She cried out in joy, "My lord, you are as wise as you are noble and true, for you have given me what every woman genuinely desires, sovereignty over herself. You will never see that hideous old hag again, for I choose to be fair from this time on."

Sources
Saul, G.B. *The Wedding of Sir Gawain and Dame Ragnell*. New York: Prentice Hall, 1934.
Sumner, Laura, ed. *The Weddynge of Sir Gawen and Dame Ragnell*. Northhampton, MA: Smith
    College Department of Modern Languages, 1924.

Cinderella and Father Frost Variants

In one Slavic variant on the Cinderella theme not often found elsewhere, the Cinderella character is forced out into the winter on an impossible task, since her stepmother and stepsister are hoping she will freeze to death. Instead, by being polite, she triumphs over obstacles, and they end up freezing instead.

Father Frost: A Folktale from Russia

This variant on the tale features a weak father so under the thumb of his new wife that he is even willing to give up his own child to death rather than fight for her. He, alone, in the story is neither rewarded nor punished. The little dog that is suddenly able to speak is a unique element of this variant.

In Soviet Russia, when celebrations of Christmas were banned, it was Father Frost who brought children presents on January 1.

In a faraway country, somewhere in Russia, there lived a stepmother who had a stepdaughter and a daughter of her own. Her own daughter was dear to her, and whatever the girl did, the mother would praise and pet her. But there was no praise to be wasted on the stepdaughter, even though she was a good, kind girl. There was nothing for her but scolding and abuse.

One bright cold day, the stepmother said to her husband, "Get your daughter away from my eyes and ears. Take her out to the forest and leave her there."

The father, who was a weak old man, meekly took his daughter out to the forest, left her there, and sped away in his sleigh so that he would not see her freeze to death. All alone, the girl sat amid the snowy forest and the heavy silence, and she prayed for help.

There came none other than the sovereign of winter, Father Frost, clad in furs, with a long, long, white beard and a shining crown on his white head. He looked down at the lovely young girl and asked, "Do you know me?"

"Be welcome, Father Frost," she said softly.

"Art thou comfortable in my realm, sweet child?"

"Indeed, I am," answered the girl, almost out of breath from cold.

Frost, cheerful and bright, kept crackling in the branches until the air became icy, but the good-natured girl kept repeating politely, "I am very comfortable, dear Father Frost."

But Frost knew all about human weakness. He was aware how few were good and kind. But he also knew that none of them could struggle too long against the power of Frost, the king of winter. This gentle, lovely girl charmed Frost so much that he decided to treat her differently from any others. Instead of giving her the quiet death of freezing, he chose to save her.

So he gave her first a caftan lined with precious furs and watched the life come back into the nearly frozen face. Then, he gave her a large heavy trunk filled with many beautiful, beautiful things—quilts light as feathers and warm to the touch, and silken garments ornamented with pearls and glinting with silver.

All this while, the stepmother was in the kitchen busy preparing the traditional meal given to the priest and friends after the service for the dead. She said to her husband, "Go out there. Bring back the body of your daughter so we can bury her."

He left meekly. But the little dog in the corner wagged his tail. "Bow wow! Bow wow! The old man's daughter is on her way home, beautiful and happy as never before, and the old woman's daughter is wicked as ever before."

"Keep still, stupid beast!" shouted the stepmother. "Here, take this pancake, eat it and say, 'The old woman's daughter will be married soon, and the old man's daughter shall be buried soon.'"

The dog ate the pancake and began anew, "Bow wow! Bow wow! The old man's daughter is coming home wealthy and happy as never before, and the old woman's daughter is somewhere around as homely and wicked as ever before."

The stepmother was furious at the dog and kicked it. But the dog repeated the same words over and over again.

Then she heard laughter, looked outside and stared in disbelief. There was the stepdaughter, looking like a princess in the most beautiful garments. Behind her, her father was barely managing to carry the heavy trunk full of richness.

Oho! The stepmother ordered her husband, "Hitch our best horses to the finest of our sleighs and drive *my* daughter to the same place!"

That he did, and he left the girl alone in the same place.

Old Frost was there, looking over his new guest. "Are you comfortable, fair maiden?" he asked.

"Let me alone, you fool" the girl snapped. "Cannot you see my feet and my hands are stiff from the cold?"

Frost asked a few more questions. But when the girl gave him nothing but insults and cruel words, he grew angry and froze her to death.

Meanwhile, the stepmother grew impatient. "Husband, go for my daughter. Take the best horses. Be careful; do not upset the sleigh. Do not lose the trunk."

The little dog in the corner said, "Bow wow! Bow wow! The old man's daughter will marry soon, and the old woman's daughter shall be buried soon."

And so it was. The stepmother wept and wept, understanding too late that it was through her own envy and meanness that her daughter had died.

As for the gentle, kind girl, the dog was right. She married a fine man and lived happily with him.

Sources
Afanas'ev, Aleksander. *Russian Fairy Tales*. New York: Pantheon, 1945.
De Blumenthal, Verra Xenophontovna Kalamatiano. *Folk Tales from the Russian*. 1903. Great
    Neck, NY: Core Collection, 1979.

The Twelve Months: A Folktale from the Czech Republic

This Czech variant is more typical of the Cinderella folktale type, with the wicked stepmother and stepdaughter. Here there is no father, just the three women, and there are twelve personified months instead of Father Frost.

Once upon a time, there lived a mother with a daughter and a stepdaughter. She was very fond of her own daughter, but she would not so much as look at her stepdaughter.

The only reason for this cruelty was that Marusa, the stepdaughter, was prettier than her own daughter, Holena. Marusa, gentle and sweet, did not know how beautiful she was, and so she never understood why her stepmother was so cross with her.

Marusa had to do all the housework, tidying up the cottage, cooking, washing, and sewing, and then she had to take the hay to the cow and look after her. She did all this work alone, while Holena spent the time adorning herself and lazing about.

At last, the mother thought, "Why should I keep a pretty stepdaughter in my house? When the lads come courting here, they will fall in love with Marusa and they will not look at Holena."

From that moment, the stepmother and her daughter were constantly scheming how to get rid of poor Marusa. One day—it was in the middle of January—Holena snapped, "Go, Marusa, and get me some violets from the forest."

"Whoever heard of violets growing under the snow?" asked poor Marusa.

"You wretched creature! Go off to get those violets, or we shall kill you!" Holena cried.

The stepmother shoved Marusa outside and slammed the door behind her.

Marusa went into the forest weeping bitterly. What could she do? They would surely kill her at home, but she would freeze to death out here. The snow lay deep, and there was not a human footprint to be seen. Marusa wandered about for a long time, tortured by hunger and trembling with cold. She begged God to take her from the world.

But then she saw a light in the distance, and she went that way. At last, she came to the top of a mountain, where a big fire was burning.

Around the fire were twelve stones with twelve men sitting on them. Three were old, with long white beards, three looked neither young nor old, and three were young and quite handsome. They sat in solemn silence. These were the twelve months of the year, and one of the old men, Great January, sat on the highest stone and held a club.

Marusa was frightened. But the fire was so appealing that she had to approach and say, "Please, kind sirs, let me warm my hands at your fire. I am trembling with the cold."

Great January nodded. "Of course, child." As she warmed herself, he asked her, "Why have you come here, my dear little girl? What are you looking for?"

"I am looking for violets," answered Marusa.

"This is no time to be looking for violets, for everything is covered with snow!"

"Yes, I know. But my sister Holena and my stepmother said that I must bring them some violets from the forest. If I do not bring them, they will kill me. Tell me, fathers, please tell me where I can find them."

Great January stood up and went to one of the younger months, March. Giving him the club, he said, "Brother, take the high seat."

March took the high seat and waved the club over the fire. The fire blazed up, the snow began to melt, the trees began to bud, and the ground under the young beech trees was at once covered with grass. Under the bushes, violets were blooming like a blue cloth spread out on the ground.

"Pick them quickly!" commanded March.

Marusa joyfully picked a big bunch. Then, she thanked the months with all her heart and hurried home.

Holena and the stepmother were amazed when Marusa came back with violets.

"Where did you get them?" asked Holena, frowning.

"They are growing under the bushes in a forest on the high mountains."

But Holena and the stepmother were not going to give up trying to be rid of the girl.

A few days later, Holena snapped, "Go, Marusa, and get me some strawberries from the forest."

"Whoever heard of strawberries growing under the snow?" asked Marusa.

"You wretched creature! Go off to get those strawberries, or we shall kill you!" Holena cried.

The stepmother shoved Marusa outside and slammed the door behind her.

Shivering, Marusa hunted through the snowy forest. To her great relief, she finally found the light she had seen the other day. Overjoyed, she came to the great fire with the twelve months sitting round it.

"Please, kind sirs, let me warm my hands at the fire. I am trembling with cold."

Great January nodded, and asked her, "Why have you come again, and what are you looking for here?"

"I am looking for strawberries."

"But strawberries do not grow on the snow," said January.

"Yes, I know," said Marusa sadly; "but my sister Holena and my stepmother bade me bring them some strawberries, and if I do not bring them, they will kill me. Tell me, fathers, tell me, please, where I can find them."

Great January arose. He went over to the month sitting opposite to him, June, and handed the club to him, saying, "Brother, take the high seat."

June took the high seat upon the stone and swung the club over the fire. The fire shot up, and its heat melted the snow in a moment. The ground was all green, the trees were covered with leaves, the birds began to sing, and the forest was filled with all kinds of flowers. The ground under the bushes was covered with ripe strawberries.

"Pick them at once, Marusa!" June commanded.

Marusa picked them until she had filled her apron. Then, she thanked the months with all her heart and hurried home.

Holena and the stepmother were amazed when they saw Marusa bringing the strawberries. They ran to open the door for her, and the scent of the strawberries filled the whole cottage.

"Where did you pick them?" asked Holena sulkily.

"There are plenty of them growing in the forest on the high mountains."

Holena took the strawberries, and went on eating them until she could eat no more. So did the stepmother too, but they did not give even one to Marusa.

Three days later, Holena ordered, "Marusa, go into the forest and get me some red apples."

"Alas, how am I to get apples for you in winter?" protested Marusa.

"You wretched creature! Go off to get those apples or we shall kill you!" Holena cried.

The stepmother shoved Marusa outside and slammed the door behind her.

Shivering, Marusa hunted through the snowy forest. But she did not wander about this time. She ran straight to the top of the mountain where the big fire was burning. The twelve months were sitting round the fire, and Great January was sitting on the high seat.

"Please, kind sirs, let me warm my hands at the fire. I am trembling with cold."

Great January nodded, and asked her, "Why have you come here, and what are you looking for?"

"I am looking for red apples."

"Red apples do not grow in winter," answered January.

"Yes, I know," said Marusa sadly; "but my sister and my stepmother bade me bring them some red apples from the forest. If I do not bring them, they will kill me. Tell me, father, tell me, please, where I could find them."

Great January went over to one of the older months, September. He handed the club to him and said, "Brother, take the high seat."

September took the high seat and swung the club over the fire. The fire began to burn with a red flame, the snow began to melt. But the trees were not covered with leaves. The leaves were wavering down one after the other, and the cold wind was driving them to and fro over the yellowing ground. This time, Marusa did not see so many flowers. But she was only looking for red apples, and at last she saw an apple tree with red apples hanging high among its branches.

"Shake the tree twice, Marusa!" commanded the month.

Marusa shook the tree, and one apple fell down. She shook it a second time, and another apple fell down.

"Now, Marusa, run home quickly!" shouted the month.

Marusa picked up the apples, thanked the months with all her heart, and ran home.

Holena and the stepmother stared when they saw Marusa bringing the apples. They ran to open the door for her, and she gave them the two apples.

"Where did you get them?" asked Holena.

"There are plenty of them in the forest on the high mountain."

"And why didn't you bring more? Or did you eat them on the way home?" snapped Holena.

"I did not eat a single one. But when I had shaken the tree once, one apple fell down, and when I shook it a second time, another apple fell down. And they would not let me shake it again. They shouted to me to go straight home."

"May you be struck to death by lightning!" Holena cursed. "Go on, get into the kitchen."

But then she bit into the apple. It tasted so delicious that she told her mother she had never tasted anything so wonderful in all her life. The stepmother liked it, too. When they had finished, they wanted some more.

"Mother, give me my fur coat. I will go to the forest myself. That ragged little wretch would eat them all up again on her way home. I will find the place all right, and I will shake them all down, however they shout at me."

Holena took her fur coat, wrapped a shawl around her head, and off she went to the forest. Her mother stood on the threshold, watching to see how Holena would manage to walk in the wintry weather.

The snow lay deep, and there was not a human footprint to be seen anywhere. Holena wandered about for a long time, but the desire of the sweet apple kept driving her on. At last, she saw a light in the distance. She went toward it, and climbed to the top of the mountain where the big fire was burning, and around the fire on twelve stones the twelve months were sitting.

Holena stepped up to the fire and stretched out her hands to warm them, but she did not say as much as "By your leave" to the twelve months. No, she did not say a single word to them.

"Why have you come here, and what are you looking for?" asked Great January crossly.

"Why do you want to know, you old fool? It is no business of yours," replied Holena angrily, and she turned away from the fire and went into the forest.

Great January frowned and swung the club over his head. The sky grew dark in a moment, the fire burned low, the snow began to fall as thick as if the feathers had been shaken out of a down quilt, and an icy wind began to blow through the forest.

Holena could not see one step in front of her. She lost her way as the snow kept on falling and the wind blew more icily than ever. Holena began to curse. And then she began to freeze. And that was the end of Holena.

Meanwhile, her mother was waiting for Holena, but all in vain.

"Does she like the apples so much that she cannot leave them? I must see for myself where she is."

So she put on her fur coat, she wrapped a shawl around her head, and went out to look for Holena. The snow was lying deep; there was not a human footprint to be seen. The snow fell fast, and the icy wind was blowing through the forest.

Marusa had cooked the dinner, she had seen to the cow, and yet Holena and her mother did not come back. "Where are they staying so long?" thought Marusa, as she sat down to work at the distaff.

In the morning, Marusa waited with breakfast. In the evening, she waited with dinner. But however much she waited, neither her mother nor her sister ever came back. Both of them were frozen to death in the forest.

So good Marusa inherited the cottage, a piece of good farmland, and the cow. She married a kind husband, and they both lived happily ever after.

Sources

Baudis, Josef. *The Key of Gold: 23 Czech Folk Tales*. London: Allen & Unwin, 1917; Iowa City, IA: Penfield, 1992.

Fillmore, Parker. *The Laughing Prince: Jugoslav Folk and Fairy Tales*. New York: Harcourt, Brace, 1921.

Cinderlad

The Cinderlad folktales feature a downtrodden hero instead of a heroine. He proves his worth through warrior victories against the king's enemies, then he returns to his disguise. In a complete reversal of the Cinderella folktales, it usually is the princess who discovers her true love under his disguise.

Cinders: A Folktale from Finland and America

This folktale shows how modern elements can enter an ancient story. The theme of the princess on the glass mountain dates back at least to the first millennium B.C.E. But the modern element of a photograph has been added here.

The hero of the tale is the traditional third son, the "useless" one the other two sons despise. His helper is the archetypal figure of the Wise Old Man.

Once, there was a king with a beautiful daughter. He placed her at the top of a glass mountain, sitting there with her photograph. And the king made it known that whoever could ride to the top of that glass mountain and receive the photograph would win the princess as his wife.

A smith who lived not too far from there had three sons. The first two were big, strapping young men eager to try their luck. They set about forging shoes to carry them to the top of the glass mountain.

The third and youngest son was a quiet boy who stayed at home tending the fire. Because he was always covered with ashes, he was called Tuhkimo, or Cinders.

What the rest of the family did not know was that Cinders was good of heart and that a mysterious old man was visiting him at night to give him good advice. On the first day of the royal proclamation, the old man said to Cinders, "Go to a place in the forest, and I will give you soldier's clothes and a silver-shod horse."

So Cinders went. And the next day, there he was, a soldier on a silver-shod horse. With all the others, he tried the climb—but the silver shoes were too slippery, and he failed. So did all the others, including his brothers.

The next day, Cinders was there again, this time in a captain's uniform and riding a horse shod in gold. With all the others, he tried the climb—but the golden shoes were too soft, and he failed. So did all the others, including his brothers.

On the third day, Cinders was there again, this time in a general's uniform and riding a horse shod in diamond shoes. Up they rode, crunch, crunch, crunch, with slices of glass flying in all directions, all the way to the top of the mountain. There, the princess gave Cinders her photograph.

Down again, Cinders rode, back to the forest to change his clothes, then back to the smithy to hide in the ashes.

Two soldiers of the king came to the smithy. "Are all the men present?"

"We are here," said the two older brothers.

"Did you try to ride up the glass mountain?"

"We did, but we failed."

"Is this all of you?" the soldiers asked.

"There is our younger brother, but he never goes anywhere."

But the soldiers insisted on seeing Cinders. As he stood, the photograph fell out of his miekko, or smock. So Cinders went before the king in all his ashes and rags.

"Here is the man who gained the photograph," the soldiers said to the king.

The court erupted with laughter. "What, that ragged fellow marry a princess?"

"Give me leave to change my clothes," Cinders said.

They let him go. And Cinders returned in the fine general's uniform, riding the horse shod with diamond shoes.

"That *was* you!" the princess cried. "It *is* you!"

So the wedding was held, and they may all be there yet.

Source

Dorson, Richard M. *Bloodstoppers and Bearwalkers: Folk Tradition of the Upper Peninsula.* Cambridge, MA: Harvard University Press, 1952. Collected by Richard Dorson in 1946 from Frank Vallin and translated into English in the telling by Aili Kolehumainen Johnson.

The Frog Who Became an Emperor: A Folktale from China

This Cinderlad story combines two major folklore elements in one. There is the beauty in the beast theme of the frog who transforms into a man. But the stronger element here is the Cinderlad theme of the seeming nobody who triumphs over the enemy, then goes back into his disguise.

Once upon a time, there lived a very poor couple. The wife was pregnant, but the husband knew he had to leave home to find a living somewhere else.

Before leaving, the husband embraced his wife one last time and gave her the last of their money.

"When the child is born," he told her, "whether it is a boy or a girl, do all you can to raise it. There may be little hope for us, but our child may be able to one day help us."

Sure enough, three months after her husband's departure, the wife gave birth—but the baby was not boy, not girl, but a frog!

It was her baby, though, even if it was . . . a frog. She did not have the heart to slay it. And within two months, the woman was glad she had not, for the frog grew amazingly large, and could all at once talk.

"Mother," he said, "my father is coming back tonight. I am going to wait for him beside the road."

And sure enough, the husband did come home that very night.

"Have you seen your son?" the wife asked anxiously.

"Where? Where is my son?"

"He was waiting for you by the side of the road. Didn't you see him?"

"No! I saw no sign of anyone," her husband answered, surprised. "All I saw was a large frog, which gave me such a fright."

"That frog was your son. He suddenly said you were coming tonight and went out to meet you."

"This is really extraordinary. No one knew I was coming. How could he have known?"

The frog hopped over to his father. "I was waiting for you, Father."

"How did you know I was coming back tonight?"

"I know everything under heaven. Our country is in great peril from invaders," he added. "Father, please take me to the emperor, for I must save our country."

"How can that be?" said the father. "You have no horse, no weapons, and no fighting skills!"

"Only take me there," the frog pleaded. "I will defeat the enemy, never fear."

The father took his frog son to the city to seek an audience with the emperor. After two days' journey, they arrived at the capital, where they saw the imperial decree displayed:

> Our country has been invaded. We are willing to marry
> Our daughter to the man who can drive away the enemy.

The frog tore down the decree and with one gulp swallowed it. Then, he went before the emperor. The surprised emperor asked the frog, "Can you really defeat the enemy?"

The frog replied, "Yes, Lord."

"How many men and horses will you need?"

"Not a single horse or a single man," answered the frog. "All I need is a heap of hot, glowing embers."

The emperor immediately commanded, "Bring us a heap of hot, glowing embers!"

The frog sat before the fire devouring the flames by the mouthful for three days and three nights.

By now, the enemy was at the walls. After the third day had passed, the frog went to the top of the city wall to look over the situation. There, ringing the city, were thousands of soldiers and horses, as far as the eye could see.

"How are you going to drive back the enemy?" asked the emperor.

"Order your troops to open the city gate."

"What! With the enemy at our door?"

"Your Imperial Highness has bidden me to drive the enemy away," said the frog. "So you must listen to me."

The emperor ordered the soldiers to throw open the gate. The invaders poured in. And the frog spat fire down on them until they fled in terror.

The emperor was overjoyed. He made the frog a general and ordered that the victory should be celebrated for several days.

But of the princess, the emperor said nothing, for he had no intention of letting his daughter marry a frog. She must marry someone else, but whom? Finally, he proclaimed that her marriage should be decided by casting the Embroidered Ball.

Men from far and wide came to try their luck, and all manner of people flocked to the capital. A tall, colorful pavilion had been built in the city square, and there the princess sat with her attendants.

The princess got to her feet and tossed the Embroidered Ball. Down it floated. All the men reached eagerly up to seize it—but the frog drew in a mighty breath and pulled the ball straight to him.

But when everyone looked around, they saw no frog but a handsome young man.

"This is the man!" cried the happy emperor. "Here is my imperial son-in-law."

Not until the frog was married to the princess did he change back to a frog again. By day he was a frog, but at night he stripped off his green skin and was transformed into a handsome young man.

The princess was delighted with their secret, but, at last, she could keep the secret no longer but had to tell her father. The emperor said to his son-in-law, "At night, I hear that you are a handsome young man. Why do you wear that hideous frog skin by day?"

"When I wear it in winter, I am warm and cozy," the frog said. "In summer, it keeps me cool. It protects me from wind and rain, and not even a fire can burn it. Why, for all I know, as long as I wear it, I will live for thousands of years."

"Give it to me!" the emperor ordered.

The frog discarded the skin and became human again. The emperor quickly put on the frog skin. But—he could not take it off again. He had become a true frog!

So it was that the man who had been a frog became emperor, and the emperor remained a frog.

Sources
Anonymous. *Folk Tales from China*. 3rd series. Peking, China: Foreign Languages, 1958.
Sanders, Tao Tao Liu. *Dragons, Gods and Spirits from Chinese Mythology*. New York: Schocken, 1983.

THE BOY WHO KNEW NO FEAR

This is mostly a European tale type of a young man who is fearless in the sense that he cannot feel fear. He is not afraid to do the most terrifying jobs or face the most hideous of foes. But he knows that other people know what fear is, and he has a burning desire to find out what it is as well. Often, he never learns. Though, in some versions, an impatient heroine pours ice water or live eels down his back so that he can at least know what it feels like to shiver and shudder.

The story was even used by German composer Richard Wagner in his 1876 opera *Siegfried* (part of the Ring cycle of operas). The hero has never known fear nor seen a woman, but when he first sees the sleeping Brunhilde, the Valkyrie heroine, and removes her armor, he recoils in his first shiver of fear and awe, crying, "This is no man!"

The Boy Who Searched for Fear: A Folktale from Slovenia

In this variant, the boy is not afraid of graveyards or trick ghosts. When he goes to the haunted house, he is not at all afraid of the devils, either, but rather kindly invites them to join his dinner. The way he learns fear is by a crow flying into his face.

Once, there was a boy who was absolutely fearless. He literally had no idea what fear was like.

His father sent him out into the graveyard at night. The boy sat on a tomb and waited, and then he lay down on a grave and fell asleep. In the morning, he told his father he had seen or felt nothing of fear.

His father said, "Well, then go out into the world, my son, and do not come back until you have learned about fear."

Off the boy went. He stopped at the last house in the village, that of the old bell ringer.

"Where are you going?" the old man asked.

"I'm going to find fear."

"Oh, I can find fear for you," said the old man. "Tomorrow, go and ring the church bell for me."

The next day, off the boy went to the church, which stood in a graveyard. He had no idea of the trick the bell ringer was pulling, tying a corpse to the bell rope.

"Hey, you, *I'm* to ring the bell," said the boy. "Stand aside."

That it was a corpse did not bother him at all.

"Don't just stand there, old bones, get out of my way."

The boy shoved the corpse aside and rang the bell. Then, he went back to the bell ringer's house.

"Were you afraid?" the old man asked.

"Of what? There was nothing but a dead man. When he refused to move, I shoved him aside," replied the boy.

"Then, I suppose you had better go on your way. Nothing here will frighten you."

So off the boy went. He traveled here, he traveled there, and, at last, he came to a castle in the middle of a dark wood. A skinny old gatekeeper met him and asked, "What are you doing here?"

"I'm looking for fear," the boy said.

"Oh my boy, you have come to the right place! This castle is bewitched. It belongs to a count, but he cannot live in it, since every night spirits roam through it and slay anyone they catch. Only when a man can spend the whole night here and survive will the castle be free of their evil."

"Ah, this is just the job for me!" cried the boy. "At last, I shall know fear."

He entered, and found the kitchen, where he began making himself some porridge.

"Look out!" cried a voice from above. "I'm coming down!"

"So, do," said the boy.

Two legs fell to the floor.

"That's all?" asked the boy.

"Look out!" cried the voice. "I'm coming down!"

"So you said," said the boy.

A torso landed at his feet.

"Two legs. A torso. No arms or head. Isn't there more of you?" asked the boy.

"Look out!" cried the voice. "I'm coming down!"

"This is boring," said the boy. "Make it all of you this time."

Two hands, a head, and a devil's forked tail fell down.

"Well, that does seem to be all of you," the boy said, and stuck the body parts together. "That's better. Now, do you want some porridge?"

"I want you! I want you for dinner!"

"Sorry. It's porridge or nothing," replied the boy.

"I am a devil! Aren't you afraid?"

"No. Should I be?" asked the boy.

The devil waved his tail, and a score of little imps tumbled down into the kitchen.

"Hey, all of you, behave yourselves!" the boy shouted.

Then, ignoring them all, he sat down and ate his porridge.

"I've got leftovers," he called. "Who's the hungriest?"

The imps sat down and ate. This was something new for them, so they added their own food and drink to the meal, and had a feast with the boy.

At last, morning came. "The spell is over," the devils said. "The castle has been redeemed from us."

They all vanished up the chimney.

When the count showed up later that morning, he was amazed to find the castle his again. "Thank you, my boy, thank you! Let me shower riches on you!"

"I'm sorry, but I can't stay," said the boy. "I still have to learn about fear."

He wandered on and on again and, at last, came to the farm of a woman with one daughter. The boy looked at the daughter, and the daughter looked at the boy, and the woman said to them both, "You would make a fine pair."

So they were wed. But the boy still complained that he did not know fear. His mother-in-law, though, was a wise woman. "I am going to bake some bread," she said, "but I need the sieve to sift the flour first. Would you please bring it to me?"

When the boy went to fetch the flour, something black and shrieking flew into his face, batting him with its wings.

"Oh!" he yelled. "Oh!"

"That is fear, isn't it?" he asked the wise woman.

"Yes, my son," the woman said, opening the window to let the crow fly out. "You have finally learned to recognize fear."

Sources

Fillmore, Parker. *The Laughing Prince: Jugoslav Folk and Fairy Tales.* New York: Harcourt, Brace, 1921.

Kavcic, Vladimir. *The Golden Bird: Folk Tales from Slovenia.* Trans. Jan Dekker. Cleveland and New York: World, 1969.

The Fearless Merchant's Son: A Folktale from Russia

This variant is unusual in that the fearless boy has a companion, a fearful laborer. With the laborer constantly in terror, the fearless boy defeats robbers, ghosts, and demons by simply taking it for granted that he will win. He only learns fear after a bucket of small fish is poured over him, making him shudder.

In a certain kingdom, there lived a merchant's son who had never learned the meaning of fear.

Wanting to know what fear was, he traveled with a laborer into a dark forest.

"We shouldn't go in there," the laborer said. "There may be wild beasts or robbers waiting to attack us."

"So what?" said the fearless young man. "Come on."

After they had gone on through the dark forest for a time, they came to a house with lights in the windows. "There, now," said the merchant's son. "We have shelter for the night."

"I don't like this," the laborer said. "No honest folks would live out here."

But the merchant's son ignored him and entered the house. It was a robbers' house, and they were just sitting down to dinner.

"Good evening, gentleman," the merchant's son said, and invited himself to dinner. He took one bite of the fish the robbers were having, then spat it out. "Bah, that is no good. I think I will help myself to some man flesh instead!"

The robbers fled, sure he was a cannibal. The merchant's son smiled at the laborer. "Come, sit down. We have dinner right here."

They traveled on the next day, and just when the night was coming on, they came to a graveyard. "Ah, a perfect place to spend the night," said the merchant's son.

"Are you joking?" cried the laborer. "The dead walk at night!"

"As long as they walk quietly, who cares?"

They laid down and rested. The laborer was wide awake and trembling, but the merchant's son slept sweetly.

Suddenly, a great, powerful ghost swept up from a grave and began to strangle the merchant's son. The merchant's son fought back with fearlessness. He rained blow after blow on the ghost until, at last, it begged for mercy.

"I will let you go," said the merchant's son, "if you bring me the daughter of the king of the thrice-ninth land."

"At once!" cried the ghost.

Soon, a carriage appeared, with a sleeping princess inside. The merchant's son did not want to frighten her, so he took her gently back home. When she did wake, the two young people were quite pleased with each other, and eventually they wed.

But still, the merchant's son did not know what fear was. He nagged his wife and he nagged his mother.

"What are we going to do?" the princess asked her mother-in-law. "How can we teach him?"

"I know how!" said the mother-in-law.

She sent the merchant's son out on a fishing trip. It was a hot day. As she had planned, he soon fell asleep in the boat. The fisherman promptly poured a bucketful of small fish all over him.

The merchant's son woke up shivering and shuddering and fell into the water. He swam to the surface and climbed back into the boat.

"So *that's* fear!" he cried. And he never nagged his wife or mother again.

Sources
Afanas'ev, Aleksander. *Russian Fairy Tales*. New York: Pantheon, 1945.
Haney, Jack V. *The Complete Russian Folktale*. Armonk, NY: M.E. Sharpe, 1999.

The Story of a Boy Who Wanted to Learn Fear: A Folktale from Germany

Here is a variant with a combination of tricks and fearlessness. The boy is unafraid of both trickery and dead men—who he thinks are still capable of feeling—and thinks nothing of playing cards with devils or riding a flying bed. He, too, learns how to shudder when a bucket of minnows is poured on him.

Once a father had two sons. The older was quite ordinary. The younger was absolutely without fear.

When the father asked this younger son what he would like to learn, the boy said that he wanted to learn to shudder. The annoyed father went to the sexton, who said he could teach the boy how to shudder.

So the sexton showed the boy how to ring the church bell. That was fine.

Then, the sexton sent the boy at midnight to ring the bell and appeared disguised as a ghost. The boy demanded fearlessly, "What are you doing here?"

The "ghost" said nothing.

"I asked you a question," the boy said.

The "ghost" said nothing.

Now the boy grew angry at the "ghost's" rudeness and pushed him down the stairs. The sexton broke his leg, and he decided to swear off trying to teach the boy anything.

The boy's father, shocked at what happened, turned the boy out into the world to learn how to shudder on his own. The boy went on his way, still complaining, "If only I knew how to shudder!"

A traveler overheard the boy and told him, "Stay overnight under that gallows. See where seven hanged men are still hanging?"

The boy agreed. The night was chilly, so he lit a fire. Seeing the hanged bodies shaking in the wind, he thought, "If I'm cold, those folks must really be freezing."

So he untied them, all seven, and brought them down. Then he stirred up the fire so they could get warm, too. But they just sat without moving, and their clothes began to catch on fire.

"Hey, be careful!" the boy said.

They said nothing, and their clothes continued to burn.

"Well, if you won't be careful, I can't help you."

So he hung them up again.

The boy went on down the road, and stopped at an inn. The innkeeper told him that he knew how the boy could learn to shudder. "There is a haunted castle up the road. If you can stay in it for three nights, you surely will learn to shudder. You also will win the hand of the king's daughter. But I must warn you, many men have tried to stay the three nights. Some have fled. Others have never come out of that castle again."

"I'll do it," the boy decided, and went to the king.

"You may bring only three things with you into the castle," the king told the boy, "and they must not be living things."

"That's fine with me," said the boy, and picked fire, a turning lathe, and a woodcarver's bench and knife.

On the first night, the boy built a nice fire in the fireplace and settled down. Suddenly, he heard wailing from a corner.

"How cold we are! How cold we are!"

"Hey, you," the boy called. "Instead of complaining, come warm yourself at the fire."

Two black cats leaped out of the corner. They warmed themselves before the fire, then turned to the boy, their eyes blazing like red flames. "Let's play a card game," they said.

"Why not?" the boy asked. "But first, let me see your paws." When he saw them, he said, "Oh, what long nails you have! They would puncture the cards. Let me trim them for you."

With that, he grabbed them both by the necks, dropped them onto the woodcarver's bench, and caught the cats' feet in the vice. "My desire to play cards is gone," the boy said, and struck them dead, then threw the bodies outside.

The boy was about to sit down again by the fire when suddenly, from every corner and side of the room came black cats and dogs wearing red-hot chains, crowding him in until he could hardly move. The noise was horrible, and they were smothering his fire.

"All right, that's enough!" the boy cried. "Away with all of you!"

Seizing his carving knife, he hacked at them. Some escaped, others were killed. At last, they were all gone. The boy threw the bodies outside. Then, he blew on the embers of his fire until it flared into life again, and sat down by it.

But by now, he was growing weary. Looking around the room, he saw a large bed in the corner. "Just what I need," he said, and lay down on it.

But just as he was shutting his eyes, the bed began to move, first around the room, then out into the whole castle.

"This is fun," the boy said. "But go faster!"

Now, the bed raced as if it was a carriage with six galloping horses, up staircases, around turns, down staircases, and back at last to where it had started. There, it flipped over on him. He pulled himself free, and said to it, "Anyone else who wants a ride can drive now."

Then, he curled up in front of his fire and fell asleep.

In the morning, when the king came to see what had happened, he was sure that the boy was dead.

"Not yet," the boy said, sitting up. "One night is over. The next two will pass as well. But . . . I still don't know how to shudder."

The second night, there he was again in the old castle, sitting by the fire, and saying once more, "If only I could shudder!"

Midnight came, and he heard a weird noise, soft at first, then growing into a loud scream. Half a man came down the chimney, landing in front of him.

"Hey, up there," the boy called, "you need another half here!"

With a roar and a howl, the other half landed with the first. The two pieces melded, and now there was one ugly fellow sitting there. Then, more eerie fellows began to fall down, one after another. With them were nine human bones and nine human skulls, and they began bowling with them.

"That looks like fun," the boy said. "Can I bowl with you?"

"If you have money."

"I have enough," he said. "But your bowling balls aren't quite round." He set the skulls in the lathe and turned them until they were perfectly round. "Now, they will roll better."

He played with the eerie men, but when the clock struck twelve, everything disappeared before his eyes. The boy shrugged, then lay down and fell asleep.

In the morning, the king asked what had happened.

"Oh, I went bowling," the boy said. "It was fun, but I never learned how to shudder."

On the third night, he again said sadly, "If only I knew how to shudder."

At midnight, six men entered, bearing a coffin. They put the coffin on the floor, and the boy took off the lid. A dead man lay inside, cold as ice.

"Wait," the boy said, "I will warm you up a little."

He took the dead man out and sat down by the fire with him. But that did not seem to help. So, he carried the dead man to the bed and put him under the covers. The dead man began to move.

"See," the boy said, "I did get you warm."

But the dead man tried to strangle him.

"Is that the thanks I get?" the boy cried. "Get back in your coffin!"

He tossed the dead man back in the coffin and slammed the lid shut. The six men carried the coffin away.

The boy sighed. "I still cannot shudder. I'll never learn how."

Suddenly, a huge old man with a long white beard was in the room with him. "You shall soon learn what it is to shudder," he cried, "for you are about to die."

"Now, now, don't boast," the boy said. "I am just as strong as you are, and probably even stronger."

"If you are stronger than I am," the old man said, "then I shall let you go. Come, let us put it to the test."

He led the boy through dark passageways to a blacksmith's forge. There, he took an ax, and, with one blow, drove one of the anvils into the ground.

"I can do better than that," said the boy, and went to the other anvil.

The old man stood close to him, watching, not noticing how his white beard hung down. The boy seized the ax and split the anvil with one blow, wedging the old man's beard in the crack.

"Now, it is your turn to die," the boy said.

He beat the old man until he promised to give the boy great riches. The boy pulled out the ax and released him. The old man led the boy back into the castle and showed him three chests full of gold in a cellar.

"Of these," he said, "one is for the poor, the second one is for the king, and the third one is yours."

The clock struck twelve, and the spirit disappeared, leaving the boy standing in the dark.

"I can find my own way out," he said, and made his way back to his fire. There, he curled up and fell asleep.

The next morning, glad to see the boy was still alive, the king said, "By now, you surely must have learned how to shudder."

"No," the boy said. "A dead man came to life here, and a bearded man showed me three chests of gold in the cellar, but no one showed me how to shudder."

The king sighed. "You have disenchanted the castle, and you shall marry my daughter."

Then, the gold was brought up, and the wedding was celebrated. The young bride and groom loved each other from the first.

But no matter how happy they were, he still was always saying, "If only I could shudder. If only I could shudder."

This finally made the princess angry. She told her chambermaid what to do to help. So the chambermaid went out to the brook and caught a bucketful of minnows.

That night, while he who wanted to learn how to shudder was asleep, his wife pulled the covers off him. Then, she poured the bucketful of cold water and live minnows on him.

He woke with a start, crying out, "This is it! This is it! I finally know how to shudder!"

And after that, they lived in peace.

Sources

Grimm, Brothers. *The Complete Fairy Tales of the Brothers Grimm.* Trans. Jack Zipes. New York: Bantam, 1987.

Thompson, Stith. *The Folktale.* Berkeley, Los Angeles, and London: University of California Press, 1977.

The Fearless Young Man: A Folktale from Sicily, Italy

In this variant, there is no supernatural element, merely tricks and a boy who never does learn fear. But he does gain a treasure.

Once, there lived a mother with her young son. Now, he was growing into a fine man, but he knew nothing of fear. And so the mother always worried that he would come to some harm because of that lack.

So the mother went to the village priest, her brother-in-law, and explained the problem. "Never mind," said the priest. "We shall teach your son about fear."

He called in a man and said, "You are to pretend to be dead. My nephew will watch over you. At midnight, you are to pretend to come alive again."

That, the priest thought, would surely send fear into the boy.

Sure enough, the boy willingly sat beside the "corpse" in its coffin in the empty church, and thought nothing of it. He even drifted off into sleep.

At midnight, the "corpse" sat up in the coffin with a terrible shriek. "Hey you, be quiet!" shouted the boy. "I am trying to sleep."

He hit the "corpse" so mighty a blow to make it lie down again that the man jumped out of the coffin and ran away.

"Oh dear," the priest said. "That did not work." And he gave the man some coins for his pains. "But I will teach my nephew about fear yet!"

So he gathered up an armful of skulls and placed one on every step up to the bell tower, and lit a candle in each skull to make it look eerie. At the top of the bell tower, he put a skeleton holding the bell rope. Then, he went back down the stairs and called to his nephew.

"Will you please go up the stairs to the bell tower and ring the bells?"

The boy agreed, and started up the stairs. He saw the eerie skulls with candles in them and said, "Oh, how clever! Now I can see my way!"

When he reached the top and saw the skeleton, he called, "Hey, you! I'm supposed to be ringing the bells, not you. Hey? Do you hear me?"

Of course, the skeleton never moved nor spoke. The boy picked it up and threw it down the stairs. Then, he rang the bells so loudly that the priest had to explain to all the startled villagers, "It was just some boy's prank."

But the priest decided to try frightening the boy one more time. So he told a man to hide near the church's well. "When the boy passes you, yell 'Six!' at him with all your might." That, the priest thought, would surely give the boy a sudden fright.

He asked the boy to bring him a mug of water from the well. The boy willingly went out into the night to the well. As he passed the hidden man, the man shouted, "Six!"

"Seven!" answered the boy, and whacked the man over the head with the mug. The man ran off, and the boy calmly brought the priest the mug of water.

"I give up!" the priest said. "You must go out into the world to find fear."

So off the boy went, with nothing but the mug. He wandered into the forest. Thirsty, he found a stream and filled the mug. But he slipped on the muddy bank of the stream, and the mug flew from his hand and shattered.

"Bah, look at all that!" the boy cried, looking at the tiny streams of water flowing in all directions. "Five hundred little streams there, 400 on that side, and 600 on the other side!"

What the boy did not know was that robbers were hiding just ahead. They heard his shout and thought that army troops were coming for them. They ran away.

The boy found their treasure and took it home with him. Now he and his mother were wealthy.

But the boy never did learn about fear.

Sources

Thompson, Stith. *The Folktale.* Berkeley, Los Angeles, and London: University of California Press, 1977.

Zipes, Jack, trans. and ed. *Beautiful Angiola: The Great Treasury of Sicilian Folk and Fairy Tales Collected by Laura Gonzenbach.* London and New York: Routledge, 2004.

DRAGON-SLAYERS
AND MONSTER-SLAYERS

Dragons are seen in different ways in the West and in Asia. Western tales generally feature the dragon as a dangerous force to be defeated. Whereas in lands such as China and Japan, dragons are viewed as forces of nature, rain or river spirits that are above human ideas of good and evil. Since Asian dragons, for the most part, appear in myths rather than in folktales, they are not included here.

Monsters generally are seen as bad or downright evil in all cultures (with some exceptions, such as in the beauty and the beast variants) and usually are the enemies of humanity.

The Lucky Ruble: A Folktale from Estonia

This folktale features several themes. First, there is the magic coin that always returns to its owner. Then, there is the theme of kindness, in which the hero rescues the three dogs. There is the grateful animal theme, in which the dogs help the hero. There is the theme of the princess to be saved from the dragon. Last, there is the theme of the hero revealing himself as the true dragon-slayer through his possession of some part of the dragon.

Once, there was a father with three sons. As he lay on his deathbed, he divided up his property among them.

The eldest son got the house and land, while the middle son got the cattle. For the youngest son, Peter, there was only one thing left. But his father whispered with his dying breath that it might prove the most useful gift of all. It was a silver ruble coin—and it was magic. It always returned to the pocket of its owner.

After the father's burial, there was no place left at home for Peter. So Peter set out into the world to find his fortune. After several days on the road seeing no one, he met a strange old man with a grizzled gray beard and only one eye.

With the old man were three dogs, and they did not seem to be too happy to be with him. He did not seem to like them, either. Peter thought the man probably was cruel to them.

"I will buy those dogs from you," Peter said, and the three dogs wagged their tails. "What are their names?"

The old man frowned. "Run-for-Food, Tear-Down, and Break-Iron. I will take one silver ruble for their worthless hides."

So Peter bought the dogs, who happily walked away with him. And sure enough, the magic ruble was in Peter's pocket again that night.

As Peter and his three dogs traveled through a forest, Peter heard the sound of a coach and four, and he politely stepped aside. But the coach stopped. A lovely young woman, a princess indeed, looked out briefly. The sorrow Peter saw in her eyes made him ask, "What is wrong?"

"I was chosen by lot," she said. "I am to be eaten by a dragon."

"No!" Peter cried.

"Please, it cannot be helped. If it is not me, some other poor woman will die."

"You will not die," Peter said. "But the dragon will!"

Peter listened to her directions on how to find the dragon, and off he went with his three dogs. Sure enough, there was the dragon, far larger than a bear, covered with dark scales, with two great wings, crooked horns, and terrible tusks and talons.

"All right, Tear-Down, let's go!" Peter cried.

Tear-Down rushed right in and caught the dragon by the throat. Peter then killed the dragon, cut off its horns and tusks, and returned to the princess.

"I will return to you in three years," he said.

But the princess's coachman was a villain. He dragged the princess from her coach and threatened her so violently that she agreed to say he had killed the dragon—she feared for her life. But the princess swore that she could marry no one for three years, and her vow was heard by her father the king.

The three years passed swiftly. On the wedding day, Peter returned. But, by this time, the coachman had won the king's ear, and so Peter was thrown into prison. But Peter still had his three dogs.

"It is your turn," he said to Break-Iron.

Break-Iron easily bit through every lock and chain and freed Peter.

"Now it is your turn," Peter said to Run-for-Food, and sent him to the princess.

The princess recognized the dog, and fed him a treat. Then, she said to her father, "This dog belongs to the real hero, the man who slew the dragon—the man I am going to marry."

She sent Run-for-Food back to Peter with a note on his collar. Peter appeared before the princess and the king with the three dogs at his side.

"This man is a nobody!" the coachman cried. "It was I who slew the dragon!"

"But I have the proof," said Peter, and he produced the dragon's tusks and horns.

The coachman was condemned to death. Peter and the princess were married and lived happily together.

As for the three dogs, well, they had done their work. And so they transformed into swans and flew away.

Sources

Kirby, W.F. *The Hero of Esthonia and Other Studies in the Romantic Literature of that Country.* London: John C. Ninmo, 1895.

Zheleznova, Irina, ed. and trans. *Estonian Fairy Tales.* Tallinn: Perioodika, 1981.

The Dragon-Slayer: A Folktale from Mexico

This story begins as a standard Donkey Skin variant, but then alters into a dragon-slaying tale in which the heroine is the one who slays the dragon. As is often the case in dragon-slaying folktales, a courtier or servant then claims to have slain the dragon, but is brought to judgment when the actual dragon-slayer reveals some token, such as the dragon's tongues.

Once, there was a father with three daughters. And as often happens in such cases, the older two daughters were jealous of the youngest, who was prettier and more clever than they.

So the sisters plotted to be rid of her. They decided to make it look as though she was a thief. So they stole their father's money and hid it under her bed.

"Father, Father, your money has been stolen!" one sister cried.

"Your youngest daughter took it," the other cried. "We saw her do it."

The father found his money under the youngest daughter's bed. He could not believe it. His youngest daughter a thief! What could he do?

"Leave my house," he said, ignoring her cries of innocence. "Leave, and never return."

So the poor girl went out into the world with nothing but a few tortillas and the clothes on her back. She wandered on for no one knows how long or far, until at last, worn out, she sat to eat one of the tortillas.

Just then, a ragged old woman came up to her. "Dear girl, I have not eaten in two days. Could I have just one of your tortillas?"

"Please, dear mother, help yourself. I only wish I had more to give you. My father threw me out of his house and ordered that I never return. Now I do not know what to do."

"I do," said the old woman. "Go down this road, and you will come to a fine kingdom, where the king will surely give you work. Take this little wooden wand, and whenever you need to know something, simply ask it, and you will instantly have the answer."

The girl thanked the old woman and went on her way. But then, the road split into three branches.

The girl took out the wand and said, "Oh mighty little wand, by all the might that Heaven gave you, tell me what lies down the road to the right."

"The road to the right leads only to the dragon with seven heads who loves human flesh," the wand replied.

She asked again, "Oh mighty little wand, by all the might that Heaven gave you, tell me what lies down the road to the left."

"The road to the left leads only to the giant named Bolumbi, who loves human flesh," said the wand.

She asked a third time, "Oh mighty little wand, by all the might that Heaven gave you, tell me what lies down the road in the middle."

"The middle road leads straight to the kingdom you seek," said the wand.

So the girl took the middle road, and sure enough, she came to the royal palace, where she asked for work. They put her to work in the kitchen.

The girl saw that the king was very sad. She asked the wand why this was, and it answered, "The seven-headed dragon has told the king that he must send his only son, the prince, to be eaten. Otherwise, the dragon will lay waste to the entire land."

"Do you know how to kill the dragon?" the girl asked.

It told her, and the girl left the palace kitchen and went off to find the dragon. The king had issued a proclamation that whoever slew the dragon would be granted any wish, but so far no one had survived to claim that wish.

As the wand had told her, the girl sang a soft lullaby to the dragon. She sang it over and over. One by one, the seven heads fell sound asleep. The girl took the wand as it had told her, and she slapped the dragon with it. Instantly, the dragon was dead. The girl cut the seven tongues from the seven heads to prove she had slain the dragon, then went back to the palace.

Now, a servant of the king saw the dead dragon and said, "Aha, this is my lucky day! I will tell the king I slew the dragon, and marry his daughter, the princess."

So he cut off all seven heads and lugged them to the palace. "Your Majesty, I have slain the dragon and here is the proof! I wish to marry your daughter."

But the girl stepped forward. "If you have slain the dragon, where are the heads' seven tongues?" She held them out. "Your Majesty, this man is a liar."

So the lying servant was put to death.

"What is your wish?" the king asked the girl.

"My wish is to marry your son, the prince."

The king looked at her in dismay. "I cannot let him marry a kitchen maid."

"Ah, but you gave your word. And kings must honor their pledges."

"You are right," the king admitted.

The girl then asked the wand for help. She appeared at her wedding in a magnificent gown of gold. The prince and she fell in love, were married, and lived happily together.

But sadly, the king now fell in love with his daughter-in-law, too. The girl asked the wand, "How can this be stopped without bloodshed?"

"You must go to the giant Bolumbi and take the little ring that he wears on his tooth. It is a wishing ring. All you need do is say, 'Turn this into that,' and it will do just that."

Off the girl went to the giant Bolumbi. She sang him to sleep just as she had done with the dragon. When he was snoring with his mouth wide open, the girl quickly snatched the ring and hurried away.

She got home just in time to see the king about to stab his son in the back. "Ring, turn the king into a wild pig!"

The king instantly became a javelina, a wild pig, and he went scurrying off into the forest.

The prince and princess, now king and queen, lived for many happy years.

Sources

Bierhorst, John. *Latin American Folktales: Stories from Hispanic and Indian Traditions.* New York: Pantheon, 2002.

Wheeler, Howard T. *Tales from Jalisco, Mexico.* Philadelphia: American Folklore Society, 1943.

Chin Timur and Mehtumsala: A Folktale from the Uighur of Central Asia

This folktale from the Uighur people combines several themes. First is the one of the casting off of babies who then are replaced with animals and the accusation of the wife as a monster. Second is the raising of the children by an animal, here a bear, which is reminiscent of the Roman myth of Romulus and Remus being raised by a wolf. Then, the Snow White theme appears as the sister is warned not to open the door but is tricked into doing so. At last, this becomes a dragon-slaying tale.

Once, there was a king with two wives.

The first wife was very jealous of the second. When the second wife gave birth to a boy and a girl, the first wife had the babies taken away and replaced with a puppy and a kitten.

"You see? She is a monster! Get rid of her!"

So the king did.

But the two children, who had been cast out into the wilderness to die, were rescued by a she-bear. She raised them as though they were her own cubs, but she never let them forget they were human.

When they were old enough, the children gave each other names. The girl named her brother Chin Timur, and the boy named his sister Mehtumsala. And when they were old enough to be on their own, the she-bear sent them back to the world of humans.

Somehow, though the tale does not say how, Chin Timur became a fine warrior, with a sword, a horse, and a hunting hound. One day, when he knew he would be away for longer than usual, he warned Mehtumsala, "Do not go out on the road. Wait for me here. I will return."

So Mehtumsala waited. When she grew bored, she climbed up onto the roof to get fresh air. But while she was up there, a cat chased a bird through the house and during the chase, the fire was extinguished. Mehtumsala hurried back inside, but there was not even an ember left to restart the fire.

"I am not supposed to go out on the road. But if I stay here, I will freeze tonight."

Mehtumsala could see distant smoke rising from another chimney. So off she went to beg a hot coal to restart her fire. She found an old woman living in that house, who gave her hot embers in a stick to restart her fire.

"Take these millet seeds," the old woman said. "Scatter them behind you as you go. Then, if you get lost, you can find your way back to me."

Mehtumsala hardly thought she would get lost, but she thanked the old woman and went home.

What she did not know was that there was no old woman. That had been a disguise. What there actually was much worse: a seven-headed dragon. That night, the dragon followed the trail of millet right to Mehtumsala's door. The dragon called out:

> Is Chin Timur home?
> Is the horse in the stable,
> The sword on the wall,
> The hound by the door?

Mehtumsala, thinking herself safe behind the locked and bolted door, replied:

> Chin Timur is not home.
> No horse in the stable,
> No sword on the wall,
> No hound by the door.

Then, to Mehtumsala's horror, the seven-headed dragon entered as though the door had been wide open. She seized Mehtumsala by her long hair and drank enough of her blood to leave the girl weak and pale, lying on the floor.

Then the seven-headed dragon left.

The next day, Chin Timur returned. He found his sister lying on the floor, weak and pale. "My sister!" he cried. "What happened to you?"

Mehtumsala wept as she told her brother what had happened.

Chin Timur burned with rage. "I will avenge you and kill that monster! Do not tell anyone I am back. I will wait in hiding. And you, my horse and hound, make not a sound. We shall find a way to slay the seven-headed dragon."

And indeed, the seven-headed dragon returned that night. She called:

> Is Chin Timur home?
> Is the horse in the stable,
> The sword on the wall,
> The hound by the door?

Mehtumsala answered:

> Chin Timur is not home.
> No horse in the stable,
> No sword on the wall,
> No hound by the door.

The seven-headed dragon swarmed into the house. "I smell another human," she snarled.

"There is only me. I washed my brother's shirts and set them out to dry. That must be what you smell."

The seven-headed dragon lunged at Mehtumsala—but Chin Timur was faster yet. With one swipe of his sword, he cut off one of the dragon's heads.

The dragon shrieked, "You got one of my heads—let's see how you handle the other six!"

Oh, that was a battle! The dragon could not get out of the house. Every time she threw herself against Chin Timur, he cut off another of her heads. Every time, the dragon tried to get out the door, Mehtumsala would cut at her with Chin Timur's second sword.

The fight lasted a day and a night, but, at last, Chin Timur had cut off six of the seven heads. The dragon turned herself into a whirlwind and shot up through the chimney.

Chin Timur ran to his horse and called his hound to him. They chased the dragon, until at last they caught up with her. They fought again, all that night.

Then, Chin Timur's hound leaped up and bit off the dragon's last head. She fell to the ground, dead.

Chin Timur went home, weary but joyous. He nursed his sister back to health, and the two had many more adventures together.

Sources

Li, Xuewei, trans. *Ada and the Greedy King and Other Chinese Minorities Folktales*. Singapore, Kuala Lampur, and Hong Kong, China: Federal Publications, 1991.

Wei, Cuiyi, and Karl W. Luckert. *Uighur Stories from Along the Silk Road*. Lanham, MD, and New York: University Press of America, 1998.

Law Da and the Dragon: A Folktale from the Akha People of Southeast Asia

The Akha are an ethnic minority who live today in parts of China, Laos, Thailand, and Myanmar (formerly Burma).

This folktale has a distant echo of the Anglo-Saxon English epic of *Beowulf*, with the hero having to slay both the dragon (instead of Grendal) and the dragon's more dangerous mother. Is this a case of cross-cultural contact, or merely a coincidence? That is up to the storyteller to decide, since there is no evidence either way.

One night, in long ago times, a baby was born to A Law and his wife. But to their shock, they saw that he had been born with only one ear, only one eye, but a full set of teeth. This baby, they decided, could not be raised. So they left him under a tree.

The next day, an old, childless couple heard a baby crying and took the boy home. They named him Law Da and raised him well. By the age of eight, he was as strong as a grown man. His adoptive parents were very poor, and so he would often go out begging for food for them.

One twilight, Law Da traveled all the way to Rock Ear Lake, too far to get home before night. The boy came to the house of an old woman, and he asked if he could stay there till morning.

The old woman welcomed him inside. But then she began to cry.

"Grandmother, what is the matter?" Law Da asked.

"You make me think of my own child."

"Has he died?" Law Da asked.

"Not yet," the old woman said sadly. "But there is no hope for him. In Rock Ear Lake, there is a dragon that eats one person a day from our village. Tomorrow, the dragon will eat my son."

"He will not!" Law Da cried. "I will kill that dragon."

"You are but a boy!" the grandmother cried. "What can you do?"

"Grandmother, I was born with special gifts. I will not let the dragon eat your son."

The next day, there was Law Da at the lake's edge. "Come fight me, dragon!"

The dragon roared up out of the water. But Law Da focused his one eye on the monster. Light blazed from the eye and dazzled the dragon so that it could not find Law Da. Instead, the dragon lashed its tail and sent a wave of underbrush onto Law Da. But the hero shielded himself with his one ear.

Then, Law Da rushed forward and hacked the dragon in half. The lake turned red with its blood.

"Everyone, hurry!" Law Da called. "Open up all the wells to drain the lake or the dragon's mother will attack us!"

When the lake was dried up, a huge fish swarmed out of the mud and thrashed its way out of sight. Law Da chased after it, but could not find it. Instead, he found a beautiful young woman sitting under a tree.

Law Da knew the young woman had been the fish, but before he could strike her, she cried pitifully, "Please let me speak."

"Speak," Law Da said.

"I was born in the Rock Ear Lake. The dragon came and forced me to be his wife. He was so much stronger that I had no choice. I did not want the villagers to die, but I could do nothing to help them. Please do not kill me."

Law Da felt pity stir in his heart, and he did not kill her.

Now, all the villagers rejoiced that Law Da had slain the dragon. But a village elder warned, "The mother of the dragon is still alive."

But no one could find her. The girl whose life Law Da had saved stayed with him and worked hard.

After some time, the ruler of the land heard about the beautiful girl who had been a fish. He had her brought to his palace. The girl pretended to fall gravely ill, and the king asked her what was wrong.

"You must kill Law Da," she said. "Kill Law Da, or I will never recover."

Law Da was taken to the palace. Now, he knew who and what the girl really was. "Do not kill me," he told the king. Then he whispered so only the king could hear, "Wait and see what happens tonight."

Sure enough, that night, the girl dropped her disguise. She became a dragon.

Law Da ordered all the doors and windows closed and locked. Then, he attacked. The light blazing from his eye dazzled the dragon, and Law Da cut her apart.

The terror of the dragons was over. Everyone could finally rejoice.

Sources
Lewis, Paul W. *Akha Oral Literature*. Bangkok, Thailand: White Lotus, 2002.
Walton, Geoffrey, ed. *A Northern Miscellany: Essays from the North of Thailand*. Bangkok, Thailand: Silkworm, 1989.

The Dragon of Kinabalu: A Folktale from Borneo

This adventurous folktale shows both Chinese and Bornean influences. Its country of origin is not known, although it was collected in Borneo. It does attempt to explain how a Chinese prince started a dynasty on Borneo without worrying about political or military history.

Once, there was a Chinese emperor with three sons, each of whom wanted the throne.

The emperor could not decide which son was best suited to rule after him. So he set them a task.

On the island of Borneo lived a dragon on Mount Kinabalu, in a lake on the mountain's very peak. The dragon had one great treasure, an enormous ruby red as the heart of fire, with which it played like a child with a ball.

"My sons," the emperor said, "you are to go to Borneo. Whichever of you can bring me that enormous ruby shall be my heir. But whoever fails must die."

First to set out was the eldest, Kwun Wang, sailing to Borneo with a mighty fleet and many soldiers. But they found that the mountain was so steep that it was nearly impossible to climb, and the dragon picked them off with ease. They fled for their lives.

Now, Sun Wang set out with a mighty fleet and many soldiers. But he, too, met with defeat as the dragon picked them off one by one.

Both brothers knew they now had only two choices: return to China and be executed or stay in exile in Borneo.

While his elder brothers were trying to decide what to do, the youngest son, Kong Wang, set out. But though he, too, took a mighty fleet, he filled his ships not with warriors but with iron cauldrons. When he reached the foot of the mountain, he used those cauldrons, piled up and up, as a staircase up to the top of the mountain. Kong Wang carried, carefully wrapped up, a large, red-hot ball of iron.

There by the lake's shore was the dragon, with glinting green scales and enormous green wings. As it played with the enormous ruby, it lashed its whiplike tail from side to side, and its fangs gleamed as though it was smiling.

For a moment, Kong Wang stood frozen at the sight of the huge beast. Then, he hurled the red-hot ball of iron straight at the dragon's face. The startled dragon dove straight into the lake—forgetting to take the enormous ruby. Kong Wang seized it, and hurried down the cauldron staircase. There, he met his two brothers, and all three decided to set sail before the dragon came after them.

But the dragon was furious. It soared down on its mighty wings, and it smashed ship after ship and ate their crews whole. At last, only three ships escaped, and those three held the three princes and the enormous ruby. In the confused escape, the ruby was on Kwun Wang's ship, and when they landed in China, he rushed to the emperor.

"I have brought you the ruby!"

But Kong Wang rushed after him, shouting, "Liar! I was the one who got the ruby!" And he told, with true details, how it had been done.

Kwun Wang and Sun Wang ran from that palace and sailed hastily away. No one knows what became of Kwun Wang. But Sun Wang landed on the shore of Brunei, where he won himself the throne.

Today, in the capital Chinese city of Beijing, it is said that the great ruby still can be seen in the Imperial Palace of the Forbidden City. Whether or not it once did belong to a dragon is something that cannot be proved.

Sources

Furness, William H. *Folklore in Borneo: A Sketch.* 1899. Whitefish, MT: Kessinger, 2003.

Rutter, Owen. *The Dragon of Kinabalu and Other Borneo Stories.* Sabah, Malaysia: Natural History Publications, 1999.

Urumba the Water Monster: A Folktale from the Mbarakwena Bushmen of the Kalahari Desert

In this monster-slaying tale, it is two boys who are the heroes, mostly because they are smart enough not to rush to the attack. Instead, they listen to the wind and learn that even the monster had to sleep.

It was said that Urumba was a water monster, one who lived in the river and had neither legs nor feet. But Urumba did not care. He caught and ate anyone who came too close to the riverbank.

In those long-ago days, only the Mbarakwena people lived in the area. One day, a little girl went down to the river for water. She never returned. Her father went down to the river to find her. He never returned.

Since the people back then could speak with Elephant, he went down to the riverbank to look. But he knew to wait till Urumba was asleep. Elephant got a drink of water, but he never found any missing people. Elephant told the people that Urumba had eaten them.

Two boys heard this story. They saw that everyone was afraid of Urumba. No one knew how to fight him. He was too powerful. But the two boys listened to what the wind had to say, and the wind told the boys that even Urumba had to sleep.

So the two boys stole down to the riverbank. They hid among the tall reeds until they saw the great, terrible bulk of Urumba, sound asleep. Then, they stabbed him with spears until he was dead.

The boys cut open his stomach, and all the people and animals that the monster had eaten came out and were happy.

Sources
Fourie, Coral. *Living Legends of a Dying Culture: Bushmen Myths, Legends, and Fables.* Pretoria, South Africa: Ekoglide, 1994. Collected from Shiamjomo, a man of the Mbarakwena people, date unknown.

Metzger, Fritz. *The Hyena's Laughter: Bushmen Fables.* Windhock, Namibia: Kuiseb-Verlag, 1995. (This contains a similar tale about Tsama Lake in Namibia, but lacks the dragon-slaying element: The people simply avoid the lake once they know about the monster.)

The Wanderer and the Dragon: A Folktale from the Gypsies of Slovakia

In this folktale, the problem of the dragon is solved in what can be seen as a singularly Gypsy way, not by rushing in with sword drawn but by sheer cleverness. The dragon is tricked into thinking that the hero is more dangerous than the dragon and must be appeased.

One day, a wanderer and his dog came to a great city. He found it in a state of mourning, hung with black cloth.

"What has happened here?" he asked.

"We are in mourning," he was told.

"Why so? Who has died?"

"It is not that. In a cave nearby lives a great dragon with twenty-four heads. Every day, he must eat a woman. If we fail to feed him, he will crush this city under his feet."

"I will help you out of that," the wanderer said. "I will go there alone with my dog."

He had such a big dog that it could have even fought the devil. With his dog at his side, the wanderer went to the dragon's cave and shouted, "Dragon! Dragon, come out here with your blind mother. Women have you eaten but will eat no more. I will see if you are any good."

The dragon was not used to someone not fearing him, and he called the wanderer into his cave. The wanderer boldly said to him, "Now, you will give me whatever I ask for to eat and to drink. And then, you will swear to me to always give that city peace, and never to eat women or men, no, not one. For if ever I hear of your doing so, I shall come back and cut your throat."

"My good man, fear not," the dragon said meekly. "I swear to you. For I see that you are a proper man. If you were not, I should long since have eaten up you and your dog. Just tell me what you want of me."

"I only want you to bring me the finest wine to drink and meat such as no man has ever eaten. If you do not, I shall destroy everything that is yours, shall shut you up here, and you will never come out of this cave."

"I will fetch a basket of meat, and cook it for you," replied the dragon.

The dragon brought him such meat as no man ever had eaten. When the wanderer had eaten and drunk his fill, then the dragon swore to him never to eat anybody, man, woman or child, again.

"Good," the wanderer said. "So let us leave it."

So he brought peace to the city. And from that moment on, the dragon never ate another human being. And if they are not dead, they are still alive.

Sources

Groome, Francis Hindes. *Gypsy Folk Tales*. 1899. Whitefish, MT: Kessinger, 2004.

Tong, Diane. *Gypsy Folktales*. New York: Harvest, 1989.

The Three Dragons: A Folktale from the Gypsies of Bohemia

This folktale from the Gypsies of what is now the Czech Republic is more traditional in its form than the former Gypsy tale. Here, there are three maidens captured by dragons, and a fearless hero who rescues them (with the aid of some good wine to strengthen him). The tale contains the theme of the broken token, the ring that is made whole when the lovers are reunited. And it has the theme of the dragon tongues as proof that the hero is the true dragon-slayer.

A king had three daughters who one day went to a pond to bathe. A dragon swooped down and carried them away to a cave in the mountains. There, they stayed, trapped, for years, with their father not knowing where they were or what had become of them.

A clever fellow named Bruntslikos went to the girls' father, and told him he would do his best to find the missing daughters. The father promised Bruntslikos one of them to wife, if he could find them.

Bruntslikos took a horse from the girls' father, and rode for a whole year through the forest. He came at last to a tavern. When two fellows there asked him where he was going, he told them the story, and they offered to go with him. Three, they thought, would make merrier company.

So off the three went, until they came to the entrance of the dragon's cave, which was a great cleft down into the rock. Bruntslikos had his two comrades lower him by a rope to fetch up one of the maidens. When Bruntslikos came down, there she sat alone.

"How came you here?" she asked. "The dragon has gone hunting, but when he returns here, you will lose your life!"

"I have no fear," he answered.

But the girl thought she would see what sort of a hero he might be. She asked him to lift a sword. But, at first, he could not even raise it from the ground. Then, he took a drink of wine she offered him, and suddenly he had the strength to freely brandish the sword.

"Now, I am strong," he said. "I will soon help you out of here."

"Do that," she answered, "and I will be your bride."

She gave him half a golden ring and kept the other half herself.

Then, the dragon came home. "I smell human flesh!" he said.

The girl asked, "But how could that be? How could it get here? Not even a bird comes here."

"Do not talk nonsense," the dragon said. "I know a man is here. You, man, come out here."

Bruntslikos had been hiding under a trough. Now, he sprang out and cried, "What do you want? I fear you not."

"Why bother telling me that?" asked the dragon. "I will soon put your strength to the test."

The dragon ate dumplings of lead. But Bruntslikos casually said, "I do not care for such dumplings. Let us drink together instead."

When they had drunk their fill, the dragon challenged Bruntslikos to wrestle with him.

"A fine idea," Bruntslikos said.

In the first bout, the dragon drove Bruntslikos into the earth to the waist, then drew him out again.

In the second bout, Bruntslikos drove the dragon into the earth to the neck, then grasped the sword and began to cut off the dragon's twelve heads. Bruntslikos struck them all off save for the middle one.

The girl cried, "Give it one smashing blow, and he will die."

So the dragon was slain and turned to pitch. But Bruntslikos took all the tongues out of the twelve heads, and put them in his pocket.

Then, he collected all the money that was there, put his new bride and himself into the basket and called to his two comrades to pull them up. When they saw the girl, they wanted her for wife. But Bruntslikos told them that there were two more maidens to be rescued.

So Bruntslikos fought and slew the next two dragons, one that had fifteen heads and one that had twenty-four heads. He rescued his bride's two sisters and brought them up to the surface. And in his pockets were all the dragon tongues.

But now, his two comrades wanted all the glory. They tossed Bruntslikos down a well and left him there. And they took the three young women back to their father.

Before this happened, Bruntslikos already had agreed with his bride that if anything happened and they were separated, she must wait for him for eight years. If he did not return by then, she would be free to wed another.

So the eighth year came, and the sorrowing young woman was to marry another man.

Then came Bruntslikos dressed like a beggar. He asked for wine, and when she gave it to him, he slipped his half of the ring into the glass, then offered it to her. When she saw the half of the ring, she threw her half into the glass, and the two halves became whole again.

With a cry of joy, she threw herself into his arms and began kissing him. The other marriage was broken off, and she was married then and there to Bruntslikos.

Just to prove his worth, he flung the dragons' tongues on the table. The people all cheered the dragon-slayer and rescuer of the princesses.

So, if they are not dead, they are living together.

Sources

Groome, Francis Hindes. *Gypsy Folk Tales*. 1899. Whitefish, MT: Kessinger, 2004.

Tong, Diane. *Gypsy Folktales*. New York: Harvest, 1989.

Iya: A Folktale from the Lakota Sioux of the American West

This folktale features a unique shapeshifting monster who disguises his huge bulk in the form of a human baby and almost gets away with his deception. He is a true monster in that he devours whole villages—but he meets his match in this tale.

Once, hunters returning to their people found a baby crying in the woods. Who had left him there? Were his parents dead?

At last, one of the men, whose wife had no child, picked up the baby and brought it home to her. She was overjoyed, as were most of the people of the tribe. Only the shaman was wary.

"It seems like a human baby," he said. "But there are evil spirits of the forest that can take strange disguises."

"We cannot leave a baby to die," the woman argued. And the shaman backed off, defeated by her fierce determination.

As night fell, the people went to sleep, one by one, until only the woman was awake, looking down at the baby sleeping in her lap, its little mouth open.

But gradually, she became aware of a strange murmuring, as of distant voices. Were these spirit voices? They seemed to rise from the earth all around her. Were these evil beings?

The shaman, meanwhile, came awake with a start. He rushed to where the woman sat. The mysterious noise was coming from the baby's open mouth.

"Put the baby down and come out here with me," the shaman ordered. The woman, alarmed and afraid, obeyed.

"What is wrong with the baby?" she asked.

"That is not a baby," the shaman said. "That is Iya the camp-eater."

Iya was a monstrous being, a giant body on spindly legs. He could not fight or run on those thin legs, but he could devour a whole camp in a gulp.

The shaman continued, "Had you fallen asleep with the rest, he would have dropped that disguise and devoured us all in our sleep. If he wakes now, he will swallow us all."

With whispers, they woke all the people and had everyone move away as silently as possible. When morning came, Iya awoke—and found himself alone. Furious, he dropped his baby disguise and stormed out into the open as his true, hideous self. Wobbling along on his thin legs, he shouted, "Run as you will! I will eat you all!"

The shaman mocked him,. "Spindly legs, you cannot catch us!"

Iya rushed forward as best he could—and all the warriors shot their arrows at him. They stabbed him with their knives.

And so died Iya the camp-eater. And he troubled them no longer.

Sources

Eastman, Charles A. *Wigwam Evenings: Sioux Tales Retold.* Lincoln: University of Nebraska Press, 1990.

Zitkala-Sa. *Old Indian Legends.* Boston, New York, and London: Ginn, 1901.

The Hunter and the Monster Bird: A Folktale from the Cherokee of Tennessee

Although no monster is slain in this folktale, the basic theme is of the hero's survival and eventual escape. Showing how a good story can arise seemingly spontaneously in more than one location and time, there is a similar story of Lugalbanda, a Sumerian epic hero of the second millennium B.C.E. in Mesopotamia.

Once a hunter was out in the woods, when he saw a Tla'nuwa, a monster hawk, overhead.

The hunter dove for cover, trying to hide from the great bird, but the Tla'nuwa already had seen him. It came surging down, sank its talons into the hunter's pack, and carried him off, high into the air.

But as it flew, the Tla'nuwa spoke to the hunter. "Do not be afraid. I am a mother with several fledglings. And I merely wish you to be a guard for them until they are old enough to leave the nest."

The hunter, without any real choice, agreed.

After he knew not how long, they finally landed in the hawk's nest on the top of a mountain. In the nest squirmed two fledglings, not yet old enough to fly. The mother Tla'nuwa set the man down gently, and then she flew away.

The hunter stood watching the fledglings, wondering if they were old enough to try attacking him. But they merely squawked and pecked at each other like any other baby birds.

Then, the Tla'nuwa returned with a deer she had slain. She gave a large portion to the hunter, and the rest to her two chicks.

So it went for many days. The hunter watched the fledglings while the mother was away, and he tried to occupy his time thinking of home and family. How he missed them! Did they think him dead?

Every day, he begged the Tla'nuwa, "Let me go home."

But every day, she answered, "Not yet. Just wait a little bit longer."

At last, the hunter knew he must make his own escape. He caught one of the fledglings and dragged it to the edge of the nest. Then, he tied himself to its leg with the thongs from his pack. He struck the fledgling several times until it finally launched itself into the air. The fledgling could not really fly, but it managed to flap its way down safely to the top of a tall tree.

The hunter quickly cut through the thongs and scrambled down the tree to the ground. He hurried home, a feather from the fledgling in his fist. But the feather was lost along the way, and he had nothing to prove what had happened to him.

He did not really care. It was good to be home again.

Source

Mooney, James. *James Mooney's History, Myths, and Sacred Formulas of the Cherokees.* 1900. Asheville, NC: Bright Mountain, 1982. Collected by Mooney from an informant named Swimmer, ca. 1900.

THE FAIRY'S MIDWIFE

The fairy's midwife is a common tale type in the Celtic, British, and Scandinavian countries—those with a strong folk belief in the fairy folk. Variants of the tale also come from cultures without strong fairy folk beliefs, such as the Swedish tale of the troll wife and the Jewish one of the demon wife. The concept that the fairies might need a mortal midwife may come from the equally strong folk belief that the fairies are seldom fertile, and thus might not be well-acquainted with the birth process.

The Fairy's Midwife: A Folktale from England

This is the basic folktale, including a human midwife, a mysterious stranger, and perilous magic ointment. This tale ends with the theme of the fairy folk being thieves, and the human midwife suffering a loss for becoming involved in fairy magic.

Once, there lived a kind old midwife, skilled in her art, one who had helped many a soul into the world.

One night about midnight, there came a frantic knocking on her door. Startled but not really alarmed, the midwife got out of bed and went to the door to see who it was who needed to be helped into the world. Odd, she could not recall any woman in the village so near to term. Hopefully, it was not a premature babe struggling to come out.

When she opened the door, there stood a strange, squint-eyed, little, ugly, old fellow. He had a look, she thought, very like a certain dark personage, who ought never to be called by his proper name. But there was no mistaking the urgency in the old fellow's voice when he asked her to come and attend to his wife, who was in childbirth.

The midwife had to wonder if she was going to be attending to the birth of a little devil. But she mounted behind the strange man on a coal-black horse, and away they sped through the black night. It was a great relief to the midwife to finally find herself at the door of a neat, normal-seeming cottage and to find her patient to be a decent-looking woman.

A healthy, very active baby boy was soon born. In its flailing about, the baby gave the midwife a good box on the ear. She had to laugh, for the babe had not yet the strength to hurt her, and she said, "The little fellow is very like his father."

The mother said nothing to this, only gave the midwife an ointment. "Rub both of the child's eyes with this."

The midwife did as she was told, wondering what marvels might be in the ointment. Overcome by curiosity, she slyly touched one of her own eyes with the ointment.

What a change she saw! The new mother was now a beautiful lady attired in white, while the babe was wrapped in swaddling clothes of a silvery gauze. It looked much prettier than before, but still maintained the elfish cast of the eye, like its father, indeed. There on either side of the bed's head sat a couple of little flat-nosed imps, scratching their heads or pulling the lady's ears.

The midwife, fearing for her safety in this enchantment, fled the house as fast as she could, and said nothing about having touched her own eye with the ointment. The sour-looking old fellow once more handed her up on the coal-black horse, and sent her home much faster than she went.

On the next market day, the midwife was startled to see the same wicked-looking fellow pilfering articles from stall to stall.

"Oho!" she thought. "You are nothing but a thief!"

She went up to him and asked after his wife and child.

The fellow frowned. "Do you see me?"

"I see you as plain as day. And I see you are busy as well!"

"With what eye do you see this?"

"With the right eye," she said without thinking.

"Take that for meddling with what did not belong to you," he cried, and struck her eye. "You shall see me no more."

From that hour until the day of her death, the midwife was blind on the right side, thus dearly paying for her curiosity.

Sources
Ashliman, D.L. *A Guide to Folktales in the English Language.* New York, Westport, CT, and London: Greenwood, 1987.
Jacobs, Joseph. *English Fairy Tales.* London: David Nutt, 1890.

The Midwife of Hafoddydd: A Folktale from Wales

This folktale begins in the standard way for this tale type, with the arrival of the mysterious stranger. But these fairy folk are nobler than those in the previous English folktale. There is no magic ointment, and the midwife is properly rewarded with gold.

Once upon a time, a midwife had but newly come to Hafoddydd, when she heard a knocking at her door.

There sat a gentleman on a fine steed. "My wife is in childbirth and needs your help. Please, come with me at once!"

He spoke with such a mixture of authority and fear that she could not do anything else but do as he bid. So she mounted behind him, and clung to him as they sped over the land as lightly as a bird. They were far and far again away before the midwife could even catch her breath.

At last, they stopped before a magnificent, brightly lit mansion. A crowd of servants appeared, and the midwife was at once helped down and led through the great hall into a splendid bedchamber. There lay the mistress of the house, struggling and in pain. The midwife forgot all about the splendor and set to work helping the poor thing through the birth.

The midwife soon held a healthy boy child, got it properly cleaned and wrapped in silken swaddling clothes, and placed the child in its mother's arms.

Plate 9.
In this "Donkey Skin" tale, when the furry skin is removed, a beautiful
young woman is revealed.

Illustration by Jesus Blasco (1919–1995). Courtesy of Private Collection/© Look and Learn/
The Bridgeman Art Library.

Plate 10.
Tales of Father Frost have become so popular that this image of him was used on a twentieth-century greeting card.

Courtesy of Private Collection/The Bridgeman Art Library.

Plate 13.
In this 1881 painting, the love-struck prince is just about to kiss and wake the sleeping princess. He has overcome the high hedge of thorns and passed through the enchanted sleeping palace. Love is about to conquer all.

Illustration by Richard Eisermann (fl. 1878–84). Courtesy of The Bridgeman Art Library/Getty Images.

Plate 14.
The evil queen, disguised as an old woman, offers to comb Snow White's lovely hair. The comb is poisoned, and if Snow White agrees, she will fall down dead until the comb is removed.

Illustration by Jesus Blasco (1919–1995). Courtesy of Private Collection/© Look and Learn/ The Bridgeman Art Library.

Plate 15.

Sadko is said to have caught the golden fish in the Lake of Ilman, with the help of the lake dwellers.

Illustration by Alexander Nikolaivich Benois (1870–1960) after set design for the opera "Sadko." Courtesy of Private Collection/Archives Charmet/The Bridgeman Art Library.

Plate 16.
Urashima Taro visits the lovely princess in the emperor's fine palace at the bottom of the sea.

Illustration by Evelyn Paul (1870–1945) from The Myths and Legends of Japan *by F. Hadland Davis. 1918. Courtesy of Private Collection/The Stapleton Collection/The Bridgeman Art Library.*

She stayed there until the lady had completely recovered. It was the merriest night she could remember, full of dancing, singing, and endless rejoicing, since there had been no heir for the lord for long and long again.

But merry a time as it was, the midwife knew at last that she must leave. The nobleman gave her a large purse, with the order: "Do not open it until you are back in your own house."

Then, he ordered one of his servants to take the midwife home, and they went back as swiftly as she had come. The servant left her at the door of her house, bowed, and left.

When she was safely inside her home, the midwife opened the purse. To her great joy, it was full of money. She lived happily on those earnings to the end of her days.

Sources
Rhys, John. *Celtic Folklore*. Vol. 1. Oxford, United Kingdom: Oxford University Press, 1901.
Sikes, Wirt. *British Goblins: Welsh Folk-lore, Fairy Mythology, Legends, and Traditions*. Boston: Osgood, 1881.

The Clergyman's Wife: A Folktale from Sweden

Since trolls are major characters in Swedish folklore, the wife to be delivered in this tale is a troll woman, but a kindhearted one. The midwife is warned against eating otherworldly food or taking otherworldly treasure, either of which would have trapped her in the otherworld forever. Instead, she receives a proper reward once she is safely home again.

There once lived a clergyman and his wife in Swedish Lappmark. While he was a fine clergyman, his wife was the finest midwife in all Sweden.

One night, there came a pounding on the door. There stood a mysterious being of such size, he could only be a troll. "Are you the midwife?" he asked.

"I am."

"Then come now, come to help Vitra."

Startled and alarmed, she had a whispered exchange with her husband, who could only tell her, "You are a midwife, and there is a woman in need, even if she is a troll."

So she went. Her strange guide led her into a mansion as elegant as could be imagined. There, in a bed with silken hangings, lay a lovely woman who could be none other than Vitra, for she was in the midst of childbirth.

Under the midwife's care Vitra soon gave birth to a fair little girl babe. In a remarkably short time, Vitra had entirely recovered, and she ordered a wondrous meal placed before the midwife. But the midwife, who was a wise and wary sort, refused to eat or take the money offered her. She knew that eating the meal or taking the money would bind her to the place.

"You are wise," Vitra said. "The next time that you enter your cowherd hut, see what you find there." Then, she sent the midwife home.

The midwife, curious, went to look in the cowherd hut. There, she found half a dozen spoons of pure silver, each engraved with her name. It is said that her family kept those spoons for a long while as an heirloom.

Sources

Hartland, Edwin Sidney. *The Science of Fairy Tales: An Inquiry into Fairy Mythology.*
   London: Walter Scott, 1891.
Hofberg, Herman. *Swedish Fairy Tales.* Trans. W.H. Myers. Chicago: W.B. Conkey, 1893.

Cherry of Zennor: A Folktale from Cornwall, England

Although this is not, strictly speaking, a fairy's midwife story, it is a regional variant. Here, it is not a midwife who uses the fairy ointment, but a teenaged servant girl, Cherry, who makes the mistake of falling for her fairy master, and daring to think he should be true to her. She keeps the sight of both eyes but is cast out of his life for using the forbidden ointment.

Once, there lived a family near the cliffside in Zenor. They had several children, but the wildest of them was their teenaged daughter, Cherry.

Now Cherry's family was far from rich. So one day, she packed up her few belongings and set out to find work.

She walked and she walked, and she tried not to think of the home she was leaving. By the time she came to the crossroads on the Lady Downs, she sat herself down on a stone and cried a bit, then thought of what work she might find, or whether she should just go home.

When she looked up, she started with surprise, for there was a fine gentleman where no one had been a moment before.

"Good morning," he said to her.

"Good morning," she replied.

"Where might you be going?" the gentleman asked.

"I left home just this morning to look for work."

"What luck!" the gentleman exclaimed. "I left home just this morning to find a nice, clean girl to keep house for me, and here you are. I am a widower with one little boy, and you could help to raise him. You will have little to do but milk the cow and look after the child. In exchange, I will see that you want for nothing. Is it a deal?"

"Yes, sir," Cherry said.

And so they went on together, with the gentleman talking so kindly to Cherry that she quite lost track of where they were or how long they had walked. They were now in tree-shaded lanes amidst bowers of lovely flowers. They came to a clear stream of water, and before Cherry could think of how to cross, the gentleman lightly carried her across, then set her back on her feet. The lane grew darker and darker, and they seemed to be going forever downhill.

Then, the gentleman opened a gate into a beautiful garden. "Here is where we live."

Oh, what a wonderful, beautiful place! Flowers of all colors surrounded Cherry, fruit like none she had seen before hung from the trees, and even the birds seemed to have sweeter songs than ever she had heard before.

Now, a child came running toward them, crying, "Papa! Papa!"

How strange! He seemed to be no more than three years old, yet there was an odd, odd look of age to him, as though he grew far more slowly than other children. But before Cherry could speak to him, an ugly old woman grabbed the boy by the arm and dragged him back into the house, muttering and glancing back at Cherry in disapproval.

"Do not worry about her," the master said. "She is known as Aunt Prudence, and is my late wife's grandmother. She will stay here only until you know your work."

Within the house, all was beauty. It was so bright and cheerful that Cherry never realized until far later that she did not see the sun.

After a fine dinner, Aunt Prudence took Cherry in hand and took her to her bedchamber, where the child also slept.

"Keep your eyes shut at night," the old woman warned, "or you might see things you will not like. Do not speak to the child at night, either. At daybreak, you are to take the boy to a spring in the garden for his bath, then anoint his eyes with an ointment I will give you. Do not, I warn you now, touch your own eyes with it. Do you understand me?"

"Yes, ma'am," Cherry said.

"Then, you are to call the cow and draw a bowl of milk for the boy's breakfast."

The next day, Cherry did as she was told. She washed the little boy in the spring and anointed his eyes with the ointment. The cow came as called, and the boy drank his milk without a word. After this, Cherry went back to the house for her own breakfast. Aunt Prudence warned her that she must keep to the kitchen and not go anywhere else in the house, and above all not try opening any locked doors.

"Very well, ma'am," Cherry said, even though she burned with curiosity. She did her work well, and had time left to help the master in his garden. But all the while, she was aware that Aunt Prudence was watching her.

"I knew it," the old woman would grumble. "I knew Robin would bring here some fool from Zenor. Bah. Better for them both if she had stayed away."

Despite Aunt Prudence's mutterings, the master and Cherry got along very well, so well, in fact, that they started stealing kisses now and then.

After Cherry had been there for some time, Aunt Prudence took her through parts of the house the girl had not yet seen. There was a dark passageway that seemed never to end. There was a room with a floor of glass and what, at first, Cherry thought were remarkably lifelike statues, then thought were surely people changed to stone. Terrified, the girl realized that, charming though Master Robin might be, this was a place of conjurers.

"Please, ma'am," she said, "I'll go no farther."

The old woman laughed mockingly at Cherry and dragged her forward to a box that looked very much like a coffin resting on a stand, insisting that the girl shine it up. Cherry set to shining the coffin with all her might, but no matter how hard she worked, the old woman would cry, "Rub! Rub! Harder and faster! Shine it up!"

Poor Cherry worked as hard as she could, so hard that she shook the box. It gave an eerie, deep, despairing groan, so unearthly a sound that Cherry fell to the floor, near to fainting.

But the master, hearing the noise, came running. He was furious at Aunt Prudence for taking Cherry where she had, and told her, "Leave this house at once!"

Then, he carried Cherry into the kitchen and restored her with some cordial. After that, the girl realized she could no longer remember what had happened, but that Aunt Prudence was gone.

"You are the mistress here now," Master Robin told her.

It was a wonderful life after that, a year that passed as sweetly as a day in summer. But there were some clouds. Cherry could remember the stone people now, and could swear that the master spoke with them. There were other days when he simply was not to be found. And every day, she grew more and more curious about that ointment that she applied to the child's eyes every day.

At last, she could stand it no longer, and touched a little of it to one of her own eyes. It burned, and Cherry hurried to the pool beneath the spring to wash her eye—when she saw at the bottom of the water, as though through a spyglass, hundreds of fine ladies and gentlemen—and there was Master Robin among them. She gasped and looked around the garden. Everywhere she looked were strange small beings, playing in the trees, running through the grass.

Master Robin returned that night, a fine gentleman on a fine horse, as though nothing strange had happened. He went straight to the enchanted room, and from it echoed strange, beautiful music. She peeped through the keyhole and saw the room full of lovely ladies—and to her shock, she saw Master Robin kiss one of them.

The next day, when Master Robin would have kissed her, she told him to stop toying with her and go kiss that lovely lady.

"Ah, you have used the ointment," he said sadly. "I am sorry. Now, you must go home."

He gave her many rich gifts, then set her on the road to home. Then, he disappeared, and Cherry sadly went on home.

Cherry's parents were amazed to see her again and delighted with all the riches she had brought with her. But she never saw Master Robin again.

Sources

Hunt, Robert. *Cornish Legends*. Truro, Cornwall, United Kingdom: Tor Mark, 1969.
———. *Popular Romances of the West of England*. London: John Camden Hotten, 1871.

The Demon's Midwife: A Folktale from the Jews of Morocco

In Jewish folklore, demons are not the evil beings they are in Christianity. Instead, they are more like nature spirits, alien to humanity but utterly amoral rather than evil. This folktale contains the motif common to many folktales of fairies—eating fairy food or taking their treasure is perilous for a human.

Once, long ago, Aviva the midwife was hurrying home after having helped yet another baby be born. But the night was very dark, and a gust of wind blew out Aviva's candle.

"Oh, no! Now, I can't see where I'm going."

Suddenly, a big white cat stepped out of the darkness and rubbed itself against the midwife's legs, purring. Aviva started to pet it, but the cat stalked away, looking back over its shoulder.

"You . . . you want me to follow you? Very well. I don't want to stay out here all night."

Sure enough, the white cat led Aviva right to her own front door. She told the cat, "God grant that as you helped me, I can someday help you."

A year passed.

One night, as Aviva sat at home, peacefully sewing, someone pounded on her door.

"No need to break it down," she called. "I'm coming."

There stood a tall, dark-eyed stranger wrapped in a black cloak. "Please, come with me," he pleaded. "My wife is about to give birth to her first child, and she needs a midwife's help."

Well, Aviva did not like the looks of that mysterious stranger, but how could she refuse a woman who needed her help? So off she and the stranger went into the night.

Whether they went a long way or a short way, Aviva could not tell in all that darkness. Only by clinging to the stranger's cloak could she keep going.

Then all at once, the darkness was brightened by hundreds of candles, and the midwife found herself entering a magnificent mansion. But she did not have time to do more than glance here and there at all the lovely things.

Before Aviva could even catch her breath, she was led into a bedroom. There lay a young woman who was about to give birth. The midwife set about her work, and soon was welcoming a healthy baby boy into the world.

But as Aviva placed the baby at his mother's breast, the young woman whispered to her, "Do you recognize me? No? I am a demon woman, and all these people are demons, too. But do not be afraid! I also was the white cat who guided you home a year ago. Now, you have helped me, so I will help you. When my relatives ask you to share their feast, refuse. When they offer to reward you, take nothing but the smallest rug that lies by the door."

Sure enough, the demons asked Aviva to join their feast. Politely, she told them that she was fasting. Next, they showed her wonderful gold and silver treasures, and told her to choose a reward. Aviva asked only for the smallest rug that lay by the door.

"My wife has warned you," the tall, dark-eyed stranger said. "Had you eaten with us, you would have been our guest forever. Had you chosen any of those treasures, you would have been our prisoner forever. But the rug cannot harm you. Come, I shall take you home."

So he did. Aviva spread out the small rug by her bedside.

"It's a pretty thing," she said, "even if it isn't a wonderful treasure."

But when she awoke in the morning, Aviva found that the rug was covered with gold coins. And each time a gold coin was removed, another took its place.

"The demon woman gave me a wonderful treasure after all."

Aviva was not a greedy woman. She shared that gold with anyone who needed help, and so she lived happily all her life.

Sources

Noy, Dov. *Folktales of Israel*. Trans. Gene Baharav. Chicago: University of Chicago Press, 1963.

Sherman, Josepha. *Rachel the Clever and Other Jewish Folktales*. Little Rock, AR: August House, 1993.

RUMPELSTILTSKIN

The mysterious helper with an ulterior motive turns up across Europe. Sometimes, the helper is a dwarf or other small male, such as an imp, or even a devil.

In all the tales, the price is a high one if the heroine cannot learn the magical helper's name: She either must wed him or must give up her firstborn child to him.

But sometimes, the cost of receiving help is far less. In one tale variant, it is three magical old women who come to the rescue, and they ask only that the heroine calls each of them "Aunt," or "Auntie."

Rumpelstiltskin: A Folktale from Germany

This folktale is the one best known and most often retold. In it, the king threatens the heroine with death if she cannot spin straw to gold (yet she agrees to marry him). It is the king who reveals the secret name that he has overheard.

Once upon a time, there was a poor miller with a beautiful daughter. He foolishly boasted to the king, "My daughter knows the art of turning straw into gold."

So the king immediately sent for the miller's daughter and ordered her to turn a whole room full of straw into gold in one night. If she could not do it, the king warned, she would die.

The poor girl was locked in the room. She sat there and cried because, for her life, she did not know how the straw would turn into gold.

Suddenly, a little man appeared before her, and said, "What will you give me, if I turn this all into gold?"

"This necklace," she said, taking it off and giving it to the little man.

He did exactly as he had promised.

The next morning, the king found the room filled with gold, and his heart became even greedier. He put the miller's daughter into an even larger room filled with straw. Again, he told her to turn it into gold in one night.

The little man came again. This time, the girl gave him a ring from her hand, and he turned all the straw into gold.

The third night, the king had the girl locked in a third room, which was larger than the first two, and entirely filled with straw. The king said to her, "If you fail, you die. But if you succeed this time, I will make you my wife."

Then, the little man came and said, "I'll do it again, but you must promise me the first child that you have with the king."

In her distress, the girl made the promise. When the king saw that this straw, too, had been turned into gold, he took the miller's daughter as his wife.

Soon thereafter, the queen delivered a child.

Then, the little man appeared before her. "I demand the child that you promised to me."

The queen begged him, "Oh please, please, let me keep my child! I will offer you great riches, any riches you wish, in my baby's place."

The little man grumbled to himself. At last, he said, "I'll return for the child in three days. If you can learn my name by then, you can keep the child."

For two days, the queen pondered what the little man's name might be, but she could not think of anything that might fit. What was she to do? She could not bear to give up her dear baby!

Then, on the third day, the king came home from a hunt and told her how, while hunting deep in a forest, he had come upon a little house. A comical little man was there, jumping about as if on one leg, and crying out:

> Today I'll bake; tomorrow I'll brew.
> Then I'll fetch the queen's new child.
> It is good that no one knows
> Rumpelstiltskin is my name.

The queen was overjoyed to hear this.

The little man appeared and asked, "Your Majesty, what is my name?"

"Is your name Conrad?" the queen asked.

"No."

"Is your name Heinrich?" she asked.

"No."

She asked once again, "Then could your name be Rumpelstiltskin?"

"The devil told you that!" shouted the little man. He ran away angrily, and never came back.

Sources

Grimm, Brothers. *The Complete Fairy Tales of the Brothers Grimm*. Trans. Jack Zipes. New York: Bantam, 1987.

Ranke, Kurt. *Folktales of Germany*. Trans. Lotte Baumann. Chicago: University of Chicago Press, 1966.

Tom Tit Tom: A Folktale from England

This is a much earthier version of the tale, what with the daughter talking about not having a pie "until it comes again," that is, after it passes through her body. The language throughout has been modernized for easier reading. The king is just as ruthless as in the German version, the girl still marries him, and it is the king who reveals the magic name.

Once upon a time, there was a woman who baked five pies. But when she took the pies out of the oven, they were so overbaked that the crusts were too hard to eat.

So she told her daughter, "Put them on that shelf and leave 'em there a bit, and they'll come again." (That is, the crusts would soften.)

But the daughter, tired and hungry, ate them all.

When it was suppertime, the woman said to the daughter, "Go get one of the pies and see if they've come again."

"No, they ain't come again."

"Not one of 'em?" asked the mother.

"Not one of 'em," said the daughter.

"Well, come again, or not come again," said the woman, "I'll have one for supper."

The girl finally admitted, "I've eaten 'em all, and you can't have one till that's come again."

Well, the woman was so angry, she could do nothing but take her spinning to the door to spin, and as she spun she sang:

> My daughter ate five, five pies today.
> My daughter ate five, five pies today.

The king was coming down the street, and he heard her sing. But what she sang he could not hear, so he stopped and asked, "What was that you were singing, my good woman?"

The woman was ashamed to let him hear what her daughter had been doing, so she sang instead:

> My daughter spun five, five skeins today.
> My daughter spun five, five skeins today.

The king said in amazement, "I have never heard of anyone who could do that. I will marry your daughter, and for eleven months out of the year she shall have all she likes to eat, and all the gowns she likes to get, and all the company she likes to keep. But for the last month of the year, she will have to spin five skeins every day, and if she does not do that, I shall kill her."

So the king and the girl were married. And for eleven months, the girl had all she liked to eat, and all the gowns she liked to get, and all the company she liked to keep. But when they were getting toward the twelfth month, she began to worry and hoped that he had forgotten all about the spinning.

But on the last day of the last month, he took her to a room in which sat nothing but a spinning wheel and a stool. And the king said, "Now, my dear, you will be shut in here tomorrow with food and flax, and if you have not spun five skeins by the night, your head will go off."

The poor girl was terrified. She had never even learned how to spin. And what was she to do tomorrow? She sat down and wept.

However, all of a sudden she heard a scraping sort of knocking low down on the door. What entered was a little black thing with a long tail. The creature asked, "What are you a-crying for?"

It could do no harm to tell him, she thought. So she told him the whole thing.

"This is what I will do," said the little black thing. "I'll come to your window every morning and take the flax and bring it spun at night."

Wary, she asked, "What's your pay?"

The little black thing looked at her slyly. "I'll give you three guesses every night to guess my name, and if you haven't guessed it before the month's up, you shall be mine."

Well, she thought, she would be sure to guess the little black thing's name before the month was up. And, at least, she would not be losing her head. "All right, I agree."

With a twirl of its tail, the creature was gone.

On the next day, the king took his wife into the room with the spinning wheel and the stool. Now, there was also the flax and the day's food. "Remember," the king said. "If that is not all spun by night, off goes your head."

Off he went, and locked the door behind him. But no sooner had the king gone than there was the little black thing sitting on the stool. "Give me the flax."

So she did. And that evening, he reappeared with five fat skeins of flax. "Here it is. Now, what's my name?"

"Is it Bill?"

"It ain't." And the thing twirled its tail.

"Is it Ned?"

"It ain't." And the thing twirled its tail.

"Is it Mark?"

"It ain't." With that, the thing twirled its tail and flew away.

When the king returned, there were the five fat skeins of flax for him. "Excellent. I will not have to kill you tonight, my dear. Tomorrow, you will have the next batch of flax and your day's food," he said and left.

Every day, the flax and the food were brought. And every day that little black thing took away the flax in the morning and brought spun skeins in the evening. And all day, the girl sat trying to think of what the creature's name might be. But she never hit on the right one.

And as it got toward the end of the month, the little black thing began to look more and more malicious. When there was only one night left, it stared at her with eyes like coals of fire and said, "Woman, there is only tomorrow night, and then you are mine!"

Well, she was terrified. Just then, though, there came the king. He saw the five fat skeins of flax and said, "I am getting glad I will not have to kill you. Let us sit for a time." But after a moment, he began to laugh.

"What is it?" she asked.

"I was out hunting today, and I reached a place in the wood I had never seen before. There was an old chalk pit, and I heard a kind of humming coming out of it. So I tiptoed to the pit and looked down. What did I see but the funniest little black thing you could ever have imagined. It had a little spinning wheel, and that was spinning wonderfully fast, and it was twirling its tail as the wheel spun. And it was singing:

> Nimmy nimmy not
> My name's Tom Tit Tot.

Well, the woman could have jumped out of her skin for joy, but she did not say a word.

The next day, there was the little black thing, come for the flax. That night, there it came back with the finished skeins of flax. The creature was grinning from ear to ear, and twirling its tail so fast it was a blur.

"All right, woman. What's my name?"

"Is it Solomon?" she asked, pretending to be afraid.

"It ain't."

"Is it Zebedee?"

"It ain't." The little black thing laughed. "Take your time, woman. Next guess, and you're mine." And it stretched out its clawed hands to her.

She backed up a step or two, then laughed and pointed at the creature.

> Nimmy nimmy not
> Your name's Tom Tit Tot.

Well, when the little black thing heard her, it gave an awful shriek, and away it flew into the dark. And she never saw it any more.

Sources

Jacobs, Joseph. *English Fairy Tales.* London: David Nutt, 1890.
Steel, Flora Annie. *English Fairy Tales.* London: Macmillan, 1918.

Mistress Beautiful: A Folktale from Germany

This folktale has a difference. Instead of straw to be spun into gold, there is a dowry granted to the heroine by a devil whose name she must learn or become his. In this tale, it is a kindhearted shepherd who tells the heroine the magic name.

Once, long ago in a city whose name we know not, there lived a poor but very beautiful young woman. She was so lovely that she was known as Mistress Beautiful.

A merchant fell in love with her and asked her to marry him. But he did not know that Mistress Beautiful was so poor.

In those days, a bride was supposed to present a rich dowry to her groom, showing her wealth. But poor Mistress Beautiful had nothing. What could she do? Where could she get a dowry?

That night, a strange dark figure appeared before her. It was a devil. "I will make a deal with you," the being said. "I will give you all the wealth you need. But you must discover my name in a year, or you become mine!"

Mistress Beautiful was sure she could discover the devil's name in a year. She married the merchant, and for a time she was very happy. But the year came and the year went. The year's end was approaching, and she still did not know the devil's name.

One night, a shepherd saw a mysterious fire burning on a hill. He saw weird, dark figures dancing about it. One of them sang loudly:

It is good, it is good!
Mistress Beautiful does not know
Does not know
That my name is Hipche, Hipche.

The next day, the shepherd hurried straight to Mistress Beautiful and told her what he had seen and heard. She laughed and filled his hands with gold coins.

That night, when the year had come to an end, the devil appeared before her and asked, "Tell me my name or I shall carry you off."

"Oh dear, oh dear, what can it be? Can your name be . . . Hipche?" she replied. With a cry of rage, the devil disappeared.

Mistress Beautiful lived happily as her merchant husband's partner, and their fortune grew as their trade increased.

Sources

Ranke, Kurt. *Folktales of Germany.* Trans. Lotte Baumann. Chicago: University of Chicago Press, 1966.

Ratcliff, Ruth. *German Tales and Legends.* London: Century Hutchinson, 1982.

The Gold Spinner: A Folktale from Hungary

In this folktale, the heroine hates spinning—and is stunned when she winds up married to a young lord who expects her to spin golden thread or die. For all that, they have a happy marriage, and it is her husband who saves the day by learning the needed name.

Once a young lord went looking for a bride. He came to the house of a widow, who had three unmarried daughters. The two elder were spinning busily, but the youngest daughter, Hanka, hated spinning and just sat sleeping in the corner.

When the young lord saw this, he was surprised. "Why do you not make that one, too, take a distaff?" he asked her mother.

"Ah, young sir," replied the mother, "I would allow her to spin with all my heart. But she is such an amazing spinner that by herself she would by morning spin up not only all our spinning materials, but all the thatch from the roof, and that into golden threads. So I must give her a holiday."

"If this is true," the young lord cried in delight, "I will marry her at once. I have flax, hemp, everything that can be spun. She could spin away to her heart's content."

The woman was delighted, and sent Hanka off with her new bridegroom in his fine carriage.

Poor Hanka! What would happen to her when her husband learned what a poor spinner she was?

"Do not be frightened," the young lord said. "At my house, I shall give you all that your heart desires, everything you want for spinning."

That only made Hanka sadder than ever.

They reached his castle, and Hanka was taken to a large room crammed full of every type of spinning material. "Here you are," the young lord said. "If you can spin all this, as your mother promised, into golden threads, we shall be wed. But if you cannot do this, you must die."

He left Hanka alone in the room. She wept, knowing she could never spin everything into golden threads.

As she sobbed, the wall suddenly opened. A little man stood before the terrified Hanka, with a red cap on his head and an apron round his waist. Before him, he pushed a little golden handcart.

"Why do you weep?" he asked. "What has happened to you?"

"I have been ordered to spin all this into golden threads by morning. And if I do not do so, they will have me put to death!"

"Is that all?" laughed the little man. "I will teach you to spin golden threads—but you must be here next year to the day. Then, if you do not guess my name, you will become my wife, and I shall carry you away in this cart. But if you guess my name, I shall leave you in peace. Well, have you agreed to this?"

What choice did Hanka have? "I agree," she said.

The little man made three circuits round her with his golden cart, seated himself under the distaff, and repeated:

> Thus, Haniczka, thus!
> Thus, Haniczka, thus!
> Thus, Haniczka, thus!

With these magic words ("Haniczka" is an endearing form of Hanka) and the gestures that went with them, he taught her to spin golden threads. Then, he vanished as quickly as he had arrived. Hanka sat and spun, sat and spun, amazed to see the golden threads appear. By morning, all was done, and she had even managed to have a good night's sleep.

In the morning, when the young lord entered the room, he was all but blinded by the glitter and would not even believe his eyes. But when he had satisfied himself that, yes, this was all gold, he embraced Hanka, and declared her his true and lawful wife.

Thus they lived. And if our young lord had previously loved his Hanka, his dear Haniczka, for the golden spinning, he loved her a thousand times more for the beautiful son that she bore him.

Alas, the joy of the wedded pair could not endure forever. Day passed after day, until finally the appointed time was nearly there. Hanka began to be more sorrowful from moment to moment. How could she endure losing both her husband and her child and become the property of an inhuman being?

At last, she could not bear to keep her secret, and she told everything to her husband as it had occurred to her on that first night. He turned pale as a whitewashed wall, and made a royal proclamation that if anyone knew the name of such a dwarf, he would give him a piece of gold as large as his head.

But though everyone in the land searched high and low, nobody saw the dwarf, and no one could tell his name. Unable to bear the suspense, Hanka's husband took his gun and hounds and went hunting.

But during the hunt, rain began to pour down, and the young lord and his party hunted simply for shelter. Finally, they saw where, out of the hole of the side shaft of a mine, puffs of smoke were rolling. But all were too afraid to look, save for the young lord himself. He went straight to the smoke hole and knelt beside it.

There below him, he saw a strange being, a dwarf in a red cap with a golden handcart before him as he twirled about in an eerie dance. From time to time, after making the circuit, the dwarf sang:

> I've manufactured a golden spinster for the young lord,
> She will try to guess my name tonight.
> If she guesses my name aright, I shall leave her.
> If she guesses it not, I shall take her.
> My name is Martynko Klyngas.

The young lord raced home, with his hunting party barely keeping pace. "Hanka, my dear Haniczka, do not worry any more!" he cried to his wife, flinging himself from his horse and running to embrace her. "I have what you need: His name is Martynko Klyngas!"

Hanka embraced and kissed her husband, then joyfully went to the room in which she had spent the first night spinning golden threads.

At midnight, there came the dwarf with the red cap and golden handcart. Running around her with the cart, he shouted:

> If you guess my name, I leave you.
> If you guess it not, I take you.
> Only guess, guess away!

"Let me guess," said Hanka. "I think your name is Martynko Klyngas."

As soon as she said this, the dwarf seized his cart, threw his cap on the ground, and departed as he had come.

Hanka breathed in peace. From that time forth, she spun no more gold, and, indeed, neither was it necessary for her so to do, for they were rich enough. She and her husband lived happily together, their boy grew like a young tree by the water's side, and they bought a cow, and on the cow a bell, and here's an end to the tale I tell.

Sources
Severo, Emoke de Papp. *Hungarian and Transylvanian Folktales*. Nepean, Ontario, Canada: Borealis, 1997.
Wratislaw, A.H. *Sixty Folk-Tales from Exclusively Slavonic Sources*. Boston: Houghton Mifflin, 1890.

The Three Aunts: A Folktale from Norway

Here is a charming variant on the Rumplestiltskin theme in which the little man is replaced by three mysterious women who help the heroine and get her out of ever having to spin again.

Once there was a poor man with one daughter. She was pretty and gentle, but since she was now nearly grown, she said she would go out into the world to earn her bread.

She came, at last, to a palace and found work there as a maid. She was so cheerful and efficient that the queen came to like her. But the other servants grew jealous. They decided to get rid of her and told the queen, "Did you know that the girl boasts she can spin a pound of flax in only twenty-four hours?"

The queen found this difficult to believe, but she sent the girl to a room filled with flax and a spinning wheel. There, she was left. The poor girl had never spun in her life and did not know what to do.

Suddenly, there was an old woman in the room with her. The woman was remarkably ugly, with a long, long nose, but she had kind eyes. "What is wrong, child?"

So the girl told her the whole story. "What am I to do? I have never even seen a spinning wheel before!"

"If you will simply call me Aunt on the happiest day of your life, I will spin this flax for you."

"Oh, done!" the girl cried in relief.

The next morning, there was all the flax neatly spun. The queen was delighted. But the servants were more jealous than before. Now, they told the queen, "She has boasted again. She claims she can weave all that flax in just twenty-four hours."

The queen found this difficult to believe, but there was the flax, and there was the room. So the queen put the girl in the room with a loom and left her there.

Just as the poor girl had never seen a spinning wheel, so she had never seen a loom. She sat there wondering what to do.

A second old woman was suddenly in the room. She, too, was remarkably ugly, with a broad, humped back. But she, too, had kind eyes. "What is wrong, child?"

"I must weave all this flax within twenty-four hours, and I do not know how to do it!"

"If you will simply call me Aunt on the happiest day of your life, I will weave this flax for you."

"Oh, done!" the girl cried in relief.

The next morning, there was fine linen fabric woven from the flax. The queen was delighted, but the servants were even more jealous than before. They whispered to the queen, "Now, the girl boasts that she can turn all that fabric into shirts in twenty-four hours."

So the girl was shut up in the room with needle and thread. She could sew, and tried her best to hurry. But there was just too much cutting and piecing and sewing to be done, and all in only twenty-four hours. What was she to do?

A third old woman was suddenly in the room. She, too, was remarkably ugly, with huge eyes, but for all their hugeness, they were kind eyes. "What is wrong, child?"

"I must sew all this linen into shirts within twenty-four hours and I do not know how I can do it!"

"If you will simply call me Aunt on the happiest day of your life, I will sew the shirts for you."

"Oh, done!" the girl cried in relief.

The next morning, there were piles of fine linen shirts. The queen was so delighted that she said, "I think you would make a wonderful wife for my son. You can spin, weave, and sew all you wish."

Well, the girl saw the prince, the prince saw the girl, and they agreed that they would love to marry. She tried not to think about having to do any spinning, weaving, and sewing.

But as they sat down at the wedding feast, an ugly old woman with a long, long nose entered. The new bride jumped up and cried, "Welcome, Auntie!"

The prince was startled that so lovely a bride should have so ugly an aunt, but he made the old woman welcome. Then in came a second ugly old woman, this one with a broad humped back. The bride jumped up again and cried, "Welcome, Auntie!"

The prince was once again startled that so lovely a bride should have so ugly an aunt, but he made the old woman welcome. Then in came a third ugly old woman, with huge eyes. The bride jumped up again and cried, "Welcome, Auntie!"

The prince was once again startled that so lovely a bride should have so ugly an aunt, but he made the old woman welcome.

The prince struggled with his curiosity, and, at last, lost the battle. "How is it that my lovely bride should have such, well, ugly aunts?"

The long-nosed old woman said, "I was once as lovely as she, but my nose got stretched from hour after hour of spinning and nodding over my spinning."

"And I," said the second old woman, "got this broad humped back from always scuttling back and forth, back and forth, over my loom."

"I," said the third, "spent all my time staring and sewing, sewing and staring, night and day, and that is why I have these huge eyes."

"I see!" the prince said. "Well, my dear wife, do not worry. You shall never have to spin, weave, or sew again!"

And, needless to say, they were both delighted. So were the three mysterious old "aunts."

Sources

Birkhauser-Oeri, Sybille. *The Mother: Archetypical Image in Fairy Tales.* Trans. Michael Mitchell. Toronto, Ontario, Canada: Inner City, 1988.

Thompson, Stith. *One Hundred Favorite Folktales.* Bloomington and Indianapolis: Indiana University Press, 1968.

The Building of the Kalundberg Church: A Folktale from Denmark

Esbern Snare, the hero of this folktale, was an actual architect, famed for the Frue Kirke (the Free Church), which he designed and built in about 1170. The folk process often attaches a folktale or cycle of folktales to an historical figure, as though tellers were trying to give credulity to the folktales.

Esbern Snare had been hired to build a magnificent new church in the city of Kalundberg at the end of the twelfth century. But while he had the talent, he soon realized he did not have the proper means to create such an elegant building.

Then one night, a troll, large and ugly as a broken boulder, came to him and said, "I will make a deal with you."

"What manner of deal?" Esbern asked.

"I can build you that church within the time needed."

"What do you want from me?"

The troll laughed, a sound like great rocks clashing together. "Nothing much. When the church is built, you must call me by name. If you cannot do that, I will take your heart and eyes."

Warily, Esbern agreed, sure that he would be able to learn the troll's name in time. But he had reckoned without the troll's building skills and speed. Soon, all was done but one half of one pillar. And Esbern was no nearer to knowing the troll's name than he had been when he had first made the agreement.

Sick at heart, Esbern wandered here and there, sure he had agreed to his own slaying. At last, weary in mind and body, he lay down to rest on a riverbank.

While he lay there, he heard a voice singing softly. It was not a human voice. A troll woman! Alert now, Esbern listened to the words she sang to her baby:

> Lie still, my child, lie still.
> Fin comes here tomorrow,
> Father of thine.
> A gift he'll bring,
> A heart and eyes,
> Esbern's heart, Esbern's eyes,
> Toys for your delight.

When Esbern heard this, hope surged back through him. He rushed back to the church. He met the troll on the way, with that final half-pillar over his stony shoulder.

"I see you," Esbern shouted, "and I name you: FIN!"

The troll was so furious that he smashed the half-pillar to dust and disappeared.

And that is why, even today, the Frue Kirke has only three and a half pillars.

Sources
Ashliman, D.L. *Fairy Lore: A Handbook.* Westport, CT, and London: Greenwood, 2006.
Keightley, Thomas. *The Fairy Mythology.* London: Bohn, 1850.

SLEEPING BEAUTY

Another familiar folktale theme is that of the "Sleeping Beauty." Although there is a similarity between her and the male figure in the "Beauty and the Beast" and "Heroine's Quest" tale types, the sleeping beauty figure is the victim of a magic spell or curse, not merely a sleeping potion. Unlike the drugged male figure, the sleeping beauty heroine generally is a passive figure, asleep and waiting for life and love to reach her.

It is sometimes, but not always, the prince's kiss that awakens the sleeping beauty. In more "adult" versions, he may awaken her by sleeping with her, or she even may become pregnant and awaken in childbirth. In all cases, though, the awakened beauty gets her prince at the end of the tale.

This tale type has inspired a Tchaikovsky ballet (first performed in 1890), a Walt Disney animated feature film (originally released in 1959), and many a psychological study.

Little Briar Rose: A Folktale from Germany

Here is the most familiar form of the folktale, at least to Western audiences. It has been the subject of a ballet, Pytor Ilyich Tchaikovsky's nineteenth-century *The Sleeping Beauty* (although there she bears the Russian version's name, Aurora); several retellings and reworkings, including Jane Yolen's 1993 novel, *Briar Rose*; and numerous psychological studies.

Once, there lived a king and queen who had no children, although they longed for one.

Then one day, while the queen was bathing, a crab crept out of the water onto the ground and said to her, "Your wish will be fulfilled. You will soon bring a daughter into the world." And that is what happened.

The king was so overjoyed at his daughter's birth that he held a great celebration. He also invited the fairies who lived in his kingdom. But because he had only twelve golden plates, one fairy had to be left out, for there were thirteen of them.

The twelve fairies came to the celebration and presented the child with gifts. The first fairy gave her virtue, the second one gave her beauty, and so on down the line, each one offering a desirable and magnificent gift.

The eleventh fairy had just presented her gift when the thirteenth fairy walked in, furious because she had not been invited. She cried out, "Because you did not invite me, in her fifteenth year, your daughter will prick herself with a spindle and fall down dead."

The parents were horrified. But the twelfth fairy, who had not yet offered her wish, said quickly, "It shall not be her death. She will only fall into a hundred-year sleep."

The king, just to be sure, promptly issued an order that all spindles in the kingdom should be destroyed.

The princess grew into a lovely, kind young lady. One day, when she had just reached her fifteenth year, she went exploring in the castle, looking for rooms she had never seen.

She finally came to an old tower. Curious, she climbed up the narrow, winding stairway that ended in a small room where an old woman sat spinning flax. The princess, who had never seen spinning before, asked the old woman if she could try her hand at it. The old woman nodded, and the princess picked up the spindle. But as soon as she touched it, it pricked her finger, and she fell down into a deep sleep.

At that same moment, everyone and everything in the castle fell asleep, from the king to the courtiers, the horses in the stalls, the dogs in the courtyard, the pigeons on the roof, the flies on the walls. The cook let go of the kitchen boy, whose hair he was about to pull. The maid dropped the chicken that she was plucking. Even the fire on the hearth flickered and stopped moving. The roast stopped sizzling.

They all slept. And a thorn hedge grew up around the entire castle, growing higher and higher, until nothing at all could be seen of it.

Time passed, and princes, who had heard about the beautiful Briar Rose, came and tried to free her. But they could not penetrate the thorn hedge. Thus, it continued for many long years.

Then one day, a prince was traveling through the land. An old man told him about the belief that there was a castle behind the thorn hedge, with a wonderfully beautiful princess asleep inside with all of her attendants. The old man added that many princes had tried to penetrate the hedge, but they had gotten stuck in the thorns and had been pricked to death.

"I am not afraid of that," said the prince. "I shall penetrate the hedge and free the beautiful Briar Rose."

When the prince came to the thorn hedge, it turned into flowers that let him pass. But after he passed, the flowers turned back into thorns.

The prince continued on into the castle. How strange it was! Horses and hunting dogs were asleep in the courtyard. Pigeons slept on the roof. The attendants were all asleep, as were the courtiers. Yes, and there, asleep, were the king and the queen. It was so quiet that he could hear his own breath.

Finally, the prince came to the old tower where Briar Rose was lying asleep. He climbed the narrow, winding stairway to the small room at the top. Upon opening the door, he was instantly smitten by the sight of the princess. He could do nothing else but bend over and kiss her.

At that moment, Briar Rose awoke, and with her the king and the queen, and all the attendants, and the horses and the dogs, and the pigeons on the roof, and the flies on the walls. The cook boxed the kitchen boy's ears. The maid finished plucking the chicken. The fire rose up and continued cooking the food. And the roast sizzled away.

The prince and Briar Rose were married not long after that. And they lived long and happily until they died.

Sources

Grimm, Brothers. *The Complete Fairy Tales of the Brothers Grimm.* Trans. Jack Zipes. New York: Bantam, 1987.

Ranke, Kurt. *Folktales of Germany.* Trans. Lotte Baumann. Chicago: University of Chicago Press, 1966.

The Ninth Captain's Tale: A Folktale from the Arabian Nights

Here is a variant on the basic sleeping beauty folktale, in which the heroine is not destined to prick her finger on a spindle, but is deathly allergic to even the smell of flax. The hero already knows the heroine from childhood, and he goes to rescue her. There are no fairies or magic gifts, good or ill.

There once was a childless woman who prayed to Allah, saying, "Give me a daughter, even if she is so delicate that she cannot bear the smell of flax!"

Soon, the woman conceived and easily bore a daughter, as fair as the rising moon, as pale and delicate as moonlight. Her parents named her Sittukhan.

When the little girl was ten years old, the sultan's son (who was not much older) fell in love with her. He begged to at least know her name. An old woman told him that the girl's name was Sittukhan and said that she would bring her to meet him.

So off the old woman went. She found the girl sitting just outside her mother's door. "What a lovely thing you are, child. Girls like you should learn to spin flax; for there is no more delightful sight than a spindle in lovely fingers."

Then, the old woman left.

At once, the girl went to her mother, saying, "Mother, take me to the flax mistress."

"Do not say such a thing!" cried the woman. "Flax is a danger to you. Its smell is fatal to you, and a touch of it will kill you."

But the girl refused to believe it. At last, her mother sent her to the flax mistress. She stayed there for a day, learning to spin. But, when a morsel of flax became lodged behind one of her nails, she fell swooning to the floor.

When her parents learned that their daughter was dead, they tore their garments in grief and went sadly to bury her. But the old woman met them. "It would be a shame," she said, "to bury so fair a girl in the dust. Build her a pavilion in the midst of the river and couch her there upon a bed, that you may come to visit her."

So they built a pavilion of marble on columns rising out of the river and planted a garden about it with green lawns. There, the grieving parents set the girl upon an ivory bed. They came there many times to weep.

Meanwhile, though, the old woman went to the king's son and said, "Come with me to see Sittukhan. She lies in a pavilion above the waves of the river."

When the prince found the girl there, dead, he began to weep at the bedside. He gently took one of her hands to kiss it—and saw the scrap of flax lodged under one of her nails. He carefully drew it out.

At once, the girl came back to life and sat up upon the ivory bed. She smiled at the prince, and whispered, "Where am I?"

"You are with me," he answered, embracing her.

And they dwelt together in love forever after.

Source

Mathers, Powys, trans. *The Book of the Thousand Nights and One Night, Rendered into English from the Literal and Complete French Translation of J.C. Mardrus.* London: Routledge and Kegan Paul, 1964.

SNOW WHITE

Yet another familiar folktale type is "Snow White," which has variants from around the world. In many of them, the heroine is warned not to open the door to strangers, but she either disregards the warning or is tricked into opening it. Despite the danger and, often, a temporary death for the heroine, there usually is a happy ending.

Snow White: A Folktale from Germany

This is the version best known in the West, mostly through many a retelling and, of course, the 1937 Disney movie *Snow White and the Seven Dwarfs* that codified Snow White's appearance for many.

In some variants, it is not a wicked stepmother, but the mother herself who envies her daughter enough to want the girl dead. The ending with the red hot shoes is the Grimm Brothers at their grimmest, and it does not appear in the earliest versions of their collection. Storytellers can add their own ending if they wish—as long as the evildoer is punished.

Once upon a time, a queen was staring outside her window while she did her embroidery. Distracted, she pricked her finger on her needle. A drop of blood fell on the snow that had fallen on her windowsill. Looking at the red drop on the white snow, she said, "I wish that I had a daughter with skin white as the snow, lips red as the blood, and hair as black as ebony."

Soon after, the queen gave birth to a daughter who looked just as she had wished. The girl was named Snow White.

Not long after, sadly, the queen died. The king took a new wife, one who was very beautiful but also very vain—and who was secretly an evil witch.

The new queen owned a magic mirror that would answer any question honestly. She often would ask, "Mirror, mirror on the wall, who is the fairest one of all?"

The mirror always would answer, "It is you."

But as Snow White grew up, the mirror answered, "Queen, while you are fair, 'tis true, Snow White is fairer than you."

The queen fell into a jealous rage, and ordered a huntsman to take Snow White into the woods and kill her, then return with the girl's heart as proof. The huntsman did take the terrified girl into the forest, but he was unable to do so evil a deed. He let Snow White go, telling her to run for her life. Then, he returned to the queen with a deer's heart. The queen ate it with great relish.

In the forest, Snow White came upon a cottage that belonged to seven dwarfs. They gave her shelter and food. In exchange, she kept their cottage neat and clean.

Meanwhile, the queen, gloating, asked her mirror, "Who is the fairest of them all?"

To her horror and fury, the mirror answered, "Queen, while you are fair, 'tis true, Snow White is fairer than you."

"That is impossible!" the queen cried. "Mirror, where is she?" The mirror showed Snow White in the cozy cottage with the seven dwarfs.

The queen disguised herself as a peddler and went to the cottage. Snow White had been warned by the dwarfs never to open the door if they were not home. But the "peddler" offered such colorful laces that Snow White was tempted and opened the door.

The peddler laced Snow White up so tightly with the laces that she fainted. Then, the queen left, sure that the girl was dead. But when the dwarfs came home, they saw the too-tight laces and cut them. And Snow White was revived.

That night, the queen asked her mirror, "Who is the fairest of them all?"

To her renewed horror and fury, the mirror answered, "Queen, while you are fair, 'tis true, Snow White is fairer than you."

"She survived! But she will not survive this time."

This time, the queen disguised herself as a gentle old woman. She coaxed Snow White into opening the door and letting her comb the girl's lovely black hair.

But the comb the "old woman" used was poisoned. Snow White fell to the floor, and the queen again went off in triumph. But when the dwarfs came home, they found the poisoned comb and removed it. And Snow White recovered.

That night, the queen asked her mirror, "Who is the fairest of them all?"

Again, to her horror and fury, the mirror answered, "Queen, while you are fair, 'tis true, Snow White is fairer than you."

"She survived! Those dwarfs must have helped her."

Now, the queen created an apple, so fair and red it was a wonder to see. But one half of it was poisoned. She took on the disguise of a countrywoman and went off to the cottage. Again, Snow White was alone, and again she was coaxed into opening the door, this time by the lovely aroma of a basket of apples.

But Snow White hesitated to taste the apple she was offered. So the "country-woman" cut the apple in half and ate the safe half, giving the other half to Snow White. This time, all that the dwarfs did could not revive Snow White. They sadly put her in a glass coffin, sure she was dead.

Meanwhile, the queen asked, "Mirror, mirror on the wall, who is the fairest one of all?"

This time, to her evil joy, the mirror answered, "It is you."

A prince came riding through the forest, and stopped short at the sight of lovely Snow White in her glass coffin. Oh, how he loved the sight of her! How he wished she lived! He begged the dwarfs to give him the coffin, and, at last, they agreed. But as the prince's servants lifted the coffin, they stumbled. The piece of poisoned apple was dislodged from Snow White's throat, and she awoke.

It was love for the prince and Snow White. He took her to his castle, and a grand wedding was planned.

Meanwhile, the queen once again asked her mirror, "Who is the fairest one of all?"

The mirror, to her shock, replied, "You, my queen, are fair, 'tis true. But the young queen is a thousand times fairer than you."

The evil queen rushed off to the wedding. There, she was seized. As punishment for her wicked ways, a pair of heated iron shoes were brought forth with tongs and placed before her. She was then forced to step into these and dance until she fell down dead.

Source
Grimm, Brothers. *The Complete Fairy Tales of the Brothers Grimm.* Trans. Jack Zipes. New York: Bantam, 1987.

Myrsina: A Folktale from Modern Greece

This folktale is an interesting combination of two tale types: "Cinderella," with the element of the months, and, more clearly, "Snow White." This tale also includes a throwback to pre-Christian beliefs in the appeal to the Sun (i.e., Apollo) to choose the most attractive sister.

Once upon a time, there lived three sisters who were orphans. The youngest was named Myrsina, or Myrtle.

One day, the two older sisters, who thought themselves great beauties, decided to find out which one was the fairest of the three. So they went outside just as the sun was rising and asked, "Sun, who is the best of us all?"

The sun answered, "One is as good as the other, but the third and youngest is the best."

When the two older sisters heard that, jealousy came alive in them. The next day, they wore their finest clothes and forced Myrsina to wear her oldest clothes.

"Sun, who is the best of us all?"

The sun answered, "One is as good as the other, but the third and youngest is the best."

Now, the two older sisters were truly angry. The next morning, they added all of their jewelry to their finery and forced Myrsina to wear dirty old rags.

"Sun, who is the best of us all?"

The sun answered for the third time, "One is as good as the other, but the third and youngest is the best."

That was the last thing the two older sisters could bear to hear. They were eaten up by envy and began to plot how best to be rid of Myrsina.

"Our mother has been dead for so many years," said the eldest. "We should go and rebury her."

"It will take time," said the second sister, "since she is buried far away on the mountain."

Myrsina, who was too young to remember any funeral, agreed to go with her sisters. She took the funeral bread and *kollyva*—the traditional offering of fruit and grain—with her.

When they had gotten into the mountain forest, the eldest sister said, "Here is the site. But—well, aren't we fools? We forgot our shovels."

"We will go back for them," said the second sister. "Myrsina, you stay here and guard the site."

There was Myrsina left all alone in the forest. She waited, and waited, and finally, when night began to fall, she knew she had been left to die, and burst into tears.

The trees took pity on her. "Do not cry," whispered a beech tree. "Let that bread you hold roll. Wherever it stops, there you stay, safe and sound."

So Myrsina set the bread rolling, and followed it down and around until it finally stopped in front of a house. She went inside, but found no one around and the place in a terrible mess. Myrsina rolled up her sleeves and set to work. She soon had straightened everything out and even had started dinner.

Then, the owners of the house came home. They were the twelve months, twelve brothers who shared the house.

"Look at this!" one month cried, "Someone has cleaned up our house!"

"And someone has started dinner!"

"Do not be afraid!" they called out. "If you are a lad, you shall be our younger brother. If you are a maid, you shall be our little sister. We shall never harm you."

Then, Myrsina came out from where she had hidden herself. She sat down with them and told them how her sisters had abandoned her.

"Then, little sister, you shall have a home with us," the months decided.

And for a time, they did. Myrsina kept the house clean and the food cooked, and the brothers treated her kindly and laughed and sang with her.

Meanwhile, though, Myrsina's two sisters found out that she was not dead and cold, but alive and happy. Envy ate them up. They baked a pie with poison in it, and set out to visit her.

"Oh Myrsina, we thought you were dead! We have been searching and searching for you!" the two older sisters exclaimed.

"I thought you had abandoned me," replied Myrsina.

"No, no, we looked everywhere for you. When we learned you were here, we came with a pie for you."

"Won't you stay and eat it with me?"

"No, no, we are in a hurry. Good-bye, Myrsina."

They hurried off.

Myrsina cut a tiny piece of the pie and gave it to the dog. Instantly, the dog fell down dead.

"Poison!" Myrsina cried, and went out and buried the pie deeply.

Months passed. The two older sisters heard that Myrsina was alive and again set out to visit her. This time, they brought a poisoned ring.

"Sister? Sister? Won't you let us in?" they implored.

"No, sisters, I will not," Myrsina replied.

"Please, Myrsina! We have our mother's ring," said the eldest sister. "On her deathbed, she said, 'If you do not want my curse, give this to Myrsina when she grows up.'"

The second sister said, "And now you are all grown up, and we do not want to go to hell from our mother's curse. So, just open a window a crack, and we will slip the ring in to you."

So Myrsina opened the window just a crack, and the sisters slipped the ring in for her. No sooner had Myrsina put the ring on her finger than she fell to the floor.

When the months came home and found Myrsina lying lifeless, they mourned so loudly, the mountains rang with their cries. Then, they dressed her in gold and placed her in a golden casket. But they did not have the heart to bury her, so they kept the casket in the house.

A young prince chanced to pass that way. He saw the golden casket and begged for it. "It is such a lovely thing. I will keep it in a place of honor."

"No, you must not. Our poor Myrsina lies dead within."

They told the prince all about the lovely maiden, and his heart ached with pity. "May I see her, for just a moment?"

So they opened the casket. The prince cried out in anguish. Such a lovely maiden, dead.

But then he saw the ring on her finger, and the red marks around the ring. Carefully, he removed the ring. As soon as he had done so, Myrsina returned to life.

Myrsina found the handsome young prince on his knees before her. And her heart went out to him.

So it happened that they were wed. And the twelve months were guests at the wedding.

As for the two older sisters? No one knows what became of them. But Myrsina and her prince lived and thrived and did good deeds.

Sources
Halliday, William Reginald. *Greek and Roman Folklore.* New York: Cooper Square, 1963.
Megas, Georgios A. *Folktales of Greece.* Chicago and London: University of Chicago Press, 1970.

The Crystal Casket: A Folktale from Italy

This tale has several unusual aspects. First is the idea that the wicked stepmother was the girl's teacher at school. Then, there is the watering of the pot of basil, a medieval motif from a rather grisly tale about a girl's lover's head buried in a pot of basil, which she waters. The seven dwarves are replaced by fairies. And the young king is besotted with the corpse, thanks to the fairies' spell.

Once, there was a widower with one daughter, Ermelina.

As it happened, the girl's teacher fell in love with the father and wanted to marry him. Sure enough, they settled the marriage in a few days.

Little did Ermelina know that the teacher would turn out to be a cruel stepmother who hated her. The girl was sent every day to water a pot of basil that sat on so narrow a terrace that with one slip she would fall to her death.

One day, a large eagle saw Ermelina and said, "Get on my back, and I will carry you away. You will be happier than with your new mamma."

Ermelina obeyed, and, after a long flight, they arrived at a beautiful crystal palace. The eagle landed and cried, "Open, my ladies, open, for I have brought you a pretty girl."

When the people in the palace opened the door and saw the lovely girl, they were amazed. They gladly took her in, where she was loved and comforted.

But the eagle flew by the terrace where the stepmother was now left to water the pot of basil. "Where is your daughter?" he asked.

"Eh!" she replied indifferently. "Perhaps she fell from this terrace to her death."

"What a fool you are!" the eagle sneered. "I carried her away because you abused her. I carried her away to my fairies, and she is very well." With that, the eagle flew away.

The raging stepmother called a witch to her. "My stepdaughter is alive and in the house of some fairies. Find me a way to kill her, lest she someday return and my husband learn the truth."

The witch put together a small basket of sweets, into which she placed a spell. She then wrote a letter as though the girl's father was giving her the present.

Meanwhile, the fairies told Ermelina, "We will be away for four days. While we are gone, do not open the door to anyone, for some treachery is being prepared by your stepmother."

Ermelina promised to open the door to no one. She added, "My stepmother has nothing to do with me."

The fairies went away. The next day, when Ermelina was alone, she heard a knocking at the door. "Knock away! I do not open to anyone," she cried.

But curiosity forced Ermelina to look out of the window. She thought she saw a servant girl from her father's house, though it actually was the witch in disguise. "My dear Ermelina, your father wept for you, thinking you dead. But he is happy now knowing you are with the fairies and has sent you this small present."

Ermelina could not resist. She took the basket, but as soon as she had tasted one sweet, she fell to the floor.

When the fairies returned, they found Ermelina dead. They saw the little piece of sweet still in her mouth, removed it, and she returned to life.

Once more, the fairies needed to leave. "Remember, Ermelina, we cured you once, but we will not do so again."

Ermelina replied that they need not worry. She would not open the door to anyone.

When the stepmother found out the girl was still alive, she threatened the witch with death. But the witch got a lovely dress, disguised herself again, and went to the fairies' house. She knocked on the door, and said, "Please open. I am your seamstress."

"No," Ermelina replied, "I will not do so."

"Come down. I must fit a dress on you."

"No, no. I have been deceived once."

"But you know me!" the disguised witch cried. "I always have made your dresses."

Poor Ermelina was persuaded by that. She opened the door and tried on the dress. But as soon as she began to button it, she fell down dead.

There, the fairies found Ermelina. This time, they had to keep their word and not save her.

Weeping, the fairies conjured up a beautiful casket covered with diamonds and put the girl in it. They put the casket on a gleaming white horse and commanded it, "Do not stop until you find someone who says to you, 'Stop, for pity's sake, for I have lost my horse for you.'"

The horse raced off at once. A young king saw it and chased after it so hard that his own horse fell dead beneath him. The king cried out, "Stop, for pity's sake, for I have lost my horse for you!"

With that, the horse stopped. When the king saw the beautiful girl dead in the casket, he brought the horse and the casket home to his palace. The king's mother knew that her son had gone hunting, but when she saw what he brought back, she did not know what to think.

The young king had the casket carried to his chambers, then called to his mother, "I went hunting, but I found a wife."

"But what is it?" she asked. "A doll? A dead woman?"

"Whatever it is, it is my wife," the young king replied, never guessing that he was under a spell.

From then on, the king did nothing but stay in his chamber. But a war was declared against his kingdom, and he was forced to leave.

He told his mother, "I wish two careful chambermaids to guard this casket. For if on my return I find that anything has happened it, I shall have the chambermaids killed."

His mother said, "Go, my son. Fear nothing, for I myself will watch over your casket. Only return in safety."

The king left, weeping at having to leave the casket. The days passed, and his mother forgot all about the casket. Then, a letter came telling her that her son had won the war, and he would be back in a few days.

The king's mother rejoiced—then she remembered the casket. She called the chambermaids to her, and said, "My son is returning, and we have not taken care of the doll!"

The chambermaids went to the king's room and saw that the doll's face and hands were covered with dust. So they washed her face, but some drops of water fell on her dress and stained it. The poor chambermaids began to weep, and they went to the queen for advice.

The queen said, "Call the royal seamstress, and have her make a dress exactly like this one. Then remove this one before my son comes home."

They did just that. When the new dress was ready, the chambermaids went to the room and began to unbutton the stained dress. The moment that they took off the first sleeve, Ermelina opened her eyes.

The poor chambermaids sprang up in terror, but one of the most courageous said to herself, "I am a woman, and so is this one." The chambermaid helped Ermelina out of the casket and asked shyly for her story. Ermelina told her, and then asked, "Where am I?"

The queen entered and did her best to explain it all. Then, she had Ermelina dressed in royal attire.

When the young king entered, he stopped in amazement, as the spell holding him captive to the casket shattered. "You are alive!" he cried. "Oh my dearest lady, you are alive! I adored you when you were dead, and now I adore you even more. Will you be my wife?"

"I will," Ermelina replied.

They arranged the wedding and, in a few days, were man and wife.

Sources

Calvino, Italo. *Italian Folktales.* New York: Harcourt Brace Jovanovich, 1980.

Crane, Thomas Frederick. *Italian Popular Tales.* New York and Oxford, United Kingdom: Oxford University Press, 2003.

TRANSFORMATION FOLKTALES

Unlike the main character in the "Beauty and the Beast" tale type, the main character in this tale is a voluntary shapeshifter who may be a human magician or a nonhuman, such as the English Hedley Kow. He or she may be able to take more than one form, or may go through a series of rebirths into various human and animal forms. If originally human, he or she is sometimes reborn as a human, but seldom as the same human that he or she once was.

The Hedley Kow: A Folktale from England

This supernatural creature is not malicious, merely a mischievous shapeshifter who likes to play tricks on humans. He might take the form of a farmer's horse, then lead the farmer into a stream, or he might shapeshift into various inanimate objects. Only once was he unable to get a shocked reaction from a human.

Once, there was a cheerful old lady who was rich only in her good cheer. Well now, one summer evening as she headed on home, she found a large black pot lying at the side of the road.

"That is an odd thing. Who could have left it here?" She looked around but saw no one. "Well, perhaps it has a hole in it, so someone tossed it away. But it would do fine as a flowerpot for my window!"

But then she took a look inside, and nearly jumped out of her skin for the shock. "It is brim full of gold coins!"

What good luck! What amazing luck!

But how was she to get the treasure home? Ah, she would fasten one end of her shawl to the pot and drag it home. "It is nearly dark out, and no one will see what I am bringing home. I do not know where I will put the thing for safety, though. Still, what wonderful luck!"

After some time, the old lady was rather tired with dragging that heavy weight, and she stopped for a moment's rest. But when she looked back, it was not a pot she was dragging, but a good-sized lump of silver!

"Oh, the twilight must have been playing tricks with my eyes and mind," she decided. "Well, this is a change for the better, since it us far less trouble to keep safe than a bunch of gold coins. Yes, it is definitely a change for the better."

So off she went toward home again, grinning cheerfully.

But soon the old lady was tired again, and she stopped to rest.

"Well, would you look at that? The twilight really has been playing tricks with me! That is a lump of iron I am dragging! What good luck, because it is just really convenient. I can sell it as easy as easy, and it is much handier than a lot of gold and silver that might bring around robbers. What good luck, indeed!"

The next time she stopped to rest and turned around to see what she was dragging, it was a great stone. "What good luck this is! How could it have known that I was just terrible wanting something to hold my door open with? Ay, if that is not a good change! It is a fine thing to have such good luck."

All in a hurry to see how nice the stone would look by her door, she trotted down the hill to stop beside her own gate and unlatch it. She turned to untie her shawl from the stone, which was lying on the path quite peacefully.

Then, all of a sudden, it seemed to give a jump and a squeal, and it grew in a moment as big as a great horse. Then, it threw down four lanky legs, shook out two long ears, flourished a tail, and went off kicking its feet into the air and laughing like a naughty mocking boy.

The old woman stared after it until it was fairly out of sight.

"Well!" she said at last. "I do be the luckiest of people. Fancy seeing the Hedley Kow, me, all by myself, and making so free with it! I do feel that grand!"

Sources
Hartland, Edwin Sidney. *English Fairy and Other Folk Tales*. London: Walter Scott, 1890.
Jacobs, Joseph. *More English Fairy Tales*. London: David Nutt, 1894.

The Soul That Lived in the Bodies of All Beasts: A Folktale from the Inuit of Greenland

> This transmutation folktale features three types of transformation. First, the man transforms himself into other men. Then, his soul lives in several animal forms. The third transformation is when he finally is reborn as human once more.

There was a man whose name was Avovang. And of him it is said that nothing could wound him.

At that time of the year when it is good to be out, and the days do not close with dark night, and all is nearing the great summer, Avovang's brother stood one day on the ice near the breathing hole of a seal. As he stood there, a sledge came dashing up. And as it reached him, the man who was in it cried a warning, "There will come many sledges to kill your brother."

The brother hurried to deliver the warning to Avovang. Sure enough, the sledges drove up to the house.

Avovang went out to meet them. But he took with him a dog's skin that had been his blanket when he was a child, placed it on the ground, and stood on it. When his enemies attacked, though they stabbed again and again, they could not wound him.

So he mocked them. "All my body bears scars, yet you could not kill me."

Since they could not kill Avovang with their weapons, his enemies dragged him to the top of a mountain, planning to throw him to his death. But each time they tried, he changed himself into another man, confusing them so much that they had to give up and leave.

After that, Avovang decided to travel to the people who lived in the south to buy wood. And so he and others set off, many sledges together. They bought the wood, and Avovang found a wife among the people of the south. Then, they all set out for home. On the way, they stopped to look for the breathing holes of seal.

The men all had a great desire to possess Avovang's wife, and they tried to kill him. They tossed him down through a seal's breathing hole into the icy sea. His new wife was so furious that she broke their wood into useless pieces and then went home.

The men, feeling guilty, drove on northward. Suddenly, a great seal rose up, right in their way, where the ice was thin and slippery. Many of the sledges fell through, and many of the men were drowned.

Then, the survivors again saw something in their way. It was a fox, and they set off in chase. But as they drove after it up an ice mountain, they fell to their death. Only two men survived and made it home.

It was the soul of Avovang, whom nothing could wound, that had changed—first into a seal and then into a fox—and avenged his own murder. After that, he made up his mind to let himself be born in the shape of every beast of Earth, so that he might one day tell his fellow men the manner of each beast's life.

At one time, he was a dog, and lived on meat, which he stole from the houses. But he grew tired of being a dog, mostly because of the beatings he got for stealing meat.

So he changed into a reindeer. That was fine for a time, once he had learned how to gallop and grow fat on a diet of moss and lichen. But then the herd was attacked by wolves. In their panic, the herd raced into the sea, where men in kayaks killed some of them, including the reindeer that had been Avovang.

But when the men began to cut open their kill, Avovang escaped and changed himself into a wolf. That was fine for a time, once he learned how to run with the pack and catch prey.

But he grew bored with being a wolf, and became a walrus. He learned how to swim as the walrus does and to eat mussels and other seafood.

Then, he wished for the air and became a raven. That was fine for a time, but he found that ravens' feet got cold.

Eventually, Avovang had become every animal of the far north. He changed once more into a seal.

He let himself be caught and killed, then crept into the body of the hunter's wife. And after a time, Avovang was born again and became once more a man.

Sources

Jenness, Diamond. *Eskimo Folklore: Myths and Traditions from Northern Alaska, the McKenzie Delta and Coronation Gulf.* Honolulu, HI: University Press of the Pacific, 2002.

Rasmussen, Knud. *Eskimo Folk-Tales.* Trans. W. Worster. London: Gylglendal, 1921.

The Transformation Chase

In this folktale type, closely related to the transformation tale type, objects and people are fluid things, able to change shape without effort. Objects such as combs turn into forests and become barriers to the pursuing villain. The hero or heroine often shapeshifts many times into different animals before finally escaping or destroying the villain.

Master and Pupil: A Folktale from Denmark

This is one of the few folktales to stress the importance of literacy and the lack thereof. This probably places the tale's earliest ancestry somewhere in the fifteenth century, when printing was bringing about more widespread literacy.

Although reading is a major point of the folktale, it otherwise follows the basic transformation tale type. That is, except for the ending, which does not conclude with romance but rather with a surprise.

There once was a boy who was very clever at reading and took great delight in it. He left his parents and went out into the world to seek service.

As the boy was walking between some earth mounds, he met a man, who asked him where he was going.

"I am seeking for service," said the boy.

"Will you serve me?" asked the man.

"Oh, yes, just as readily you as anyone else," said the boy.

"But can you read?" asked the man.

"As well as the priest," said the boy.

"Then I cannot have you," said the man. "In fact, I want a boy who cannot read. His only work would be to dust my old books."

The man then went on his way and left the boy looking after him. "It was a pity I did not get that place," the boy thought. "All those books . . . that was just the very thing for me."

Making up his mind to get that situation, he hid behind one of the mounds and turned his jacket outside in, so that the man would not recognize him so easily. Then, he ran along behind the mounds and met the man at the other end of them.

"Where are you going, my boy?" asked the man, not noticing that this was the same one he had met before.

"I am seeking for service," said the boy.

"Will you serve me?" asked the man.

"Gladly," said the boy.

"Can you read?" asked the man.

"No, I do not know a single letter," said the boy.

The man took the boy into his service, and all the work he had to do was to dust his master's books. But as he did this, he had plenty of time to read them as well.

They were magic books, and the boy read away at them until at last he was just as wise as his master—who was a great wizard—and could perform all kinds of magic. Among other feats, he could change himself into the shape of any animal or any other thing that he pleased.

When he had learned all this, the boy did not think it wise to stay there any longer. So he ran away home to his parents again.

Soon after this, there was a market in the next village. The boy told his mother that he had learned how to change himself into the shape of any animal he chose.

"Now," he said, "I shall change myself to a horse, and father can take me to market and sell me. I shall come home again all right."

His mother was frightened by the idea, but the boy told her that all would be well. He changed himself to a horse—a fine horse, too—and his father got a high price for it at the market. But after the bargain was made and the money was paid, the boy changed again to his own shape when no one was looking, and returned home.

The story spread all over about the fine horse that had been sold and then had disappeared. At last, the news came to the ears of the wizard.

"Aha!" he said. "This is that boy of mine who befooled me and ran away. But I shall have him yet."

The next time there was a market, the boy again changed himself into a horse, and was taken there by his father to be sold. The wizard saw the horse and knew at once what he was seeing. So he bought the horse.

The first thing the wizard did was lead the horse to a smith to get a red-hot nail driven into its mouth. Because after that was done, it could not change its shape again.

When the horse realized what was to be done to it, it changed itself into a dove and flew up into the air. The wizard at once changed himself into a hawk and flew up after it.

The dove now turned into a gold ring, which fell into a girl's lap.

The hawk now turned into a man and offered the girl a great sum of money for the gold ring. But she would not part with it, saying that it had fallen down to her from heaven. The man kept offering the girl more and more for it, until at last she was ready to agree.

The gold ring changed into a grain of barley, which fell on the ground.

The man then turned into a hen and began to search for the grain of barley.

But the barley grain changed itself to a cat and took off the hen's head with a single snap.

The cat put on human shape, bowed to the amazed girl, and left.

Sources

Asbjornsen, Peter Christen, and Jorgen Engebretsen Moe. *Popular Tales from the Norse*. Trans. George Webbe Dasent. New York: G.P. Putnam, 1896.

Kvideland, Reimund, and Henning K. Sehmsdorf, eds. *Scandinavian Folk Belief and Legend*. Minneapolis: University of Minnesota Press, 1988.

Master and Pupil (or the Devil Outwitted): A Folktale from the Republic of Georgia

In this variant transformation folktale, it is a devil—not a magician or magic books—who teaches the boy his trade as a shapeshifter. The transformation chase occurs, but again it ends without any romantic interest at all.

Once, there lived a peasant with one son, who needed to learn a trade. So off they went, father and son, seeking a master to teach the son a trade.

Along the way, they stopped to drink from a stream. Out of the water came a devil in man's form.

"What do you wish?" he asked. "I am Vakhraca. What is your trouble?"

"My son must learn a trade," said the peasant.

"Give him to me. I will teach him for one year, and then come for him. If you know him, he will go with you. If you do not know him, then he will be mine and mine forever."

The peasant agreed to the proposal and went home.

A year passed by, and the peasant returned for his son. There was a crowd of boys all alike. To his horror and sorrow, he could not recognize his boy.

But the boy recognized his father. He whispered to him, "We are all going to be turned into doves and fly. I shall be in the lead on the way out, and the last on the way back. So you can find me."

So it happened. The devil was furious when the peasant pointed to the right dove. That fool of a boy had tricked him! But there was nothing he could do but let the peasant and his son leave.

They came to a place where nobles were hunting with greyhounds that were failing to catch any game.

The boy said to his father, "Go into the wood and raise a hare. I will turn into a hound and seize it before the eyes of these nobles. The nobles will want to buy me. Ask a high price and sell me to them. Then, I shall seize the first opportunity to escape and overtake you on the road."

The father went into the wood and started a hare. His son turned into a hound, pursued the hare, and, just before the eyes of the nobles, pounced on it. They crowded around the peasant and insisted upon buying the hound. The peasant asked a high price, which they paid in exchange for the hound.

The nobles attached a cord to the hound's neck and went away. When they had traveled a little way along the road, a hare started from the thicket. They let the hound loose and sent him after it.

When the hound had chased the hare a long way, and had lost sight of the nobles, he changed again into a boy. He set after his father and soon overtook him.

A little later, they saw another party of nobles hunting with falcons that failed to catch any game. The boy changed himself into a falcon and brought down a fine pheasant right before the nobles. They insisted that the peasant sell them the fine falcon. The peasant again asked a high price, to which the nobles agreed and paid him in exchange for the falcon.

The peasant went on his way. The nobles, after traveling some distance, sent the falcon in pursuit of another pheasant. The falcon flew after the bird.

When the falcon was out of the nobles' sight, he again changed into a boy and rejoined his father.

Now, as the father and son went along, the son said, "I will change into a magnificent horse. Take me to town and sell me. But remember this: Do not sell me to a man with eyes of two different colors. If you do, do not give him the bridle. If you give him the bridle, I will not be able to free myself from him."

But the father, overwhelmed with offers for the splendid horse, did sell it to a man with eyes of two different colors—and the man got the bridle as well. It was, of course, a trap, and the master was delighted to have his pupil in his power once more. He shut the horse in a dark room and locked the door.

The prisoner thought and grieved, grieved and thought. But he could puzzle out no way of escape. Until suddenly, he noticed a sunbeam entering the dark room through a tiny hole. Perfect! He changed into a mouse and ran out.

The master saw him and chased him as a cat. Just when the cat was about to catch the mouse, they came to a stream, and the mouse changed into a fish.

The master turned into a net and followed him. Just when the net was about to catch the fish, the fish changed into a pheasant and flew away.

The master pursued him as a falcon. Just when the falcon was about to put its claws into the pheasant, the pheasant turned into a red apple and rolled into the king's lap.

The falcon changed into a knife in the king's hand. Just when the king was going to cut the apple, it changed into a pile of millet spread on a cloth.

The master changed himself into a brood hen, and began to eat the millet. When it had left one grain, this grain turned into a needle, and rolled in front of the hen.

The hen changed into a thread in the eye of the needle. As the thread was about to hold back the needle, the needle ran into the fire and burned it.

The boy thus escaped from the devil, went home to his father, and lived happily ever afterwards.

Sources

Papashvily, George, and Helen Papashvily. *Yes and No Stories: A Book of Georgian Folk Tales.*
    New York: Harper and Brothers, 1946.
Wardrop, Marjory. *Georgian Folk Tales.* London: David Nutt, 1894.

The Pupil Who Bested the Master: A Folktale from Libya

This transformation chase folktale begins with a romance. The hero then learns his shapeshifting trade from a devil, and the traditional shapeshifting chase follows. A romantic ending fulfills the promise of the beginning.

There was a young man who had fallen in love with the governor's daughter. But the governor would not let anyone marry his daughter who did not know a decent trade.

So the young man tried his hand at being a blacksmith's apprentice. But he accidentally hit the blacksmith instead of the anvil and was sent away.

He tried his hand at being a cobbler's apprentice. But he accidentally stabbed the cobbler with the awl instead of piercing the shoe leather and was sent away.

The young man wandered on, trying to find a trade that would suit him. At last, he came to a grand mansion. But no one was around.

He entered the mansion and found a herd of sheep, a herd of goats, and a herd of cattle, all being tended by a devil. The devil took a liking to the young man and invited him to stay.

So the young man stayed and was taught the magic arts. Here was a trade at which he was good!

One day, the devil left his mansion. Before he left, he gave the young man the keys. "You may go anywhere you wish, through six rooms. Only the seventh you may not enter."

As soon as the devil was away, the young man opened the door of the seventh room. To his horror, he saw a row of dead men hanging from ropes. He went down the row and found one man still alive and hastily cut him down. The man was near death, but he lived long enough to warn the young man.

"The devil teaches his victims the magic arts and then hangs them."

The young man fled all the way back home. He told his mother that now he had a trade. He had mastered the magic arts.

Unfortunately, the devil had been looking for the young man, and finally caught up with him. The young man ran away and transformed himself into a mansion. But the devil touched the mansion, and it fell apart.

The young man turned into a mule. But the devil threw a halter on him and dragged him to the seaside, meaning to drown him.

The mule transformed into a fish and dove into the sea. But he devil dove after him.

The fish transformed into an eagle and soared up into the sky. But the devil became a larger eagle and soared up after him.

The eagle transformed into a ring and fell at the feet of the governor's daughter. She picked it up and put it into her jewelry box.

The devil appeared at the governor's door and bargained for the ring. But when the ring was brought to him, it turned into a pomegranate. The devil grabbed it, and the pomegranate broke apart, spilling out its many seeds.

Instantly, the devil became a chicken, pecking up the seeds. But one seed turned into a knife and cut the chicken's throat.

Then, the knife turned into the young man. This time, the governor was delighted to let him marry his daughter.

Source

Noy, Dov. *Folktales of Israel*. Trans. Gene Baharav. Chicago: University of Chicago Press, 1963. Recorded by M. Ohel from Menahim Mevorakh, a Jewish immigrant from Libya.

The Magician and His Disciple: A Folktale from India

This variant has some unusual elements, and it is more complex than most folktales of this type. This is the only tale of this type that begins with a deposed king. The magician here is a wicked guru who seeks to keep the wiser son as his slave, but he is tricked by the boy.

What follows is an extended transformation chase, followed by a romantic interlude, then continued as a transformation chase. The ending is first a romance and then a righteous ending, as the son returns his father to his throne.

A king, vanquished by foes, fled with his wife and two sons to a distant land, where he became a beggar. The hardships of his life did not bother him, but he did worry about his children.

One day, the former king went to a learned guru and pleaded, "You must take my children under your wing and give them a proper education. I am poor. I cannot offer you money. But I can give you one of my children as repayment."

The guru agreed and kept the children with him. The king returned to his beggar's life.

The guru sent the older boy to graze cows and taught him little skills like counting. The younger boy, though, was far smarter than the older one. When the guru showed him one thing, he learned ten things. He even became expert in the arts of magic. Very soon, he was better than his guru.

One day, the younger son, who now was a young man, looked into the far distance with his inner eye to see what his parents were doing. Ah, his heart melted for them and the hardship they endured. He also learned about his father's promise to give the guru one of his sons in return for a proper education. But the clever guru had taught his elder brother only to be a cowherd and had educated only him, the younger of the two. There must be some trick, some treachery in this arrangement.

The young man thought, "If I do not do something about this right now, my parents will lose me and die in poverty."

He changed at once into a bird, flew to his parents' place, then changed back into himself and entered their hut. The old king and queen were full of joy. They touched his hair, fondled his face, held his hand, and blessed him.

"What brought you here?" they asked. "Is everything all right?"

The young man said, "Father, something is strange. The guru has taught me everything, but he has neglected my brother. He sends him out every day with the cows. I know you have promised to give one of us to him. When the time comes, offer to give the guru my brother and ask for me. He will give you every kind of excuse—how wonderful my brother is, how much smarter and better educated he is. But you must be stubborn. Insist that you want only the younger son. I will take care of the rest."

With that, he changed into a bird, and flew away.

The old king awaited an auspicious day and hour. And then he went to the guru.

The guru had dressed the older brother in silk, brought him to the schoolroom, made him sit in front as if he were a top-ranking student, and spread big books in front of him. As for the younger brother, he was dressed in rags and made to sit with the stupidest pupils.

The guru showed the father both his sons and said, "Look, of your two sons, the older son is brilliant. He learns everything before you even mention it. He has become a great scholar. But the younger fellow listens to nothing I say. Nothing enters his head. He does not want to do anything. He grazes cattle. You can have one of these two. Tell me which one you want."

The king remembered what his younger son had told him when he came as a bird. He replied, "Wise sir, you have taught at least one of them some good sense. You have taken a lot of trouble over them. That is a great thing. I will give you the smart fellow, the older brother. I will take the stupid one. The younger fellow will adjust to our poverty better."

In spite of all the guru's persuasions, the king insisted on taking the younger son, and he finally did so.

When they reached home, the young man was hungry, but since his father had spent all day in travel, he had not gone out that day to beg. So there was no food at home. The parents told him how they lived, showed him how little they had. That night, they all drank water and went to bed hungry.

Early next morning, the young man heard a town crier make an announcement, "A reward, a reward for anyone who will bring a rooster to fight the palace rooster!"

The young man woke up his father at once and said, "Father, let us make some money. I will become a rooster. Take me to the palace and sell me for 1,000 rupees." And he changed into a rooster.

His father nervously took the rooster to the palace. The local king gave the old man 1,000 rupees as a reward and a new turban as a special gift. The servants brought an iron coop and covered the rooster with it.

As soon as the servants were gone, the rooster turned into a bandicoot, burrowed a hole in the ground, and returned to his parents as their beloved son.

That evening, the palace was ready for the cockfight. But when they picked up the iron coop, the rooster was gone and there was nothing but a big rat hole in the ground. The servants ran to the king and told him that a bandicoot had eaten up the rooster. The king sighed.

"It is a shame that in such a solid palace as ours there are bandicoots and rats that make burrows. I am ashamed to live here. Tear it down and build a stronger palace!"

Meanwhile, the 1,000 rupees the parents got for the rooster did not last very long. The young man said, "Father, in this town there is a merchant named Ratnakara. He fancies horses. I will change into a rare breed of horse. You can sell it to him for 1,000 rupees." Then, he changed into a rare breed of horse called *Pancakalyani*, "the breed of five virtues."

The old king took the horse to the merchant Ratnakara. The merchant knew at once what a splendid horse it was. He said, "This looks like a valuable horse. But we must get its quality, the condition of its teeth, and the whorls on its body examined by experts."

Then, he sent for the guru, who had taught him much about horses. The guru came down and carefully examined the horse's mouth and teeth and every inch of its body all the way down to the tip of its tail.

It did not take the guru long to discover that the horse was no other than his own pupil, who was now playing tricks on people. So, here was the pupil who thought he would outwit the master. The foolish young man must be destroyed!

The guru told the merchant, "This is a rare breed, no doubt about it. But there are things wrong with its quality, the whorls are not right. The science of horses says that only a *sanyasi* can ride it safely. So I will buy it. Why don't you give me a gift of 1,000? Giving a Brahmin such a gift will earn you merit."

Ratnakara gave him the money. The guru gave the bewildered old king the 1,000 rupees and bought the horse.

Then, the guru mounted the horse and rode it into pits, onto boulders, until the horse was dying of fatigue and thirst. Then, he took it to a small creek. But as soon as the horse touched water, he changed into a fish and glided away.

The guru saw what was happening. At once, he called his disciples, telling them to get poison to pour into the creek.

The young man, who was now a fish, knew he would be killed if he stayed in the water. He saw an untouchable, a man of the lowest caste, about to cut up a dead buffalo. The young man quickly left his fish form and entered the carcass of the dead buffalo. When the untouchable turned around, he saw the dead buffalo get up and walk away.

"A demon!" the untouchable yelled. He started running, panic-stricken, screaming, "A demon has entered the dead beast!"

The guru knew at once that this was another of his pupil's tricks. He stopped the untouchable, and told him, "If you run like this, this demon buffalo will destroy you. You must kill it now. I will help you."

They quickly captured the fleeing animal and forcibly tied it to a tree. The guru told the untouchable, "Strike now with your knife."

The young man thought he was lost—but then he saw a many-colored parrot lying dead in the bole of the tree. Just as the untouchable was swinging his knife at him, the young man entered the parrot's body and flew up into the sky.

The guru took the form of a Brahmany kite and gave chase to the parrot.

But after all, the pupil was young, the guru was old. Though the kite had large wings, he could not move them fast enough. The parrot flew farther and farther away.

As he flew over a palace, the parrot saw a princess on the terrace, shaking out and drying her long hair in the sunshine after a bath. She was exquisitely beautiful. The parrot flew down and perched right on the back of her hand.

"Oh, how wonderful!" she cried. "What a lovely bird you are!"

"Yes, I am," the parrot replied.

"You have been trained to talk. How charming!"

When the kite saw her take the bird in, he knew that his enemy had eluded him. He flew on, hatching new plots.

The princess loved the many-colored parrot, and she took great care of it, never letting it out of her sight. She would bathe, eat, and sleep in the company of the parrot in the cage.

After several days, the younger son, who was now a parrot, waited one night until the princess was asleep and came out of the cage. He changed into his human form, and then tenderly stroked the princess's silken hair. And then, not daring to do more, he returned to the cage as a parrot.

In the morning, when the princess woke up, her hair was in disarray. She could still remember the touch of a man's hand. Had that been a dream? Or had someone come into her bedroom?

All the doors of her chamber were still shut. The sentinels outside were still there. Not even a fly could have come in past the wakeful sentinels and the bustling maids. Who could have entered her bedroom? If it had not been a dream, he would surely come again, and this time she would catch him.

That night, she went to bed early and lay there pretending to be asleep. At midnight, the parrot came out of the cage and turned into the young man. He came to her bed—but the princess jumped to her feet. Catching him by the hands, she asked, "Who are you? You were a parrot. How did you become a man?"

Caught in the act, he had to tell the truth. He told her about his whole life, then said, "I had to stroke your hair. You are so beautiful that I . . . I love you."

As he blurted out his love, the princess, too, loved him. "You are my husband from this moment. I will help you in any way I can," she promised.

"Princess, tomorrow my guru will come to this palace in the guise of an acrobat. He wants to kill me. He will please your father with his marvelous acrobatic feats and ask for a reward. When your father offers him gold and silver, he will refuse it and ask for the parrot in your bedroom. Your father will send maids to get the parrot. You must refuse. He will send maids again and again, many times. Then, you get into a rage and break the neck of the parrot in front of them all."

"Won't that kill you?" she cried in horror.

"It will not even hurt me. But my guru will not stop there. He will ask for the necklace of pearls around your neck. At that point, tear off the pearl necklace and throw it down. I will do the rest."

After this, they tenderly embraced, and then he went back to the cage as a parrot.

Sure enough, the next day, the guru did visit the palace in the guise of an acrobat. He showed the king and the court some amazing tricks. The delighted king held out a handful of gold coins.

But the acrobat would have none of it. He said, "Your Highness, your daughter has a many-colored parrot. That is what I would like to have."

The king sent maids to the balcony, where the princess sat watching. She refused to yield the parrot each time the maids came to her. When at last the king insisted, she came down, pretended to throw a tantrum, and twisted the parrot's neck, killing it then and there.

The acrobat now asked for the pearl necklace that only he noticed had appeared magically around her neck. In her pretended rage, she pulled it off and spilled the pearls on the court floor.

The pearls turned into little worms. The acrobat ran toward them, quickly changed into a hen, and began to peck at the worms and devour them.

At once, the young man, who was now one of the worms on the floor, abruptly changed into a tomcat. He caught the hen by the neck.

The guru cried out from within the hen, "Ayyo, I surrender. Let me go now. Remember, you were once my pupil."

The young man screamed from within the cat, "No, you are full of lies. I am going to kill you so that you will not bother me or anyone else again."

The king, who had recovered his poise sooner than the others, asked, "Who are you? What is with all these shapes?"

The hen squeaked, "Ask the cat."

The cat explained the whole story. The king said, "A guru, even such a wicked one, should not be killed. Let him go. He will not bother you anymore."

The young man decided that by now he was confident enough of his powers to counter anything the guru did. So he showed mercy and let the guru go. Both of them gave up their animal forms and became human again.

The king married his daughter to the young man and gave half his kingdom as dowry. The young man brought home to the palace his elder brother from the guru's place. He sent palanquins to his parents, who had seen life at its worst, a king and a queen who had lived as beggars. He waged war against his father's old enemies and won back his father's kingdom for him.

Everyone was happy—even though the guru never did dare go near the prince again.

Sources

Beck, Brenda E.F., Peter J. Claus, Praphulladatta Goswami, and Jawaharlal Handoo, eds. *Folktales of India*. Chicago: University of Chicago Press, 1987.

Ramanujan, A.K. *A Flowering Tree and Other Oral Tales from India*. Berkeley and London: University of California Press, 1997.

The Master-Maid: A Folktale from Norway

In this transformation chase tale, the hero could never succeed without the help of the master-maid, the woman he loves, who has picked up magical talents from her time as the giant's prisoner.

But the tale continues on after the chase, taking on a new theme—the forgotten bride who must set out on the heroine's quest to regain her true love. It also takes on a third theme, that of the clever woman who outwits three would-be suitors.

Once, there was a king who had many sons. The youngest of the sons had no place at home, so he went out into the world to try his luck.

After traveling for many days, the young prince came to the house of a giant. He was hired by the giant as a servant.

In the morning, the giant had to go out to pasture his goats. As he was leaving the house, he told the prince to clean out the stable.

"That is your only work for the day. But it must be done well. And you must on no account go into any of the rooms that lead out of the room in which you slept last night. If you do, I will take your life."

"Well, this is an easy master, but a bit of a strange one," the prince said to himself. "What could be in those rooms he does not want me to see?"

He went into the first room. A cauldron was hanging from the walls, bubbling away, although no fire was under it. What could be inside it? As the prince looked into it, a lock of his hair dipped into the mysterious soup and came out copper.

"Now there is a strange thing!" the prince said.

He went on into the next room. There, he saw another cauldron boiling away without a fire under it. The prince carefully dipped the end of another lock of hair into it, and it came out silver.

"What a strange soup this is!" the prince said

He went on into the third room. There, too, a cauldron was hanging from the wall, boiling, exactly the same as in the two other rooms. The prince dipped a lock of hair in, and it came out brightly gilded.

"If he boils gold here, what can he boil in there?" the prince said, and he went into the fourth room. There was no cauldron here, but on a bench sat the most beautiful young woman the prince had ever seen.

"In heaven's name, what are you doing here?" said she who sat upon the bench.

"I took the place of servant here yesterday," said the prince.

"If you have come to serve here, may you soon have a better place!" she cried.

"Oh, but I think I have got a kind master," said the prince. "He has not given me hard work to do today. When I have cleaned out the stable, I shall be done."

"And you think that an easy task?" she said. "Hear me. If you clean it out in the normal way, ten pitchforksful will come in for every one you throw out. But I will teach you how to do it. You must turn your pitchfork upside down, and work with the handle, and then all will fly out of its own accord."

"Thank you! I will do it that way," replied the prince.

He sat beside her, and they talked. And they realized that they loved each other, sudden as that. They decided that when they got out of this place, they would marry.

So the first day of the prince's service with the giant flew by. When evening was drawing near, the young woman said, "You had best clean out that stable now, before the giant comes home!"

When he got there, the prince first tried to work in the normal way. But the maiden had been right: More came in than went out. So he did what she had taught him, turning the pitchfork around and working with the handle. And in the twinkling of an eye, the stable was as clean as if it had been scoured.

When the prince had done that, he went back again into the room in which the giant had given him leave to stay.

The giant came home with the goats. "Have you cleaned the stable?" he asked.

"Yes, now it is clean and sweet," replied the prince.

"I shall see about that," said the giant. He went around to the stable, but it was just as the prince had said.

The giant came back grumbling, "You certainly have been talking to my master-maid, for you never got that out of your own head."

"Master-maid! What kind of a thing is that, master?" asked the prince, making himself look quite stupid. "I should like to see that."

"Well, you will see her quite soon enough," said the giant.

On the second morning, the giant again had to go out with his goats. He told the prince that on that day he was to fetch home his horse, which was out on the mountainside. When the prince had done that he might rest himself for the remainder of the day.

"For you have come to a kind master, and that you shall find," said the giant. "But do not go into any of the rooms that I spoke of yesterday, or I will tear off your head."

"Yes, indeed, you are a kind master," said the prince. "But," he thought, "I will go in and talk to the master-maid again."

So he went to her, and they talked for a bit. Then, she asked him what he had to do that day.

"Oh, not very dangerous work, surely," said the prince. "I have only to go up the mountainside after his horse. There is no great art in riding a horse back to his stable. I have certainly ridden friskier horses before."

"None like this," said the master-maid. "But I will teach you what to do. When you go near the horse, fire will come from its nostrils. Take the bridle that hangs by that door and fling the bit right into his open jaws. Then, you will have a horse so tame that you can lead it by one finger."

"I will do this," replied the prince.

Then, the prince again sat in there the whole day by the master-maid, and they chatted and talked of one thing and another. But the first thing and the last, now, was how happy and delightful it would be if they could but marry each other and get safely away from the giant. The prince nearly forgot all about the giant's horse, but the master-maid reminded him.

So the prince took the bridle and strode up the mountainside. It was not long before he saw the horse. It stood breathing fire at him, then charged him with open jaws. The prince threw the bit straight into the horse's mouth, and it stood as quiet as a lamb. The prince had no difficulty getting the horse home to the stable. Then, he went back into his room again.

Toward evening, the giant came home. "Have you fetched the horse back from the mountainside?" he asked.

"That I have, master, and put him in the stable, too," replied the prince.

"I will see about that," said the giant. He went out to the stable, but the horse was standing there just as the prince had said. "You certainly have been talking with my master-maid, for you never got that out of your own head."

"Yesterday, master, you talked about this master-maid, and today you are talking about her again. Heaven bless you, master, why will you not show me the thing?" asked the prince, who again pretended to be silly and stupid.

"You will see her soon enough," said the giant.

On the morning of the third day, the giant again had to go into the woods with the goats. "Today, you must go underground and fetch my taxes," he said to the prince. "When you have done this, you may rest for the remainder of the day, for you shall see what an easy master you have come to." And then he went away.

"Well, however easy a master you may be, you set me very hard work to do," thought the prince. "But I will see if I cannot find your master-maid." And he returned to her. When the master-maid asked him what the giant had set him to do that day, he told her that he was to go underground and get the taxes.

"You must tell me how to do it," said the prince, "for I have never yet been underground. And even if I knew the way, I do not know how much I am to demand."

"You must take that club and knock on the rocky wall," said the master-maid. "Then someone sparking all over with fire will come out. Tell him your errand. When he asks you how much you want, say, 'As much as I can carry.'"

"Yes, I will do that," replied the prince.

Then, he sat there with the master-maid the whole day, until the master-maid reminded him that it was time to be off to fetch the taxes before the giant came home.

So the prince set out on his way with the club, and he knocked on the rocky wall with it. Then, came one so full of sparks that they flew out of his eyes and his nose. "What do you want?" he growled.

"I am here on the giant's behalf, and demand the tax for him."

"How much are you to take?" said the other.

"I ask for no more than I am able to carry with me," said the prince.

"It is well for you that you have not asked for a horse load," said the fire-sparking being. "Come with me."

The prince followed him into the mountain, and what a treasure he saw! Gold and silver were lying inside the mountain like heaps of stones. He got a load that was as large as he was able to carry, and with that he went his way.

In the evening, when the giant came home with the goats, the prince was in his room.

"Have you been for the tax?" the giant asked.

"Yes, that I have, master," replied the prince. "The bag of gold is standing there on the bench."

The bag was so full that gold and silver dropped out when the giant untied the string.

"You certainly have been talking with my master-maid!" snarled the giant, "and if you have I will wring your neck."

"Master-maid," said the prince. "Yesterday, my master talked about this master-maid. Today, he is talking about her again. And the first day of all, it was talk of the same kind. I do wish I could see the thing myself."

"Yes, yes, wait until tomorrow," said the giant, "and then I myself will take you to her."

The next day, the giant took the prince to the master-maid. He instructed the master-maid, "Now, you shall kill him and boil him in the great big cauldron, and when you have the broth ready give me a call," said the giant.

Then, the giant lay down on the bench to sleep. Almost immediately, he began to snore so that it sounded like thunder among the hills.

The master-maid took a knife, and cut the prince's little finger, and dropped three drops of blood upon a wooden stool. Then, she took all the rubbish she could lay her hands on and put it in the cauldron.

Then, the master-maid filled a chest with gold dust, a lump of salt, and a water flask. She also took a golden apple and two gold chickens. Then, she and the prince raced away, down to the sea, where there rested a little ship. They took it and away they sailed.

Now, when the giant had slept a good long time, he began to stretch himself on the bench on which he was lying. "Will it soon boil?" he asked.

"It is just beginning," said the first drop of blood on the stool. So the giant lay down to sleep again, and he slept for a long, long time.

Then, he began to move about a little again. "Will it soon be ready now?" he asked.

"Half done!" said the second drop of blood, and the giant lay down to sleep once more.

When he had slept again for many hours, he began to move and stretch himself. "Is it not done yet?" he asked.

"It is quite ready," said the third drop of blood.

Then, the giant sat up and rubbed his eyes. There was no one else in the room.

"Ah well, the master-maid has just gone out for a little while," thought the giant.

He took a spoon, and went off to the cauldron to have a taste. But there was nothing in it but rubbish all boiled up together.

When the giant saw this, he understood what had happened, and fell into a terrible rage. Away he went after the prince and the master-maid, so fast that the wind whistled behind him. It was not long before he came to the water, but he could not get over it.

"Well, well, I will soon find a cure for that. I have only to call my river-sucker," said the giant.

So the giant called to his river-sucker, and it came and lay down, and drank one, two, three draughts. And with that, the water in the sea fell so low that the giant saw the master-maid and the prince out on the sea in their ship.

"Now, you must throw out the lump of salt," the master-maid told the prince, and he did. It grew up into a great mountain stretching right across the sea so that the giant could not come over it, and the river-sucker could not drink any more water.

"Well, well, I will soon find a cure for that," said the giant.

So the giant called to his hill-borer to come and bore through the mountain so that the river-sucker might be able to drink up the water again.

But just as the hill-borer had made the hole and the river-sucker was beginning to drink, the master-maid told the prince to throw one or two drops out of the flask. When he did this, the sea instantly became full of water again. And before the river-sucker could take one drink, the two young people had reached the land and were safe.

They decided to go to the prince's father. But the prince thought it was too far for the master-maid to walk there.

"Wait here the least little bit of time, while I go home for two of the horses in my father's stable," he said. "It is not far off, and I shall not be long away. But I will not let my betrothed bride go on foot to the palace."

"Oh no, do not go. For if you go home, you will forget me!"

"How could I forget you? We have suffered so much evil together, and love each other so much," the prince replied.

He was so determined that at last the master-maid had to yield. "But when you get there," she said, "you must not even greet anyone, but go straight into the stable, and take the horses, and come back as quickly as you can. For they all will come round about you. But you must behave just as if you did not see them. And on no account must you taste anything. For if you do, it will cause great misery both to you and to me."

"I promise," the prince replied.

But when the prince got home to the king's palace, one of his brothers was just going to be married, and the bride and all her kith and kin had come to the palace. They all thronged around the prince, and questioned him about this and that, and wanted him to go in with them.

But he behaved as if he did not see them, and went straight to the stable, and got out the horses, and began to saddle them. When they saw that they could not get him to go in with them, they came out to him with meat and drink. But the prince refused to touch anything, and he would do nothing but saddle the horses as quickly as he could.

At last, however, the bride's sister rolled an apple across the yard to him, and said, "As you will not eat anything else, at least take a bite of that, for you must be both hungry and thirsty after your long journey."

Without thinking, he took up the apple and bit a piece out of it. But no sooner had he got the piece of apple in his mouth than he forgot the master-maid and that he was to go back to fetch her.

"What am I doing here with these horses?" he wondered. Putting the horses back in their stalls, he went into the palace. There, it was settled by the king that the prince should marry the bride's sister, she who had rolled the apple to him.

The master-maid sat waiting for the prince for a long time, but no prince came. So she started forward alone. When she had walked a short distance, she came to a little hut that stood all alone in a small wood, hard by the king's palace.

"May I stay here for a while?" she asked the old crone who lived there.

Now, the old crone was an ill-tempered and malicious troll. At first, she said, "No. Again, no."

But finally, the master-maid coaxed the old crone into saying, "Very well, yes. For now." She was thinking as a troll thinks, that this human looked nice and tasty.

The hut was as dirty and black inside as a pigsty, so the master-maid said, "I will smarten this up a little so that it will look a little more like what other people's houses look inside."

"Humph," the old crone said.

But the master-maid ignored that. She took out her chest of gold and flung a handful of it into the fire. And the gold boiled up and poured out over the whole of the hut, until every part of it, both inside and out, was gilded.

When the gold began to bubble up, the old crone fled as if the Evil One himself were pursuing her. She ran straight into a tree, hit her head, and died on the spot.

The next morning, the sheriff came traveling by there. He was astonished to see the gold hut shining and glittering. He was still more astonished when he caught sight of the beautiful young maiden. The sheriff fell in love with her at once, and, on the spot, he begged her to marry him. He would not listen to her say no, and he would not go away.

But then the master-maid cried, "I have forgotten to see to the fire."

"Why should you do that?" asked the sheriff. "I will do that!" So he went to the chimney in one bound.

"Just tell me when you have got hold of the shovel," said the master-maid.

"I have hold of it now," said the sheriff.

"Then you may hold the shovel, and the shovel you, until day dawns," said the master-maid.

So the sheriff had to stand there the whole night. When the day began to dawn, and he had power to throw down the shovel, the sheriff ran away as fast as he possibly could.

The next day, an attorney passed by and saw how brightly the hut shone and gleamed through the wood. He too, went to see who lived there. And when he entered and saw the beautiful young maiden, he fell even more in love with her than the sheriff had done, and he began to woo her at once. The attorney, too, would not listen to her say no, and he, too, would not go away.

But suddenly the master-maid cried, "I have forgotten to lock the back door!"

"Why should you do that?" asked the attorney. "I will do it."

"Tell me when you have got hold of the door latch," said the master-maid.

"I have hold of it now," cried the attorney.

"Then you may hold the door, and the door you, until day dawns."

At first, the attorney began to abuse the master-maid, and then to beg and pray. But the door did not care for anything but keeping the attorney where he was until break of day. As soon as the door let go its hold of him, the attorney ran away.

On the third day, the bailiff came by. He, too, saw the gold house in the little wood, and he, too, felt that he must go and see who lived there. When he caught sight of the master-maid, he became so much in love with her that he wooed her almost before he greeted her. The bailiff, too, would not listen to her say no, and he, too, would not go away.

But suddenly the master-maid cried, "I have forgotten to bring in the calf!"

"No, indeed, you shall not do that," said the bailiff. "I am the one to do that."

"Tell me when you have got hold of the calf's tail," said the master-maid.

"I have hold of it now," cried the bailiff.

"Then, may you hold the calf's tail, and the calf's tail hold you, until day dawns," said the master-maid.

So the bailiff had to bestir himself, for the calf would not stand still all night. When daylight began to appear, the bailiff was so glad to leave loose of the calf's tail that he left on the spot, though he was too tired to run.

On the following day, the wedding was to take place in the king's palace. The elder brother was to drive to church with his bride, and the brother who had been with the giant was to accompany her sister, who was to be his bride.

But when they had seated themselves in the coach and were about to drive off from the palace, one of the trace pins broke. And, though they made one, two, and three to put in its place, each trace pin broke in turn, no matter what kind of wood they used to make them. This went on for a long time, and they could not get away from the palace, so they were all in great trouble.

Then, the sheriff, who also had been invited to the wedding, said, "In that wood lives a maiden. And if you can get her to lend you the handle of the shovel that she uses to make up her fire, I know very well that it will hold fast."

So they sent off a messenger to the maiden who begged so prettily that they might have the loan of her shovel handle that they were not refused. Now, they had a trace pin that would not snap in two.

Then, the bottom of the coach fell into pieces. They made a new bottom as fast as they could. But, no matter how they nailed it together or what kind of wood they used, no sooner had they got the new bottom into the coach, than it broke again.

Then, the attorney, another guest at the wedding, said, "That same maiden has a remarkably strong door. And if she lends even half of it to you, I am certain that it will hold together."

So again they sent a messenger to the maiden, who begged so prettily for the loan of the porch door of which the attorney had told them that they got it at once. Now they had a bottom for their coach that would not break into pieces.

They were just setting out again, but now the horses seemed unable to draw the coach. They had six horses already. Now, they put in eight, and then ten, and then twelve. But the more horses they put in, the less good it did. The coach never stirred from the spot. It already was late in the day, and to church they must and would go, so everyone was in a state of distress.

Then, the bailiff said, "That same maiden has an amazingly strong calf. It could certainly pull the coach."

So off the messenger went again, this time asking for the loan of the calf. The master-maid let him take it.

They harnessed the calf to see if the coach would move. Move it did. Away they sped, over rough and smooth, over stock and stone, sometimes on the ground, and sometimes in the air. When they came to the church, the coach spun like a spinning wheel, and everyone just barely managed to get out alive. When they got back in again, the coach went quicker still, so that they barely knew how they got back to the palace.

When they were seating themselves at the table for the wedding feast, the youngest prince said, "I think we should have invited the maiden who lent us the shovel handle, the door, and the calf. Without them, we should never have got away from the palace."

The king agreed. And so he sent a royal escort to greet the maiden and invite her to the palace.

"Greet the king, and tell him that, if he is too good to come to me, I am too good to come to him," replied the master-maid.

So the king had to go himself. And the master-maid went with him immediately. As the king believed that the maiden was more than she appeared to be, he seated her in the place of honor by the youngest bridegroom.

When they had sat at the table for a short time, the master-maid took out the cock and the hen, and the golden apple that she had brought away with her from the giant's house, and set them on the table in front of her. Instantly, the cock and the hen began to fight for the golden apple.

"Oh! Look how those two there are fighting for the golden apple," cried the prince.

"Yes, and so did we fight to get out of the mountain," said the master-maid.

In that instant, the prince knew her again, and he gave a great cry of joy. The one who had rolled the apple to him turned out to be a troll, and she was put to death.

Now, there was a truly joyous wedding. And, weary though they were, the sheriff, the attorney, and the bailiff kept celebrating, too.

Sources

Asbjornsen, Peter Christen, and Jorgen Engebretsen Moe. *East o' the Sun and West o' the Moon.* Trans. George Webbe Dasent. New York: Dover, 1970.

Kvideland, Reimund, and Henning K. Sehmsdorf, eds. *Scandinavian Folk Belief and Legend.* Minneapolis: University of Minnesota Press, 1988.

The Grateful Prince: A Folktale from Estonia

This folktale begins with a familiar theme, that of the man who promises to a stranger (a spirit or demon in most versions) the first living thing that greets him, thinking he can always give up a dog—then being met first by his son, who he must send away. The folktale then follows the more familiar transformation chase story, when the young hero and heroine are united and flee together.

Once upon a time, the king of the Golden Land lost his way in a forest and could not find his way out.

At last, he came across a stranger, who asked, "What are you doing here, my friend, in this gloomy forest?"

The king replied, "I have lost my way and am trying to find the road home."

The stranger smiled. "If you will promise to give me the first living thing that meets you when you return to your palace, I will show you the right way."

The king said, "Why should I run the risk of losing my good hunting dog? I can find my way home by myself."

The stranger shrugged and went away. But the king wandered about in the woods until his provisions were exhausted, amd he was unable to discover the least trace of the right path.

Then, the king met the stranger met a second time. The stranger said, "Promise me the first living thing that meets you on your return to your palace, and I will show you the right way."

But the king stubbornly refused to promise anything yet. He once more explored the forest backwards and forwards, seeking the right path. At length, he sank down exhausted under a tree, sure he would die in that place.

Then, the stranger, who was none other than the Old Boy, the Devil, himself, appeared to the king for the third time. "Do not be a fool. How can you be so fond of your dog that you are unwilling to part with him to save your life? Only promise me what I require, and your life will be saved."

"My life is worth more than 1,000 dogs," the king agreed. "The welfare of a whole country and people is at stake. I will grant your request, if you will only take me home."

No sooner had the king said that than he found himself on the edge of the forest, and he could see his palace. He hurried there. But the first thing to meet him at the gate was not a hound, but the nurse with his son, who stretched out his arms to the king.

After his first horror passed, the king exchanged his son for the daughter of a peasant. The little boy was raised in the home of the poor people, while the little girl slept in the royal cradle.

In a year's time, the Old Boy appeared and demanded his due, and he took the little girl with him. The king rejoiced and ordered a great feast. He saw that the prince and his foster parents wanted for nothing. But he did not dare bring the boy home yet, not while the deception might yet be discovered.

In the meantime, the prince grew up to boyhood, and he finally learned of how he had been switched with a girl baby. He could not stop thinking about how an innocent girl was suffering the consequences of his father's thoughtlessness in his place. At last, he disguised himself as a peasant boy and entered the forest.

Now, he started crying, "Oh what an unfortunate boy I am! Who will show me the way out of this wood? I see no human soul anywhere!"

Sure enough, here came the stranger. "I know this forest well, and can direct you anywhere you please, if you will promise me a good return."

"What can I promise you?" the prince cried. "I have nothing but my life. My parents are dead, and even my clothing belongs to my master."

"Well now," said the stranger with a grin, "since you have no real ties, why not enter my service? I happen to be in need of a handy workman for my small household, and I have taken a fancy to you. You shall have fresh food every day, meat twice a week, and when you work out of doors, butter or herrings as a treat. And I will give you a full suit of summer and winter clothing, besides two acres of land for your own use."

"That will suit me," said the crafty prince. "I will go with you."

The Old Boy seemed well pleased at having made such a good deal. He started off on the road with his new servant without observing that his companion dropped a pea from his pocket at every ten or fifteen paces.

The sun was high in the heavens when they reached a large stone. Here, the Old Boy stopped, looked sharply round on all sides, whistled loudly, and then stamped on the ground three times with his left foot. A secret door opened under the stone and revealed an entrance into darkness.

The Old Boy seized the prince's arm, and said roughly, "Follow me!"

They were in utter darkness, on a path that led deeper and deeper into the earth. After some time, there was a glimmer of light, and then they seemed to be in another land.

But when the prince looked around, he could find neither sun nor sky, only a mass of shining clouds overhead in this eerie new world. There was land and water, trees and plants, animals and birds. But nothing seemed quite the same as anything he had seen before.

But what seemed strangest was the silence. When a bird sang, there was no sound. When a dog barked, there was no sound. The Old Boy did not speak a word, and when the prince tried to speak, he felt his voice die away in his throat.

Then suddenly, wonderfully, there was sound again, as the Old Boy said, "They are expecting us at home." The prince heard what sounded like a sawmill at work, but the Old Boy merely said, "My old grandmother is fast asleep and snoring."

They reached a vast homestead with many outbuildings. There was an empty dog kennel at the gate.

"Creep in there," said the Old Boy, "and lie quiet until I have spoken to my grandmother about you. She is very self-willed, like most old people, and cannot bear a stranger in the house."

The prince crept into the dog kennel. After a while, the Old Boy called him out of it and said, "Take good note of the arrangements of our household. And be careful not to go against them, or you might fare very badly":

> Keep your eyes and ears both open,
> But your mouth fast closed,
> And obey without a question.
> Think whatever pleases you;
> Never speak without permission.

When the prince crossed the threshold, he saw a beautiful maiden, and he thought, "If he has many such daughters as this, I should be glad to become his son-in-law. The maiden is just to my taste."

The fair maiden laid the table without saying a word, set the food upon it, and then modestly took her place by the hearth. She took out needles and worsted, and began to knit a stocking.

The master sat down alone at the table. He did not ask either the prince or the maid to join him, nor was anything to be seen of the old grandmother. The Old Boy's appetite was amazing. In a short time, he had made a clean sweep of everything on the table, though it would have been plenty for at least a dozen people.

When at last he was done, the master said to the maiden, "Scrape out what is left at the bottom of the pot and kettle, and you and the new servant content yourselves with the fragments. But throw the bones to the dog."

The prince was disheartened at the thought of such a meal, but he soon found that there was quite a nice meal still to be had from the scrapings. During supper, he stole many glances at the maiden. But whenever he was about to speak, he met her imploring glance, warning him to silence.

So the prince allowed his eyes to speak, and he gave expression to this dumb language by his good appetite. For the maiden had prepared the supper, and it must be pleasant to her to see that the prince appreciated her cookery.

After supper, the Old Boy told the prince, "You may rest for two days after your long journey and look around the house. But come to me tomorrow evening, and I will arrange your work for the next day. For those in my household always must set about their work before I get up myself. The maiden will show you your lodging."

The prince opened his mouth to answer. But the Old Boy shouted, "If you break the house rules, you will find yourself a head shorter! Hold your jaw and off to bed with you!"

The maiden beckoned the prince to follow, unlocked a door, and signed to him to enter. The prince thought he saw a tear glisten in her eye. He would have been only too glad to comfort her, but he knew it was not time to break any rules.

"This cannot be his daughter," he thought. "No, this kind, lovely girl must be the one who was brought here in my place and for whose sake I undertook this foolhardy enterprise."

The prince did not fall asleep for a long time. When he did, he dreamed of all sorts of unknown dangers. But it was always the lovely maiden who came to his aid.

When the prince awoke the next morning, he found the maiden already at work. He helped her to draw water from the well and carry it into the house. He chopped wood, kept up the fire under the pots, and helped her in all her work.

In the afternoon, the prince went out to look around, and was much surprised that he could find no trace of the old grandmother. He saw a white mare in the stable and a black cow with a white-headed calf in the enclosure. And in other locked outhouses, he thought he heard ducks, geese, and other fowl.

That day, the meals were just as good as the previous night's supper. He would have been very content with his position, except that it was so very hard to hold his tongue with the maiden opposite him.

On the evening of the second day, the prince went to the master to receive his instructions for the next day's work. The Old Boy said, "I will give you an easy job for tomorrow. Take the scythe and mow as much grass as the white mare needs for her day's provender and clean out the stable. But if I should find the manger empty or any litter on the floor, it will go badly with you."

The prince thought, "I shall soon be able to manage this work." He had never handled a plow or scythe before, but he had been curious enough to watch how the country folk managed those tools. "And I am quite strong enough."

But when the prince was about to go to bed, the maiden whispered to him, "What work has he given you?"

"I have an easy task for tomorrow," answered the prince. "I have only to mow grass for the white mare, and then clean out the stable."

"Oh, no!" the maiden said, "The white mare is the master's grandmother, and she is an insatiable creature, for whom twenty mowers could hardly provide the daily fodder. And another twenty would have to work from morning until night to clear the litter from the stable.

"Take my advice and follow it exactly. When you have thrown a few loads of grass to the mare, you must plait a strong rope of willow twigs in her sight. She will ask you what this is for, and you must answer, 'To bind you up so tightly that you will not feel disposed to eat more than I give you, or to litter the stable after I have cleared it.' "

The maiden hurried away without giving the prince time to thank her. He repeated her instructions to himself several times, and then he went to sleep.

Early next morning, the prince set to work. He plied the scythe lustily and soon had so much grass that he could rake several loads together. He took one load to the mare. But when he returned with the second, he found with dismay that the manger was already empty, and there was half a ton of litter on the floor. The prince saw now that he would have been lost without the maiden's good advice, so he began to plait the rope of willow twigs.

Seeing him do this, the mare asked in astonishment, "My dear son, what do you want with this rope?"

"Oh nothing at all," he answered. "I am only going to bind you up so tightly that you will not eat more than I choose to give you or drop more litter than I choose to carry away."

The white mare sighed deeply. But it was clear that she understood him, for long after midday, there was still fodder in the manger and the floor remained clean.

Presently, the master came to inspect the work. When he found everything in good order, he was surprised, and asked, "Are you clever enough to do this yourself, or did anyone give you good advice?"

But the prince was on his guard, and he answered, "I have no one to help me but my own poor head and a mighty God in heaven."

The Old Boy was silenced, and he left the stable grumbling. But the prince was delighted that everything had gone so well.

In the evening, the master said, "Tomorrow, as the maiden has plenty to do in the house, you must milk the black cow. But take care not to leave a drop of milk in the udder. If I find that you have done so, it might cost you your life."

As the prince went away, he thought, "If there is not some trick in this, I cannot find the work hard."

But when the prince was about to go to bed, the maiden whispered to him, "What work do you have to do tomorrow?"

"I have a whole holiday tomorrow," answered the prince. "All I have to do tomorrow is to milk the black cow and not leave a drop of milk in the udder."

"Oh, no!" she said with a sigh. "Know, dear young stranger, that if you were to milk the black cow from morning until evening, the milk would continue to flow in one unbroken stream. I am convinced that the old man is bent on your ruin. But fear nothing, for as long as I am alive, no harm shall happen to you, if you will remember my advice, and follow it exactly."

"When you go milking, take a pan full of hot coals and a smith's tongs with you. When you reach the place, put the tongs in the fire and blow the coals to a bright flame. If the black cow asks what this is for, answer her as I am about to whisper in your ear."

Then, the maiden crept away, and the prince lay down to sleep.

The prince got up almost before dawn the next day. He went to the cow house with the milk pail in one hand and a pan of live coals along with a smith's tongs in the other.

The black cow asked, "What are you doing, my dear son?"

"Nothing at all," he replied. "But some cows have a bad habit of keeping back milk in their udders after they are milked. In such cases, I find hot tongs useful to prevent the chance of any waste."

The black cow sighed deeply. The prince then took the pail, milked the cow dry, and when he tried again after a while, he found not a drop of milk in her udder.

Some time after, the master came into the cow house. As he also was unable to draw a drop of milk from the black cow, he asked angrily, "Are you so clever yourself, or did anyone give you good advice?"

But the prince answered as before, "I have no one to help me but my own poor head and a mighty God in heaven."

The Old Boy went off in great vexation.

When the prince went to the master in the evening, the latter said, "There is still a heap of hay in the field that I should like under cover during dry weather. Bring the hay home tomorrow, but take care not to leave a particle behind, or it might cost you your life."

The prince left the room well pleased, thinking, "It is no great job to bring hay home. I have only to load it, and the mare must draw it. I will not spare the master's grandmother."

But when the prince was about to go to bed, the maiden asked in a whisper what his work was for the morrow. The prince said smiling, "I am learning all sorts of farm work here. I have to bring home a heap of hay tomorrow and take care not to leave a scrap behind."

"Oh, no!" she sighed. "If you were to set to work for a week, with the help of all the inhabitants of a large district, you could not remove this heap. Whatever you took away from the top would grow up again from the ground directly. Mark well what I say."

"You must get up tomorrow before daybreak and lead the white mare from the stable, taking with you some strong cords. Then, go to the haycock, fasten the cords round it, and bind them to the mare. When this is done, climb on the haycock, and begin to count one, two, three, four, five, six, and so on. The mare will ask what you are counting, and you must answer her as I whisper."

Then, the maiden hurried off, and the prince went to bed.

When the prince awoke next morning, he remembered the maiden's good advice. So he took some strong ropes with him, led out the white mare, and rode her to the haycock. There, he found that the so-called haycock contained at least fifty loads. And the prince did all that the maiden had told him.

When the prince was sitting on the heap and had counted up to twenty, the white mare asked in surprise, "What are you counting, my dear son?"

"Nothing at all," said he. "I was only amusing myself by counting up the packs of wolves in the forest. But there are so many that I cannot reckon them all up."

He had hardly spoken when the white mare darted off like the wind, and the haycock was safely housed in a few moments.

The master was not a little surprised, when he came out after breakfast, to find that the new laborer already had finished his day's work. He asked the same question as before and received the same reply, and he went off, shaking his head and cursing.

In the evening, the prince went as usual to inquire about his work, and the Old Boy said, "Tomorrow, you must take the white-headed calf to pasture. But take care that he does not run away or it might cost you your life."

The prince thought, "There are many ten-year-old farm boys who have whole herds to manage, so surely I cannot find it so very difficult to look after one calf."

But when the prince was about to go to bed the maiden came to him and whispered, "This calf is so wild that he would run three times round the world in a day. Take this silk thread and bind one end to the left foreleg of the calf and the other to the little toe of your left foot. And then the calf will not be able to stir a step from your side, whether you are walking, standing, or lying down."

Then she left him, and the prince lay down to sleep. But it vexed him to think that he had again missed the chance to thank her for her good advice.

The next morning, the prince followed the maiden's advice and led the calf to the pasture by the silken thread. The calf remained peacefully by his side, and, in the evening, he led it back to the stall.

There, the Old Boy met him angrily and, after the usual question and answer, went off in a fury. The prince thought it must be the mention of the holy name that kept him under restraint.

Late in the evening, the Old Boy gave the prince a bag of barley and said, "I will give you a holiday tomorrow, and you may sleep as long as you like. But you must work hard tonight instead. Sow me this barley, which will spring up and ripen quickly; then you must cut it, thresh it, and winnow it, so that you can malt it and grind it. You must brew beer of this malt, and when I wake tomorrow morning, you must bring me a jug of fresh beer for my morning drink. Take care to follow my instructions exactly or it might easily cost you your life."

This time, the prince thought he could not possibly escape death. He whispered to the maiden, "Alas, my last hour has come, and we must part forever. I am the only son of a great king, but now all hope and happiness are at an end." He told the maiden what task the Old Boy had given him, and he was startled to see her smile.

"My dear prince," she said, "you may sleep quietly tonight and enjoy yourself all day tomorrow. Take this little key, which unlocks the third henhouse, where the Old Boy keeps the spirits who serve him. Throw the bag of barley into the house and repeat word for word the commands that you have received from the master. Then add, 'If you depart a hair's breadth from my instructions, you will all perish together. But if you want help, the door of the seventh pen will be open tonight, in which dwell the most powerful of the old man's spirits.'"

The prince carried out all her instructions, and then he lay down to sleep.

When the prince awoke in the morning and went to the beer tub, he found it full of beer. He filled a large jug with the foaming drink and brought it to his master.

But instead of thanks, the Old Boy shouted in fury, "That is not from you. I see you have good friends and helpers. All right! We will talk again this evening."

In the evening, the Old Boy said, "I have no work for you tomorrow, but you must come to my bedside tomorrow morning and shake hands with me."

The prince was amused at the Old Boy's queer whim, and he laughed when he told the maiden of it.

But when she heard it, she said urgently, "Now, you must look to yourself, for the old man intends to eat you tomorrow morning, and there is only one way of escape. Heat a shovel red hot in the stove and offer it to him instead of your own hand."

Then, she hastened away, and the prince went to bed.

The next morning, the prince took good care to heat the shovel red hot before the old man awoke. At last, he heard him shouting, "What has become of you, you lazy fellow? Come and shake hands with me."

But when the prince entered the room with the red-hot shovel in his hand, the old man cried out with a whining voice, "I am very ill today, and cannot take your hand. But come back this evening to receive my orders."

The prince loitered about all day, and he went to the Old Boy in the evening and found him very friendly. The Old Boy said, "I am well pleased with you. Come to me tomorrow morning with the maiden. For I know that you have long been attached to each other, and I will give her to you as your bride."

The prince would have liked to shout for joy. But by good luck, he remembered the strict rules of the house and kept silent.

But when he spoke to his new betrothed of their good fortune, he saw the maiden turn as white as the wall with terror. She gasped, "The Old Boy has discovered that I have been helping you, and he means to destroy us both. We must fly this very night, or we are lost."

"Take an axe, and strike off the head of the white-headed calf, then split the skull in two with a second stroke. In the brain of the calf, you will find a shining red reel, which you must bring me. I will arrange whatever else is needful."

The prince hesitated for a second, then thought, "I would rather kill an innocent calf than both myself and this dear girl. The peas I sowed must have sprung up by this time, so that we cannot miss our way."

He found the cow and the calf lying asleep near together. When he struck off the calf's head, the cow groaned aloud, as if she had had a bad dream. He hurried to split the calf's skull with the second blow, and the red reel fell out of its brain, shining like a little sun. The prince wrapped it carefully in a cloth and hid it in his tunic.

The prince found the maiden waiting for him at the gate with a small bundle on her arm. He gave her the reel, and she said, "Now, we must hurry."

The maiden unraveled a tiny piece of cloth from the reel, and its light lit up the darkness like a lantern. As the prince had expected, the peas had all sprung up, their leaves different from wild forest plants, so that they could not miss the way.

As the prince and the maiden hurried along, she told him that she had once overheard the Old Boy say to his grandmother that she was a princess whom the Old Boy had stolen from her parents by a trick. The prince knew the real story, but he kept silence, rejoicing that he had succeeded in freeing the maiden.

Meanwhile, the Old Boy had discovered that the two were missing, and he searched everywhere for them. Then, he found the dead calf and knew what had happened. He flung open a spirit house and shouted, "Bring them back to me just as you find them!"

The spirits flew forth like the wind.

The fugitives were crossing a wide meadow, when the maiden suddenly cried, "The reel moves in my hand—we are being pursued!"

When they looked back, they saw a black cloud rushing toward them with great speed. Then, the maiden turned the reel thrice in her hand and said:

> Hear me, reel, and reel,
> Oh, hear me.
> I would become a brook,
> And my love a fish swimming in it.

Instantly, the prince and the maiden were both transformed. The maiden flowed away like a brook, and the prince swam in the water like a little fish. The spirits rushed past, then turned after a time and flew back home. But they did not touch the brook or the fish.

As soon as the pursuers were gone, the brook became a maiden and the fish a young man. And they continued their journey in human form.

When the spirits returned, weary and empty-handed, the Old Boy asked if they had not noticed anything unusual on their journey.

"Nothing at all," they answered, "but a brook in a meadow, with a single fish swimming in it."

"That was them! That was them!" the Old Boy shouted. He let out more spirits and told them to drink up the brook and capture the fish. The spirits flew off like the wind.

The fugitives were just approaching the far edge of the meadow, back into forest, when the maiden cried, "The reel moves again in my hand."

They looked around and saw another cloud in the sky, darker than the first, with eerie red borders.

"These are our pursuers," the maiden cried, and turned the reel three times round in her hand, saying:

Hear me, reel, and reel,
Oh, hear me.
Change me to a wild rose briar,
And my love a rose upon it.

Instantly, the maiden was changed into a wild rosebush, and the prince hung upon it in the form of a rose. The spirits rushed away over their heads and did not return for some time. But they saw nothing of the brook and the fish, and they did not trouble about the wild rosebush.

As soon as their pursuers were gone, the rosebush and the rose again became a maiden and a prince. And they hurried away.

"Have you found them?" the Old Boy cried when the spirits returned and crouched before him.

"No," answered their leader; "we found neither brook nor fish on the plain."

"Did you see nothing else remarkable on the way?" the Old Boy asked.

"We saw nothing but a wild rosebush on the edge of the wood, with a single rose upon it."

"Fools!" cried the Old Boy "There they were! There they were!"

He sent out his most powerful spirits to search for the fugitives. "Bring them to me just as you find them, for I must have them, dead or alive. Tear up the accursed rosebush by the roots and bring everything else with you that looks strange."

And the spirits rushed forth like a tempest.

The fugitives were resting in the shade of a tree, when the maiden cried out, "We are being pursued, and the danger is close at hand, but the wood still hides us from our enemies."

Then, she turned the reel over three times in her hand, saying:

Hear me reel, and reel,
Oh, hear me.
To a puff of wind transform me,
To a gnat transform my love.

Instantly, they were both transformed. The maiden rose into the air as a puff of wind, and the prince sported in the breeze like a gnat. The mighty host of spirits swept over them like a tempest and returned some time afterwards, as they could find neither the rosebush nor anything else remarkable.

But the spirits were hardly gone before the youth and the maiden resumed their proper forms. And the maiden cried out, "Now we must make haste, before the Devil himself comes to look for us, for he would know us under any disguise."

They ran on for some distance, until they reached the dark passage, which they easily climbed by the light of the reel. They were breathless by the time they reached the great rock.

But the maiden again turned the reel three times round, saying:

Hear me, reel, and reel,
Oh, hear me.

> Let the rock aside be lifted,
> And for us a portal opened.

Instantly, the rock was lifted, and they found themselves once more upon mortal earth.

"God be praised," cried the maiden, "we are saved. The Old Boy has no further power over us here, and we can guard against his cunning. But now, my friend, we must part. Do you go to your parents, and I will go to mine."

"By no means," replied the prince, "I cannot part from you, and you must come with me and become my wife. You have passed days of sorrow with me, and now it is only right that we should enjoy days of happiness together."

The maiden used the magic reel to provide them both with suitable clothing. But as they neared the palace, they learned that the king had died, repenting bitterly of his thoughtless promise and of his treachery in delivering a poor innocent maiden to the old rascal, for which God had punished him by the loss of his son.

The prince and maiden both mourned the king's death, and they saw that he was buried with great honors. For, the prince whispered to the maiden, had it not been for that trickery, they never would have met and fallen in love. Then, as was proper, he and she mourned separately for three days of fasting.

On the fourth day, the prince presented himself to the people as their new ruler. Then, he assembled his councilors and told them all that had befallen him—and did not forget to say how the clever maiden had saved his life. Then, the councilors all exclaimed with one voice, "She must become your consort and our queen."

With that, the maiden entered, dressed in the regal robes the reel had provided. All the people supposed that she must be the daughter of some very wealthy king from a distant country, and neither the new king nor his new queen told them anything else.

Then, the wedding festivities began and lasted four weeks. The new king and queen lived together in happiness and prosperity. And since they used the magic reel only to help the people, everyone lived for many a pleasant year.

Sources

Kirby, W.F. *The Hero of Esthonia and Other Studies in the Romantic Literature of that Country.* London: John C. Ninmo, 1895.

Zheleznova, Irina, ed. and trans. *Estonian Fairy Tales.* Tallinn: Perioodika, 1981.

The Obstacle Flight: A Folktale from the Native Peoples of Alabama

> This variant on the transformation chase has no romantic interest. Instead, the story focuses on the female protagonist and the monster's wife, who helps the heroine escape through various transformations.

Big Man-eater was a monstrous being who lived with his wife on the other side of the ocean from where humans were. But when he grew hungry for human flesh, Big Man-eater got into his canoe and came across.

Once, when Big Man-eater had reached the human side, a young girl who lived with her three brothers went out for water. When she reached the water, Big Man-eater was there in his canoe, and he had with him some pretty little puppies.

"Come here and look at them," he said. But when the girl got into the canoe, he put out to sea with her and brought her to his wife.

The next day, Big Man-eater went hunting all day, but he came home without having killed anything. He said to the girl, "Cut off a piece of your body and roast it for me."

But instead, his wife slipped the girl a piece of non-human flesh. The girl roasted it and gave it to Big Man-eater, and he ate. The same thing happened the next day.

On the following day, when Big Man-eater went hunting again, his wife said to the girl, "We can only put him off so long. If you stay here, he will devour you. Run away. Run along upon this good trail and return, and then run along upon this other good trail and return."

When the girl returned, the woman gave her a huckleberry, a blackberry, and a piece of sugar cane, plus some mud. "Run along upon this old trail," she told the girl. "When he has nearly come up to you, throw down a huckleberry and go on. The next time he has almost caught you, throw down a blackberry and go on. Then, throw down the sugar cane. After that, throw down the mud and go on."

Big Man-eater came back before it was late, and he called out "Girl!"

He could not find the girl. He asked his wife, but she said, "I cannot see at all. She is somewhere about."

Then, Big Man-eater said, "She has run away from me."

He hunted for his chunk stone, a magical stone that could track people. Not finding the stone, he asked his wife, "Where did you put that thing?"

"I cannot see at all," she answered.

Then, Big Man-eater hunted for the magical stone all over until he found it under the bed. He placed it on one of the good trails. It ran off out of sight, and he followed it. But because the girl had run back and forth, the stone went back and forth, too. Only when Big Man-eater put it on an old trail did it run off in the right direction.

Meanwhile, the girl threw down a huckleberry, and a whole wall of huckleberry plants sprang up. Big Man-eater came to them and started eating the berries.

"No, no, I must run on."

But the girl had thrown down a blueberry, and now there were thickets of blueberry bushes. Big Man-eater came to them and started eating the berries.

"No, no, I must run on."

But the girl had thrown down the sugar cane, and now there was a whole canebrake. Big Man-eater reached the canebrake. This time, he followed the chunk stone around the canebrake, then ran on.

When Big Man-eater had nearly overtaken the girl, she cried out, "Elder brothers, elder brothers, I am nearly caught!"

Her three brothers heard her and, taking their bows and arrows, went to meet her. They shot Big Man-eater with their arrows and finally hit his vital spots: his ankle and his head.

Big Man-eater fell down, and everyone, even the girl, hit him until he was dead. Then, they burned the monster's body until nothing was left but ashes. These became blackbirds and bees, and flew away.

Source
Swanton, John R. *Myths and Tales of the Southeastern Indians.* Bureau of American Ethnology Bulletin no. 88. Washington, DC: Smithsonian Institution, 1929.

The Girl and the Evil Spirit: A Folktale from the Tundra Yukaghir of Siberia

Here is a transformation chase with a twist: What seems like an evil spirit turns out to be a good spirit, a young man spirit, and the tale ends with a romantic ending.

There lived a girl who had no man and no parents, but she was rich in reindeer and other property.

So she walked about, singing magic songs. When her reindeer strayed too far, she would merely sing for them, and they would come back. She would sing, and when she came back to her home, she would find the fire burning, the food cooked, and everything ready. Thus, she lived on without work, care, or trouble.

One day, the girl saw that half the sky was darkened, and the darkness was racing nearer and nearer. It was an evil spirit. One of his lips touched the sky, the other dragged along the ground. Between was an open mouth, ready to swallow up whatever came in its way.

"Ah!" said the girl, "my death is coming. What shall I do?"

She took her iron-tipped staff and fled.

The evil spirit gave chase. He was gaining on her. She pulled out a small ivory comb from her pocket and threw it back over her shoulder. The comb turned into a dense forest. The girl ran onward.

When the evil spirit reached the forest, he swallowed it, chewed it, and gulped it down. He digested it and then defecated. The dense forest turned again into a small ivory comb.

After that, the evil spirit continued his pursuit. He was gaining on the girl, as before. She loosened from her waist a red handkerchief, which became a fire extending from heaven to earth.

The evil spirit reached the fire. He went to a river and drank it completely dry. Then he came back to the fire and poured the water upon it. The fire was extinguished. Only a red handkerchief lay on the ground, quite small and dripping wet.

After that, the evil spirit gave chase again. He gained steadily on the girl. She struck the ground with her iron-tipped staff, and, all at once, she turned into an arctic fox. In this form, she sped on, swifter than ever. The big mouth, however, followed after, wide open, and ready to swallow her.

The girl struck the ground with her iron-tipped staff, turned into a wolverine and fled swifter than ever.

But the evil mouth followed after.

She struck the ground with her iron-tipped staff, and turned into a wolf and sped away swifter than ever. But the evil mouth followed her.

She struck the ground with her iron-pointed staff, and turned into a bear, with a copper bell in each ear. She ran off swifter than ever.

But the big mouth followed and gained on her steadily.

Finally, the big mouth came very near, and it was going to swallow her.

Then, the girl saw a tent covered with white skins. She summoned all her strength and rushed on toward that tent. She stumbled at the entrance and fell down, exhausted and senseless.

After a while, the girl came to herself and looked about. On each side of her stood a young man, their caps adorned with large silver plates. She looked backward and saw the evil spirit had turned into a handsome youth, fairer than the sun. He was combing and parting his hair, making it smooth and fine. The girl rose to her feet.

The three young men came to the girl and asked her to enter the tent. The one who had appeared in the form of the evil spirit said, "We are three brothers, and I am the eldest one. I wanted to bring you to my tent. Now, you must tell us which of us you will choose for your husband."

She chose the eldest, and married him, and they lived together. The end.

Source

Bogoras, Waldemar. *Tales of Yukaghir, Lamut, and Russianized Natives of Eastern Siberia.* Anthropological Papers of the American Museum of Natural History, Vol. 20, part 1. New York: Trustees of the American Museum of Natural History, 1918. Collected from John Korkin, a Tundra Yukaghir man, on the western tundra of the Kolyma, spring 1985.

Fundevogel (Foundling Bird): A Folktale from Germany

In this odd folktale, it is a boy and a girl who escape a cannibal cook through their ability—which is never explained—to change shape.

Once, a forester went into the forest to hunt when he heard the crying of a baby—and the sound was coming from the top of a tree.

Sure enough, there was a little boy up there. Clearly, some large bird of prey had carried the child off and then left him there.

The forester rescued the child and took him home to be a brother to his little girl, Lina. He called the foundling Fundevogel, or Foundling Bird. The children grew up together, and they loved each other dearly.

The forester, however, had an old cook. One evening, the cook took two pails and began to fetch water, and did not go once only, but many times, out to the spring.

Lina saw this and asked, "Why are you fetching so much water?"

The cook said, "Early tomorrow morning, when the forester is out hunting, I will heat the water, throw in Fundevogel, and boil him in it."

The next morning, the forester went out hunting. When he was gone Lina said to Fundevogel, "The cook is planning to fill the kettle with hot water, throw you into it, and boil you. Let us go away together."

When the water in the kettle was boiling, the cook went into the bedroom to fetch Fundevogel. But both the children were gone. Alarmed, the cook said, "What happens when the forester comes home and sees that the children are gone? They must be followed instantly to get them back again."

Then, the cook sent three servants after the children to catch them. The children, however, were sitting just outside the forest, and they saw the three servants running.

Lina said to Fundevogel, "Never leave me, and I will never leave thee."

Fundevogel said, "Neither now, nor ever."

Then, said Lina, "Do thou become a rosebush, and I the rose upon it."

When the three servants came to the forest, nothing was there but a rosebush and one rose on it. But the children were nowhere to be seen.

"There is nothing to be done here," they said.

The servants went home and told the cook that they had seen nothing in the forest but a little rosebush with one rose on it.

Then, the old cook scolded and said, "You simpletons, you should have cut the rosebush in two and should have broken off the rose and brought it home with you. Go and do it at once."

They had therefore to go out and look for a second time. The children, however, saw them coming from a distance.

Lina said to Fundevogel, "Never leave me, and I will never leave thee."

Fundevogel said, "Neither now, nor ever."

Then, said Lina, "Then do thou become a church, and I will be the chandelier in it."

So when the three servants caught up, they saw nothing but a church, with a chandelier in it. They said, "What can we do here? Let us go home."

When they got home, they told the cook they had found nothing but a church with a chandelier in it.

And the cook scolded them and said, "You fools! Why did you not pull the church to pieces and bring the chandelier home with you?"

Now, the old cook got to her feet and went with the three servants in pursuit of the children. The children, however, saw from afar that the three servants were coming, with the cook waddling after them.

Lina said to Fundevogel, "Never leave me, and I will never leave thee."

Fundevogel said, "Neither now, nor ever."

Then, said Lina, "Be a fishpond, and I will be the duck upon it."

The cook, however, came up to them, and when she saw the pond, she lay down by it, and was about to drink it up. But the duck swam quickly to her and seized her head in its beak. The duck drew her into the water, and there, the old witch had to drown.

Then, the children went home together, and were heartily delighted. And if they are not dead, they are living still.

Sources

Grimm, Brothers. *The Complete Fairy Tales of the Brothers Grimm.* Trans. Jack Zipes. New York: Bantam, 1987.

Ranke, Kurt. *Folktales of Germany.* Trans. Lotte Baumann. Chicago: University of Chicago Press, 1966.

The Story of Aja: A Folktale from the Krobo of Ghana

Although this folktale does not feature an actual chase, it does feature the traditional shapeshifting duel of this tale type. It also features a test—in this case that of shooting an arrow through seven bags of sand. Such tests turn up in folktales and myths alike, for example, the test of the suitors in the Greek *Odyssey* and Rama's test in the Hindu *Ramayana*.

Once, there lived a woman named Ajanye, and her son was Aja. Aja had magical powers, including useful ones such as finding water where there seemed to be none and finding game in empty places. But Aja knew that in the forest there was an evil beast with just as much magic. It would turn into an antelope and then lure hunters to their death.

Aja was wise to that trick. He saw the antelope and shot it. But it did not die. Instead, it changed into a man, hoping to lure Aja into its grasp. But Aja knew it was still the evil beast, so he shot the man. This time, the evil beast died.

Aja cut open the evil beast and took its heart. Then, he buried the rest. He brought the heart home and told his mother that it must stay very dry. If any water touched the heart, there would be trouble.

Ajanye took good care of the heart. Each day, she put it out in the blazing sun to keep it dry. But one day, a sudden rain shower began. And before Ajanye could get to the heart, it was wet—and it was gone.

The heart was the evil beast's seat of power. Now, the heart turned into a beautiful woman and went to the village. She was so very lovely that all the men wanted to marry her.

But the beautiful woman said she wanted to be sure she picked the best man possible. She told them all that she would test them. So she got seven bags of sand and put them all together in a row. The man who could shoot one arrow through all seven bags would be the one she would marry.

All the men tried. Some shot through four bags, some shot through five, and the chief even shot through six. But no one could shoot through all seven.

Aja heard about this, and he was suspicious. He stole a hair from the woman's head and wrapped it around his arrow. And then he cast a spell.

> It should go through one.
> It should go through two.
> It should go through three.
> It should go through four.
> It should go through five.
> It should go through six.
> It should go through seven.

Aja shot, and the arrow went right through all seven bags of sand. So he won the woman.

But even as he was suspicious of her, so she was suspicious of him. This was, she realized, the man who had killed the evil beast whose heart had created her.

Aja took the woman home. But he refused to sleep in the same room with her. He waited to see what she would try.

Sure enough, while Aja pretended to sleep, the woman came into his room and transformed into a lioness. Aja turned himself into a sheet, so she thought he was not in the room.

The woman tried again the next night, appearing in his room as a venomous snake. Aja turned himself into a tiny gnat, and she failed to see him.

This went on for several nights, until Aja grew weary of the game. He went off alone, making sure that the woman heard that he was doing this.

Sure enough, the woman turned into an eagle and soared down to attack. But Aja turned into a fierce fire. The eagle plunged into it—and that was the last of the evil beast.

Today, though, it is still said that if an eagle is seen circling over a fire, that is the evil beast still hunting Aja in vain.

Source

Berry, Jack, collector and trans., and Richard Spears, ed. *West African Folk Tales*. Evanston, IL: Northwestern University Press, 1991.

The Four Sisters and the Mountain Lion: A Folktale from the Osage of the American Midwest

In this feminist folktale, four fearless and very effective sisters are the protagonists. They outwit a hungry mountain lion that chases them by using their magical abilities. This folktale fits the tale type, although in this variant, it is not the sisters, but the objects and world around them, that are transformed.

Once, there were four sisters living together. They shared the work. One did the hunting, one did the cooking, one made the large straw mats used in camp, and one made the small straw mats used in meals.

One day, the hunter went out and saw a mountain lion. In those days, the mountain lion was larger than it is today and would eat people. The hunter hurried back and told the three other sisters that it was time to change their camp. So they put deer antlers in the fire and started out.

The mountain lion came to their camp. Where were the sisters? "I should have caught them by now," he said.

He started out on their trail. But the deer antlers called, "Where are you going, old man-eater?"

The mountain lion turned back and hunted about the camp again. But all he found were the antlers.

"A trick!" he snarled.

He set out after the four sisters.

But the first sister stamped her foot, and apples appeared. The mountain lion stopped to eat them. Then, he hurried on.

But the second sister stamped her foot, and berries appeared. The mountain lion stopped to eat them. Then, he hurried on. He had nearly caught up to the sisters.

But the third sister stamped her foot, and a ravine opened up between the sisters and the mountain lion.

"Hey, you!" called the mountain lion. "How did you get across the ravine?"

"On a log," they called back.

They set a log across the ravine. The mountain lion started across it.

But the fourth sister stamped her foot, and the log snapped in half. Down fell the mountain lion. And that was the end of him.

Source
Dorsey, George A. *Traditions of the Osage*. Publication no. 88, Anthropological Series. Vol. 7, no. 1. Chicago: Field Columbian Museum, 1904.

UNDERSEA KINGDOMS: ADVENTURES IN THE LANDS UNDER THE WAVES

In folktales of this type, a human male is taken under the waves to an undersea kingdom. In some of these tales, time flows differently, and if he returns to land, the man dies of old age or illness. In other tales, the hero escapes without penalty.

In the case of Sadko, it is his marvelous music that first ensnares and then frees him. In other stories, the hero simply asks to be returned to the human world and is returned.

The Sea Nymph: A Folktale from Sweden

This is a sinister variant of the undersea kingdom folktale type. It does not have even a remotely happy ending.

One night, there was a happy gathering of fisherman celebrating the day's good catch. One of the men was newly married. But then, something eerie occurred.

A woman's beautiful, pale hand, dripping wet, reached in through the barely open door of their hut. It was the newly married man who could not resist taking that hand, even though the others shrank back from it. He instantly was dragged away into the night.

The next day, the fishermen searched everywhere for the man. But he had disappeared without leaving so much as a footprint. The incoming tide had washed away all signs of where he might have gone.

The man's sad wife waited for him for three years without a word from him or a clue as to where he had gone. After the three years, he was declared legally dead, and she agreed to marry again.

It was during the wedding ceremony that the first husband appeared again. He was clad in flowing robes and dripping wet. He told his story to the entire wedding party:

"I should never have taken that hand. But it was so beautiful that I could not help myself. I thought that I must see the woman herself. And she was beautiful, indeed. But she was never a human woman. She was a sea nymph, and she dragged me under the sea with her.

"I was sure she meant to drown me, and I held my breath for as long as I could. I could not free myself from her grip, however, and I silently said farewell to life.

"But I did not drown. She took me to the kingdom that lies under the sea, where all is strange and beautiful. I was crowned with gold and wore necklaces of pearls, and remembered nothing at all of mortal life. I would have lived there forever, becoming one of them, those sea beings. But one of them chanced to mention seeing a wedding procession in my hometown, Kinnar.

"Instantly, I remembered who and what I was. I begged to be allowed to return. I was allowed to come, though I was warned not to step inside a house. But I will risk that."

He took a daring step inside, toward his former bride.

Suddenly, a horrifying storm swept into being, and waves swept over them all, tearing down the house. When the others had cleared away the wreckage, there lay the man, dead.

Sources

Booss, Claire, ed. *Scandinavian Folk and Fairy Tales: Tales from Norway, Sweden, Denmark, Finland, Iceland*. New York: Avenel, 1984.

Hofberg, Herman. *Swedish Fairy Tales*. Trans. W.H. Myers. Chicago: W.B. Conkey, 1893.

Sadko: A Folktale from Russia

The folktale of Sadko still is very popular in Russia—there is even a Sadko Restaurant in St. Petersburg. Oddly enough, it is the only Russian folktale with a mercantile hero that was not changed or banned during the era of the Soviet Union.

In the nineteenth century, this story was put beautifully into verse by Russian poet Alexander Pushkin, and it became an opera by Nikolai Rimsky-Korsakov in 1896.

Sadko was a poor man but a wonderful musician. He played the *gusli*, a type of zither, so sweetly only the hardest of hearts would not be moved.

Unfortunately, the merchants of his home city, Novgorod, did have those hard hearts. They ignored him. Sadko often spent time by the shore of Lake Ilmen, playing his music and wondering what he could do to earn a living.

While Sadko lingered there, his music and songs charmed Volkhova, the beautiful daughter of Tzar Morskoi, the King of the Sea. Indeed, Volkhova fell in love with Sadko. It was she who whispered to him that he should make a masterful wager with the merchants that he could find a golden fish in the lake.

So Sadko wagered his life against the wealth of all the merchants' ships. The merchants thought it a fool's wager, since no one had ever seen a golden fish. But Sadko promptly scooped one out of the lake. Grudgingly, the merchants agreed that he had won.

Now a wealthy merchant himself, Sadko sailed off on his first trading voyage, leaving his dear wife, Lubava, to wait for his return. He visited much of Europe and made several successful trades. But as the ships sailed back to Russia, the wind failed.

It was then that Sadko realized that he and the sailors had not made any sacrifices to Tzar Morskoi, king of the sea. In order to save the sailors, Sadko sacrificed himself and jumped into the water.

Instantly, a brisk breeze filled the sails of the ships. They sailed away toward home.

But Sadko did not drown. Instead, he found himself easily floating down to the bottom of the sea and into the palace of Tzar Morskoi.

The tzar and his wife had heard about Sadko's music, and they wanted him to play for them. Sadko obeyed. His music so delighted them that they decided he should stay with them forever. They even offered him the hand of Princess Volkhova.

But Sadko sadly told them all that he could not stay and marry the sea princess. He still loved his human wife, Lubava.

There are two different endings to the folktale, neither one is right nor wrong.

The first ending: A mysterious man appeared. He was not one of the sea people but was either a priest or a saint, or so Sadko thought. Whoever he was, he made the sea people all sleep so that Sadko could escape back to the human world.

The second ending: Princess Volkhova herself stole Sadko away and helped him to the surface near Novgorod, because she loved him so much that she could not bear to see him unhappy. In fact, the sea princess loved Sadko so much that she wept herself into mist and became the River Volkhova, which today flows from Lake Ilmen to the sea.

Both endings conclude with a wealthy Sadko and his wife together again and living happily ever after.

Sources

Afanas'ev, Aleksander. *Russian Fairy Tales.* New York: Pantheon, 1945.
Haney, Jack V. *The Complete Russian Folktale.* Armonk, NY: M.E. Sharpe, 1999.

Urashima Taro: A Folktale from Japan

This folktale, which is very popular even today in Japan, combines two common folkloric themes. The first is that of the kingdom under the sea. The second is the theme that time passes at a different rate in fairy realms. What seems like only a day in Faerie to a mortal visitor actually may be a year or a century in mortal time.

There are three possible endings to this folktale. All of them are perfectly authentic, and a storyteller is free to pick the one he or she prefers.

Once, there was a kindhearted young fisherman named Urashima Taro. One day, as he was heading out for the day's fishing, he saw some children tormenting a small green turtle.

"That is not right," he scolded the children and chased them away. Then, Taro picked up the turtle he had rescued and gently returned it to the sea. He thought no more about it.

But the next day, a great green turtle swam up to him (although some tales claim it was a great boat instead). It told him, "That small green turtle you rescued yesterday was the daughter of the Emperor of the Sea. She wishes to see you to thank you."

"But I cannot breathe underwater!" Taro protested.

"You can with our magic," the turtle told him.

So Taro climbed onto the back of the great green turtle. He was carried smoothly down and down to the bottom of the sea, straight to the fine coral and shell palace known as the Palace of the Dragon, Ryugu-jo. There, Taro met the emperor, a person of great dignity, and the princess, a lovely young woman.

Taro stayed with the princess joyfully for three days. But then, he remembered his life on the land and his aging mother. He said to the princess, "This has been a wonderful time, but I do need to return to the land."

"I shall grieve to see you go," the princess said.

But when Taro insisted, she finally agreed. She gave him a mysterious box and said, "You may go, and I wish you well. But you must never open this box."

Taro agreed, and the huge green turtle took him back to the land.

But how strange it was! Everything had changed, and there was no one he knew. They told him that, yes, there once had lived an Urashima Taro, but that had been 300 years ago!

Overwhelmed with shock and grief, Taro wandered by the seashore. With nothing left to him, he opened the box. Instantly, he was overcome by immense old age. The sea princess had been trying to protect him by keeping his old age safely in that box.

And here the tale splits into three parts. One ending says that poor Taro crumbled to dust. One ending says that he became a crane, flying over the land. And the third ending says that he grew gills, leaped into the sea, and was young again, living on forever with the princess.

Sources

Dorson, Richard M. *Folk Legends of Japan*. Rutland, VT, and Tokyo, Japan: Charles E. Tuttle, 1962.

Seki, Keigo, ed. *Folktales of Japan*. Trans. Robert J. Adams. Chicago: University of Chicago Press, 1969.

Hasang: A Folktale from the Hui Muslims of China

As with the folktale of Sadko, this tale, too, features a hero with great musical talent who is not appreciated by his own people—in this case, by his family. Like Sadko, he visits the undersea world. But unlike Sadko, he brings back a bride from that world and lives happily with her.

Long ago, in a poor village, lived an old couple with seven sons.

Now that the sons were grown, their father said to them, "It is time for you to go out into the world and learn a trade. Then, we will no longer need to live in poverty."

Off the seven brothers went, until they came to a road that split into seven different branches. At each branch stood a pine tree. The seven brothers agreed that these trees would represent their fates. As long as a tree thrived, so did that brother. But if a tree died, then the brother had, too.

Then, they set on down the seven paths. Three years later, all the trees were thriving, and the seven brothers came back, each eager to demonstrate the skill he had learned. One brother was a tailor, one was a shoemaker, one was a weaver, one was a baker, and so on down the line, delighting their parents.

Then, it was the turn of the seventh son, Hasang. He took a zither out of his pack and began to play it.

"What is this?" the father shouted. "I sent you out to learn a useful trade and you return playing a zither? You cannot live by that! You are not my son. Get out!"

So poor Hasang wandered alone, stopping finally by the seaside to play his zither. His music was so wonderful that birds and beasts stopped and listened. Even the sea seemed to calm itself.

An old man suddenly appeared and strode straight to Hasang. "How splendidly you play! Would you be kind enough to teach my daughter how to play the zither?"

"Of course I would," Hasang said. "But, old sir, who are you, and where do you live?"

The old man beamed, and his eyes began to glow with golden light. "I am the Dragon King of the Sea. And I live in my Dragon Palace at the bottom of the sea."

Hasang could not refuse so powerful a being. The Dragon King brought him safely down to the Dragon Palace. It was a strange, beautiful place of gold and pearl. The Dragon King's daughter was beautiful, too, and intelligent as well. She mastered playing the zither in only a short time, and soon she could play almost as well as Hasang.

Hasang went before the Dragon King. "Honored One, I can teach your daughter no more. She has mastered the zither. May I now go home?"

At first, the Dragon King was reluctant. After all, Hasang and his daughter seemed to truly like each other. And keeping such music in the Dragon Palace would be splendid.

But Hasang continued to plead. At last, the Dragon King said, "You may leave when you wear holes in these copper shoes."

Dismayed, Hasang had no idea how to wear out shoes of copper. But an old man came to him in a dream and told him to kick the threshold every time he entered or left a room. That would break off the toes of the shoes. Then, the Dragon King would want to offer him riches.

"Refuse everything. Ask only for the peony flower," said the old man in the dream.

Hasang awoke. He did as the dream had told him, kicking the threshold every time he entered or left a room. Sure enough, that did break off the toes of the copper shoes.

"I must let you go," the Dragon King said. "But what would you like as a reward? I have gold and silver, pearls and fine gems. What would you like?"

"I would like only the peony flower," replied Hasang.

The Dragon King stared at him. "Very well," he said to Hasang at last. "Take the peony flower, but treat it well."

Puzzled, Hasang took the peony flower. When he got home, he found a house in which to live. He set the flower in a vase and fell asleep.

When Hasang awoke, the flower was gone. In its place was the Dragon King's daughter.

"I am called Peony Flower," she told Hasang.

"My zither playing has won me the greatest of fortunes!" Hasang cried.

They were married soon after, and lived happily together. And for many a night after that, sweet zither music filled the air.

Source
Li, Shujiang, and Karl W. Luckert, eds. *Mythology and Folklore of the Hui, a Muslim Chinese People.* Albany: State University of New York Press, 1994. Story collected in 1982 by Yang Big from Yang Zhouwen in Ningxia and Shaanxi.

The Ruler of the Sea: A Folktale from the Yupit of Siberia

The Yupit are a group of the Inuit people who live on the Siberian side of the Bering Straits, much as the Inuits on the Alaskan coast do. These Inuit people share related languages and folktales. To the Yupit, the seahorse is a symbol of good luck.

Long ago, there lived a man and his wife with their young son. The man was old, and he knew he would have no further children. So every day, when he went to fish, he tried to catch some seahorses and tie them to his belt for luck. And he prayed that nothing bad would ever happen to his son.

But one day, the boy went down to the shore by himself and wandered along looking at all the sea life. Then, he saw an enormous crab. What a wonder this was! He would catch it and bring it home, and everyone would know what a great hunter he was.

But, instead, the crab caught him in its great claws. No matter how hard the boy struggled, he could not pull free. The crab dragged him into the ocean and down into its depths.

When the old man and his wife realized that their son was lost, the old man lost all interest in living. At last, he went down to the shore and walked into the water, determined to end his life.

But the old man did not drown. Wondering, he kept walking along the sea bottom, until he found himself in a land under the sea.

He saw a man sitting in an earthen hut, weaving a net. The man asked him, "Were you in a shipwreck, too?"

"No. I have come here because I have lost my only son," said the old man.

"Go to the Ruler of the Sea in the center of the village. He has your son."

So the old man went to the center of the village. There sat an enormous man, with shaggy hair that covered his face completely. "Why are you here?" the Ruler of the Sea asked in his deep voice.

Two young boys sat behind him. One of them, the old man saw, was his son.

"I have come for my son," said the old man.

"I will not give him back. He came here into my hands by himself."

"I will do whatever you wish," the old man cried. "Only give me back my son!"

The Ruler of the Sea shook his head. "I want nothing from you. I will not give him back."

The old man thought. What could he possibly offer? Then he remembered the seahorses he wore at his belt and removed them.

"Look at these seahorses. See how lucky they are. Take them, but only give me back my son."

The Ruler of the Sea was pleased with the seahorses. "Very well," he said. "I would rather have these than the two boys. Take them both and go. Close your eyes and take three steps."

The old man and the two boys closed their eyes and took three steps. When they opened their eyes again, they were back on the seashore near their village.

They went home. And now, since the second boy had no family, the old man had two sons.

Source

Dolitsky, Alexander. *Tales and Legends of the Yupik Eskimos of Siberia*. Trans. Henry N. Michael. Juneau: Alaska-Siberia Research Center, 2000. Collected in 1948 by G.A. Menovshchikov from Amnona, a young woman of the village of Naukan.

Hero Tales

A hero is the man, woman, or child who is the protector of the people or of individuals, the person who is willing to stand up to evil and fight for the right. In our real world, there are many heroes, such as the firefighters and police who gave their lives to save others during the terrible events on 9/11. There are doctors who risk their lives to go into war zones to save people.

In the world of folklore, most hero tales refer to heroic characters that never existed in the real world but instead came from the dreams of storytellers or the oppressed. Although some tales may be about real people to whose history folklore has added heroics—Davy Crockett made his own fantastic additions to his story, as have others.

This section is divided into the following chapters:

- Folklore heroes—those who exist only in folktales and ballads.
- Legendary heroes—those who actually existed, but about whom folktales built up around the historic facts.
- Tall tale heroes—those who may or may not have existed but have grown larger than life through implausible tales.
- Heroic outlaws, such as Robin Hood.
- And even a few antiheroes, such as the "Master Thief."

FOLKLORE HEROES

Folklore heroes may have a basis in history, but they are more likely to be purely imaginary characters representing the dreams of a people or a culture. For instance, Ilya Murometz, from Russian folklore, is an idealized version of the Russian peasant hero.

Ilya Murometz and the Robber Nightingale:
A Folktale from Medieval Russia

Ilya Murometz is one of the most popular of the folk heroes of the *byliny*, the Russian folk ballads. He is not a noble or a tzar, but a man of the people, a commoner of great strength and determination. He remained a popular figure through the age of the Soviet Union, and his tales are still told in modern-day Russia.

Ilya Murometz, or Ilya of Murom, the city near where he had been born, lived the first thirty years of his life sitting helplessly, his legs useless to him.

But then one day, when he was sitting alone while his mother and father were out working in the fields, three mysterious men came to visit. Some say they were saints or angels, other claim they were magicians. But whatever and whoever the three men were, when they had gone on their way, Ilya could walk firmly on his feet. He became conscious that he now possessed vast strength.

So Ilya made himself a warrior's equipment and a steel spear. Then he saddled a good horse, worthy of a hero.

Before he left, he asked for a blessing from his mother and father. "Honored mother and father, let me go to the golden city of Kiev, there to kneel to Prince Vladimir of Kiev."

Ilya's parents gave him their blessing. So it was that the hero started on his journey.

He traveled far on into the forest, until he came to a robbers' camp. The robbers wanted to take his horse. But Ilya simply shot an arrow from his bow and sent it flying for a wondrously far distance, and the robbers promptly left him alone.

He rode on toward the golden city of Kiev. But he came first to the city of Chernigof, which was being besieged by pagan enemies. Ilya charged into the enemy army and defeated them all. The prince of the city and his people did Ilya much honor.

Then, Ilya rode on once more toward Kiev, this time, on the direct road between the two cities. What Ilya did not yet know was that the road had been beset for years by the robber who was known as Nightingale for his whistling, which could kill anyone who heard it.

As Ilya rode into the forest, Nightingale the robber saw him and felt a sudden foreboding. Before Ilya approached very closely, the robber began to whistle vigorously, but the hero's heart was not terrified. The robber began to whistle still more vigorously, but that never stopped the hero. Ilya drew his good bow and fired an arrow that took out Nightingale's right eye. The robber tumbled down like a sack of oats.

Ilya took Nightingale the robber, bound him fast to his steel stirrup, and rode on toward the famous city of Kiev. When Ilya arrived, he rode straight to the prince's palace and knelt to the prince.

The Prince of Kiev asked him, "How do men name you, and of what city are you a native?"

"My lord," the hero replied, "men call me Little Ilya, but by my father's family I am an Ivanof, a native of the city of Murom, of the village of Karatcharof."

"By what road did you ride from Murom?"

"By that of Chernigof. And under the walls of Chernigof, I defeated an innumerable host and delivered the city of Chernigof. Thence, I proceeded by the direct road and took captive the mighty hero, Nightingale the robber. I led him here bound to my steel stirrup."

The prince was sure this was untrue since Ilya was a peasant, and he grew angry. But two of his *bogatyri*, his knights, Alesha Popovitch and Dobrynya Nikititch, assured the prince that it really was so. Prince Vladimir promptly had a ceremonial cup of wine brought to Ilya as an apology.

Now, the prince wanted to know what the robber's whistling was really like. Ilya enveloped the prince and princess in a sable mantle, took them under his arms, summoned Nightingale the robber, and commanded him to give his deadly whistle with half strength.

But Nightingale the robber whistled with his full deadly whistle. The sound stunned all but Ilya with the force of it, so that all but Ilya collapsed. For this, Ilya slew him.

When the court had recovered, Prince Vladimir named Ilya Murometz a true bogatyri and welcomed him to their ranks.

Sources

Afanas'ev, Aleksander. *Russian Fairy Tales*. New York: Pantheon, 1945.
Haney, Jack V. *The Complete Russian Folktale*. Armonk, NY: M.E. Sharpe, 1999.

St. George and the Dragon: A Folktale from England

Who was the historical St. George? His history has become so totally entwined with folklore that it is unknown if there ever was an actual saint with that name. The cult of St. George, including his glory as dragon-slayer, spread all across Europe and the Near East, even incorporating a tale first told about King Arthur, that Sir George would return when Christians were in need. St. George became the patron saint of England, and his name was shouted as a battle cry.

But it is as dragon-slayer that St. George is best known in the popular mind. The familiar theme of the princess rescued from the dragon is found in this folktale type, possibly as an echo of the Greek myth of Perseus rescuing Andromeda.

The end of the folktale, with the hero riding off into the sunset, should be familiar to anyone who knows the traditional ending of many a Western hero folktale, such as in the 1953 film *Shane*.

Once, during the time when St. George was a wanderer, in the days when Christianity had not yet spread to all the Roman lands, a terrible dragon came to live in a marshland near the city of Silene, in what was then the Roman province of Libya.

The citizens watched the dragon devouring all it could eat and devastating the farmlands. No one could manage to drive the dragon away or slay it, because its breath was poisonous. To placate the dragon, the citizens offered it two sheep every day. But soon there were no more sheep to offer, and the hungry dragon was ready to eat the entire population.

So the citizens decided that the only possible next step was to offer the dragon a human victim. These were chosen by lot so that none might be unfairly picked.

One day, the fatal lot fell upon the king's only daughter. The horrified king offered riches, even half his kingdom, if his daughter could be spared this dreadful fate. But all the people refused. Why should his child be spared if their children already had been slain and, worse still, eaten?

So the king yielded to what must be. He dressed his daughter in rich bridal attire, weeping. "Alas, my dear, I thought to see you with a fine husband, and myself reborn in grandchildren. Instead, I can but wish I had died before this."

His daughter, also weeping, embraced her father and told him, "I ask only for your blessing."

"That you have," he replied.

Then, the princess was led to the swamp, and left there, all alone. But she was not alone for long. St. George—he was simply George in those days—happened to ride by, and saw the forlorn princess.

"Why do you weep?" he asked. "And who has left you in such a terrible place?"

But she answered, "Good youth, fly from here! Ride as fast as you can lest you perish with me."

"Then mount behind me, and we shall be away from here."

"No, no, it is too late for that! The dragon is coming for me!"

St. George seized the lance from its mountings on his saddle and did battle with the dragon. Never did he give the dragon a chance to breathe its poison on him, and never did he give it a chance to close its terrible jaws on him or his brave steed.

At last, St. George transfixed the dragon with his lance. But he did not kill it.

He asked the princess for her silken girdle, the sash about her waist, then tied one end about the dragon's neck and put the other end into her hand. She was a pure maiden, and her innocence added to the strength of that frail sash. Together, they led the now-docile dragon back to town.

The people drew back in terror, but St. George told them not to fear. If they would all become Christians, he would slay the dragon.

They did, then and there. And so St. George slew the dragon.

The grateful king offered St. George half the kingdom and the hand of the princess. But St. George told him to give the reward to the poor, mounted his horse, and rode away.

Sources

Baring-Gould, Sabine. *Curious Myths of the Middle Ages.* New Hyde Park, NY: University Books, 1967; New York: Oxford University Press, 1978.

Hole, Christina. *Saints in Folklore.* New York: William Morrow, 1965.

Sir Gawain and the Green Knight: A Folktale from the Arthurian Cycle of England

Although Sir Gawain might not have been the perfect, pure knight, he was without a doubt a hero. This folktale, which was originally part of the Cuchulain stories of ancient Ireland, became attached to the knight, with some changes, such as the interlude with the Green Knight's wife.

It was at the fine court of King Arthur, when he was feasting with his knights of the Round Table. Suddenly, the great doors to the hall crashed open, and a strange figure rode into the hall.

The stranger was a mighty man, dressed from head to toe in green armor, and he bore a terrible axe. "Who is master here?" he proclaimed.

King Arthur bid him welcome. "Join our feasting if you come in peace."

"I come to learn who among this company has the courage to test his strength against mine."

The hall fell silent. All the knights were looking at the terrible axe and the Green Knight's mighty build. He laughed. "What, are you knights or mere children playing?"

"I shall fight you myself!" the king cried in anger.

But King Arthur's nephew, Sir Gawain, sprang to his feet. "Sire, it is the honor of all the knights that is at stake. I will fight you, Green Knight."

The Green Knight smiled. "The terms are simply this, sir knight. First, you shall take your sword and strike my bare neck. Then, a year and a day later, I shall do the same to you."

That seemed a strange way for the Green Knight to die. But Sir Gawain struck as he was commanded, and the Green Knight's head went flying off.

But the Green Knight calmly picked up his head and replaced it. "Remember your promise," he told Sir Gawain. I shall see you in the Green Chapel a year and a day from now. You will find it if you hunt. And then, I shall return this favor."

Gloom fell upon the company as the Green Knight rode away. But Sir Gawain meant to keep his word, and he set out on his hunt for the Green Chapel.

It took him a year, but, at last, he came to a fine castle. The lord of the castle said, "You are very near to the Green Chapel. Rest here today, and I will show you the way tomorrow. But you must give me anything you receive at my castle."

So weary was Sir Gawain from his journey that he did not ask any questions. He fell sound asleep. When he woke, he found no other soul in all the castle except for one woman, the loveliest of women. She smiled at him and said, "My lord has left me here while he goes hunting. Will you be my knight?"

"As a knight, I am at the service of all who need me."

"Then you are my knight. We must seal this pledge," she added, and kissed him. But Sir Gawain drew back from anything else, since he was an honorable knight and this was a married lady.

All that morning, Sir Gawain was polite to the lovely woman, even when she kissed him again and yet again. Then, she said, "The day is almost done, and my husband will be home. But here is a gift for you so you will never forget me." She gave him her pretty belt, all of lace, and Gawain took it.

Sure enough, the lord of the castle returned that night. Sir Gawain said, "This is what I received on your behalf," and kissed him three times.

The lord of the castle seemed not at all surprised. "Come," he said, "I will take you to the Green Chapel."

The Green Chapel was in a wild, lonely place. When Sir Gawain looked around for his guide, he found himself alone.

Then, suddenly, the Green Knight loomed up before him. "I see that you have kept your word. It is exactly a year and a day since we last met."

"The knights of the Round Table always keep their word," Sir Gawain replied. "Now, let us not delay."

He knelt and waited for the fatal blow. But the axe merely grazed his neck.

"Do not toy with me!" Sir Gawain cried. "The pledge was for one blow and one blow only."

"True enough, and you would not have been hurt at all if you had kept your word. Did you not promise to give me everything you received at my castle?"

The Green Knight was the lord of the castle! Blushing, Sir Gawain remembered the lacy belt the lady had given him, and he held it out to the Green Knight. "Your lady wanted me to keep this."

The Green Knight gave a great bark of a laugh. "She is my partner in this trickery! She did what I bade her. Keep the belt, sir knight, as a reminder that all may not be as it seems."

With that, he turned back into the lord of the castle. "I am Bernlac de Hautdesert, and my magic was taught to me by the great Merlin. I am satisfied now that the knights of the Round Table are brave—and that at least one of them keeps his word."

Sources

Armitage, Simon, trans. *Sir Gawain and the Green Knight*. New York: W.W. Norton, 2007.
Tolkien, J.R.R. *Sir Gawain and the Green Knight, Pearl, Sir Orfeo*. New York: Del Rey, 1979.

Hayk, Founder of Armenia: A Folktale from Armenia

In Armenia, Hayk is seen as a folkloric culture hero—a hero of a people. He also is said to have been the founder of Armenia. There is no way of knowing now if there ever was a man named Hayk.

In this tale, both biblical and Greek mythologic influences can be seen in the giant known as Be'l, whose name is probably a corruption of the ancient Near Eastern deity Baal and who is referred to as a Titan, one of the Greek mythological giants.

In the ancient days, there lived a giant known as King Be'l, Be'l the Titan, who ruled as king of Babylon. He thought of himself as superior to all races of humankind, and wished them all to worship him.

But one man, Hayk, son of Japheth, refused to submit to King Be'l and refused as well to call him a god. Now, this Hayk was very strong and handsome, and an extremely powerful archer and warrior. King Be'l massed troops in Babylon and went against Hayk to kill him.

Hayk had sons and grandsons at the time, and he was patriarch of the country of Ararad. His grandson, Kadmos, fled to Hayk to warn him, "King Be'l is coming against you. I, with my wife and children, have come to you as fugitives."

Hayk gave them shelter, and amassed his men against the invasion. Hayk went to fight King Be'l, but he was unable to confront the Titan king because of the vast number of Be'l's gigantic armored men.

Now, when Hayk struck at King Be'l, Be'l wanted to seize him with his own hands. But Hayk evaded him and fled. In hot pursuit, Be'l went after him with his weapons bearer.

Hayk stopped, calling back, "Why do you pursue me? Return to your own place if you do not wish to die today. I tell you now, my arrow will not miss its mark."

Be'l replied, "I pursue you in person so that you do not fall into the hands of my young men and perish. Surrender to me, and you shall live in my house in peace, looking after the young hunters."

Hayk scoffed at that offer. "You are a dog from a pack of dogs, you and your people. I will empty my quiver at you."

The Titan king was fully armored, with a great bronze shield as well, and he laughed at the thought of any arrow so much as touching him. But Hayk's bow was like the branch of some mighty tree, and the arrow he released from its great arc shot right through the bronze shield, through the bronze armor, and straight into the body of King Be'l.

The giant who had thought himself a god fell and died. His troops fled, and pursuing them, Hayk and his men took many horses and camels.

From then on, Hayk and his people remained in Ararad. Today, the land is known as Armenia.

Sources

Aghajanian, Alfred, ed. *Armenian Literature: Comprising Poetry, Drama, Folklore, and Classic Traditions.* IndoEuropeanPublishing.com, 2007.

Downing, Charles. *Armenian Folk-Tales and Legends.* Oxford, United Kingdom: Oxford University Press, 1993.

Kandebayi the Hero: A Folktale from Kazakhstan

Kandebayi shows one of the characteristics of a true culture hero, a hero of his people: miraculously swift growth. His horse also is a hero's steed; it grows with magical speed and is able to speak.

The curious might like to know that one mule in 10,000 actually is fertile. That part of the folktale is not fantasy.

Once, a poor fisherman and his wife were delighted to learn that she was, after many childless years, pregnant.

The baby was a boy, and he grew miraculously quickly. At six days, he could laugh. At ten days, he could run. And by the time he was six years old, he had become a young man strong enough to outwrestle a grown man or drag an ox out of a muddy bog, and skilled enough as a hunter to bring down any game.

One day, Kandebayi went hunting. He found a wolf killing a pregnant mule. He caught the wolf by the tail and hurled it aside with such force that it was slain. The mule was already dead, but Kandebayi cut her open and rescued her colt. He carried the little animal home and raised it.

The colt, too, grew with remarkable speed, turning swiftly into a true hero's steed that no one could catch and only Kandebayi could ride. Kandebayi named his steed Keerkula, and it could talk.

Now that Kandebayi was a man, he showed kindness and generosity to all. And one day, he met a weeping child, a little boy herding sheep.

"Why are you crying?" he asked the boy.

The boy, who looked to be no more than six or seven, replied, "Wouldn't you weep if your parents had been kidnapped?"

"Come, little one, tell me the whole story."

"My father is named Batuer, and I am his only child. An enemy robbed us of all our livestock save these few sheep. Then, the enemy returned and captured both my father and my mother, and rode off with them."

"I will get your parents back," Kandebayi vowed.

He went with the boy to the nomad camp of the boy's people. He brought the people a deer he had killed, and they welcomed him with great generosity.

Kandebayi asked if anyone knew where the boy's parents had been taken, but no one knew. But one man said there had been a strange event at dusk on the previous night. Six swans had flown overhead, and they had sung:

> Is kindhearted Kandebayi here?
> Is Keerkula in his hands?
> Does their glow light up the land?
> Are his horse's hoofs on the move?

So Kandebayi went out at dusk and stood waiting. When the six swans sang their song, he answered them:

> I am kindhearted Kandebayi.
> Keerkula is in my hands.
> Our glow lights up the land.
> My horse's hoofs are on the move.

The swans swooped down and tried to beat Kandebayi with their wings. He leaped up and caught one swan by the leg. But it pulled free, leaving only a golden shoe in his hand, and all six swans flew away.

Kandebayi mounted Keerkula and they sped after the swans. How long they raced, for long or short, the chase ended when their way was blocked by a mighty mountain.

"My dear friend," Keerkula said to Kandebayi, "I sense that the place you seek is near. Climb the mountain and you will find a river. There is an island in the river, and there is the home of Heavenly King. It is he who has imprisoned the two you seek, thrown them into Hell, and barred the door.

"On the far side of this mountain, you will find a giant cowherd. He gladly will accept money, so pay him, exchange clothes with him, and take his cattle.

"Now, before we part, pull a hair from my tail. When you need me, light the hair from my tail, and I will appear."

Kandebayi pulled a hair from Keerkula's tail, and then he climbed the mountain. He met the giant cowherd on the far side of the mountain and gave him money. They exchanged clothes, and Kandebayi went on, herding the cattle before him.

Kandebayi drove the cattle straight to the river, but the cattle refused to cross. So he began tossing them across.

A young woman, the king's youngest daughter, saw him and cried, "Do not do that! Just shout, 'Water, open a road.'"

So Kandebayi shouted, "Water, open a road."

The water parted, and he drove the cattle onto the island.

There, Kandebayi heard the king telling his two sons, "Today, the black mare will foal. For nine years, she has had a foal, but every one has vanished in the night. I want you to stand guard."

So the two sons stood guard. But they were lazy, and soon they were asleep.

Kandebayi stayed awake. He saw the mare give birth to a colt with a golden tail. But a black cloud swooped down over the colt and carried it away. Kandebayi leaped, but all he got were golden hairs from the colt's tail.

In the morning, the king asked his sons what they had seen.

"We saw nothing," they said.

"They saw nothing," Kandebayi said, "because they were asleep. I saw the mare give birth to a colt with a golden tail, but a great black cloud carried the colt away. All I caught were these golden hairs."

He held up the golden hairs, and they gleamed brightly.

"The three of you go hunt for that colt," the king commanded. "Bring it back here, or do not bother coming back at all."

Kandebayi did not wait for the two brothers. He crossed the river again and burned the hair from Keerkula's tail. Instantly, Keerkula was before him. They rode off like the wind.

Then, Keerkula said, "We are nearing Fire River. The place you seek is on the far side. Close your eyes, my friend, and do not open them again until I tell you, or we shall both die."

Kandebayi shut his eyes tightly. He felt hot air, then he felt scorching heat, and then, he felt cool air again. Keerkula said, "Open your eyes."

Kandebayi found that they were on an island. There, nine golden-tailed horses, adult down to colt, were eating grain from a golden trough.

Keerkula said, "On top of that poplar tree is the Sumulue bird. We must not be here when he returns. Take the golden trough, and the horses will follow you. They will be unable to cross Fire River, so we must take a different route.

"That will put three obstacles in our path. First, there shall be seven demons. Then, there shall be a white lion. Last, there shall be a witch. It is up to you to see that we overcome all three."

Kandebayi put the golden trough before him on Keerkula's back, and the horses all followed. They came to a mountain—and out of it rushed seven demons, all fangs and claws and horns.

Kandebayi dismounted and put down the golden trough. Then, he seized an enormous log that none but a hero could lift, and swung it, slaying all seven demons at a blow. He took their eyes as proof he had slain them, then picked up the golden trough and remounted Keerkula.

Off they rode, Kandebayi and Keerkula and the nine horses, jumping easily over six cliffs. Then, their path was blocked by a huge white lion, roaring savagely from its sharp-fanged mouth.

Kandebayi leaped from Keerkula's back and drew his sword. As the lion roared again, Kandebayi charged, swung his sword, and cut the lion neatly in half. He took the lion's gleaming white fangs as proof he had killed it, then remounted Keerkula.

They traveled on, the hero, his steed, and the nine horses, up and down steep mountainsides, across rivers, through piles of rocks. Suddenly, a thick cloud descended on them. Out of it stepped a beautiful girl in clothing covered with glittering gems.

"You must be weary," she said soothingly. "Come, rest in my home."

She was just too beautiful, too richly dressed to be real. This, Kandebayi realized with a shock, was the witch in disguise. He quickly drew his sword and beheaded her—and yes, the disguise was gone, and the beheaded evil witch remained. Kandebayi took her head to prove she was dead.

At last, they returned to the island of Heavenly King. The king was amazed and overjoyed to see the nine horses. And he ordered a great feast for Kandebayi. During it, the two princes returned empty-handed and thin as blades.

"What is your story?" Heavenly King asked Kandebayi.

"I have come here for only two things, oh Heavenly King. The first is to rescue two kidnapped people, husband and wife. The second is to return this golden shoe, which I pulled from one of six singing swans."

Heavenly King laughed. "Yes, I kidnapped the pair. I did so because Batuer is the most obstinate man in the world, and he dared to threaten me. Those six swans are my daughters, and I had sent them to find you. You pulled the shoe from my sixth daughter.

"I hoped that you would slay the seven demons, the white lion, and the evil witch for me. If you can do so, I will gladly free Batuer and his wife. Yes, and you may marry my sixth daughter."

Now it was Kandebayi's turn to laugh. "I already have done just that." He took out his trophies—the demon eyes, the white lion's fangs, and the evil witch's head.

The king kept his word. Kandebayi and sixth princess were wed. At their wedding feast, they gave Batuer and his wife many treasures.

Then, they all returned to Batuer's village, where he and his wife were reunited with their son. They all lived happily. And wherever Kandebayi was, there no enemy dared come.

Source

Li, Xuewei, trans. *Ada and the Greedy King and Other Chinese Minorities Folktales.* Singapore, Kuala Lampur, and Hong Kong, China: Federal Publications, 1991. Tale collected by Li Yong from an unnamed Kazakh informant.

The Girl Who Avenged Her Uncles: A Folktale from the Chippewa of Wisconsin

Although this folklore heroine is nameless and just a child, she is definitely a heroic character. She is not afraid to take on an evil, and apparently child-molesting, sorcerer and kill him.

There once were ten brothers who lived with their niece, who was still a little girl.

One day, the brothers all went out hunting. The oldest said to the girl, "You know that we will be gone all day. If there is any trouble, hide under that great wooden bowl, and no one will be able to find you."

After the brothers had left, the little girl did hear voices just outside. From the safety of the overturned wooden bowl, she heard men planning to attack the ten brothers. When the brothers came home, she warned them.

"We will stay and fight them," the brothers said.

But there were too many of the enemy. They killed all ten brothers, then cut off their heads, and left only the bodies behind.

After the fighting, the little girl crept out of hiding. She set out to find the ones who had slain her uncles. She followed their trail all the way to their village.

The people in the village were having a great dance to celebrate taking the ten heads. The little girl joined in the dance as though she was one of those people.

The *manido*, the bad old man, the magical man, who had led the war party, fell in love with the girl even though she was still just a child. He asked her to talk with him. He boasted about everything.

But the little girl knew that this was her chance to avenge her uncles. So she asked if there was anything that bothered the manido. He said that if a woman's clothes were placed near his head, he would die. But since he never slept, no one could get near him.

Now, the little girl had one small magic, and that was the ability to make anyone fall asleep. She sang even that evil manido asleep. Then, she took off her skirt and placed it on his head. Taking out her knife, she cut off his head, and made a bag out of her skirt.

The head could still talk. "You played quite a trick on me, little girl."

The rest of the manido's body, still active with magic, went back to the dance, but everyone that headless body touched fell dead. The head said, "If you let me go, I will bring your uncles back to life."

The little girl knew that could not be. Her uncles had been dead for far too long. And she would not be tricked.

She took the enemy head back to her village. By that time, it was dead.

Everyone praised the little girl for her bravery. The chief of the village took the little girl under his care. When she was old enough, she married his son.

Source

Barnouw, Victor. *Wisconsin Chippewa Myths & Tales and Their Relation to Chippewa Life.*
    Madison: University of Wisconsin Press, 1977. Tale collected by Ernestine Friedl at Court
    Oreilles in 1942 from Delia Oshogay, with interpreter Maggie Lamorie.

Sam Hart and His Brave Gray Mare: A Folktale from Massachusetts

There are two heroes in this folktale, Sam Hart and his nameless gray mare. Horse
racing in the New World officially began in 1662, on what was to become Long Island, New York (very near to the site of the current Belmont racetrack). But informal
horse races were held whenever two horsemen chanced to meet.

There once was a horseman and horseplayer named Sam Hart. He often was to
be seen at horse races wherever they were held, though he lived in the town of
Woburn.

But of all the horses he knew, Sam Hart loved his own gray mare the best. She
was a beautiful mare, with a deep chest, good, strong legs, and a fine love of racing. In fact, Sam raced his gray mare against anyone who dared stand a horse
against her, and the mare always won.

Then, one summer evening, a stranger approached on a fine black steed. Sam's
horseman's eye took in the black steed's fine lines, but he thought, "My mare's
more than a match for him."

The rider was richly dressed as any gentleman, but he had a cruel, hot gleam
in his eyes. "My steed can beat any horse," he boasted, "and he shall easily beat
that old gray nag of yours."

"You think so?" Sam said. "What odds are you offering?"

"How does three to one sound to you? And I will even give your mare a head
start."

That sounded fine to Sam. They agreed that the race would be from Central
Square to Woburn Common, and that the black steed must catch the gray mare's
tail in his teeth before they reached the Common.

Sam agreed. Off went the horses, racing fiercely over the ground, seeming almost to fly.

The gray mare was at full gallop, yet Sam thought uneasily that the black steed
was gaining. Why, he could almost feel the black steed's hot breath—no wonder,
because there were flames coming from its nostrils!

Now, Sam knew who his opponent was, and he changed his racing plans in an
instant. He turned the gray mare's head not toward Woburn Common, but toward
the nearest church.

So swiftly were Sam and his gray mare going that they made three circles of
the church before Sam could slow his mare enough to get her and him safely onto
holy ground.

The black steed followed close behind. He had his mouth open, showing sharp
white teeth. . . .

But not a hair of the gray mare's tail did he get. Instead, the black steed sat
sharply back on his haunches, almost as though the edge of holy ground were a
solid wall.

Sam managed to pull up his panting gray mare. He soothed the mare with a hand on her neck.

The rider of the black steed was clearly now none other than the Devil himself. "You cheated one whose business is cheating. Take your money." He hurled the money at Sam.

"Luck to you, but I will not say good or bad." With that, the Devil was gone.

Some say he left the black steed behind and that Sam put it in his stable. But no horseplayer would have raced such a horse and taken such a wager. For to ride the Devil's horse surely would send Sam's soul where he had no wish to go.

Sources
Brean, Herbert, et al., eds. *The Life Treasury of American Folklore.* New York: Time, 1961.

Skinner, Charles M. *Myths & Legends of Our Own Land.* Vol. 1. Philadelphia and London: J.B. Lippincott, 1896.

LEGENDARY HEROES

These are the folktales about heroes who actually existed, but around whom folktales have been circulated. The folk process seems to take over in such cases, making people want their heroes to become larger than life. Some of these hero folktales, such as those about Davy Crockett, were originated by the man himself but have since entered into the folk tradition, with changes, additions, or subtractions made to the tales.

Davy Crockett: A Folktale from the American Frontier

The real Davy Crockett (1786–1836) was a frontiersman who served as a U.S. senator and died in the Battle of the Alamo. But Crockett built up his own legends and tall tales. Other folktales grew up around him after his death.

By now, it is difficult to separate some of Crockett's tales from the others, but they are good stories either way. This particular tale, however, is known to have started with him. It is from his writings, only some of the spelling has been modernized for easier reading, and the text, originally one long paragraph, has been divided up.

One January morning, it was all so cold that the forest trees were stiff and they couldn't shake, and the very daybreak froze fast as it was trying to dawn. The tinderbox in my cabin would no more catch fire than a sunk raft at the bottom of the sea.

Well, seein' daylight was so far behind time I thought creation was in a fair way for freezing fast. So, thinks I, I must strike a little fire from my fingers, light my pipe, and travel out a few leagues and see about it.

Then, I brought my knuckles together like two thunderclouds, but the sparks froze up before I could begin to collect 'em, so I walked, whistlin' "Fire in the Mountains!" as I went along in three double quick time.

Well, after I had walked about twenty miles up the Peak O' Day and Daybreak Hill, I soon discovered what was the matter. The Earth had actually frozen fast on her axis, and couldn't turn round; the Sun had got jammed between two cakes of ice under the wheels, and there he had been shinin' and workin' to get loose 'til he froze fast in his cold sweat.

"C-r-e-a-t-i-o-n!" thought I, this are the toughest sort of suspension, an' it mustn't be endured. Somethin' must be done, or human creation is done for.

It was then so ante'luvian an' premature cold that my upper and lower teeth an' tongue was all collapsed together as tight as a frozen oyster. But I took a fresh twenty-pound bear off my back that I'd picked up on my road and beat the animal against the ice 'til the hot oil began to walk out on him at all sides.

I then took an' held him over the Earth's axis an' squeezed him 'til I'd thawed 'em loose, poured about a ton onto the Sun's face, give the Earth's cogwheel one kick backward 'til I got the Sun loose—whistled "Push along, keep movin'!" an' in about fifteen seconds the Earth gave a grunt, an' began movin'.

The Sun walked up beautiful, salutin' me with such a wind o' gratitude that it made me sneeze. I lit my pipe by the blaze o' his topknot, shouldered my bear, an' walked home, introducin' people to the fresh daylight with a piece of sunshine in my pocket.

Sources
Crockett, Davy. *Davy Crockett's Almanac*. New York: Cozans, 1854.
Eastman, Max. "Davy Crockett as Demigod." *Scribners Magazine* (July 1936): 10.

Daniel Boone: A Folktale from Kentucky

The historic Daniel Boone (1734–1820) was an American pioneer who explored much of Kentucky and the surrounding regions. He also fought in the Revolutionary War. As with other historic figures, the folk process added folklore to his actual history. Boone became a popular figure as a result of contemporary books that made him into a swashbuckling adventurer—he scoffed at such nonsense.

An interesting point is the folktale's link to a folk ballad, "Polly Vaughn," an Irish ballad known in the New World at that time. In the ballad, a young man hunting at night thinks he sees a swan, and instead he shoots his true love, Polly, who is dressed in white (or, in some versions, who has very white skin).

One night, Daniel Boone and a friend decided to go out hunting. At night, you went fire hunting. That meant taking a fire pan, one full of burning pine knots or other burning stuff, and shining it into the dark forest. If there was a deer nearby, the firelight would reflect in its eyes, confuse it, and give the hunters a chance to shoot it.

This time, though, the eyes that Boone saw were blue. He aimed his rifle, then lowered it again. This was too amazing: He had never seen a blue-eyed deer.

A rustling of bushes told him the deer had fled, and he pursued it, wild with curiosity. At last, Boone caught up with it in a moonlit meadow—and found that it had been truly fortunate he had not shot at that deer, because it was not a deer at all, but a blue-eyed young woman!

Her name was Rebecca, and she was the daughter of a neighbor. Smitten by this blue-eyed "deer" he had been too amazed to shoot, Boone wooed and won Rebecca, and they were married.

Sources
Coffin, Tristram Potter, and Hennig Cohen. *The Parade of Heroes: Legendary Figures in American Lore*. Garden City, NY: Anchor/Doubleday, 1978.
Leeming, David, and Jake Page. *Myths, Legends and Folktales of America: An Anthology*. New York and Oxford, United Kingdom: Oxford University Press, 1999.

George Washington: A Folktale from Virginia

The historic George Washington (1732–1799), the first president of the new United States, was an excellent politician and military man, but he was no more or less honest than the next man.

It was the folk process—and possibly a touch of political propaganda—that created a larger-than-life character, someone of amazing integrity. This folktale dates to at least the turn of the nineteenth century, and it is still very much a part of public belief.

The young George Washington grew up on his father's Virginia farm. There, his father often would tell him that truth was one of the finest virtues, something lovely to be in a boy's heart and words. By contrast, his father would say, a liar is a man accursed, dreaded by all.

"But I never tell lies," the young boy said.

"No, I am delighted to say, my son, you do not."

When the boy was six years old or so, he was given the wonderful gift of a hatchet. Many a boy in those days was trusted with knife or hatchet at that age. And of course, like every other boy, the young Washington had to try his hatchet out on everything he could cut. Sticks, branches—what fun!

But then he saw his father's lovely cherry tree. Its trunk was just too tempting, and the boy gave it a great cut with his hatchet.

The next morning, his father saw what had happened to his favorite cherry tree, and said to his son, "Come here, George. Do you know who cut it down?"

The boy did not hesitate. He remembered his father's lessons. "I did it, Father. I cut down the cherry tree with my hatchet."

He expected to be punished, but instead his father hugged him. "Keep to the path of honesty, my son. For that is worth more than 1,000 cherry trees."

Sources

Botkin, B.A. *A Treasury of American Folklore.* New York: Crown, 1944.

Hardin, Terri. *A Treasury of American Folklore: Our Customs, Beliefs, and Traditions.* New York: Barnes & Noble, 1994.

Abraham Lincoln: A Folktale from Washington, D.C.

This folktale is not about the living president, but about his ghost. It shows how a beloved figure in American history was fitted into the category of "the hero's return," just as folktales from England mention the return of King Arthur.

It is said that the ghost of President Abraham Lincoln still lingers in the White House—appearing only when the nation is in peril.

President Franklin D. Roosevelt and his wife, Eleanor, were in the White House during the Great Depression and the following World War II. They used what had been Lincoln's bedroom as a study for the first lady.

Eleanor often was aware of someone watching her, and she was sure it was Lincoln's ghost, although she never caught a glimpse of him. A clerk, though, was sure he saw Lincoln sitting on the bed.

While spending a night at the White House during the Roosevelt presidency, Queen Wilhelmina of the Netherlands was awakened by a knock on the bedroom door. Answering it, she was confronted with the ghost of Lincoln staring at her from the hallway.

The next president, Harry S. Truman, once responded to a 3 A.M. knock on his door and found no one there. He attributed the knock to Lincoln.

Perhaps the most startling of visits happened while British Prime Minister Winston Churchill was at the White House, during World War II. Churchill loved to take long, hot baths and smoke a cigar. Naked, and with his cigar, he walked into his bedroom—and found Lincoln standing by the fireplace, leaning on the mantle.

Churchill said, without a moment's pause, "Good evening, Mr. President. You seem to have me at a disadvantage." Lincoln smiled and politely disappeared.

But mystery surrounds Lincoln's funeral train as well. Soon after his assassination, Lincoln's body was transported by train, the Lincoln Special, from Washington to Illinois for burial. The train made several stops along the route to allow the nation to honor their president. And many people reported that their clocks stopped when the Lincoln Special passed their town.

But even that phenomenon was not impressive enough for a hero's final journey. Since then, citizens of Urbana and Piqua, Illinois, have claimed to see a ghostly train forever repeating that final journey.

Sources

Lee, Edward. *Haunted House: And Other Presidential Horrors.* Hiram, GA: Overlook Connection, 2007.

Oates, Stephen B. *Abraham Lincoln: The Man Behind the Myth.* New York: Harper & Row, 1984.

Antoine Barada: A Folktale from Nebraska

Antoine Barada (1807–1887) was a real man, born to a French trapper and an Omaha Indian woman. He was an important figure in Nebraska history, and his deeds include the settling of the town that now bears his name, Barada. He also may have been one of the supporters of the Underground Railroad, which helped runaway slaves escape to freedom.

But folktales seem to have gathered around Barada primarily because he was a man of great strength and height.

Antoine Barada was a huge man, maybe seven feet tall, a giant in those days, and a man of great strength. He always was being called upon by those needing his help. He could load hogs just by picking them up and putting them in the wagon. And he could help build a barn by easily lifting the heaviest of beams into place.

One day in St. Louis, Barada was challenged to prove his strength. So he simply lifted a stone that weighed, people say, 1,700 pounds, as if it was nothing.

Barada also worked on the railroad. In Nebraska, he got fed up with the lazy railroad crew. He grabbed a heavy hammer and threw it across the Missouri River with such force that the earth buckled when the hammer landed, creating Nebraska's Missouri River breaks.

Still angry, Barada slammed his fist down on a metal pile so hard that it sank into the earth and struck water. All of Nebraska would have been flooded if Barada had not plugged up the hole again.

Barada also was active in the Underground Railroad. He used his strength to help slaves on the road to freedom by carrying them, several at a time, across the Missouri River.

Later in life, Barada's great strength started to fail, making him no more than an ordinary man.

Sources

Edwards, L.C. "Antoine Barada." In *History of Richardson County, Nebraska: Its People, Industries and Institutions.* Indianapolis, IN: B.F. Bowen, 1917.

Welsch, Roger J. *A Treasury of Nebraska Pioneer Folklore.* Lincoln: University of Nebraska Press, 1984.

Aliquispo: A Folktale from the Oneida of the Northeast

This legend of a heroic woman saving her people is partly true, though the ending is pure folklore.

In the days before the Europeans came, the Oneida and the Mingoes were great enemies. The Mingoes would invade Oneida villages, burn the crops, kill the men, and carry off the women and girls.

During one such raid, some of the Oneida managed to escape, hiding in a cave in the side of a cliff. But there was neither food nor water in the cave, and soon it became a case of starving or dying at the hands of the foe.

A great council was held to decide what to do. A young woman named Aliquispo stepped forward. She said that powerful spirits had come to her in a vision and told her to save her people.

"Stay here," she told the Oneida. "I shall lead the enemy down below us. Then you can crush them."

Aliquispo left her people and let herself be captured by the Mingoes. She hinted that she knew where the Oneida were hiding. The Mingoes tortured her to be sure that she was telling the truth. Nothing they could do would shake her, but, at last, she pretended to give in.

"I will lead you to them by a secret way."

They bound Aliquispo's hands and forced her ahead of them. As soon as she had led them all to the land below the cliff, she shouted, "My people, destroy your enemies!"

The Mingoes killed Aliquispo—but they, in turn, were killed by the rocks thrown down by the Oneida.

Aliquispo had died to save her people. From her hair grew woodbine, the healing herb, and from her body grew honeysuckle, which is still called by the Oneida "brave woman's blood."

Sources

Leeming, David, and Jake Page. *Myths, Legends and Folktales of America: An Anthology.* New York and Oxford, United Kingdom: Oxford University Press, 1999.

Wonderly, Anthony. *Oneida Iroquois Folklore, Myth, and History: New York Oral Narrative from the Notes of H.E. Allen and Others.* Syracuse, NY: Syracuse University Press, 2004.

John Henry: A Folktale from West Virginia

Was there actually a real John Henry, the steel-driving man? It may well be so, although most of the facts have been overwritten by folklore. Scanty evidence indicates that he may have been born as a slave in Missouri in the 1840s and would have been freed after the Civil War. What makes it difficult to be sure of the right man, though, is the fact that the records of the Chesapeake and Ohio Railway, where he was said to have worked, list more than one African American worker named John Henry.

But there is no reason not to believe that there might, indeed, have been a contest between man and machine as is described in this folktale and in popular folk ballads.

John Henry was said to be the strongest man alive.

Working on the building of the Chesapeake and Ohio Railroad in mountainous West Virginia, John Henry spent every day drilling holes by hitting steel spikes into rocks. And no one could keep up with him for speed and accuracy. So it was that the railroad was being built at a good speed, thanks to him.

But ahead of the railroad now stood an obstacle, the Big Bend Mountain. Since it was too large and would be too costly to go around, the C&O bosses agreed that the best way to overcome this problem was to drill right through the mountain, a mile and a quarter of tunneling.

The work took three years, and many men died from sheer exhaustion or from rockfalls or cave-ins. But John Henry, that mighty man, kept going, drilling with his favorite fourteen-pound hammer. And no one else could keep up with him.

Then, the bosses decided to speed up the work by bringing in a steam-powered drill, one that was said to be faster and stronger than any man. John Henry said he doubted that, and the other workers backed him up. And so it was that a contest was set up between man and machine.

The steam drill was run by the foreman. John Henry had nothing but his own muscles and two twenty-pound hammers, one in each hand.

The contest began. Both man and machine drilled away, often hidden by clouds of dust.

At the end of the time, John Henry had drilled twice as many holes as the steam drill. He had won—but the stress killed him. John Henry fell dead on the spot.

But wherever men work, John Henry's name will be remembered as the man who beat the machine.

Since John Henry's story is so closely linked with the many ballads about him, following is the folk song version, in the public domain:

The Ballad of John Henry

Some say he's from Georgia,
Some say he's from Alabam',
But it's wrote on the rock at the Big Ben Tunnel,
That he's an East Virginia man,
That he's an East Virginia man.

John Henry was a steel drivin' man,
He died with a hammah in his han',
Oh, come along boys and line the track,
For John Henry ain't never comin' back,
For John Henry ain't never comin' back.

John Henry he could hammah,
He could whistle, he could sing.
He went to the mountain early in the mornin'
To hear his hammah ring,
To hear his hammah ring.

John Henry went to the section boss,
Says the section boss what kin you do?
Says I can line a track, I kin histe a jack,
I kin pick and shovel, too,
I kin pick and shovel, too.

John Henry told the cap'n,
When you go to town,
Buy me a nine-pound hammah,
An' I'll drive this steel drill down,
An' I'll drive this steel drill down.

Cap'n said to John Henry,
You've got a willin' mind.
But you just well lay yoh hammah down,
You'll nevah beat this drill of mine,
You'll nevah beat this drill of mine.

John Henry went to the tunnel,
And they put him in lead to drive.
The rock was so tall and John Henry so small
That he laid down his hammah and he cried,
That he laid down his hammah and he cried.

The steam drill was on the right han' side,
John Henry was on the left.
Says before I let this steam drill beat me down,

I'll hammah myself to death,
I'll hammah myself to death.

Oh the cap'n said to John Henry,
I bleeve this mountain's sinkin' in.
John Henry said to the cap'n, Oh my!
Tain't nothin' but my hammah suckin' wind,
Tain't nothin' but my hammah suckin' wind.

John Henry had a cute liddle wife,
And her name was Julie Ann,
And she walk down the track and nevah look back,
Goin' to see her brave steel drivin' man,
Goin' to see her brave steel drivin' man.

John Henry was on the mountain,
The mountain was so high.
He called to his pretty liddle wife,
Said ah kin almos' touch the sky,
Said ah kin almos' touch the sky.

Who gonna shoe yoh pretty liddle feet,
Who gonna glove yoh han',
Who gonna kiss yoh rosy cheeks,
An' who gonna be yoh man,
An' who gonna be yoh man?

Papa gonna shoe my pretty liddle feet,
Mama gonna glove my han',
Sistah gonna kiss my rosy cheeks,
An' I ain't gonna have no man,
An' I ain't gonna have no man.

Then John Henry told huh,
Don't you weep an' moan,
I got $10,000 in the First National Bank,
I saved it to buy you a home,
I saved it to buy you a home.

John Henry took his liddle boy,
Sit him on his knee,
Said that Big Ben Tunnel,
Gonna be the death of me,
Gonna be the death of me.

John Henry took that liddle boy,
Helt him in the pahm of his han',
And the last words he said to that chile was,

I want you to be a steel drivin' man,
I want you to be a steel drivin' man.

John Henry ast that liddle boy,
Now what are you gonna be?
Says if I live and nothin' happen,
A steel drivin' man I'll be,
A steel drivin' man I'll be.

Then John Henry he did hammah,
He did make his hammah soun',
Says now one more lick fore quittin' time,
An' I'll beat this steam drill down,
An' I'll beat this steam drill down.

The hammah that John Henry swung,
It weighed over nine poun',
He broke a rib in his left han' side,
And his intrels fell on the groun',
And his intrels fell on the groun'.

All the women in the West
That heard of John Henry's death,
Stood in the rain, flagged the east bound train,
Goin' where John Henry dropped dead,
Goin' where John Henry dropped dead.

They took John Henry to the White House,
And buried him in the san',
And every locomotive come roarin' by,
Says there lays that steel drivin' man,
Says there lays that steel drivin' man.

Sources

Chappell, Louis W. *John Henry: A Folk-Lore Study.* Port Washington, NY: Kennikat, 1983.
Coffin, Tristram Potter, and Hennig Cohen. *The Parade of Heroes: Legendary Figures in American Lore.* Garden City, NY: Anchor/Doubleday, 1978.

Yorimitsu: A Folktale from Japan

There was an historic Minamoto no Yorimitsu (944–1021 C.E.) Also known as Minamoto no Raiko, he served the Fujiwara clan and was known for his military exploits and for quelling various bandit uprisings.

Yorimitsu served as a commander of a regiment of the Imperial Guard and then as a secretary in the War Ministry. He finally inherited Settsu Province from his father. But the folk process took over the historic story, adding more fantastic exploits to his name.

Yorimitsu already was a known sword master when the dreadful *oni,* or demon, Shuten Doji began rampaging through Kyoto. Some stories claimed that
the oni had once been human, but he had become a demon through his lust for
killing.

The emperor ordered Yorimitsu to slay the oni. Yorimitsu and his four most
trusted men disguised themselves as *yamabuse,* or Buddhist monks who lived in the
mountains and had fallen from grace. Then, they headed for the oni's mountain
home.

On their way, Yorimitsu and his followers met three mysterious old men. The
mysterious old men actually were three local gods in disguise, who saw in the
hero the best way to be rid of the oni. They gave him a magic helmet and a bottle of
a magical beverage that would make the drinker sleep.

The pretend fallen yamabuse went straight to the castle of Shuten Doji, acting
like men wanting to join the oni's service. They were invited to the oni's banquet
and served human flesh. They ate without questioning or flinching so that Shuten
Doji would believe their false identity.

The oni did believe. And when Yorimitsu offered him a drink from his bottle,
the oni drained it and fell asleep.

Yorimitsu and his four followers ran the oni through with their spears and cut
off his head. But onis do not die so easily.

Shuten Doji fought back, and the disembodied head hurled itself at Yorimitsu
and closed its powerful jaws on his head. Yorimitsu would have died, but the
magical helmet protected him.

At last, the life ebbed from the oni. The date of the oni's death is said, by Japanese folk tradition, to be (in Western years) January 25, 990.

But that was far from the last of Yorimitsu's adventures. Next, he set out to
investigate reports of a giant flying skull.

Yorimitsu and his trusted followers did find the skull and chased it, but it
escaped them. During the chase, though, the hero found an incredibly strong boy
named Kintaro, who joined his band.

The search for the skull got them nowhere. At last, they decided to stop for the
night at a house they had come across. It was run by a beautiful young woman
(though some tales claim it was a young servant boy).

Yorimitsu felt ill, and the young woman brought him medicine to help him. But
every time he tasted it, Yorimitsu felt worse, and he knew that this was a trap.

He waited for the young woman's visit, and then lashed out with his sword.
The illusion was broken, and she fled, no longer in woman form but revealed as a
hideous *tsuchigumo,* a giant spider.

The spider's web snared Yorimitsu, but his followers tore him free. Then, they
tracked the giant spider by its trail of blood.

The spider had fled to its cave. Yorimitsu's sword was named Kumokirimaru,
which means Spider-Cutter. So it was Yorimitsu who battled the tsuchigumo and,
eventually, with one great slash, he cut her open.

But there was a final horror, because from the split dead body of the giant spider poured out thousands of spiders, as large as human children. Yorimitsu and
his followers cut and slashed and fought until at last all were dead, and they could
finally claim victory.

Sources
Dorson, Richard M. *Folk Legends of Japan.* Rutland, VT, and Tokyo, Japan: Charles E. Tuttle, 1962.

Seki, Keigo, ed. *Folktales of Japan.* Trans. Robert J. Adams. Chicago: University of Chicago Press, 1969.

Bakaridjan Kone, Hero of Segu: A Folktale from Mali

There actually may have been such a man as Bakaridjan Kone. Once the magical elements are removed, the history of a great warrior living in the seventeenth century C.E., when Segu was at the height of its strength, is plausible.

Segu was not a country as we know it but a collection of related city-states in what is now known as Mali.

In the days before the hero's birth, Bakaridjan's father abandoned his family and moved to Segu City to join the court of King Da Monzon.

When the father heard that his wife, Kumba, had given birth to a son, he legally should have gone home for the naming ceremony. But he refused to go.

When King Da Monzon heard about this, he sent cowrie shells to Kumba so that there could be a proper naming ceremony. The king even gave the child a name: Bakaridjan. By doing this, he was saying, "I adopt this child."

The years passed. King Da Monzon began to worry about which of his sons should inherit his throne. And what if a hero from some other kingdom came to usurp his throne before his sons were grown? So the king consulted his diviner, who told him that there was no threat from any grown man.

"But," the diviner added, "there is a boy who will someday be able to take the throne if he wishes it. I advise you, oh king, to test all of your sons."

So the king did just that. He stabbed his spear into each son's foot, hard enough to hurt but not enough to cripple. Each boy cried out in startled pain—except for Bakaridjan. This, the king realized, was the one destined to be capable of overthrowing him.

The king's sons were less than happy about this. Indeed, the eldest son told his father, "I will kill Bakaridjan for you."

After that, there were several attempts to slay Bakaridjan, but the boy escaped them all. At last, though, he was tricked into hand-to-hand combat with the king's eldest son, and he was forced to slay him.

The king had to accept pressure from the court that Bakaridjan had been acting in self-defense, so he did not punish the boy. He merely sent him back to his home village of Disoro Nko.

In Disoro Nko, the boy continued to grow strong, and he soon had a following of other boys who wished to be heroic, too. They were ready to face the coming-of-age ceremonies to become men.

But before the ceremonies could take place, the enemy Fula people performed a great cattle raid, and they took all the livestock of the land back with them. The king ordered a war party out to return the livestock. Bakaridjan set out after them, but he soon saw the party returning in defeat.

Bakaridjan stole the king's horse, spear, and gun. And alone, the young man rescued all the livestock and drove it back to Segu.

Now, even the king could not ignore him. The fully grown Bakaridjan became a brave warrior, conquering many cities for his king. And he became well-known as a hero with great courage.

But one foe proved to be something of a problem, and that was a water djinn, or genie, named Bilissi. Bilissi started claiming cattle from the king and the people alike as his right, and Bakaridjan challenged him.

Although Bilissi used magic against Bakaridjan, the hero finally slew the djinn. But then, Bakaridjan fell, stricken by one of the djinn's sorceries, unable to move one side of his body. It took fully eighty of the king's magicians to cure him.

But magic left a mark on Bakaridjan that the magicians could not remove. He and two other men became intrigued by a woman, Aminata, who could not decide which one of the three she liked the best.

So the three suitors were set a test. The one to bring back the gun of a dangerous man named Dosoke Zan would win Aminata's hand.

Dosoke Zan, however, knew magic. He tricked the other two men. And when Bakaridjan came up against him, the hero knew he could not win against magic. For the first time in his career, he went home in disgrace.

That did not last too long. Bakaridjan was sent on a mission to capture the fine cattle that roamed a neighboring region. That region's king, hearing that the hero was coming, had all the cattle driven inside the city-state's walls.

Bakaridjan promptly spread the rumor that he had died, and hid, waiting. Sure enough, the warriors and the cattle both came out from behind the walls. Bakaridjan killed the warriors, took the cattle, and returned home, once more with honor.

Many other heroic deeds did Bakaridjan perform. He never did try to overthrow his king. And the king gave him a permanent place of honor at court.

Sources

Courtlander, Harold, and Ousmane Sako. *The Heart of the Ngoni: Heroes of the African Kingdom of Segu.* Amherst: University of Massachusetts Press, 1994.

Jackson, Guida M. *Traditional Epics.* New York and Oxford, United Kingdom: Oxford University Press, 1994.

Hua Mulan: A Folk Ballad from Ancient China

There might have been an historic Hua Mulan. Although the major folk ballad about her dates to approximately the sixth century C.E. and no longer exists save in a twelfth-century C.E. reconstruction, she actually might have lived in the fourth century C.E., during a time of trouble from would-be invaders.

The stories about Mulan claim that she disguised herself as a boy and fought alongside male warriors. Since history tells of many women who did the same, Mulan may have been such a warrior. Tradition, incidentally, claims (without actual proof) that the poet who told Mulan's tale was a woman.

Many films have been made about Mulan, most of them in China. The exception is the 1998 animated version made by Walt Disney Pictures.

Following is the anonymous ballad itself, in an anonymous translation into English.

Ode of Mulan (Anonymous)

Ji-ji, again ji-ji (the happy cricket sings),
Mulan faces the door, weaving.
You can't hear the sound of the loom's shuttle,
You only hear Daughter's sighs.

They ask Daughter who's in her thought,
They ask Daughter who's on her memory.
"No one is on Daughter's thought,
No one is on Daughter's memory."

Last night, I saw the army notices,
The Khan is calling for a great force.
The army register is in twelve scrolls,
And every scroll has Father's name.

Father has no adult son,
Mulan has no older brother.
"Wish to buy a saddle and horse,
And serve in Father's place."

In the East Market, she buys a steed.
In the West Market, she buys a saddle and saddle blanket.
In the South Market, she buys a bridle.
In the North Market, she buys a long whip.

At dawn, she bids farewell to Father and Mother,
In the evening, she camps on the bank of the Yellow River.
She doesn't hear the sound of Father and Mother calling
    for Daughter,
She only hears the Yellow River's flowing water cry *jian-jian*.

At dawn, she bids farewell to the Yellow River,
In the evening, she arrives at the summit of Black Mountain.
She doesn't hear the sound of Father and Mother calling
    for Daughter,
She only hears Mount Yan's nomad horses cry *jiu-jiu*.

She goes 10,000 miles in the war machine,
She crosses mountain passes as if flying.
Northern gusts carry sound of army rattles,
Cold light shines on iron armor.

Generals die in 100 battles,
Strong warriors return after ten years.

On her return, she sees the Son of Heaven,
The Son of Heaven sits in the ceremonial hall.

Merits are recorded in twelve ranks
And grants 100,000 strong.
The Khan asks her what she desires.
"Mulan has no use for a high official's post.
I wish to borrow a 10,000-mile camel
To take me back home."

Father and Mother hear Daughter is coming.
They go outside the city wall, supporting each other.
When Older Sister hears Younger Sister is coming,
Facing the door, she puts on rouge.

When Little Brother hears Older Sister is coming,
He sharpens the knife, quick, quick, for pig and sheep.
"I open the door to my east room,
I sit on my bed in the west room."

"I take off my wartime gown,
And put on my old-time clothes."
Facing the window, she fixes the cloudlike hair on her temples,
Facing a mirror, she dabs on yellow flower powder.

She goes out the door and sees her comrades.
Her comrades are all shocked.
Traveling together for twelve years,
They didn't know Mulan was a girl.

"The male rabbit's feet kick up and down,
The female rabbit's eyes are bewildered.
Two rabbits running close to the ground,
How can they tell if I am male or female?"

Sources

Jackson, Guida M. *Traditional Epics*. New York and Oxford, UK: Oxford University Press, 1994.
Zhang, Song Nam. *Ballad of Mulan*. Union City, CA: Pan Asian Publications, 1998.

TALL TALE HEROES

A tall tale is a story, usually a folktale, that makes a fantastic claim to explain something natural, or to tell about a character who is larger than life. A tall tale always is obviously fiction.

The tall tale heroes, for the most part, come from America and Australia. These are the heroes with fantastic strength or size, men who never actually existed, but who represent the folkloric ideals of various types of workers. There is the giant Paul Bunyan for the loggers, Pecos Bill for the cowboys, and so on. The tales always are deliberately, wildly improbable, with the tall tale heroes taking on everything from logjams to tornadoes and conquering seemingly unconquerable foes.

Paul Bunyan: A Folktale from Michigan and Wisconsin

Folklorists have argued back and forth for about fifty years as to whether the giant logger Paul Bunyan is an authentic folk figure or a literary creation. Apparently, the first stories about him appeared in 1914 in commercial publications of the Red River Lumber Company of Minnesota. They may, indeed, have been literary creations.

But no matter what his origins, there is no doubt that by now the giant Bunyan and his great blue ox, Babe, have entered the folklore pantheon of tall tale heroes. Numerous stories about the two have been and continue to be collected from the logging camps of northern Michigan and Wisconsin.

Now, Paul Bunyan, it is said, was over seven feet tall, and he was strong as he was tall.

With him was his great ox, Babe, who was, some say, seven feet from horn tip to horn tip, while other stories claim the ox was a full fourteen feet from horn tip to horn tip. Whatever the claims, both Bunyan and Babe were big. Babe was a bright blue, having slept outside one winter during a seven-day storm of blue snow that permanently dyed the ox's coat.

One day, Paul Bunyan was driving a large bunch of logs down the Wisconsin River. Just when the logs had reached the Dells, they jammed. It was a terrible jam. The logs were piled up nearly 200 feet high and went back a full mile upriver.

At the time, Bunyan and Babe were at the back of the jam. They saw that the loggers were having a terrible time trying to free the logs. So Bunyan told them to stand back and let Babe and him work.

Bunyan took Babe to the front of the jam, where he had the great ox stand in the river. Then, he strolled to the back of the jam. Standing on the riverbank, he fired his rifle at Babe.

Now, an ordinary ox would have fallen dead on the spot. To Babe, it was the merest sting, and the ox thought it was flies biting him.

So Babe started switching his tail. Bunyan fired again, and Babe began switching his tail in a full circle, like a mighty propeller.

Sure enough, the force of that powerful circular switching was so strong that the whole logjam went sailing back upstream and straightened itself out. Bunyan took Babe out of the river, and the logs floated back down the river without jamming.

Sources

Coffin, Tristram Potter, and Hennig Cohen. *The Parade of Heroes: Legendary Figures in American Lore.* Garden City, NY: Anchor/Doubleday, 1978.

Felton, Harold W., ed. *Legends of Paul Bunyan.* New York: Alfred A. Knopf, 1948.

Hardin, Terri. *A Treasury of American Folklore: Our Customs, Beliefs, and Traditions.* New York: Barnes & Noble, 1994.

Old Stormalong: A Folktale from New England

Old Stormalong was said to have been the greatest sea captain in all New England, even if he was considerably larger than life.

It began in the early 1800s, when Cape Cod, Massachusetts, was hit by a terrible storm. As the last wave surged back from the beach, the villagers heard the sound of a baby crying—a baby with a voice louder than any baby anyone had ever known.

Sure enough, the villagers found the castaway baby. But to their amazement, he was nearly eighteen feet long as he crawled toward them.

What could they do? They got the biggest wheelbarrow they could find on all Cape Cod, joined hands to lift the baby into it, and wheeled him into town. There, it took no one knew how many gallons of milk to feed him.

Since the villages had no way of knowing the baby's rightful name, they dubbed him Alfred Bulltop Stormalong. Needless to say, Old Stormalong, as a baby, was nicknamed Stormy.

Well, as Stormy grew older, he fell in love with the sea. By the time he was twelve, he bid Cape Cod farewell and took off for Boston and its seaport. There, he headed straight toward the biggest of all the Yankee clipper ships at dock. Her name was *The Lady of the Sea.*

So Stormy signed aboard as the biggest cabin boy in the history of sailing. And soon enough, he proved that he was the best cabin boy as well.

The Lady of the Sea was anchored off the coast of South America. But when the captain commanded the crew to hoist anchor, nothing happened. The cabin boy, knife between his teeth, dove overboard.

Soon after that, the ship was tossed about by terrific waves. Then, just as suddenly, the sea went calm again. There was the cabin boy, climbing the anchor chain back onto the ship. Then, he yanked up the anchor with ease.

What had happened? An enormous octopus had grabbed the anchor. But the bigger Stormy had persuaded it to let go.

Stormy's next encounter was with a kraken, a huge sea monster. But the kraken managed to escape from Stormy. That so depressed Stormy that, one day, when *The Lady of the Sea* dropped anchor in Boston, he announced that he had decided to give up his seafaring life to go out west.

So Stormy became a farmer. But it was not long before he grew homesick for the sea. After a few years out west, now a grown man, a giant of a man, indeed, he headed on back to Boston Harbor.

Alfred Bulltop Stormalong had big plans. In fact, he was set on building the biggest clipper ship in the world. So big was *The Courser* that only the Mohave Desert was large enough for the cutting and sewing of her sails. Soon *The Courser* was taking cargoes all over the world.

So big was *The Courser* that it took four weeks to get all hands on deck, and the sailors had to ride horses to get from bow to stern. The ship's masts were so tall that they had to be hinged to let the moon pass. So broad was that clipper ship that once she hit an island in the Caribbean and hurled it into the Gulf of Mexico. And when that island slammed into the coast of Panama, it drilled the Panama Canal.

But the most famous adventure took place while the ship was sailing the English Channel—and got stuck. Captain Stormalong had the crew break out every bar of soap on board and use the soap to grease the sides of the ship. Sure enough, the ship made it through. And the sign of its passing can still be seen in the white cliffs of Dover.

Stormalong did encounter the kraken again. And this time, he won, forcing the monster into a whirlpool from which it never escaped.

How old Stormalong died, no one knows for sure. One version of the story claims that he died during a trans-Atlantic race and was buried at sea. Another version states that Stormalong and his ship were caught by the last wind of a hurricane and lifted up into the sky.

Sources
Jagendorf, M. *New England Bean Pot: American Folk Stories to Read and to Tell.* New York: Vanguard, 1948.

Osborne, Mary Pope. *American Tall Tales.* New York: Scholastic, 1992.

Febold Feboldson: A Folktale from Nebraska

This tall tale hero is the hero of the Great Plains farmers. He is a larger-than-life Swedish farmer who can kill off mosquitoes or make it rain—all useful traits for a farmer in Nebraska.

No one can say how or when this powerfully built giant of a Swede came to the Nebraska Great Plains from his native land, but it must have been during the hottest of Nebraska summers. It was so hot, in fact, that the mountain ranges were melting down into foothills.

That summer, the mosquitoes were so bad that Febold Feboldson took shelter in an old boiler with a hammer as weapon. Every time one of those mosquitoes stuck its stinger through the boiler, Feboldson would hammer it sideways, so that the bug was stuck. Then, he finished off the last of them with one blast from his shotgun.

Something about the region must have appealed to Feboldson, heat and mosquitoes aside, because he decided to settle there in Nebraska.

He became a master farmer, and could fix anything—even a drought. He built enormous bonfires around all the lakes, hot fires that evaporated the lakes and formed clouds. Soon, there were so many clouds that they got so heavy with water they turned to rain.

But now there was another problem: The water just was not hitting the ground, because the air was too hot. Feboldson thought about it a bit, and then got some frogs. He got one to croak, and then they all began croaking. And the rain came down to end the drought.

Sources
Beath, Paul R. *Febold Feboldson: Tall Tales from the Great Plains.* Lincoln: University of Nebraska Press, 1948.
Welsch, Roger J. *A Treasury of Nebraska Pioneer Folklore.* Lincoln: University of Nebraska Press, 1984.

Pecos Bill: A Folktale from the American West

Can Pecos Bill really be considered a folklore hero? Stories about him by Edward O'Reilly first appeared in 1919 and were put into an anthology, *The Saga of Pecos Bill*, in 1923. Other writers added to his tales in various magazines and in two movies: Warner Brothers' *Melody Time* in 1948 and Disney's *Tall Tale: The Unbelievable Adventures of Pecos Bill* in 1995.

Over time, Pecos Bill seems to have left the literary world and taken on a life of his own. And, as with other tall tale heroes, that life has been embellished by folklore.

Born in the 1830s, Pecos Bill was the youngest of eighteen children of a Texas pioneer.

He was so tough even as a baby that he used a bowie knife as a teething ring. As a toddler, he made wild animals his playmates.

Then, while the boy was still very young, he fell out of his parents' wagon as they were crossing the Pecos River and was swept away by the current. Finally swept onto land, he was rescued by coyotes and raised as one of their own.

Years later, one of Pecos Bill's brothers found him still living with the coyotes. The brother had a hard time convincing him that just because he could hunt and howl, he was not a coyote himself.

Once Pecos Bill was returned to what civilization was available in Texas at that time, he became an excellent cowhand. It is he who was credited with inventing the branding iron and the use of cowboy songs to soothe the cattle.

But more notable by far than his cowboy skills were his amazing feats. Pecos Bill could ride a cyclone as though it were a bucking bronco, rope an entire herd at one time, and use a rattlesnake as a whip. He even harnessed the Rio Grande River to water his ranch.

Pecos Bill had a favorite horse he called Widow Maker. That horse was as mean as could be. But Pecos Bill was so tough that he often rode a mountain lion instead.

Somewhere along the line, ol' Pecos Bill met and fell in love with a woman named Slue-Foot Sue, who he found riding down the Rio Grande River on a catfish as large as a whale. Courting her, Pecos Bill shot all the stars out of the sky, leaving only the Texas Lone Star. Then, he proposed to Slue-Foot Sue.

Alas, Slue-Foot Sue tried to ride Pecos Bill's horse, Widow Maker. And Widow Maker, jealous, bucked her off. Slue-Foot Sue landed on her bustle, which bounced her higher and higher, until she hit her head on the moon.

After days of bouncing, one story claims, Pecos Bill had to shoot Slue-Foot Sue to put her out of her misery. A milder version has Sue survive, but she swears off cowboys, including Pecos Bill.

Poor Pecos Bill. He never did get married.

Sources

Botkin, B.A. *A Treasury of American Folklore.* New York: Crown, 1944.

Emrich, Duncan. *Folklore on the American Land.* Boston and Toronto, Ontario, Canada: Little, Brown, 1972.

Crooked Mick: A Folktale from Australia

The Speewah of Australia does not actually exist. It is an imaginary place without known boundaries, and it can be placed wherever a storyteller wishes it to be.

Just as the Speewah is not real, neither are the adventures of Crooked Mick. But that does not stop the tales from being told, or even a movie, *Crooked Mick of the Speewah* (2005), from being made.

Some folks say that the Speewah lies just over there. Others claim it lies west of the sunset.

On the Speewah, there are dust storms so thick people that can walk on them, and the crows fly backwards to keep the dust out of their eyes. There are trees so tall that the tops have hinges to let the sun pass. During the day, the Speewah is so hot that the freezing point is 99 degrees. Then at night, even the mirages freeze over.

This was Crooked Mick's home. When he was born, he began to grow so quickly that his father got worried and tried to slow his growth down by ring-barking the boy's legs as though he was a tree. It did not work. But it did leave him with a limp that gave him the name of Crooked Mick.

Now, Crooked Mick was so big he had to go outside just to turn around. But he was a master sheep shearer.

He could shear at least 500 sheep a day, and he worked so fast that his shears would get red hot. Then, he would drop those shears into a pot of water to cool them, and grab another pair. So fast was he that he had a dozen more sheep sheared between the time the boss said the job was done and the time Crooked Mick could hang up his shears.

He certainly was a master sheep shearer.

Sources

Macdougall, A.K., ed. *Australian Folklore. Two Centuries of Tales, Epics, Ballads, Myths and Legends.* Sydney, Australia: Reed, 1990.

Parker, K. Langloh. *Australian Legendary Tales.* London: Senate, 1998.

HEROIC OUTLAWS
AND BOLD ANTIHEROES

These are the daring but usually good-hearted outlaws of folklore, those who skirt the law but always do right when it comes to the poor or the downtrodden. They may be historical figures, such as Jesse James, whom the folk process has turned into a Robin Hood figure, or quasi-historical figures, such as Robin Hood. But they are always outside the law, yet almost always working for good.

Even a president of the United States, Theodore Roosevelt, noticed this phenomenon, commenting in the *Journal of American Folklore* (vol. 79, 1966) that, "there is something very curious in . . . [the American] sympathy for the outlaw, Jesse James taking the place of Robin Hood."

Robin Hood: A Folktale from England

Was there ever actually a Robin Hood? Scholars have argued the issue back and forth without coming to a definite conclusion. There certainly were outlaws during the tenth and eleventh centuries, men hiding in the woods and preying on the rich, and one of them might have been giving to the poor as well.

But the codified image of Robin Hood and his Merry Men robbing the rich and giving to the poor was built up over the centuries, until the basic story that was told in ballads and folktales, and later in motion pictures—from Douglas Fairbanks's 1922 *Robin Hood*, through Errol Flynn's 1938 *Adventures of Robin Hood*, down to the parody of Mel Brooks's 1993 *Robin Hood: Men in Tights*—became the "correct" version. Since the stories of Robin Hood are so well-known, only a summary of the basic tale is given here.

When King Richard I, Richard the Lionheart, rode to the Crusades, he left his brother Prince John to rule. Those were troubled times for England. And many a man lost his life or his lands, and many were thrown into outlawry.

One of those men was Robin Hood. Originally a nobleman (though some tales claim he was a commoner), he fell afoul of the harsh laws and took to the shelter of Sherwood Forest. There, he built up a band of outlaws who took his code of robbing the rich to give to the poor and of never harming a woman.

A master archer, Robin Hood also was a bit of a trickster, risking his life to win archery contests in disguise. With him were such figures as the tall Little John, Robin's cousin Will Scarlet (nicknamed for his love of red), the minstrel Alan a' Dale, and the outlaws' priest, Friar Tuck. Maid Marian, Robin's love, may have been added to the basic tale later on, but she certainly seems to be part of the story to everyone who knows of Robin Hood.

In many of the stories, the ending comes with the return of King Richard to

England. In some versions, he is scolded by Robin for abandoning his throne. But in all versions, Robin and his band are pardoned by the king.

The main villains of the story, aside from Prince John, usually are the Sheriff of Nottingham and Sir Guy of Gisborne. In fact, one version of Robin's death says that he was bled to death by an abbess who was a relative of the latter.

Sources

Bellamy, John. *Robin Hood: An Historical Enquiry.* Bloomington, IN: Indiana University Press, 1985.

Blamires, David. *Robin Hood: A Hero for All Times.* Manchester, United Kingdom: The John Rylands University Library of Manchester, 1998.

Steckmesser, Kent L. "Robin Hood and the American Outlaw: A Note on History and Folklore." *Journal of American Folklore* vol. 79 (1966): 348–355.

Hereward the Wake: A Folktale from Anglo-Saxon England

Hereward was an Anglo-Saxon leader of the eleventh century. The fact that he lived around 1070 is the only date we have for him. We also know that he led a resistance movement against the Norman Conquest, and was, as a result, labeled an outlaw by the Normans. He used the Fens of eastern England as his base of operations so successfully that he eventually made peace with the Normans and was given back his lands. That much about him is fact. The title "Wake," signifying "watchful," may date from after his death.

But the folklore process soon began. Legend placed Hereward's base of operations on the Isle of Ely. That may or may not have been true. But as early as the beginning of the twelfth century, folkloric adventures for Hereward had been created. The authors of various chronicles featuring his adventures are not known, but it is clear that the romanticized Hereward captured the English imagination.

Forced to temporarily flee to Cornwall, Hereward found that King Alef had betrothed his fair daughter to a terrible Pictish giant. Worse, he had done that by breaking off her trothplight with Prince Sigtryg of Waterford, son of a Danish king in Ireland. The princess feared the giant, and she was in love with Prince Sigtryg.

Hereward, ever chivalrous, picked a quarrel with the giant and killed him in fair fight. Whereupon, the king threw Hereward into prison.

That night, however, the princess arranged for her gallant Saxon rescuer to be freed. She begged him to speed to her beloved Prince Sigtryg.

After many adventures, unfortunately not recorded, Hereward reached Prince Sigtryg, who hastened to return to Cornwall with the young hero. But to the grief of both, they learned, on their arrival, that the princess had just been betrothed to a wild Cornish hero, Haco. The wedding feast was to be held that very day.

At once, Prince Sigtryg sent a troop of forty Danes to King Alef, demanding the fulfilment of the trothplight between himself and the king's daughter and threatening vengeance if it were broken. To this threat, the king returned no answer, and no Dane came back to tell of their reception.

Plate 17.

A Renaissance painting from Germany shows St. George in the act of slaying a dragon.

Illustration by Lucas Cranach, the Elder (1472–1553). Courtesy of The Bridgeman Art Library/ Getty Images.

Plate 18.
Davy Crockett stands proudly. The folk hero added to his legendary
exploits with his own tall tales.

*Illustration by James Edwin McConnell (1903–1995). Courtesy of Private Collection/© Look
and Learn/ The Bridgeman Art Library International.*

Plate 19.
The Lincoln Special, the funeral train that transported Abraham Lincoln's body from Washington to Illinois for burial, is said to still travel the rails as a ghostly train.

Courtesy of Private Collection/Peter Newark American Pictures/The Bridgeman Art Library.

Plate 20.
These larger-than-life statues of Paul Bunyan and Babe the Blue Ox stand over the town of Lake Bemidji, Minnesota. The town claims to be Bunyan's birthplace.

Plate 21.
Old Stormalong battles the giant octopus.

Illustration by Oliver Frey (1948–). Courtesy of Private Collection/© Look and Learn/ The Bridgeman Art Library.

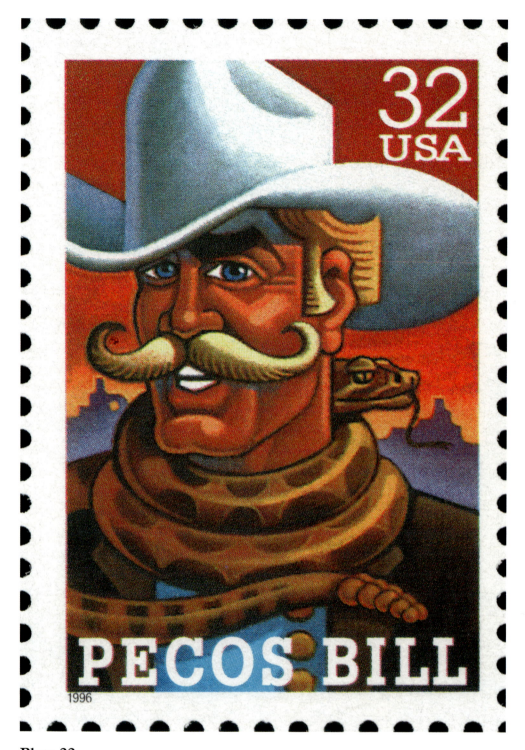

Plate 22.
This United States postage stamp features an illustration of Pecos Bill.

Courtesy of Blank Archives/Hulton Archive/Getty Images.

Plate 23.
In a classic scene from the Robin Hood folktales, Robin Hood and Little John meet and fight on the bridge. John knocks Robin in the water, and the two men become fast friends.

Illustration by Howard Davie (fl. 1914–1944), from Robin Hood and his Life in the Merry Greenwood, *by Rose Yeatman Woolf, published by Raphael Tuck, 1910–1920. Courtesy of Private Collection/The Bridgeman Art Library.*

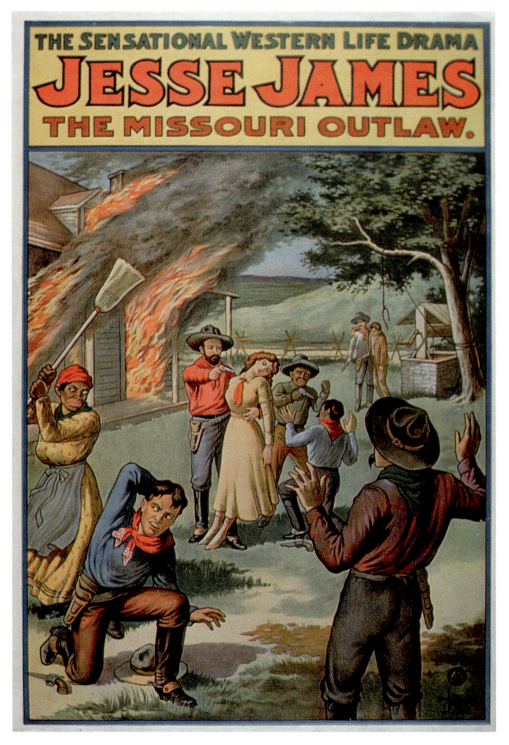

Plate 24.
Jesse James may have been a notorious outlaw, but folk culture turned him into a hero.

Illustration by the American School, from a twentieth century advertisement. Courtesy of Private Collection/Barbara Singer/The Bridgeman Art Library.

Prince Sigtryg would have waited until morning, trusting in the honor of the king. But Hereward, not trusting the king at all, disguised himself as a minstrel and gained access to the bridal feast.

At the feast, Hereward soon won applause with his beautiful singing. The bridegroom, Haco, offered the "minstrel" any boon he liked to ask, but Hereward demanded only a goblet of wine from the hands of the bride.

When she brought the wine to him, Hereward slipped the betrothal ring from Prince Sigtryg into the goblet and said, "I thank thee, lady, and would reward thee for thy gentleness to a wandering minstrel. I give back the goblet, richer than before."

The princess gazed into the goblet and saw her ring. She then looked again at the minstrel and was hard put not to laugh, knowing that rescue was at hand.

While men feasted, Hereward listened and talked. He found out that the forty Danes were prisoners. They would be released on the morrow when Haco was sure of his bride—but only after they had been blinded. Haco was taking his lovely bride back to his own land. And Hereward saw that any rescue, to be successful, must be attempted on the march.

Hurrying back to Sigtryg, Hereward told all that he had learned. The Danes planned an ambush in the ravine where Haco planned to blind and then set free his captives.

The Cornishmen, with the Danish captives, passed first without attack. Next, came Haco, riding grim and ferocious beside his silent bride, he exulting in his success, she eagerly looking for any signs of rescue.

As they passed, Hereward sprang from his shelter, crying, "Upon them, Danes, and set your brethren free!"

Hereward struck down Haco and smote off his head. There was a short struggle, but soon the rescued Danes were able to aid their deliverers, and the Cornish guards were all slain. The men of King Alef, never very zealous for the cause of Haco, fled. And the Danes were left masters of the field.

Prince Sigtryg had, in the meantime, seen to the safety of the princess. And now, with Hereward, he escorted her to the ship, which soon brought them to Waterford and a happy wedding.

The Prince and Princess of Waterford always recognized in Hereward their deliverer and best friend. In their gratitude, they wished him to dwell with them always. But the hero was hardly ready to settle down in exile. He had deeds of arms to win.

Sources
Ebbutt, M.I. *The British: Myths and Legends.* 1910. London: Senate, 1994.
Kingsley, Charles. *Hereward the Wake.* London: Macmillan, 1895.

Jesse James: A Folktale from the American West

The historic Jesse James was the most notorious of bank and train robbers in the West in the last half of the nineteenth century. Not too much could be said for him except for a touch of gallantry: He never would rob a woman, but merely would kiss her.

His death came at the hand of a member of his own gang, Robert Ford, who wanted the reward and is said to have shot James in the back. (Ford, incidentally, was then shot in revenge by another member of James's gang.) But the folk process turned James into a Robin Hood figure, a helper of the poor.

One summer day, Jesse James was riding his fine black stallion down a country road, when he heard the wailing of an old widow woman from her shack.

He rode up to her and asked politely, "Ma'am, what's wrong?"

"I cannot pay the mortgage," she told him in despair. "And my landlord is coming to put me out of my home because of it."

"Do not worry," Jesse said, and he handed her the required amount.

He rode on down the road and rested his horse awhile in the cool shade of some bushes. Some even might have called it hiding.

There went the landlord. To the landlord's surprise, the old widow woman handed over the mortgage. Grumbling a bit, the landlord rode on down the road. Soon, he was near the bushes where Jesse waited.

Out rode Jesse with his black mask on and his ugly gun out. He demanded the money. The landlord quickly surrendered it and galloped away.

So it was that Jesse lent his money for a bit, gave happiness to a poor widow woman, and went on his way without any loss to himself.

Sources

Coffin, Tristram Potter, and Hennig Cohen. *The Parade of Heroes: Legendary Figures in American Lore*. Garden City, NY: Anchor/Doubleday, 1978. Collected by Margaret Gillis Fish from L.C. Rogers of Montgomery, Alabama, March 1948.

Emrich, Duncan. *Folklore on the American Land*. Boston and Toronto, Ontario, Canada: Little, Brown, 1972.

Railroad Bill: A Folktale from the American South

Railroad Bill actually was an African American man named Morris Slater, who, in 1892, refused to register his rifle in Florida, and exchanged shots with the deputy sheriff before escaping.

Slater then became famous for jumping on freight trains to steal goods, throwing cans of food and other goods off the boxcars, then jumping off and collecting his loot. He would sell the goods cheaply to the poor, and sometimes he even gave them away. Slater eluded the law for several years, but the law finally caught up with him. He was shot to death in 1896. That much is fact, including his nickname being Railroad Bill. But, as often happens, folklore began to surround the facts.

Morris Slater was soon known across northern Florida and southern Alabama as Railroad Bill. Pretty soon, his escapes and escapades made people sure that he possessed supernatural powers.

He might have been a conjurer, stories claimed, trained in the powers of hoodoo. And he might even have been a shapeshifter who could change himself into an animal and escape that way. In fact, it even was said that Railroad Bill turned himself into a dog and joined the sheriff's pack of hounds to "chase himself" all the way to his girlfriend's house. There, he left the pack and stayed nice and peaceful, while the posse and dogs continued their search.

The stories claimed that Railroad Bill could catch bullets in his bare hands, and that he could be slain only by a silver bullet. He also was magically skilled with a pistol. Once, he shot the buttons right off a brakeman's coat without harming the man.

Even after he was said to have been shot dead by the law, stories claimed that whoever handled Railroad Bill's body died of blood poisoning. Or maybe he never did die, but roamed on freely in the shape of a fox, or a hound, or even an eagle.

Many a ballad was created about Railroad Bill. Following is part of one that is very much in the public domain and has many variants.

The Ballad of Railroad Bill

Railroad Bill, Railroad Bill,
He never worked, and he never will,
And it's ride, ride, ride.

Railroad Bill's a mighty mean man,
Shot the light out of the poor brakeman's hand.

Railroad Bill, up on a hill,
Lightin' a seegar with a $10 bill.

Got a thirty-special in a forty-five frame,
I can't miss 'cause I got dead aim.

Sources
Botkin, B.A. *A Treasury of American Folklore.* New York: Crown, 1944.
Emrich, Duncan. *Folklore on the American Land.* Boston and Toronto, Ontario, Canada: Little, Brown, 1972.

Stagolee/Stackalee: A Folktale from Missouri

An African American from Missouri, Lee Sheldon was known as Stagolee/Stackalee—or sometimes as Stack Lee, or just Stack—and he was a carriage driver and a pimp. The facts behind the folklore built around him are simple and grim. In 1895, a story in the *Globe-Democrat* of St. Louis, Missouri, reported that

William Lyons, 25, a levee hand, was shot in the abdomen yesterday evening at 10 o'clock in the saloon of Bill Curtis, at Eleventh and Morgan Streets, by Lee Sheldon, a carriage driver . . . Both parties . . . had been drinking . . . and an argument was started, the conclusion of which was that Lyons snatched

Sheldon's hat from his head. The latter demanded its return. Lyons refused, and Sheldon...shot Lyons in the abdomen. When his victim fell to the floor Sheldon took his hat from the hand of the wounded man and coolly walked away. He was subsequently arrested....

But the folk process was not satisfied with that stark account, especially in the African American community. Soon, the hero of the story took on supernatural strength.

Stagolee, or Stack for short, came into this world both double-jointed and with a veil over his face. The gypsy woman who helped deliver him knew that the veil was a clear sign that the baby was "born to raise hell":

> Gypsy told Stack's mother,
> Told her like a friend,
> Your double-jinted baby
> Won't come to no good end.

Sure enough, the baby grew into a bad, wild man. Some say he could change his shape or walk barefoot on hot coals without harm.

Some even said that Stack sold his soul to the devil, and in exchange, the devil gave him a magic Stetson hat. Now, Stack was mad about Stetson hats, and he already had several, but this one, of oxblood leather, was never to be lost. If Stack did lose it, the devil warned, he would lose his life as well.

What followed were wild days. Stack ran briefly with Jesse James, but that did not suit him, so he escaped in the form of a horse.

Heading on out to San Francisco, he ran into a racist bartender who refused to serve him. Stack warned him, "You either fix me up with that gin or I pulls down this bar!"

The bartender did not believe him. So Stack took hold of the bar with both hands, set himself, and pulled down the whole building. Some say it was an earthquake, but others say it was just Stack getting angry.

Stack left the West soon after that, and settled in St. Louis. And that is where his doom caught up with him.

One night, Stack was gambling with a man named Billy Lyons. And Lyons stole the magic Stetson hat from Stack.

Mad beyond thought to lose that magic hat, Stack opened fire and blasted Billy down. That got Stack in prison.

But there is one last tale to tell. For when Stack went down to hell, he gave the devils there so fierce a fight that they threw him out before he murdered them all.

Stack is no longer with the living. But no one can say where he went.

Sources

Botkin, B.A. *A Treasury of American Folklore.* New York: Crown, 1944.

Emrich, Duncan. *Folklore on the American Land.* Boston and Toronto, Canada: Little, Brown, 1972.

The Master Thief

The hero of this worldwide folk motif is hardly a hero in any conventional sense. He is a classic antihero who probably is so popular in so many cultures because he gets the better of the wealthy or the self-important.

Efflam the Master Thief: A Breton Folktale

This Breton folktale follows much of the standard "Master Thief" tale, except that this master thief has a sister, who is his partner in crime and winds up with as much of a good reward as does the master thief.

Once, there was a man with two offspring, a boy named Efflam and a girl named Henori. Efflam was the older of the two, and so he set out into the world to find himself something to do.

But Efflam had not gone far into the forest before he heard thieves chattering as if they had not a care in the world. Quickly and quietly, Efflam climbed a nearby tree to hear what the thieves were saying.

One of the thieves had a magic cloak that would take him wherever he wished to be. The second thief had a magic hat that made him invisible. The third had magic shoes that let him move like the wind.

"Call yourselves thieves, do you?" Efflam muttered. "If I had those gifts, I would be a master thief."

So he sprang down from the tree, shouting in his loudest, fiercest voice, "Thieves! Thieves!"

As Efflam had planned, the three thieves were so frightened, sure the law had found them, that they dropped their magic gifts and fled. Efflam picked up the gifts.

From that day on, Efflam found it no trouble to steal whatever he wished. And no one was the wiser, save for his father and sister, with whom he shared his prizes.

But this was no challenge to a master thief. One day, Efflam heard of the king's treasure house, and he said to himself, "Now, there is a challenge worthy of me!"

That night, with the help of his three magic gifts, Efflam robbed the king's treasury. And he got far away with no one the wiser, save for his father and sister.

Soon, though, the king learned of the theft and decided to set traps all around. This time, Efflam's father decided to go stealing with his son—and got caught and beheaded by the traps. Efflam quickly took anything that might identify his father from the body and fled.

When the king found the headless body, he had no way to identify the thief. He decided to have the body sent around town in a cart, and anyone who mourned would be arrested.

Efflam warned his sister not to mourn. But when she saw their father's body, she could not keep from crying. So Efflam quickly cut her hand with his dagger, not badly, just enough so that when the soldiers came running in, she could say, "I cut myself, and it hurt so much I wept."

Now that the king's plan had failed, he had the body nailed to a wall of his palace. He set two guards to watch it.

Efflam and his sister disguised themselves as wine merchants, put sacks of drugged wine on a donkey, and set out for the palace. They let a sack fall and break open, and left it. When they returned, both guards had drunk from it and had fallen sound asleep. The brother and sister took down their father's body and buried it honorably.

When the king found the body gone, he raged up and he raged down. "That thief thinks he is too clever for me! Very well, I shall put on display a pure white goat in the middle of the town square. Let us see what our thief does then!"

But with his magic gifts, Efflam stole the goat and was away with it without a soul seeing him. "I have brought us a tasty dinner," he told his sister.

The king sent out a guard disguised as a beggar. If he so much as smelled goat meat cooking, he was to mark the door of that house with a white cross.

But when the king went looking for that white cross, he found that every door had a white cross chalked on it!

Now, the king found that he was beginning to admire the clever thief. "Very well, I shall now put my royal crown on display. Let us see him steal that!"

Of course, Efflam stole it as easily as he had stolen the goat.

By now, the king was beginning to think that it might be a good thing to have this mysterious thief on his side. So he put his daughter, the princess, on display. "Whoever can steal her shall wed her!" he proclaimed.

Efflam stole the princess, and took her home. There, they talked, and Efflam, the princess, and Henori became friends.

When the king found them, the princess said, "Efflam and I will be married. And you, father, shall marry Henori."

That was fine with everyone. And from that day on, Efflam stole no more.

Sources

Proust, Pierre-Yves. *Legendes, Contes et Recits des Pays Bretons.* Marseilles, France: Editions Autre Temps, 1995.

Soupault, Ré, ed. *Breton Folktales.* Trans. Ruth E.K. Meuss. London: G. Bell & Sons, 1971.

The Butler's Clever Son: A Folktale from Scotland

Here is a variant in which the boy apprentices himself to a thief to learn a trade and becomes a master thief. It happens because the laird orders his butler to find the butler's son an honest trade—but the boy is not an honest fellow.

Now, this was in the days of lairds, or lords, and their servants. This one laird had a butler who was an honest man. But the butler had a son who was a born thief. When the laird of the manor found this out, he told the butler to send his son away to learn a trade.

Off the son went to learn a trade. But the first man he met was a thief, and so the son signed on with him.

"Watch and learn," the thief told the boy. He took them into a watch store, and by distracting the owner, managed to slip a gold watch up his sleeve, then leave.

But the boy was a better thief. "Did you see that fellow? He slipped a gold watch up his sleeve, smooth as can be!"

While the watchmaker ran in vain after the thief, who already had gotten away, the boy calmly took a whole shelf of watches and just as calmly strolled off. When he met up with the thief again, he showed the man how much finer a thief he was.

Well, the thief decided he would get even with the boy for that. He told him, "There is a fine house to rob. I will lower you into the cellar on a rope so you can see if there are valuables down there."

So he did. But while the boy was down there, the thief pulled up the rope and left him stuck there.

But the boy was not out of tricks. He saw the hide of a cow with the hoofs and horns still attached and wrapped himself up in it. Then, he began to howl most terribly.

When the servants came to investigate, they saw a horrible horned figure standing on two legs. "It's the Evil One himself!" they cried.

"Indeed it is," the boy said in a hissing voice. "And if you do not throw me down the keys to the house, I shall send you and it down to the flames below!"

Well, they threw down the keys and fled. The boy helped himself to some of the house riches, and then he strolled away.

Casting off the disguise, the boy went home. But both his father and the laird saw him, and the laird was furious. "You could not have been away long enough to learn a trade."

"Oh, but I did," the boy said. "I am a fine thief."

"Are you, now? Here is a deal for you. I will put a bullet through your head with my own gun if you cannot steal the sheet out from under myself and my wife tonight."

"I can and will," the boy said.

There was a body in the churchyard that had been buried only a day past. The boy dug it up and changed clothes with it. Then, he took a ladder and climbed it with the corpse over his shoulder. He carefully pried open the laird's bedroom window and stuck the corpse's head inside.

The laird woke. He saw what he thought was someone trying to enter, and thought it must be the thieving boy. "You have lost," he said, and fired a shot clean through the corpse's head. The force of the shot sent the body crashing to the ground. The laird rushed out of bed to get rid of the body.

Meanwhile, the boy had stolen into the manor. He muttered in the laird's voice, "The brute is heavier than I thought. I need something to put him in so I can drag him away. Give me a sheet."

Now, the wife thought this was, indeed, her husband, and she passed him the sheet from their bed. The boy hurried off.

The laird returned. "What's this?" he cried. "Where is the sheet from our bed?"

"I gave it to you as you asked!" the wife replied.

"I never said that!"

"You did!"

That was when the laird realized the boy had won their contest. He never said another word about it.

And the boy went off into the wide world as a master thief.

Source
Bruford, Alan, and Donald A. MacDonald. *Scottish Traditional Tales*. Edinburgh, United
   Kingdom: Polygon, 1994. Recorded from Samuel Thornburn, Isle of Skye, by James Ross,
   July 1953. Published from the original transcription made by Ross in 1953.

Ko-Tieke-Iti, Little Tieke, the Dancing Thief: A Folktale from the Maori of New Zealand

Little Tieke, the thief of the story, is as much a trickster as he is a thief. And, like any good master thief, he can get himself out of trouble with a trick.

There once were two brothers, Big Tieke and Little Tieke. Big Tieke was a fisherman. Little Tieke was a thief, and a very good, tricky one. He knew how to get out of trouble even if he got caught.

One day, after Little Tieke had stolen one kumara, or sweet potato, too many, the farmers lay in wait for him. They cornered him in a storage shed, and dragged him out.

The farmers debated about killing Little Tieke. But he was not at all worried.

"Do not kill me until I have danced for you," he said.

All right, then, the farmers decided. "Let us see you dance."

So he started to dance, chanting as he did:

> Little Tieke, little Tieke,
> Watch him dance from far away.

So the farmers watched. And with each step, though none of them realized it, Little Tieke was a step farther away from them.

At last, he laughed and said, "That is all!"

And since he was too far away by then to be caught, he simply ran away. That is all.

Sources
Orbell, Margaret. *The Illustrated Encyclopedia of Maori Myth and Legend*. Christchurch, New
   Zealand: Canterbury University Press, 1995.
———, ed. and trans. *Traditional Maori Stories*. Aukland, New Zealand: Reed, 1992.

The Best Thief: A Folktale from Spanish New Mexico

This variant on the "Master Thief" theme features three sons—one a tailor, one a shoemaker, and one a thief—who all work together to help the thief succeed. This story features many of the same themes as the tale "The Butler's Clever Son" from Scotland, including the "killing" of the thief.

There once was a poor man and wife who could not raise their three sons. So they gave them into the care of the boys' godfathers.

One boy's godfather was a tailor, so the boy learned to make fine suits of clothes.

One boy's godfather was a shoemaker, so the boy learned to make shoes of the softest leather.

The third boy's godfather was a thief. One day, the thief said to the boy, "Let us see which of us is the better thief."

He led the boy to a tree with a bird's nest in it. There was a bird in the nest sitting on its eggs. "I will steal the eggs right out of the nest without the bird even knowing it," said the godfather thief. "Then I will put them back, and it will be your turn."

So the godfather thief climbed the tree and stole the eggs right out from under the bird without the bird knowing it. He put the eggs in his pocket.

But the boy was right behind him without the godfather thief knowing it. The boy took the eggs out of the godfather thief's pocket and slipped them into his own pocket. Then, he went back down the tree, again without the godfather thief knowing it.

When the godfather thief climbed down, he said to the boy, "Here are the . . ."

"Are these the eggs you are hunting?" the boy asked.

"You are definitely the better thief," the godfather thief said. "Return the eggs and go home. I can teach you nothing more."

All three sons came home. Their parents were delighted with the tailor and the shoemaker. But they were very alarmed when they learned that the third boy was now a thief. The thief, however, promised them that he would never harm anyone in his craft.

Now, the king of that land soon heard how fine a tailor and shoemaker were in that home, and that the third son was a master thief. He sent for all three. The tailor and shoemaker found work right away. But the king had the thief brought before him.

"Is it true that you are a thief?" the king asked.

"I am a master thief," the boy replied.

"Let us test you. I will send twelve soldiers to a certain place. Each will have a burro loaded with coins. You are to take that money without the soldiers knowing it. If you can bring the coins to me, you will be welcome to stay in my palace, as I can always use a clever man. If you fail, you will be hung."

The thief asked his two brothers to make him a figure that looked like a dead man, big enough for him to hide inside. Then, he stole out of the palace ahead of the soldiers. As the night came on, the thief hung the figure from a tree and hid inside it.

Soon, the soldiers saw the "dead man" hanging from the tree, and they said a prayer for him. Then, the soldiers began arguing over where they should spend the night, and the thief heard all their plans. He followed them and waited until they were all settled down for the night.

Then, the thief began whooping and hollering like a pack of angry Apaches, and the soldiers ran for their lives. The thief took the money and returned to the king.

"There you are, Your Majesty," he said cheerfully.

The king was amazed. But he said, "I want to give you another test. The soldiers know about your trick, so it will not be so easy for you to steal the money away this time."

The thief only smiled. He went to his two brothers and asked them for twelve priests' robes. His brothers made them, and the thief set out before the soldiers and dressed himself as a priest.

When the night was beginning to fall, the thief, dressed as a priet, met the soldiers and made a holy sign. "Blessings on you, my sons."

"Won't you spend the night with us, Father?" the soldiers asked.

"No, no, I have to go on to say Mass."

"At least stop and have a drink with us."

So the thief took a bottle of whiskey out of his robes. He drank only coffee, but the soldiers finished off that whiskey. They finally were so drunk that they all fell asleep. The thief took off their soldiers' uniforms and dressed them as priests. Then, he took the money.

The next morning, the soldiers woke up with much moaning and groaning, and found themselves dressed as priests. They hurried back to the king's palace, but the people at the royal church thought they were priests, and tried to get them to say Mass. By the time the soldiers had gotten away from there, the thief already had reached the king.

"There is your money, Your Majesty!" the thief said.

The queen shook her head and murmured to the king, "This one could steal the sheet right off our bed, and we would not even know it."

"Now there is a good test," the king said. To the thief, he announced, "If you can take the sheet from my bed, I will give you half my fortune. But if you fail, I shall be forced to hang you."

"That is a fair deal," the thief said.

Off the thief went to his two brothers. He needed another life-sized figure of a man, he told them. This one, he filled with a pig's intestine, full of pig blood.

That night, the thief slowly pushed the figure into the room, making it look as though the figure was stealing inside.

"There he is!" the queen whispered.

The king drew his sword and struck the figure. It collapsed, and the pig blood poured out of it.

"Too bad," said the king. "He was clever, but not clever enough." He slung the figure over his shoulder and took him out to be buried.

As soon as the king was gone, the thief went into the royal bedchamber, keeping to the shadows. "Ay, he was heavy!" he said. Getting into bed, he told the queen, "Move over." He kept telling her to move over until he had removed the sheet. Then, he said, "I had best check to see if they have buried him."

He left the room.

Now, the king returned. "He was heavy!"

"You just told me that!" said the queen.

"No, I just got here!"

"You were here!"

The king lit all the lamps. "Whose blood is that?" he wondered.

Then, he saw that the sheet was gone.

The next day, the thief came before the king. "Here is your sheet, Your Majesty. Oh, and that was pig's blood you spilled."

When the king heard how the theft had been done, he gave the thief a place as the royal thief, the fellow who would steal whatever was needed. And with a tailor, a shoemaker, and a royal thief in the family, the three sons and their parents soon were quite wealthy.

Source

Hayes, Joe. *Cuentos de Cuanto Hay: Tales from Spanish New Mexico.* Albuquerque: University of New Mexico Press, 1998. Collected by J. Manuel Espinos from Patrocina Roybul, Penasco, New Mexico, ca. 1930.

The Thieves Who Tricked Each Other: A Folktale from the Akamba of Kenya

Sometimes there are two master thieves in a story, who try to trick each other, like a pair of con men. That is the case in this story.

Once, there were two clever thieves, Mulu and Kitoo. Each thief worked alone. But one day, the two thieves happened to meet. Mulu had a honey barrel. Kitoo had a tobacco barrel.

"Greetings, fellow," said Kitoo. "What is in that barrel?"

"Honey," said Mulu. "I plan to sell it to buy tobacco."

"And I plan to sell this tobacco to buy honey!" Kitoo exclaimed.

"Let us merely switch barrels," said Mulu.

So they did, and each man went home.

But when Mulu opened the tobacco barrel, all he found was a thin layer of tobacco over a barrel-full of cow dung. And when Kitoo opened the honey barrel, all he found was a thin layer of honey over a barrel-full of cow dung.

The two thieves rushed off to fight.

But when they met, they began to laugh instead. "We are both equally clever," said Kitoo.

"We were pulling the same trick," said Mulu.

And they became fast friends and the cleverest team of thieves in all the land!

Sources

Klipple, May Augusta. *African Folktales with Foreign Analogues.* The Garland Folklore Library. New York and London: Garland, 1992.

Mbiti, John, ed. *Akamba Stories.* The Oxford Library of African Literature. London: Oxford University Press, 1966.

Tales of Kindness Repaid and Hope and Redemption

These folktales may be wonder tales or contain wonder in them, but they also may be more realistic teaching tales. They are the moral tales, featuring what each culture finds good or bad, but they usually teach a lesson without being didactic.

Tales of kindness repaid often show the worth of treating animals well, especially when the animals turn out to be supernatural creatures who will then help the protagonist. There also are tales of kindness to beggars; they also often turn out to be supernatural beings who will help the protagonist. But woe to the hard-hearted person who ignores animals or beggars in need, for that person likely will wind up with an unhappy ending.

Tales of hope and redemption deal with sinners reforming or innocent folks, such as fairy folk, learning that they, too, can worship freely and hope for redemption. These are the closest to religious folktales, but such tales usually do not specify a particular religion and are common to many cultures.

FOLKTALES OF KINDNESS REPAID

In this folktale type, the protagonist does a kind deed with no thought of reward. He or she is rewarded because of such selfless kindness.

Kindhearted Ferko: A Folktale from Hungary

This folktale is a case in point for being kind to animals, even snakes. Because the hero has a kind heart, he ends up with a treasure.

Once, there was, where there was not, beyond the Glass Mountains, a widow with one son, Ferko.

Now, when Ferko was not needed to help his mother with her chores, he loved to go down to the water's edge and skip stones or just watch the waves. But one day, he went down to the water's edge in time to see some children toss a cat into the waves.

"No!" he said. "That is cruel! That cat is too small to swim." And he dove in and rescued the cat.

"That is our cat," said the children. "You must pay us for her."

So Ferko paid them one of his precious copper coins and took the poor, wet cat home. That was all right with his mother, since there were mice in the house. But she was sorry he had spent any of their precious money.

The next time that Ferko went to the water's edge, he saw some children toss a dog into the waves.

" "No!" he said. "That is cruel! That dog is too young to swim." And he dove in and rescued the dog.

"That is our dog," said the children. "You must pay us for him. And this time, we want *two* copper coins."

So Ferko paid them two of his precious copper coins and took the poor, wet dog home. That was all right with his mother, since they now had a guard for the house. But she was sorry he had spent any of their precious money.

The next time that Ferko went to the water's edge, he saw the children toss a tiny snake into the waves.

"No!" he said. "That is cruel! That snake is too tiny to swim." And he dove in and rescued the snake.

"You must pay us," the children insisted. "We want three copper coins from you, or we will take the snake from you and kill him."

Ferko could not fight all of them. With a sigh, he gave them three precious copper coins.

But this time, when his mother saw what he had brought home and learned what he had spent precious money on, she shouted at Ferko and slapped him, and scolded him, and beat him. This went on for so long that finally Ferko tucked the tiny snake into his shirt and set out into the world to find his fortune.

As they wandered here and wandered there and wandered over seven king-doms wide, the snake began to grow. Now, it was so big, it traveled next to Ferko. Now, it grew again, and said to Ferko, "You have cared for me, my kind master. Let me care for you. Come, sit on my back."

So Ferko settled himself on the gleaming scales. The snake started forward, slithering with speed through forest and over water. At last, the snake stopped in a small thicket.

"Now, my master, do you see that hollow tree? Take the flute you find inside and blow one clear note. That will summon the Twelve-Headed Dragon. Do not say a word until after I talk to her. Then, she will ask you what you want. Say that you wish nothing but the golden ring."

Ferko agreed. He blew one clear note on the flute. Almost at once, there was a wild whirling of air that nearly threw him to the ground. The Twelve-Headed Dragon was landing.

"Mother!" cried the snake. "I was caught by an eagle and dropped by some children. They would have killed me, but this young man saved my life."

The Twelve-Headed Dragon turned all twelve of her heads to look at Ferko. Her eyes were fierce and golden. But her voice was gentle. "Do not fear me, little human. You saved my son's life. What reward do you wish?"

"Only the golden ring," Ferko said.

"Not that! I will give you diamonds, I will give you all the treasure you can carry."

"Only the golden ring," Ferko replied once again.

"Very well. Put it on your finger, twist it three times, and see what happens."

With that, the Twelve-Headed Dragon and her son vanished.

Ferko twisted the ring three times. Three giants appeared and asked, "What is your wish?"

"I wish you . . . to take me back to my mother," Ferko told them.

Instantly, he was there. Ferko twisted the ring backwards three times, and the giants vanished. "Mother!" he shouted. "I have brought back a treasure."

He showed her the ring and told her of the three giants. From that day on, they could have whatever they needed.

It was all because of Ferko's kindness to a snake.

Sources

Degh, Linda, ed. *Folktales from Hungary.* Chicago and London: University of Chicago Press, 1969.

Severo, Emoke de Papp. *Hungarian and Transylvanian Folktales.* Nepean, Ontario, Canada: Borealis, 1997.

The Tiger and the Man: A Folktale from Ghana, West Africa

Usually in folklore, affairs between tigers or other predatory animals and human beings end sadly for one or the other. This tale of true kindness is an exception to the rule.

Tigers are, of course, not native to Africa. But in West African storytelling, as well as in Caribbean storytelling, any predatory cat may be called a tiger.

O nce, a kindhearted hunter came upon an injured tiger. The tiger was sure the man would kill him, and it prepared to die.

But instead, the hunter said, "Hello, tiger. Do not be afraid or try to attack. I want to help you."

The amazed tiger let the hunter examine him.

"Aha," said the hunter, "here is the trouble. You must have escaped from a wire trap."

"I did," replied the tiger

"Well, there is a wire still twisted around your leg. There, you are free of it now."

"I would like to invite you to my cave to meet my family," the tiger said.

Now, it was the hunter's turn to be uneasy. But he thought, "A kindness for a kindness."

Sure enough, the hunter had a lovely visit with the tiger's wife and cub.

"Won't you let me return the favor?" he asked the tiger. "Come meet my family."

Now, it was the tiger's turn to be uneasy. But he thought, "A kindness for a kindness."

Sure enough, the tiger and his family had a lovely visit with the hunter's wife and child, and the human child and the tiger cub played together.

Then, a few months later, the hunter's father died. To the hunter's amazement, the tiger came to offer condolences.

But on the way home from the funeral, the tiger narrowly escaped being killed by wicked hunters. He played dead, wondering if these wicked hunters were with the hunter who he had befriended, and he told his cub to play dead, too.

But when the kindhearted hunter saw the tiger and his cub lying there, seemingly dead, he burst into tears, and so did his son.

The tiger cub could not stand it. He jumped up and started playing with the boy. The tiger and the hunter laughed. Their friendship was true.

And it was a kindness for a kindness.

Sources

Asihene, Emmanuel. *Traditional Folk-Tales of Ghana*. Lampeter, United Kingdom: Edwin Mellen, 1997.

Spears, Richard, ed. *West African Folk Tales*. Collected and trans. by Jack Berry. Evanston, IL: Northwestern University Press, 1991.

The Amir Kheyyun and the Golden Fish: A Folktale from Iraq

In this unusual folktale of kindness, a young prince is kindhearted, but he is afraid of women. His kindness to a trapped fish that is really a female magician in disguise leads to her and her mate helping the prince to get over his fear and to find the maiden who steals his heart. Another unusual moment is the removal of a curse that was placed on her.

N ow, there was a sultan of sultans whose name was Hajji Ali. He had but one son, the Amir Kheyyun, a handsome young man of some twenty years.

The Amir was brave and thoughtful. He had a good heart. Indeed, he had only one flaw: He feared that women were evil. His father did his best to change his son's mind, pointing out that his mother certainly had not been evil, nor had his grandmother been evil.

But the Amir would not listen. The truth may have been that, deep within him, he knew little of women and feared what he did not know. So stubborn was he about not being wed that, at last, his father threw him into prison, hoping that that would teach the young man some wisdom.

It happened, one day, that a fisherman caught in his net a wonderful fish of gold. The fisherman knew that the Amir was in prison, and he decided to take the wonderful golden fish to him to cheer up the young man. So he put the golden fish in a bowl of water, and took it to the Amir.

The Amir was delighted. He made a pool for the fish and sat watching it swim about. But the fish would not cease swimming frantically back and forth.

"Like me, it is a prisoner," the Amir realized. "The poor thing needs the freedom of the river." And he asked for a chance to return the golden fish to the river.

As the Amir threw the fish into the river, he said, "May God leave you with your lover." He added with a sigh, "And may he leave me with a lover."

Now, when the fish had landed in the river, she swam hastily off to a cave beneath the waters. There she changed to woman shape and embraced her lover, who also was a magician.

"Where have you been?" the magician asked.

"I was caught in fish shape," the woman magician answered. "But the Amir returned me to the river and told me, 'Go to your lover.' My love, he is a kindhearted young man, and he, too, wishes a lover."

So they sent softness into the Amir's heart. He remembered one princess from a neighboring country, Aliya bint Rejab. And he thought that she was not evil but good, and sudden love burned in his heart.

But the Amir knew that his father the sultan already was making plans to wed him to his cousin.

The magician knew this, and thought, "I must reward the Amir for freeing my beloved."

So the magician took on the shape of a dervish, a wandering wise man, and he said to the Amir, "I know your deepest desire. You wish to wed Aliya bint Rejab."

"Oh, master of miracles!" the Amir cried. "Help me to find her."

So they mounted horses and left the prison, and no one saw them go. They rode to the palace where Aliya lived. The dervish magician and the Amir stole in like two cats, straight to her quarters. Aliya saw the Amir and loved him as suddenly as he had fallen in love with her. She left with them.

But when they were safely away from the palace, the dervish stopped. "Is it not written that if two are partners in labor, they must share the reward? I shall divide this girl. Which half would you like?"

Both the Amir and Aliya cried out, "No! Do not do this!"

But the dervish suddenly held a sword and was about to strike—when the head of a snake appeared out of the mouth of the girl. The dervish pulled it out and slew it. "There. That was a curse someone had placed on you. But now, you are both free and peace be with you both."

With that, the magician vanished. The Amir took Aliya home, and they were wed. And the sultan rejoiced.

Soon, the sultan let his son rule in his place. And that son proved a wise and just ruler, and he and Aliya had many children, beautiful as moons.

Source

Campbell, C.G. *Tales from the Arab Tribes: The Oral Traditions Among the Great Arab Tribes of Southern Iraq.* London, New York, and Bahrain: Kegan Paul, 2007. Transcribed by the author from Hamud, a storyteller of the Muntafiq tribe.

The Kettle of Good Fortune: A Folktale from Japan

> This folktale of kindness to a fox is related to the transformation folktales in that the fox takes on several shapes to repay a human couple for their kindness.

Once, there lived a poor but kindhearted old husband and wife. Every day, the old man would go into the woods to cut firewood, then sell it in town, and that was how they managed to live.

One day, when the old man was heading out, he saw some boys who had caught a fox. They were tormenting it and planning to kill it. "Stop that!" he cried. "That is no way to act. I will buy the fox from you."

The boys happily took the old man's coins and gave him the rope holding the fox. The old man led the fox to a thicket, then released it. "Go have a good life," he said, "and stay out of reach of bad boys!"

The fox scurried off.

The next day, when the old man headed out, he found himself confronted by the fox. It said to him, "I am more grateful than I can say to you for saving my life."

"I do not need any reward," the old man said. "Your thanks are enough."

"But I wish to help you. Good grandfather, at the temple they need a teakettle but do not have one. I will turn myself into a teakettle, and you can sell it at the temple. Will you do that?"

Before the old man could answer, the fox had turned itself into a lovely metal teakettle. What was there for the old man to do but take it to the temple? There, the priest bought the teakettle from him for a larger sum than the old man had ever seen in his life. He returned home full of joy.

Meanwhile, the priest told his acolytes to polish the teakettle with sand. They began with enthusiasm—but they stopped short when the kettle complained, "That hurts! Be gentle, please!"

The acolytes ran to the priest, crying, "It talks! That teakettle talks!"

"Nonsense," said the priest. "It is just the sound metal makes when it is being polished. You only think it sounds like words."

That night, though, the teakettle vanished. "Alas," said the priest. "Some thief must have stolen it."

But the teakettle had become a fox again, and it hurried off to the old man. "I am back, grandfather. They were treating me too roughly for me to stay. Now, I am going to turn into a geisha and make some more money for you."

The old man protested, "You do not need to—"

But the fox already had changed into a lovely geisha and went off to join others. The fox stayed a geisha for a year, then it grew bored and came back to the old man with the money the fox geisha had made.

"Now, I am going to become a horse," the fox said. "Take me to a rich man and sell me. You will not see me again, but do not worry about me! I will not stay a horse for long."

So the old man took the fox, who had become a handsome horse, to a rich man and sold him. The rich man did not treat the horse well, and, the next day, it vanished.

But the old man and his wife were happy, and they went on being kind and friendly to all. And every day, they would say a prayer for their friend, the fox.

Sources

Dorson, Richard M. *Folk Legends of Japan*. Rutland, VT, and Tokyo, Japan: Charles E. Tuttle, 1962.

Seki, Keigo, ed. *Folktales of Japan*. Trans. Robert J. Adams. Chicago: University of Chicago Press, 1969.

The Kind Giver and the Grudging Giver: A Folktale from the Ainu of Japan

Not only is this a folktale of kindness repaid, it is a traditional type in that the kind man is rewarded, while the stingy one, who just wants a reward, is punished. The folktale again features the theme of being kind to animals—in this case, puppies.

The Ainu are the aboriginal people of northern Japan, having lived there for an unknown but lengthy time. Their ethnicity is unknown as well, but they are not Japanese.

There was a fisherman who had laid his net across a river and caught many fish.

A raven came and perched beside him. It looked to be so worn and weary, nearly starving, that the man felt great pity for the bird.

"Here you are, poor raven," he said, giving it a fish.

The raven ate with great joy. The fisherman gave the raven a second fish and a third, and it ate those, too.

"I am very grateful," the raven said, "for having been fed on fish by you. If you will come with me to my old father, he, too, will thank you. So you had better come."

The man followed the raven, walking as it flew, until they finally came to a large house, into which the raven disappeared. The man followed, and he found himself facing an old man and woman, divine beings, and a girl, also a divine being. All three of them were ravens in human form.

The divine old man said, "Thank you for feeding my daughter with good fish. You are here so I may reward you nicely."

He held out two puppies, one gold-coated, the other silver-coated. The fisherman took them in his arms, smiling at them. Maybe they would grow up to be fishing dogs?

But the divine old man, clearly pleased at the fisherman's delight, said, "There is more to this gift. The golden puppy excretes gold and the silver puppy excretes silver. Treat them kindly, and you shall be rewarded, indeed."

The fisherman took the two puppies home and treated them well. Sure enough, the golden puppy excreted gold, and the silver puppy excreted silver. The fisherman became comfortably rich by selling the metal, and he and the puppies lived happily together.

Another man tried to imitate him. But he had a hard heart and got everything wrong. The fish he threw at the raven, without any kind words, was muddy. When the man got to the divine man's home, the divine man was angry at him, but he still gave him two puppies with the understanding that the man must treat them properly.

But the man was only interested in gold and silver. He fed the puppies carelessly on anything he could find. When they excreted, he got nothing but dung, and the two puppies ran away, back to the divine old man.

So it was that the hard-hearted man got nothing but dirt. And the kindhearted man got gold, silver, and the love of two happy puppies.

Sources

Chamberlain, Basil Hall. *Aino Folk-Tales*. London: 1888. Collected from Ishanashte, July 20, 1886.

Shigeru, Kayano. *The Ainu: History, Culture and Folktales*. Rutland, VT, and Tokyo, Japan: Charles E. Tuttle, 2004.

The Kind Maiden and the Fish: A Folktale from the Hausa of West Africa

Here is a tale that combines two themes, "Cinderella" and "The Maiden Without Hands." But unlike the first tale, the heroine prospers through kindness. And unlike the second tale, the loss of her hands is quickly fixed by the fish to whom she showed kindness.

Once, there was a man whose first wife had died and who had married a second time. The man also had a daughter, kind and gentle. But the stepmother did not like her.

One day, the man brought home a fish alive in a bucket of water, so it would be fresh for dinner. The stepmother said to the daughter, "Go to the river and clean that fish. But do not let it go, or you shall be beaten!"

The daughter went to the river. But the fish said, "Oh maiden, will you not set me free to go care for my young ones?"

"Very well, go," she said, sure that the fish would never return.

But it did return. "Now, kill and clean me."

"No," she said. "You may go free."

"I heard what the woman said to you," the fish said. "You will be beaten if you let me go."

"Fish, swim away," said the daughter.

The fish said, "Goodbye, then, for now. Tomorrow morning, you must come here again."

So the daughter went home, and she was beaten. But she thought of the fish alive and free, and that helped her get through it.

The next morning, the daughter hurried back to the river. There was the fish, and there were all the relative fish. "Do you see?" said the fish to the other fish. "This is the kind maiden who saved my life. I wish you all to thank her."

So they did. And they said, "Whenever you need help, come to us."

Now, the king of the land was holding a great feast. Only the daughter could not go, since she had only rags to wear. She went down to the river and asked, "Fish, can you help me?"

The fish brought her finery to wear, and off she went to the feast. There, she and the king met and fell in love. He wished her to become his wife. And what he said was law.

But the stepmother spread evil tales about the king's wife to the women of the palace. And one night, the women seized the new wife and cut off her hands. Her maid, who was her friend, listened when the wife said, "Go to the fish and tell them what has happened."

The maid went. The fish agreed that the one who had done them no harm should suffer no harm. The maid helped the king's wife down to the river. And the fish magically restored her hands.

As she and her maid were returning, the jealous women started mocking her, saying, "She is useless, she has no hands!"

But the king's wife waved her hands at them, and went back to her husband. And no one dared harm her again.

Source

Tremearne, Arthur John Newman. *Hausa Superstitions and Customs: An Introduction to the Folk-Lore and the Folk.* 1913. London: Frank Cass, 1970.

The Kindhearted Girl: A Folktale from the Ojibway

This folktale from the Ojibway people begins with the traditional scene between a beggar and the kind sister and the cruel sister. It then twists into a bride-test folktale, in which the kind girl is rewarded when the beggar drops his disguise.

There were two sisters, older and younger, both beautiful and sweet of voice. But the older sister had a hard heart, while the younger was as kind as she was beautiful.

One day, a ragged old beggar came to them. The older sister said, "Go away! We have nothing for you."

The younger sister said, "No, wait. We do have enough food to feed you."

As the ragged old beggar ate, the younger sister frowned at the sight of his tattered old pair of moccasins. "You cannot walk much farther in those," she said. "Here, take this pair. I made and embroidered them myself."

The old beggar blessed her kindness and left.

The next day, the girls' father called to them both, "Come outside. There is a fine young man who seeks a bride."

They hurried outside. Handsome he was, indeed, tall and slender. "I will be your wife!" cried the older sister.

But the younger sister stared at the moccasins on the young man's feet, the ones she had given to the old beggar. "Did you rob that old man?" she cried.

He laughed. "I *was* that old man. It was a test to see which sister would be the kindest to me. And I choose you, the kindhearted girl, as my wife."

Sources

Erdoes, Richard, and Alfonso Ortiz, eds. *American Indian Myths and Legends.* New York: Pantheon, 1984.

Johnston, Basil H. *Tales the Elders Told: Ojibway Legends.* Toronto, Ontario, Canada: University of Toronto Press, 1993.

The Two Chests: A Folktale from Austria

Here is a traditional European folktale type, about a kind and an unkind daughter. The kind daughter helps the three beings—in this case, an oven, a frog, and an apple tree—and comes away with the gold. The unkind daughter never returns. The only element lacking from the usual format is the three beings helping the kind girl to escape.

Once, there was a woman with two daughters. The older one was mean to everyone. The younger one was kind to all.

The day came when there was no longer enough food in the house to feed three people. The youngest girl sadly packed up her few belongings and set out into the world to find her fortune.

She came to an old oven, left abandoned in the forest. "Help me, please," it called to her.

The girl cleaned the oven up as best she could, and she even lit a fire in it.

"Thank you," the oven said. "Take the path straight ahead and stay on it."

So she did. Soon, she came to a little green frog sitting sadly on a pile of leaves.

"Help me, please," the frog said. "There is a nice spring under all these leaves, but I cannot clear them away."

So the girl cleared away the leaves. Soon, the spring was flowing once more, and the frog could jump into the brook it formed.

"Thank you," the frog said. "Do not turn aside from the path."

The girl nodded, and she set off once more. Soon, she came to an apple tree so laden down with fruit that its branches bent nearly to the ground.

"Help me, please," it called to her. "Pick these apples before the weight of them breaks my branches."

So the girl picked the apples, placing them in a neat pile on the ground for any traveler who might be hungry.

"Thank you," said the tree. "The house is just ahead."

So it was, a cottage in the middle of the forest. In the doorway, an old woman sat and spun flaxen threads. At her feet lay a dog and a cat.

"What do you want here?" the old woman asked.

"May I find work here?" the girl asked. "I can keep a house tidy."

"Good! Sweep up all the dust. Put the lighter dust in the chest to the left and the heavier dust in the chest to the right."

That she did. The girl worked day after day, and her only companions were the dog and cat. The old woman never said a word to her. But after three years had come and gone, the old woman finally broke her silence.

"You have served me well. Now, pick a chest and take it home."

A chest of dust? That seemed very strange. Or was there treasure under the dust? The girl saw the coldness in the old woman's eyes and knew better than to ask. "I pick the lighter chest," she said.

"Fortunate for you that you did," the old woman said.

So the girl left with the lighter chest and went back to her mother and sister.

"What did you bring?" they asked.

"Nothing much," the girl said. But when she opened the chest, gold coins spilled out.

The mother and sister soon had the whole story out of her. They ran off to get chests of gold coins for themselves. But they refused to help the oven, the frog, and the tree, and they did not sweep the old woman's floor very well. And they never returned.

Meanwhile, the girl found a nice young man to marry, and she and he lived happily ever after.

Sources

Egan, Joseph B. *New Found Tales from Many Lands*. Philadelphia: John C. Winston, 1929.

Simpson, Jacqueline. *European Mythology*. New York: Peter Bedrick, 1987; London: Hamlyn, 1987.

The Flute Player and the Shojo: A Folktale from Japan

This folktale has a charming theme, that the *shojo* should enjoy the young man's music, and that he should be kind enough to play for her without being afraid of her. He is rewarded for his kindness in a useful way, too.

Once, a young and talented flute player went down to the shore to practice without disturbing anyone.

Suddenly, he sensed that he was not alone. The flute player looked up to see an odd young woman. She looked almost human, but her long red hair betrayed her.

"Are you a *shojo*?" he asked.

"Yes, I am a female shojo," she told him. The shojo were strange water beings with long red hair and a love of wildness. "Please, I do not mean you any harm. I heard your flute, and . . . oh, I have never heard any flute music before. We have nothing like it under the sea. Please, won't you play some more for me?"

"Was this a trick?" the flute player thought. There was genuine sorrow in the shojo's eyes, as though she was sure he was going to refuse or run away.

"No," he thought, "he could not be so cruel." The flute player sat and gave the shojo a lovely concert. When he was done, she bowed to him.

"Thank you." She pulled out one of her long red hairs and gave it to him, along with a fish hook. "From now on, you shall never go hungry. Use the hook and my hair, and you will never need bait."

With that, the shojo dove back into the sea.

After that, it was true. The flute player could catch whatever fish he wanted, without bait, and he never went hungry.

Today in Japan, there is a fishing site called Shojo. Tradition claims it is where the young flute player first played for the female shojo.

Sources

Dorson, Richard M. *Folk Legends of Japan*. Rutland, VT, and Tokyo, Japan: Charles E. Tuttle, 1962.

Seki, Keigo, ed. *Folktales of Japan*. Trans. Robert J. Adams. Chicago: University of Chicago Press, 1969.

The Boy and the Bears: A Folktale from the Tewa of the American Southwest

This is a clear example of how a familiar European folktale, "Goldilocks and the Three Bears," can be altered to fit a different culture. It also can be used to explain why the Tewa people do not kill bears.

Once, there was a family with three sons—one grown, one nearly grown, and one very young. The very young boy often was left out of things, and he always was told to just stay put.

One day, the older boys went to gather wood. Their younger brother tagged along after them. "Stay here," they told him. "We will come for you on the way back."

But it was a long time for a little boy to wait. At last, he was sure they had forgotten all about him.

The little boy looked for a place to hide. It was the den of Bear Mother and her two bear cubs. Inside were three bowls of berries. The little boy was hungry, and he ate from each bowl. Then he was sleepy, so he lay down on one cub's bed and fell fast asleep.

Bear Mother and her two cubs returned. "Who was eating from our bowls?" one cub cried.

"Who is that sleeping in my bed?" the other cub cried.

The little boy woke up and was frightened.

"Do not be afraid," Bear Mother told him gently. "Who brought you here?"

"My brothers left me in the woods, and I was looking for them," the little boy replied.

"Well, you can stay here tonight," Bear Mother told him. To her cubs, she said, "This is your younger brother. Stay with him. And do not make him cry!"

Bear Mother went out to look for the little boy's parents. She heard them calling for him, so she sent the little boy out to meet them.

The little boy's parents hugged their son. "Where have you been?" they asked.

He told them the whole story, and all about how kind Bear Mother had been to him.

His mother was happy to hear how well Bear Mother had treated her son. And from that day on, no one hunted bears because of Bear Mother's kindness to a little lost child.

Source

Parsons, Elsie Clews. *Tewa Tales.* New York: American Folk-Lore Society, 1926. Collected from Informant 1 of San Juan [Pueblo], who said that this was a Mexican story.

The Generous Man and the Miser:
A Folktale from Bosnia and Herzegovina

Generally, in folktales, when there is a generous man and a miser, the miser gets punished. In this folktale, the kindhearted man is rewarded, and the miser is punished. That such a tale comes from such a troubled part of the world shows that folklore survives even warfare.

Once, there lived a kindhearted, generous man. Next door to him lived a miser. They traveled together for a time. But the miser used up all the generous man's coins and none of his own, and then he left.

The generous man wandered for a time, trying to figure out what to do. He came to a town where the mills had been abandoned for lack of water. Having nowhere else to sleep, the generous man crawled into one of the mills, curled up behind the millstone, and tried to sleep.

But at midnight, the man was awakened by the sound of laughter and music. He peeked warily over the edge of the millstone and had to bite back a gasp. A troop of merry devils was there, dancing, singing, and laughing.

Then, one of them said, "Now let us tell stories of the old days!"

"Yes, yes, remember when the river flowed and this mill was working?" cried another devil. "If only the silly humans knew that a large stone fell across the spring that feeds the river, right at the crossroads of the town. All they have to do is move it, and they would have water again."

"Oh yes," said another devil, "and what about that crook of a barber, the one who always overcharges everyone? If only the fool knew to lift up a slab from the floor, he would find the seven bags of gold we hid there!"

The man waited until dawn. Then, the devils disappeared, and he went straight into town, straight to the office of the vizier, who ran the local government. "Give me forty men," the generous man told him, "and you will have water again."

So the vizier gave him the men. They dug and dug until they found the stone. They lifted it out—and water instantly began to flow.

The vizier called the generous man to him. "What reward do you wish?"

He replied, "I would like the shop where the thieving barber lives."

So the vizier bought the shop and gave it to the generous man, who dug up the stone slab and found the seven bags of gold coins. Now, he was a wealthy man and opened several shops. But he always was generous to anyone in need.

One day, he saw a poor beggar, and realized with a shock that this was his old neighbor, the miser. "Come, my friend," he called. "Sit and dine with me."

But all the miser wanted to know was, "Where did you get your wealth?"

So the generous man told him about the mill and what he had overheard.

The miser ran straight to the mill and lay down behind the grindstone.

But when the devils appeared, they had no more stories to tell. Instead, they played a game of "catch the human" and ate the miser.

Source

Marshall, Bonnie C. *Tales from the Heart of the Balkans.* Englewood, CO: Libraries Unlimited, 2001.

The Fate of the Cruel Master and the Kind Servant: A Folktale from China

This Chinese folktale is clear and to the point: The maid is kind, and she is rewarded, while the wealthy man and his wife are cruel and end up transformed into silly animals.

Once, there lived a wealthy man and his wife. They had everything save children.

That was probably to the best—at least for the children—since the man and woman were cruel and hard of heart. They never gave to charity, and if any beggar was foolish enough to come to their door, the man chased him away, shouting, "You should have perished rather than come here!"

One day, the man bought himself a maid servant. Better for her he had not. He treated her like the lowest of slaves. But she bore it all, knowing that complaints would only get her beaten again. She ate nothing but what leavings she could scrape together, and she wore whatever rags she could sew together. But the worst of it was that she had a kind heart and hated to see how her master treated those who needed help.

Then one day, when the master was not home, a poor beggar came to the door. He was met not by the cruel master but by the maid servant. "Please," the weary old man said, "a scrap of food, just whatever you can spare."

The maid servant had put together, grain by grain, a small bag of rice. "Here, take this. But please hurry away. My master is very cruel, and if he sees you, he will beat you."

The beggar slipped a handkerchief into her hand. "Wash your face with this every morning. But let no one else use it."

Just then, the master and his wife returned. "What are you doing, slave?" he shouted at the maid servant. "What have you given that creature?"

The master and his wife would have beaten the beggar, but he hurried away. Instead, the maid servant received yet another beating.

"Never mind," she told herself. "I was finally able to help someone else."

Every morning after that, she used the handkerchief to wash her face. The bruises vanished, and her skin grew soft, white, and lovely. The master and his wife wanted to know why this was happening.

Finally, the maid servant could not keep quiet any longer. "My face is soft and clean because I wash it with the handkerchief I got from that beggar in exchange for the rice I had gathered from the grains you wasted!"

"Give us that!" shouted the master, and he tore the handkerchief from her hands.

The master and his wife washed their faces with the handkerchief—and they instantly turned into monkeys. They ran off into the forests and were never seen again.

And because that beggar actually had been one of the Immortals in disguise, the maid servant inherited all the property. She became a lovely, kindhearted lady who never forgot those in need.

Sources

Anonymous. *Folk Tales from China*. 3rd series. Peking: Foreign Languages, 1958.
Eberhard, Wolfram. *Folktales of China*. Chicago and London: University of Chicago Press, 1965.

The Farmer and the *Tikbalang:* A Folktale from the Philippines

In non-Christian regions of the Philippine Islands, folk tradition claims that there are many weird, sometimes perilous nonhuman beings living in the shadows and in the forests. The *tikbalang* is one of them. This part-horse, part-man being can be very dangerous, even close to demonic, taking human lives or souls. But in this story, kindness is returned for kindness.

Once, in Lian, a quiet and remote part of the islands, there lived a hardworking but kindhearted farmer. He was a fearless man as well and believed that the nonhuman beings of the region had as much right to exist as did the humans.

One day, the farmer had finished his work and was trudging his tired way back home. It would be so nice if he had a helper, he thought, but he had no children and could not afford to hire someone.

Ahead of him, he saw someone else sitting on a rock, head down. A fellow farmer? No.

As the farmer drew near, he saw that it was a *tikbalang*. Although its arms were manlike and ended in manlike fingers, its body was covered with coarse black fur. And its long black mane hung in tangles over its horsey face. The being looked so weary that the farmer could not fear it.

"How is it with you?" he asked the tikbalang.

The tikbalang looked up at him with its great, dark eyes. It said nothing but made only the softest of whinnies.

"Oh, I see the problem. You made the mistake of trying to get through some bramble bushes, didn't you? Those tangles must be uncomfortable. I would say you need a good grooming. Very well," said the farmer, sitting beside the tikbalang, "let us be friends, even if we cannot talk to each other."

The farmer began to comb out the tangled mane, gently removing brambles as if he was working on a mortal horse. The tikbalang gave its softest whinny again, as if thanking him.

"There," the farmer said at last, having removed all of the brambles. "I see I have three strands of your mane that came out. May I keep them to make snares for quail? Yes? Thank you."

The farmer bowed politely to the tikbalang and went on his way. But the next day, when he was working wearily, he heard the sound of hoofs. The tikbalang was there.

All that season, the tikbalang came every day to help the farmer with his fields. When the crops were harvested, the tikbalang even pulled the farmer's wagon to the village market—before sunrise, of course, so no one else could see.

After that, every time the tikbalang needed his coat groomed, he would come to the farmer. And every time the farmer needed help, the tikbalang would appear.

It was an odd friendship, but never was the farmer in danger. For the friendship had begun with a kindness for a kindness.

Sources
Ramos, Maximo D. *Legends of the Lower Gods*. Quezon City, Philippines: Phoenix, 1990.
———. *The Creatures of Philippine Lower Mythology*. Quezon City, Philippines: Phoenix, 1990.

The Dog That Changed Shape: A Folktale from the Winnebago of the American Midwest

In this folktale of the Winnebago people, the kindhearted young man clearly is being tested by the panther to see if he is worthy. Equally clearly, he is, indeed, worthy.

Once, there was a kindhearted young man. He took no interest in hunting or warfare.

It was not that he could not hunt or fight. He just did not like to do these things. He would go with the other young men and help them build a lodge. Then, when they went out to hunt or fight, he simply would stay at the lodge.

Now, one day, the young man found a poor, skinny, abused little tan dog. "Poor thing," he said. "I will take care of you."

He treated the dog well, healing its bruises and feeding it until it was no longer skinny. Since the other young men of the village usually were out hunting or looking for fights, he spent a great deal of time talking to the dog, not caring that it could not answer him.

Then, it happened that the hunters did not return. "I wish you could tell me where they are," he said to the dog.

And the dog answered him, "I can. The hunters noticed enemy tracks heading this way. They decided to wait. They said that if the enemy killed you, it would not matter."

As the young man looked at the dog in wonder and shock, the dog continued, "Do not worry, my brother. They shall not kill us, nor need you fight. Go to sleep, and know that I will be watching over you."

The young man went to sleep. He awoke as the dawn came, and the dog said, "Stay in the lodge, even when you hear the enemy's war whoop. I will fight them— but do not look at me when I do."

Soon after, the dog went out, and the young man heard the fighting begin. He heard strange sounds, snarling and screams, and he wondered what was happening out there. But the dog had told him not to look.

Still, it did sound like a strange fight out there. Maybe he could take one quick peek?

The moment the young man peeked outside, he heard the dog give a yip of pain. It came limping into the lodge with an arrow in its paw. "I told you not to look!" the dog said.

"I am sorry," the young man told the dog, pulling out the arrow.

"Never mind, never mind. I am really started now. I am going back out there, and I am going to finish it."

"I am going with you," said the young man. "You were hurt because of me."

So they fought together. But the dog was no longer a little tan dog. It had become a huge, raging panther. The young man was amazed, but he fought as well as the panther.

Soon the enemy men were all dead. The young man took their scalps to prove they were dead, and he went home to the village, the great panther at his side.

Everyone there was astonished to see the young man alive. The other hunters had told them that he had been killed. Now, it was clear that they had been afraid to fight, and he had not been afraid.

The panther said to the young man, "You were kind to me when I was in dog form. Now, I have been kind to you. I am leaving now."

From that day on, the young man was known as a brave warrior who picked his fights. And he and the panther often met in secret and spoke together as friends.

Sources
Radin, Paul. *Culture of the Winnebago: As Described by Themselves*. Baltimore: Waverly, 1949.
Smith, David Lee. *Folklore of the Winnebago Tribe*. London and Norman: University of Oklahoma Press, 1997.

The Grateful Dead

Nowadays, the title "The Grateful Dead" is more likely to conjure up an image of a rock band than of folklore. But the band took its name from the folkloric theme of the grateful dead—that is, the ghost or spirit of a man whose unburied body the protagonist buries properly and who then does the protagonist a good deed in return. This is a specific folktale type of a kindness for a kindness, and it is popular around the world.

The Bird Grip: A Folktale from Sweden

This is one of the most complex variants of the "grateful dead" tale type, with a traditional beginning of three sons setting out on a quest, the youngest being the most worthy. But, then, the tale brings in the grateful dead element, which becomes the means by which the youngest son succeeds.

Once, long ago and far away, there was a king with three sons.
One day, the king went blind, and no one at court could restore his sight. But an old wise woman said that the song of the bird Grip would cure him. She added that the bird was being kept in a cage by another king.

The king's eldest son proclaimed, "I will bring the bird Grip to you, Father!"

But on his way, the prince chanced to stop at a merry inn, an inn so very cheerful that it gave him much delight. And he forgot all about his journey.

Now, it was the turn of the second son. But on his way, he, too, came to that merry inn, and he joined his brother in the joviality. And he, too, forgot all about his journey.

Only the youngest son was left. "Do not worry, Father," he said. "I will find the bird Grip and bring it to you."

The youngest prince came to the merry inn and heard his two brothers calling to him. But he refused to enter.

He went on and came to a house in the woods. There, he stayed for the night.

But the night was disturbed by moans and shrieks. The prince asked, "Who is making that noise?"

One of the maids told him that the cries came from a dead man who had been slain by the furious innkeeper when he had been unable to pay the bill, and whom the innkeeper refused to bury since there was no money for the funeral.

The prince went to the innkeeper and said, "I will pay the dead man's bill, and pay for a decent funeral, too."

The innkeeper took the money, and the dead man was decently buried. But the prince did not like the look in the innkeeper's eyes. It warned him that the man might try to kill him for his money.

"I am not staying here," the prince said to the maid. "I will leave the right amount, but I need to find a way out of here."

"I will help you if you get me out of here and help me to find another place," the maid said.

"Agreed," the prince replied.

The maid told him the host kept the key to the stables under his pillow. She stole it and returned to the prince. They went off together, and the prince kept his word, getting her a place at a good inn before he went on.

The prince traveled through the forest for some time, long or short, without finding any trace of the bird Grip. Then, a fox darted out of the underbrush and stopped in front of him.

"I can help you," it said. "I know where the bird Grip is kept. Follow me."

The prince agreed, since he was not having any luck on his own. Soon, they came to a great castle.

"That is where the bird Grip is kept," the fox said.

The fox gave the prince three seeds of grain. "Drop one in the guardroom," the fox said. "Drop one in the room with the cage, and drop one in the cage itself. Then, you can safely take the bird Grip—but you must not stroke it."

The prince dropped the first grain in the guardroom, and all the guards fell asleep. He dropped the second grain in the room with the cage, and the guards there fell asleep, too. He dropped the third grain in the cage, and the bird Grip put its head under its wing and slept.

But it was such a lovely bird, and its feathers looked so wonderfully soft that the prince could not stop himself. He stroked the bird and . . .

The bird Grip woke in a flash and began squawking and screaming. The guards woke up, seized the prince, and threw him into prison.

While the prince was sitting in prison, sorry he had disobeyed the fox's orders, the fox appeared. "Do not look so glum, my friend. This time, listen to what I say. At your trial, you are to answer 'yes' to every question."

"I will," said the prince.

So he did. The prince was brought before the king, who looked at him with cold eyes. "Are you a master thief?" the king asked.

The prince answered, "Yes."

"Excellent. I will pardon you if you can carry off the world's most beautiful princess, who lives in the next kingdom."

The prince remembered what the fox had told him, and he said only, "Yes."

"Do not worry," the fox told the prince. "Here are three more grains, for the guards in the guardroom, for the maids in the princess's chambers, and for the princess in her bed. But remember this: You must not kiss the princess."

The prince dropped the first grain in the guardroom, and all the guards fell asleep. He dropped the second grain in the princess's chambers, and all her maids fell asleep, too. But when he approached the princess's bed, he froze. Oh, she was the most beautiful young woman he had ever seen! And he could not help but kiss her.

The princess woke with a scream. All her maids woke, and they screamed, too, and the guards came rushing in to arrest the prince. Once again, he was thrown into prison.

The fox appeared. "Ah well, this could be worse. Do the same thing at this trial. Say 'yes' to every question."

This king did not look any kinder than had the last. "Are you a master thief?" he asked the prince.

"Yes," the prince said.

"Then I will pardon you if you can bring me the horse with the four golden shoes, who is kept in the next kingdom."

"Yes," the prince said.

Off he went with the fox. "Here are three more grains," said the fox when they had reached the next kingdom. "One is for the guards in the guardroom, one is for the grooms in the stable, and the third is for the horse in its stall. Whatever you do, you must *not* touch the golden saddle. If you do, I will be unable to help you."

The prince dropped the first grain in the guardroom, and all the guards fell asleep. He dropped the second grain in the stable, and all the grooms fell asleep, too. He dropped the third grain in the stable, and the horse with the four golden shoes grew tame as a kitten. The prince led him out of his stall.

But then, the prince saw the golden saddle. What a magnificent thing! He started to reach out a hand—but then something hit his hand, and the prince led out the horse without the saddle.

The fox appeared at his side. The prince confessed to him, saying, "I almost touched the saddle."

"I know. Who do you think it was who struck your hand away? Now, let us go win the princess for you."

This time, the prince followed the fox's advice perfectly. He carried off the princess. Then, on he rode to the castle in which sat the bird Grip. Once again, the prince followed the fox's advice perfectly, and he carried off the bird.

"Very good," said the fox. "Now, I have one more warning: Do not ransom anyone, or it shall mean trouble for you."

The prince rode on, and he discovered that his brothers had gone into debt at the inn and were to be hanged. Yes, the fox had warned him, but the prince knew he could not leave his brothers to die. He paid off their debt.

What the prince did not expect was that his brothers would be so jealous of his success that they wanted him dead. They threw him into a den of lions and took the bird Grip, the horse, and the princess, threatening to kill the princess if she did not say they had won her and the horse and the bird.

When the brothers reached home, they pretended to be sorrowful and told their father, "Our brother, alas, was hung for debt."

But the bird Grip did not sing, the horse with the golden shoes would let no one in the stall, and the beautiful princess locked herself in her room and would let no one in.

Meanwhile, the prince was sure his time had come. But the fox appeared, and the lions backed off and did not harm him. The fox led the prince out of their den. He did not scold the prince, but said only, "Sons who would forget their father also will betray their brother."

"I understand," the prince said sadly.

"Now you must do something for me," the fox said. "You must cut off my head."

"No! I cannot do that!"

"You must. I will kill you if you do not do it."

"Very well," the prince said. Drawing his sword, he quickly cut off the fox's head. Instantly, the fox was gone. In his place stood a misty figure.

"I am the spirit of the dead man whose debts you paid."

The spirit faded into the air.

The prince disguised himself as a horseshoer and went to the castle. He tamed the horse with four golden shoes. Then, hearing that the bird Grip would not sing, he declared, "It needs something. If I could see it, I would find out what it wants."

He was led into the castle. There, the prince called to the bird, "Bird Grip, sing!"

It began to sing, and the princess came out of her locked room to smile at the prince.

Hearing the bird Grip sing, the king's sight recovered in a moment, and he recognized the horseshoer as his youngest son. He banished the older sons, but the youngest prince married the princess, and they lived happily ever after.

Sources

Hofberg, Herman. *Swedish Fairy Tales.* Trans. W.H. Meyers. Chicago: W.B. Conkey, 1893.
Kvideland, Reimund, and Henning K. Sehmsdorf, eds. *Scandinavian Folk Belief and Legend.* Minneapolis: University of Minnesota Press, 1988.

Fair Brow: A Folktale from Italy

This folktale features a hard-hearted father and a kindhearted son. The son proves his worth in the "grateful dead" theme. He is rewarded with a bride and gold enough to settle accounts with his father.

Once, there lived a merchant who loved to make money. But his son was a gentle, kindhearted young man, and the merchant despaired of him.

"Here are some coins," the merchant said. "Go off and make more money, and make me proud of you."

But on the way to the market, the young man found a strange scene. A dead man was lying by the side of the road, and guards were watching the corpse.

"What happened here?" the young man asked.

"He died without paying off his debts, so he has been denied burial."

"That is not a just thing," said the young man.

The young man paid off the dead man's debts with the money his father had given him, and he paid for an honorable burial as well.

When he got home, his father wanted to know what he had done with the money. The son told him, "I ransomed a dead man so he could be buried."

The merchant cried in anger, "You wasted that money!"

But he decided to give his son another chance.

"Here are more coins. This time do not waste the money on a dead man, but make more money."

But when the young man reached the market, he stopped short at the sight of the loveliest young women he had ever seen. She had large, dark eyes and long, silky black hair. She was a slave. But when the young man managed to whisper to her, he learned that she was actually the kidnapped daughter of the Sultan of Turkey.

"I will free you," the young man said.

He bought the lovely young woman, and then freed her. She and he fell in love and got married. He took her to his father's house and said, "This is how I spent my money. Father, this is my wife."

But the merchant was so furious that the money had been lost, he drove them both out of his house.

"Do not worry," the young woman told her husband. "I am a fine artist. I will paint, and you will sell the paintings, and we shall make a living. You must not tell anyone where they come from, though!"

But in the marketplace, the sultan's men recognized the style of the paintings. They asked the young man if there were more paintings. He led them to his house—and they seized his wife and carried her off.

The young man set out to find her. He traveled to Turkey. There, he met an old man who fished with him. But they were captured by Turkish soldiers and sold to the sultan as slaves.

The old man was made a gardener, and the young man was told to carry bouquets to the sultan's daughter, whom the sultan had imprisoned in a tower as punishment for marrying without his permission. The young man sang as he worked, and one day his wife recognized him by his singing.

They escaped together with a great deal of treasure. They freed the old man, too.

Once they were safe, the old man said that they must divide the treasure.

"You may have half," the young man said.

"Is your wife also half mine?" the old man asked.

"No, of course not!" said the young man. "Here, take three quarters of the treasure."

The old man laughed. "I do not need any treasure. I am the dead man whose debts you paid."

With that, he vanished.

The young man and his wife returned to his father, who was amazed to see the riches they had brought back. But the young man and woman knew that the greatest riches they had found were each other.

Sources

Calvino, Italo. *Italian Folktales.* New York: Harcourt Brace Jovanovich, 1980.

Crane, Thomas Frederick. *Italian Popular Tales.* New York and Oxford, United Kingdom: Oxford University Press, 2003.

The Spirit Fox: A Folktale from the Yaqui of the American Southwest

This "grateful dead" variant features a man who is saved from murder by his false wife and her lover thanks to his kindness to a dead man.

Once, there lived a man named Ba'ayoeria. He and his wife lived apart from everyone else.

Ba'ayoeria was not a hunter. He made a living from collecting roots for medicines and food, and blossoms for use in tanning hides and others for medicines. He would load them in skin sacks and set out on a journey to visit other people, with whom he would exchange his goods for dried fish, clams, oysters, and salt.

Once, on his traveling, Ba'ayoeria found a dead body left unburied in the wilderness. He had no idea who this man had been, but just the same, Ba'ayoeria decided that the man deserved a decent burial. He buried the body, then went on his way.

One day, when Ba'ayoeria traveled in search of roots, a fox passed in front of him and stopped, gazing at him. Ba'ayoeria went on his way, looking back now and again at the fox who still was watching him.

This happened on the second day, too.

On the third day, at the same place, the fox spoke. "Listen to me, Ba'ayoeria. There is a great danger coming to you, and I want to save you. Your wife has been sleeping with another man, and tonight they plan to kill you as you sleep."

Ba'ayoeria, stunned, asked, "Who are you?"

"I am the soul of that lost body you buried," said the fox. "In gratitude, I came to give you my warning."

"Thank you, whoever you were."

Ba'ayoeria went home. His wife seemed sad and nervous, but she refused to tell him what was wrong. So he said, "Let us change places. You sleep in my place, and I will sleep in yours."

But Ba'ayoeria did not sleep. Late at night, his wife's lover entered quietly. He thought that the woman was Ba'ayoeria and stabbed down with his lance. Ba'ayoeria then killed the man.

Much later, Ba'ayoeria married another woman, one who was true to him. And he continued his work of trading roots and flowers.

Source

Giddings, Ruth Warner. *Yaqui Myths and Legends.* Anthropological Paper no. 2, University of Arizona, 1959. Tucson: University of Arizona Press, 1959.

The Spirit of the Unburied Man: A Folktale from Poland

This "grateful dead" variant quickly becomes a transformation chase folktale, showing how two basic tale types can be combined.

A poor young scholar, who had found no jobs and little wisdom in town, was going down the road out of town when he saw, there by the town's outer walls, the unburied body of a man. The scholar had few coins, but he gave them gladly to see the poor body properly buried and not left in open disgrace. He said prayers for the stranger and then went on his way out into the world.

The scholar stopped to rest for the night under the shelter of a vast oak tree. When he awoke in the morning, he was astonished to find a sack of gold coins beside him. How had it gotten there? Who could have left it? There was no one around. He thanked whoever his benefactor had been and then traveled on.

Ahead lay a river, so wide there was a ferry for its crossing. The scholar stepped on board, but when the two ferrymen saw his sack of gold coins, greed overwhelmed them. In the middle of the river, where the current was the most dangerous, they grabbed the sack and threw the scholar overboard.

The scholar would have drowned in the swift waters, but a wide plank surged under him and carried him safely to the shore. There, the plank vanished, and a man's voice said from the empty air, "I am the spirit of he whom you buried. I left you the coins in gratitude. But do not worry about their loss. Now, I shall teach you something far more useful. I will teach you how to transform yourself into a hare, a deer, and a crow."

The scholar quickly learned the spell. Now he could transform himself with ease.

He wandered on, and came to a royal palace. They had no use for a scholar, but they did need archers, and since he was good with a bow, he became one of the royal archers.

Now, the king had a beautiful daughter, but she lived on an island in the sea, in a castle of copper. She possessed a magic sword: Anyone who wielded it could defeat an army. The king needed the magic sword now, since an enemy was about to attack. But he had done such a good job of hiding his daughter away that no one knew how to reach her. So the king proclaimed that whoever could reach the princess and bring the sword home should have her hand in marriage and inherit the throne.

"I can do that," the scholar-archer declared. "I ask only a letter from you, Sire, so that the princess knows I come from you."

He was given that letter, and set out, first as a hare, then as a deer, speeding through the forest, all the way to the shore of the vast sea. He did not know, though, that another archer had been following him.

Now, the deer became a crow, and he flew straight to the island. The scholar-archer transformed back into himself and entered the copper castle. He presented the king's letter to the princess, and he was smitten with love for her at that moment.

The princess, too, gave her heart to him. "But how did you get here?" she asked.

The scholar-archer showed the princess how he could transform into a hare, a deer, and a crow. Each time, the princess secretly took a little fur from the hare and the deer and a feather from the crow.

The princess gave him the sword, and off he flew with it back across the sea. Then, he raced with it through the forest as a deer and then as a hare.

But that other archer had been waiting. He shot the hare, and took the sword and letter from him, then hurried before the king, claiming that it had been he who had gotten the sword. The king had no reason not to believe him.

The king took the sword, and single-handedly defeated the entire enemy army. Returning joyfully to the royal palace, he sent for his daughter, telling her she would be married to the archer.

The princess came eagerly enough, but she sat in despair, weeping, when she saw it was not the same man, but a liar. All she could do was postpone the wedding for a year and a day.

For a year, the scholar-archer slept in the body of the hare. At the end of the year, he was awakened by the spirit of the man he had buried and was magically returned to life. The spirit told him all that had happened.

"Tomorrow is the princess's wedding day. You must hurry there, but be wary of the false archer who will try to slay you again."

The scholar-archer raced to the palace, where the princess saw him and cried out in joy. The false archer turned dead-white with shock.

"It is I, not he, who won the sword," the scholar-archer announced, "he who tried treacherously to kill me."

He showed how he had won the sword, changing to hare, then deer, then crow. When he changed to a hare, the princess placed the fur she had taken onto his back, and it grew fast. When he changed to a deer, the princess placed the fur she had taken onto his back, and it grew fast. When he changed to a crow, the princess placed the feather she had taken onto his wing, and it grew fast.

The false archer was put to death. The true scholar-archer was wed to the princess. And if she wept this time, it was for joy.

Sources
Gerould, Gordon Hall. *The Grateful Dead: The History of a Folk Story.* London: David Nutt, 1908.
Wratislaw, A.H. *Sixty Folk-Tales from Exclusively Slavonic Sources.* Boston: Houghton Mifflin, 1890.

TALES OF HOPE AND REDEMPTION

Tales of hope and redemption are unexpectedly upbeat tales. They show that, for those who are basically good of heart, there always is a chance for a literal happy ending.

The Drunkard Who Freed Souls: A Folktale from Byelorussia

This is a good-natured folktale about the perils and unexpected rewards of drinking. Another theme is how devils may be tricked for a heavenly cause.

Once, there was a drunkard. He was not a bad man, just one who liked to drink a bit too much.

Then the drunkard died, and he went to hell. There was a reason for this, but the devils did not know that.

The devils put the drunkard to work stirring a huge cauldron of boiling water full of 300 souls. Now what the devils also did not know was that these 300 souls were minor sinners who were having their sins boiled away.

An angel came down to the drunkard and explained the situation to him. The drunkard agreed to help.

"But," he said, "the devils will never believe I let this happen unless I get drunk."

The angel agreed that this was one time when letting him get drunk was within the divine rules. So, the angel gave the drunkard a full bottle of vodka, which the drunkard (with a wink at the angel) downed. Then, he let the angel take the 300 purified souls to heaven, and lay down for a nap.

The devils came rushing up. "Where are the 300 souls?"

The drunkard opened one eye. He pointed to his mouth. What he meant was that he had drunk too much to speak clearly. But as he and the angel had planned, the devils thought it meant he had eaten all 300 souls.

"We cannot let him stay here!" they cried. "He has been here only a night, and already we have lost 300 souls to him! If he goes on like this, we will be out of business in a month!"

So the devils kicked him out of hell. And, of course, now quite sober, the former drunkard went happily up to heaven.

Source
Cortes, L., trans. *Byelorussian Folk Tales*. Minsk, Byelorussia: Vysheishaya Shkola, 1983.

A Single Good Deed: A Folktale from the Jews of Kurdistan

Although all of the Jews living in the troubled region between Turkey, Iran, and Iraq have by now emigrated to Israel, their folktales have been recorded. This tale shows how a single, honest good deed can help balance out wicked deeds.

There once was a wicked man who never did anyone any good.

The time came for that wicked man to die. But he prayed to the heavenly court for another chance. Surely, he would be able to redeem himself.

The man was granted a second chance. But he found it impossible to redeem himself. And so he died again.

Once again, he prayed to the heavenly court for one more chance. He pointed out that he had never had anyone to teach him right from wrong and he had never really hurt anyone. Surely this time, he would be able to redeem himself.

He was granted one last chance. Alas, he could not truly redeem himself. He tried and failed. And so he came to die, this time with no reprieve.

Now as it happened, the wicked man had managed to commit one small good deed. Next to him in judgment was a righteous man who had committed one small sin. It was decided that the wicked man would have one hour in heaven because of his one good deed, and then down he would go to Gehenna. It also was decided that the righteous man would have one hour in Gehenna because of his one sin, and then he would go up to heaven.

"That is not fair!" the wicked man cried. "Yes, I have earned my fate, I will not argue that. But this is a good man, and that was one tiny sin. I am willing to give up my one hour in heaven and give it to this good man so he may go directly to heaven."

"Now why couldn't you have been so good in your lifetime?" one of the angels said.

But divine justice ruled that this genuinely good act on the part of the wicked man, done with no hope of reward, overcame a great many sins. So both souls, righteous and wicked, entered heaven together.

Source

Sabar, Yona. *The Folk Literature of the Kurdistani Jews: An Anthology*. London and New Haven, CT: Yale University Press, 1982. Recorded by Rahamim Hakimzadeh from his father, Sulayman.

The Fiddler Who Went to Hell: A Folktale from Russia

There is a common folktale type of a fiddler outplaying the devil, and there is even a belief that the violin—or fiddle—is the devil's own instrument. However, in this odd tale, the fiddler accidentally tumbles into hell, tricks the devils by making sure all his fiddle strings break, and manages to save a rich but not totally unredeemable soul from hell.

Once, a fiddler was coming home from a festival when he stepped on a weak spot in the earth. Down he tumbled. He landed with a thump in a dark place. Someone was sitting there. "Where am I?" the fiddler asked.

"The last place you would want to be. This is hell."

"But you are a man, not a devil. Who are you?"

"I was a man, a very wealthy one. But I never gave to the poor nor used my money for good. And I died before I could tell my family where my money is hidden. Oh, I wish I knew that they were happy! I wish they were giving money to the poor!"

Just then, a horde of devils came rushing up. The fiddler hid, struggling not to make a sound as the devils beat the rich man with whips. And all the time, they mocked him for finding charity in his heart too late.

When the devils were gone, the fiddler whispered, "Where is the money? I swear by the Good Lord that I will tell your wife."

"Yes, and tell her to give generously to the poor! Swear that, too."

"I so swear," said the fiddler.

But before the fiddler could climb back out of hell, the devils came rushing in and caught him. "Aha! A live one!"

"I am a fiddler," he replied. "Let me entertain you."

"You had better," the devils said.

So he jumped up on a rock and began fiddling. He fiddled high and he fiddled low, and it seemed to him that it was only three hours. But, in fact, three years had passed on Earth.

At last, he exclaimed, "Well now, this is fine! Well, usually, a string or two breaks—blessed be the Lord. Oh, I spoke too soon. There go all the strings." All of the strings on his fiddle had broken just as he had said that blessing.

"Sorry," the fiddler said. "I cannot play without strings."

So the devils brought him a whole batch of fiddle strings. But every time the fiddler said, "Blessed be the Lord," the strings broke.

"That is it," said the fiddler. "All the strings are broken."

"You are just trying to get away!" the devils shouted.

"Well, maybe I am, maybe I am not. Why don't you send a devil with me to be sure?"

The fiddler knew what he was doing. It was nearly daybreak up in the mortal world, and as soon as the sun began to rise, poof, the devil was gone.

The fiddler went straight to the rich man's house and told his widow the whole story. They dug up the money and gave it away to the poor by the handfuls.

One poor woman, now able to help her family, said, "God bless the one who gathered this money."

The fiddler grinned. That should do it.

He was right. The rich man who had repented in hell now was gone up to heaven.

Sources
Afanas'ev, Aleksander. *Russian Fairy Tales*. New York: Pantheon, 1945.
Haney, Jack V. *The Complete Russian Folktale*. Armonk, NY: M.E. Sharpe, 1999.

The Dead Bridegroom: A Folktale from Karnataka, India

Karnataka is a region of southwestern India. This folktale shows how piety—and a little help from a sympathetic goddess—can overcome all obstacles, including, in this case, death.

Once, there lived a king with only one son, a fine young man named Jayasekhara. The king planned for his son to have a wonderful marriage. But, tragically, the prince died of a sudden illness.

His father, the king, went mad with grief. He cried that he still would see his son married. Word went out throughout the kingdom that the king wanted a bride for his son.

There was a poor Brahmin, a man of high caste, but one who was rich in children and poor in money. He thought that if he gave his daughter Lalita to the king, there would be riches enough to keep the rest of his family from poverty forever. So, even though his wife fought him about sacrificing their daughter like this, the Brahmin dragged Lalita to the palace and offered her as the dead prince's bride.

So the young woman was married to a dead man. Poor Lalita knew her fate was to light the funeral pyre and join her dead husband on it. But there came such a sudden downpour that the king and his courtiers fled, leaving Lalita alone with the corpse.

For the first time, she looked at the dead prince, and a little cry of pity escaped her. Oh, he had been so fine and handsome a young man. She could have loved him. They could have had a wonderful marriage. Now, there was nothing for them.

She burst into tears.

"Do not weep, child," said a voice.

Lalita turned to see an old woman. "Why should I not? The man I could have loved is dead."

"Weep not. If you perform Jyoti-Puja, the Worship of Light, your husband will return to life." With that, the old woman disappeared, leaving a heavenly fragrance behind her. It had been the goddess Parvati who had visited Lalita.

Lalita wasted no time. She cleaned the floor and placed a wooden plank on it. She decorated the floor around it with *rangoli*, designs made of white powder. She spread rice on the plank and placed a pair of lamps upon it, lit them, and worshipped the Force of Light. Then, she fell asleep near the lamps.

She woke with a start. The prince took a breath, another, then sat up as though waking from deep sleep.

"What strange dreams I have had," Jayasekhara began. Then, he stared at Lalita. "Oh lovely one, are you really my wife?"

"Oh my love, I am!" she cried.

To this day, girls who live in Karnataka work the same ceremony, with unmarried ones praying for good husbands and married ones praying for their husbands and themselves.

Source
Chandran, Praphulla Satish. *Folk Tales of Karnataka.* New Delhi, India: Sterling, 1985.

A Prayer Answered: A Folktale from Cuba

In this eerie folktale from Cuba, a cruel man is punished, and a wife is rescued by a most unexpected source—showing that kindness can, in a way, sometimes come out of evil.

There was a man known as Scarface for the long scar that ran down his face. But his soul was crueler than the scar.

Now Scarface had a wife, and he had children, but that did not soften his heart. He beat them whenever he wished, and he treated them like slaves.

In those days, there was no way for a wife to escape her husband, nor to protect her children. But every day, Scarface's wife would pray, silently so her husband would not overhear, "Please, dear Lord, help my children. Help me."

No one dared to interfere. Everyone was afraid of Scarface.

Yet every day, his wife would silently pray, "Please, dear Lord, help my children. Help me."

Then one twilight, a magnificent jet-black coach drawn by coal-black horses pulled up in front of their house. A tall, elegantly dressed man climbed out.

Was this man a doctor? No one else would dress so elegantly. Had Scarface actually fallen ill? Or had he finally killed his family? There was something almost eerie about the stranger's eyes, almost as if they held their own reddish glow.

The stranger rapped on the door with the handle of his ebony cane, and Scarface's wife opened it. "Can I help you, sir?"

"I have come to see the patient."

"But—but no one here is ill!"

"Is he not?"

There was something chilling in the simple words. The wife stood aside, and the stranger approached Scarface's bedside where he lay napping.

"Scarface," the stranger said.

Scarface's eyes flew open. "Who are you?"

The stranger smiled thinly, and his eyes now burned with hellish fire. "Do you not know me, Scarface? I am the Devil, and I have come for your shriveled soul."

"No!"

"Oh, yes."

The Devil's hands, now ending in long talons, closed about Scarface's chest and squeezed. No human heart could endure such treatment, and with a final gasp of agony, Scarface was dead.

"Your prayers were heard," the Devil said to the new widow. "Sometimes good and evil do work to the same ends."

With that, he disappeared.

Sources

Bierhorst, John. *Latin American Folktales: Stories from Hispanic and Indian Traditions.* New York: Pantheon, 2002.

Bueno, Salvador. *Cuban Legends.* Trans. Christine Ayorinde. Kingston, Jamaica: Ian Randle, 2003; Princeton, NJ: Markus Wiener, 2003.

The Man Who Became a Fox: A Tale from the Ainu of Japan

In this folktale, a bad man is taught a lesson through a transformation into an animal, and he learns the lesson well.

There was a certain man who was a liar and a swindler. Everywhere the man went, he made it his business to do nothing but tell lies and extort things from people. When he had finished with the people of one place, and he wanted to extort people again, he would go on to another place. While walking along, he used to think of what lies he could tell.

One day while walking along, he heard a voice, his own. But he was not saying anything that sounded like human words. He was saying something that sounded like the call of a fox, "Pau! Pau!"

When he looked at his own body, he saw that he was no longer human. He was a fox. Oh no! If he returned to his own village, or went to another place, the dogs would kill him!

Lost and alone, he lay down weeping under a large oak tree. At last, he fell asleep. He dreamt that there was a large house, and a divine woman came out of it.

"Oh, what a bad man!" she scolded him. "What a villain! You have become a bad god, a devil, as divine punishment for your misdeeds. Why do you come and stand near my house? I am this tree, which is made the chief of trees by heaven. It would defile me to have you die beside my house, so I will turn you into a man again and send you home. Behave yourself from now on. There may not be another reprieve for you!"

With that, a branch came crashing down, and he woke with a start, greatly frightened. But—he was a man again.

He bowed to the tree. Then, straight-backed and determined, he went home. And never again did he harm another living soul.

Source

Chamberlain, Basil Hall. *Aino Folk-Tales*. London: 1888. Translated literally as told by Penri, July 19, 1886.

The Water Man and the Priest: A Folktale from Sweden

A priest in this folktale is taught a lesson by his own pride. He realizes that any being who is playing a psalm, even a supernatural being, has a right to make a joyful noise unto the Lord.

Once, long ago, a priest set out to visit a mill that was not part of any parish, so that he could help the people there practice their faith.

Along the way, the priest saw nothing less amazing than a water being, a man, playing on his fiddle. What made it the most amazing was that the water being was playing a psalm.

"What good does that playing do you?" the priest snapped. "You can expect no Godly mercy."

The startled water being promptly stopped playing. He looked so sorrowful that the priest rethought what he had said.

"Who am I to judge you who were making a joyful noise unto the Lord?" he said. "God knows mercy, after all."

"Is that so?" said the water being happily. "Then, shall I play even more joyfully than before."

And the priest went his way, a wiser and more merciful man for that odd encounter.

Sources

Hofberg, Herman. *Swedish Fairy Tales*. Trans. W.H. Meyers. Chicago: W.B. Conkey, 1893.

Kvideland, Reimund, and Henning K. Sehmsdorf, eds. *Scandinavian Folk Belief and Legend*. Minneapolis: University of Minnesota Press, 1988.

The Mound Folk and Salvation: A Folktale from Norway

The *huldre* are the fairy folk of Norway, who are said to live in the hollow hills. This folktale shows them practicing religion and believing in salvation as much as do the humans.

Once, long ago, a man went up into the mountain pastures near Kasa, Norway, to hunt for his horses. He came to an earthen mound and paused there to look around for the animals. As he stood there, he heard some beings inside the mound singing psalms and praying.

Now, the man already was in a foul mood from not finding his horses. At last, he shouted, "No matter how much you sing and pray, you will not find salvation!"

With that, he hurried off, never realizing that what the mound had been was a *huldre* church. But from that day on, wherever he went, he heard soft, barely audible lamentation.

The noise went on, and it went on. At last, the man went back up to that same earthen mound and shouted with all his might:

"Yes! You will find salvation if you sing and pray! Now, in God's name, leave me alone!"

He thought he heard joyful laughing from within the mound. But after that, the huldre folk did, indeed, leave him in peace.

Source

Kvideland, Reimund, and Henning K. Sehmsdorf, eds. *Scandinavian Folk Belief and Legend*. Minneapolis: University of Minnesota Press, 1988. First collected by Knut Hermundstad from Ingeborg Larsdatter Oydgarden in Vang, Norway, 1955.

Tannhauser: A Folktale from Medieval Germany

There actually was a Tannhauser who lived in the thirteenth century, and he was a *minnesinger*, or minstrel. But by the sixteenth century, folklore began accreting around history. The folk story of Tannhauser and his stay with the pagan goddess Venus became well-known in Germany—enough so that, in the nineteenth century, it inspired German composer Richard Wagner to write an opera about Tannhauser.

Tannhauser the noble knight-minstrel wandered many lands. But at last, he wandered out of this world and into another.

It was the underworld realm of Venus, pagan goddess of love, and her ladies and servants, a lush place of the senses and sensual delight.

Venus herself, in all her beauty, called to Tannhauser, and asked him to stay with her and be her love. She so won over the noble knight that he forgot all vows but the one he swore to her, to stay forever in the Cave of Venus, knowing nothing but sensual joy.

But endless pleasure came to be a bore, and suddenly Tannhauser recalled the world above, the human world. He begged Venus to let him go, but she would not. No matter how he pleaded, she refused.

Then, at last, Tannhauser remembered another queen, and he called upon the Virgin Mary for help. Venus had no choice but to let him go.

Once he was returned to mortal soil, Tannhauser went on pilgrimage to Rome and the Holy City. Some say he met the pope, others that he met a bishop, still others that he spoke only to a priest. But when Tannhouser confessed his sin and begged for forgiveness, the pope, or bishop, or priest pointed to his staff and said, "Sooner shall this dead wood grow green and burst into leaves than you gain forgiveness for your sin."

Sorrowing, Tannhauser left. But three days after that cruel verdict, the dead staff burst into leaves and flowers. Clearly, the Lord had forgiven Tannhauser when men had not.

They searched everywhere for the noble knight, but never found him. Some say he returned to the Cave of Venus, not knowing that he had already been forgiven for his sin and would, indeed, one day enter the Kingdom of Heaven.

Sources
Hulpach, Vladimir, Emanuel Frynta, and Vaclav Cibula. *Heroes of Folk Tale and Legend.* Trans. George Theiner. London, New York, Sydney, Australia, and Toronto, Ontario, Canada: Hamlyn, 1970.
Lindahl, Carl, John McNamara, and John Lindahl, eds. *Medieval Folklore: A Guide to Myths, Legends, Tales, Beliefs, and Customs.* New York: Oxford University Press, 2002.

Tales of Fools
and Wise People

Why are folktales of these two, fools and wise people, combined in this section? Because fools can be wise, and wise people can be fools.

The reason for the popularity of foolish folktales is probably the human need to laugh at someone else's folly. And what could be funnier than seeing the pompous or the mighty—or the politician or other so-called important folks, for that matter—brought down by foolishness?

Wisdom tales are as popular around the world as fool tales. The same characters that seemed like fools may be wiser than the wise—as in the Indian and Caribbean tale of the three wise men who bring a tiger back to life and are eaten by it, while the fourth man, thought a fool, is wise enough to climb a tree.

Other wisdom tales may show the humble in a good light and the mighty as foolish. Or they may show that true wisdom lies in good sense and a kind heart.

TALES OF FOOLS

Around the world, every culture has its "fool" or "noodle" stories. There is something very satisfying to the human psyche to realize that, however foolish a move one might make, there is always someone far more foolish.

There are several main categories of fool tales. In this chapter they have been divided up into their basic groupings.

Fools Who Think They Are Dead

In this folklore tale type, the foolish man is given a silly reason to believe he is dead. He then has to have it proven to him that a dead man cannot talk, give directions, or feel pain. Since many of the folktales, such as those from Indonesia and other parts of Asia, are similar, only one example is given.

The Very Foolish Man: A Folktale from India

This folktale can be seen as a story of a silly man or as a satire on false prophets. But it also shows that there is a limit to a wife's patience and to a silly man's foolishness as well.

Once, there was a man who was very foolish, indeed. He decided to cut off a branch of a tree. So he sat on the branch, and started sawing away.

A neighbor saw this and advised him, "If you sit on the branch you are cutting off, you will fall off with it!"

"Do not tell me what to do!" the foolish man snapped.

Sure enough, the branch came off, and the foolish man fell down with it. He went running after his neighbor. "You are a prophet!" he cried. "You said I would fall, and I did."

"It was merely common sense," the neighbor said, and he tried to walk on.

But the foolish man caught his neighbor by the legs. "Please, oh wise one, tell me when I am going to die."

"I cannot do that," the neighbor replied.

But the foolish man refused to let go. "Please! Tell me when I am going to die."

Annoyed, the neighbor pulled a thread loose from his clothing. "Here. Keep this thread safe. When it breaks, you will die." With that, the neighbor went on his way.

The foolish man rushed home, and he put the thread carefully in a box. But every day, he took it out to look at it. And every day, the thread grew a little more frayed from being handled. At last, it broke.

"Oh, no!" the foolish man cried. "I am dead! I am dead!"

His wife said, "Dead men do not speak. You cannot be dead."

The foolish man fell flat and would not say another word. No matter what his wife said or did, he refused to move. At last, she grew angry at the whole silly thing and ordered that her "dead" husband be taken to the cemetery.

As they headed off with the "dead" man resting on a flower-strewn bier, a stranger stopped the procession. He wanted to know how to get to a nearby village.

"I know!" the "dead" man cried, sitting up.

The stranger fled in fear.

"I spoke!" the foolish man said in amazement. "Why, I must not be dead at all!"

He hopped down from the bier and went home.

Sources

de Souza, Eunice. *101 Folktales from India*. New Delhi, India: Puffin, 2004.

Ramanujan, A.K. *Folktales from India*. New York: Pantheon, 1991.

The Four Wise Men and the Tiger

This Indian folktale spread to the Caribbean with Indian immigrants. Following are the Indian version and one from Trinidad and Tobago to show how a tale basically may stay the same but may change in the details.

The Tiger Makers: A Folktale from Kannada, India

The Brahmans are the highest caste in India, and they are often well-educated. But in this case, the Brahmans are not all as wise as they think they are.

Once, there were four wise Brahmans, men of the highest caste. They wandered from place to place, showing off their wisdom.

One day, they found a bone in the forest.

The first Brahman said, "I can make a full skeleton from this bone." And so he did.

The second Brahman said, "I can put flesh and skin on this skeleton." And so he did. There before them stood a tiger, complete down to the whiskers on his face and the stripes on his coat.

The third Brahman asked, "Do you think that is amazing? I can give this tiger life!"

The fourth Brahman cried, "We believe you. Do not do it!"

The third Brahman said, "What is the use of having all this power if I do not use it? You just watch."

The fourth Brahman said, "First, watch me climb this tree." And he quickly climbed up the nearest tree.

The third Brahman brought the tiger to life. It promptly pounced on him and ate him. Then it ate the first and second Brahman as well.

The fourth Brahman waited until the tiger was gone. Then, he climbed down from the tree and sadly walked on.

Which of them was truly wise?

Sources

Olivelle, Patrick, trans. *The Panchatantra: The Book of India's Folk Wisdom*. New York: Oxford University Press, 2002.

Ramanujan, A.K. *Folktales from India*. New York: Pantheon, 1991.

Ryder, Arthur, trans. *The Panchatantra Translated from the Sanskrit*. Chicago: University of Chicago Press, 1958.

Three Wise Fools: A Folktale from Trinidad and Tobago

This folktale is very similar to the previous one from India. Since there are Indian immigrants living in Trinidad and Tobago, this might explain the similarity.

The big difference, though, is the irony here. The three men who think themselves wise are fools. The fourth man, who they call a fool because he cannot read, turns out to be wiser than them.

One day, four men went on a journey. Now, the first three thought themselves very wise. They had read many books. The fourth man could not read a word, so the first three thought him a fool.

As the four men walked along, they came to the bones and skin of a dead lion. The three wise men decided to show off to their friend, the fool.

"I shall put these bones back in their proper order," said the first wise man.

"And I shall put the flesh back on the bones, and the skin back on the flesh," said the second wise man.

"And I," said the third wise man, "will bring the lion back to life."

"What will you do?" they asked the fool.

"I will climb a tree," he said.

The three wise men laughed at their friend, the fool.

Then, they went ahead and brought the lion back to life. And it ate them.

The fool, up in the tree, was safe. Once the lion was gone, he climbed back down and went home.

Now, who was a wise man and who was a fool?

Source

Parmasad, Kenneth Vidia. *Salt and Roti: Indian Folk Tales of the Caribbean, a First Collection*. Trinidad and Tobago: Sankh Productions, 1984.

Foolish Rulers, Politicians, and Other Important Folks

This type of story is definitely popular around the world, since it often is the only chance a downtrodden people have to let off steam and say what they really think about their own leaders. There also is the satisfaction of the small man getting the better of the powerful and pompous.

The Foolish Man and the Royal Minister: A Folktale from Cambodia

The *Gatiloke* of Cambodia, the original source of this tale, is a collection of ancient folktales derived from the teachings of Buddhist monks. It was an oral collection passed down for possibly thousands of years until it was at last written down in the Cambodian language in the nineteenth century.

Once, there was a foolish but kindhearted man.

One day, he was riding his buffalo to market with a basket of rice riding behind him on the buffalo. The road was muddy, and the buffalo struggled on through it. The foolish man felt sorry for the beast.

"Poor buffalo! First, I ride you, and I am a heavy burden. Then, I add a second burden of the basket of rice. I must do something for you."

Then, he saw some girls walking along with baskets balanced on their heads. Aha! Now he knew what to do!

"If I carry the basket of rice on my head, then my buffalo will have less of a burden."

So, he took the basket of rice from behind him, balanced the basket on his head, and rode on.

Meanwhile, the king of the land had grown weary of his courtiers and bored with his jester's tricks. He said to his minister, "Go find me a truly foolish man. I will pay him to entertain me."

Off the minister went. But he could not find a single foolish soul. Then, he saw the foolish man riding his buffalo with a basket of rice balanced on his head. Now, that looked properly silly!

"Hey there," the minister called. "Why are you carrying the basket on your head? Why not put it on the buffalo's back behind you?"

"Because I love my buffalo," the foolish man said. "He works so hard for me. I am a heavy load for him to carry. But if I set this basket of rice on his back, he will then have to bear two heavy loads. So I carry the basket on my head."

The minister blinked. "That is very wise," he said.

He returned to the palace and told the king, "I could not find a single foolish man. All I found was a kind man who sat on his buffalo and carried the basket of rice on his head to make the load lighter for the poor animal."

"I think I have found my fool," the king said, looking directly at his minister.

Source
Carrison, Muriel Paskin, and the Venerable Kong Chhean. *Cambodian Folk Stories from the Gatiloke*. Rutland, VT, and Tokyo, Japan: Charles E. Tuttle, 1987.

The Foolish King: A Folktale from the Dominican Republic

This folktale is reminiscent of the biblical tale of the Tower of Babel, which may have inspired it. There are similar folktales of such arrogance and foolishness from around the world.

Once, there was a foolish king. He wanted to catch the moon.

But how could he even reach the moon? The king decided that he would have all his carpenters build boxes and pile them up so that he could climb them like a great ladder.

So all the carpenters built boxes and piled them up. But they were not tall enough to reach the moon. So the carpenters built more boxes. But there still were not enough to reach the moon.

"We have no more wood!" the carpenters told the king.

"Go into everyone's home and take their boxes!" the king ordered.

So they did. They took all of the boxes in the city and piled them up on top of the other boxes. But there still were not enough to reach the moon.

"We have run out of boxes in the whole city!" the carpenters cried.

"Then cut down the trees, all of them!" the king ordered.

So the woodsmen cut down all of the trees. The carpenters made boxes out of the wood. They piled them up, and up, and up.

"Wonderful!" cried the king.

He carefully climbed up the rickety pile of boxes, up and up and up. He reached up to the moon—but no matter how he stretched and strained, he could not reach it.

"More boxes!" the king cried. "I need more boxes!"

"There are no more boxes!" the carpenters cried. "And there is no more wood to be had to build more boxes!"

Then, the king had an idea. "So take some boxes from the bottom of the pile and add them to the top!"

"Are you sure, Your Majesty?"

"Take boxes from the bottom of the pile and add them to the top!" he ordered.

So they did.

Down came the whole tower of boxes, and down came the king. And that was the end of the foolish king.

Source

Andrade, Manuel J. *Folklore from the Dominican Republic.* Memoirs of the American Folk-Lore Society. Vol. 23. New York: American Folk-Lore Society, 1930.

The Foolish Astrologer: A Folktale from Kerala Province, India

This is one of the folktales in which the humor comes from seeing the high and mighty brought low by their own sheer stupidity. In the real world, there actually have been such cases of careless workers gesturing too wildly or winding up cutting off the wrong branch.

Once, there was a Panikar, an astrologer, who was very good at his trade.

But he grew bored with seeing other people's fortunes and grew more interested in tending his fruit trees. He was particularly proud of his banana trees, and would circle them, looking for ripe fruit or any problems.

What was this? One branch of a banana tree was empty of fruit and leaves. What had been eating them?

Hah, a squirrel! The furious Panikar tried to chase the squirrel away, but whenever he got too near the animal, it simply jumped to another tree.

Finally, he thought he had isolated the squirrel in a coconut tree and climbed up after it. But the squirrel, of course, was not trapped. It simply made a great leap into another tree.

The Panikar, being no lightweight squirrel, found himself in a branch that was slowly sagging down from the trunk. He was stuck! It was too high to jump down safely, but he could not climb up the branch back to the trunk, either.

"Help!" he called to his wife.

She came running out to see what was wrong and just managed to laugh. "Oh dear," she said. "What do you want me to do?"

"Pile up some hay! Pile it up so I can land safely in it!"

"How much do you need?"

Here was where the Panikar proved he was just as foolish as anyone else. "This much!" he exclaimed, spreading his arms wide.

And, of course, the moment he let go of the branch—down he fell!

Source

Beck, Brenda E.F., Peter J. Claus, Praphulladatta Goswami, and Jawaharlal Handoo, eds. *Folktales of India*. Chicago: University of Chicago Press, 1987. Collected in May 1980 by T.M. Mohan from M.K. Velappakutty in Kerala Province, India.

Foolish Towns/Peoples

The label of "fools' towns" has been attached to several places in the world—sometimes for political reasons (the people of Gotham, England, are said to have acted like fools to trick King John), sometimes because everyone seems to need someone else to look down on. Some of the most familiar "fools' towns" include Chelm, Poland; Gotham, England; Lagos de Moreno, Mexico; and Schwartzenborn, Germany. But there are others.

The Silly Folks of Cumae: A Folktale from Ancient Greece

Some of the earliest written tales about foolish towns or cities date to the fifth century B.C.E. and are about the citizens of the Greek city of Cumae, which lay on the coast of what is now Italy.

When the men of Cumae heard that they were going to be visited by a very important man, they grew very excited. But they had only one bath in the whole town! How was their important visitor going to keep himself clean?

At last, they came up with an answer. They filled the bath with fresh water, and then lowered an open grating into the bath, cutting it in half. That way, they were sure, half the water would be kept clean for his sole use.

But not all the men of Cumae were so honest. There was a thief in town who had stolen some clothes. He planned to sell them in the marketplace. But what if the original owner recognized them?

The thief smeared the stolen clothes with pitch to disguise them. He could not understand why no one wanted to buy them.

But there were wise men in Cumae, too, such as the scholar who heard a story that ravens lived for 200 years. He rushed right out and bought a raven to see if the story was true.

The same fellow saw some sparrows in a tree. He quietly spread his robe under the tree and then shook the tree, sure that the sparrows would fall like ripe fruit. The sparrows, of course, had another idea, and the bewildered man watched them simply fly away.

Sources

Clouston, W.A. *The Book of Noodles: Stories of Simpletons; or, Fools and Their Follies.* London: Elliot Stock, 1888; Detroit, MI: Gale Research, Book Tower, 1969.

Hansen, William F., ed. *Anthology of Ancient Greek Popular Literature.* Bloomington: Indiana University Press, 1998.

Hiding the Bell: A Folktale from Germany

Folklore also has labeled Schwartzenborn, Germany, as a town of fools. To which war the following tale attaches is not known.

Once, the people of Schwartzenborn were faced with a dilemma.

There was a war going on. Bells and other metal items were being seized and melted down to make weapons. But the good people of Schwartzenborn did not want to lose their lovely town bell, the bell that called out the hours for everyone. They must, they decided, hide it in a safe place.

But where would a safe place be? Not in a barn, they decided, nor in the church, and certainly not in anybody's house.

Aha! They had the solution! They loaded the heavy bell into a boat and rowed out to the middle of the town lake. Then, they carefully lowered the bell over the side and solemnly watched it sink.

"No one will know where it is now," one citizen said.

"How will *we* know where it is?" another asked.

Now, there was a problem. They must have a sign of some sort so they could find the bell again.

Aha! They had the solution! They would simply mark a notch on the boat at the spot where they had lowered the bell overboard.

Source

Ranke, Kurt. *Folktales of Germany.* Trans. Lotte Baumann. Chicago: University of Chicago Press, 1966.

The Newfies: A Folktale from Newfoundland, Canada

In Canada, foolish people are said to come from Newfoundland, one of the Maritime Provinces. The somewhat derogatory nickname for them is "Newfies." People being people, there is a second division. Those who live in towns are often known as townies, and those who are fishermen are often called baymen. It is mostly the townies who tell Newfie jokes about the baymen.

Notice the similarity to the Schwartzenborn folktale about dropping the bell in the lake and marking the boat. A good folk joke travels.

Two Newfie baymen went out in their fishing dory one day. They came to a spot they had not been to before and dropped their lines.

What a great spot! In no time at all, the boat was full of fish.

"This is some spot," said one bayman. "We will have to mark it so that we can do as well next time out."

"That is right," the other bayman said. "And I know how to do it."

He cut a notch in the gunnel, just where his line had been.

"That is no good," said the first bayman. "Got to find another way."

"Why is that?" asked the other bayman.

"Well, we may not be using the same boat tomorrow."

Sources
Fowke, Edith. *Folklore of Canada*. Toronto, Ontario, Canada: McClelland and Stewart, 1976.
Reader, H.J. *Newfoundland Wit, Humour and Folklore*. St. John's, Newfoundland: Macy's, 1982.

The Fool of a Mayor and His Foolish Council: A Folktale from Switzerland

The town of Werligen is quite real. It does not figure as a town of fools in many folktales, but the town was not spared completely. Why this tale was attached to it may have to do with some medieval satire about the local government. A similar tale was attached to the town of Schwartzenborn, Germany.

Once, the town of Werligen had a fool for a mayor and fools for the city council, too. They had a fine new town hall built. But when it was done, why, it was pitch black inside. They had forgotten all about adding windows to the plan.

"What can we do now?" the councilmen cried.

"We must have light in here!"

"But windows are expensive!"

"I know the answer!" cried the mayor.

They all went outside with big, open sacks and let the sun shine into the sacks. Then, they tied up the sacks and hurried back into the town hall. They opened the sacks—but no sunlight poured out.

"What went wrong?" the mayor wondered.

But no one knew.

It was not until the next election, when the people of Werligen got rid of the foolish mayor and the foolish council, that windows were cut in the walls of the town hall and light could enter.

Sources

Duvoisin, Roger. *The Three Sneezes and Other Swiss Tales*. New York: Alfred A. Knopf, 1951.
Muller-Guggenbuhl, Fritz. *Swiss Alpine Folk Tales*. London: Oxford University Press, 1958.

The Spotted Wood People and the Horse: A Folktale from the Lipan Apache of the American Southwest

In Lipan Apache folklore, the foolish people of the folktales are called the Spotted Wood People, those who were created just before human beings. They are said not to have much sense.

Other branches of the Apache people also have their foolish people and very similar tales about them. The Jicarilla Apache, for instance, call them the Traveling People.

Once, a group of Spotted Wood People went on a raid. They went out for a little bit, but all they found was part of a rawhide hobble that had been used to hobble a horse.

Why, this was a wonderful trophy! It was almost as good as getting a horse!

Then, they did find a horse, the one who had broken his hobble and gotten away. They took the horse with them. But what did you feed a horse? None of them knew.

One man tried to feed it meat. The horse refused to eat.

Another man tried to feed it gravy. The horse refused to eat.

They tried every type of food that they, themselves, ate. The horse refused to eat.

"What are we going to do? The horse will not eat anything!"

While they were arguing, no one remembered to tie up the horse. The horse grew bored and started to graze.

"Oh, that is what it eats!" everyone cried. "It eats grass!"

So they all started pulling up grass and ran to give it to the horse.

They startled the horse. It galloped away.

"Oh well," said the Spotted Wood People. "At least we now know what a horse eats."

Sources

Erdoes, Richard, and Alfonso Ortiz, eds. *American Indian Myths and Legends*. New York: Pantheon, 1984.
Opler, Morris Edward. *Myths and Legends of the Lipan Apache Indians*. New York: American Folk-Lore Society, 1940.

Scaredy-Cat Fools

There are some folktales about fools who are easily frightened by what is commonplace to others. A good storyteller should easily have the audience laughing at every error.

Bouki at the Market: A Folktale from Haiti

The following folktale is a classic example of a fool who is afraid of his own shadow. Bouki, sometimes known as Konpe Bouki (*konpe* being the Haitian Creole title for "godfather" or just a close male friend), is a stock fool figure in Haitian folklore. There are many tales about him, his foolishness, and his greedy appetite for meat.

One day, Konpe Malis, the wise one of the family, could not go to the market, since his mother was sick and needed tending. Konpe Malis had no one to send but Bouki. Oh, he did not wish to send that foolish, greedy fellow to the market! But there was no choice, because there was no food in the house.

So Konpe Malis said to Bouki, "I am sending you to the market. You are to buy charcoal for the fire, vegetables, rice, beans, and yes, a nice piece of beef. But I know you, Bouki. Don't you dare eat up that meat, or I swear that I will beat you!"

Well, this time Bouki was determined to be good, not foolish or greedy. He bought everything, even a nice piece of beef. Oh, how he hungered for the beef! But he said to it, "I will not eat you. I will show Konpe Malis how good and wise I am."

So Bouki started off for home at a swift walk. But—oh, no, a strange dark little man was following him!

Bouki was frightened. "Go away, little man!"

The little man said nothing.

Bouki walked even faster. The little man was right behind him.

Bouki began to run. The little man stayed right behind him.

"What do you want?" Bouki cried over his shoulder. "The charcoal? Here it is!"

He threw the charcoal at the little man and ran on. But the little man stayed right behind him.

"What do you want?" Bouki cried over his shoulder. "The vegetables? Here they are!"

He threw the vegetables at the little man and ran on. But the little man stayed right behind him.

"What do you want?" Bouki cried over his shoulder. "The rice? The beans? Here they are!"

He threw the rice and the beans at the little man and ran on. But the little man stayed right behind him.

All that was left in Bouki's basket was the nice piece of beef. "Oh, no, I am not going to give this up!"

He ran even faster than before—but the little man was right behind him.

"All right, all right, take the beef! Here! Just leave me alone!"

He threw the beef at the little man, reached home and hid under the bed.

Konpe Malis pulled him out. "Why are you hiding? And where is the food I sent you to get?"

"A little man was following me all the way! I had to throw all the food at him or he would have eaten me up!"

"What little man?" Konpe Malis asked. "Come show him to me."

Shaking with fear, Bouki led Konpe Malis outside. And there, indeed, was the little man. Instead of beating Bouki, Konpe Malis had to laugh.

Bouki had been afraid of his own shadow.

Sources

Courtlander, Harold. *The Drum and the Hoe: Life and Lore of the Haitian People*. Berkeley and Los Angeles: University of California Press, 1960.

Louis, Liliane Nerette. *When Night Falls, KRIC! KRAC!: Haitian Folktales*. Englewood, CO: Libraries Unlimited, 1999.

Who Am I?

There also are world folktales about foolish people who change their clothes (or have their clothes taken by a practical joker) and who then cannot identify themselves.

Who Am I?: A Folktale from the Jews of Poland

Now, it is not that the people of Chelm were fools. No, it was simply that foolish things kept happening to them.

Once, the Rabbi of Chelm was staying overnight at an inn with some of his students. One of the students asked the innkeeper to wake him just before dawn, since he had an early train to catch.

Sure enough, as good as his word, the innkeeper woke the student just before dawn. It was very dark in the inn, and the student did not want to wake anyone. So he rummaged about in the dark for his clothes and slipped them on.

Off the student hurried through the dark streets to the train station. It was still cold out, and he wrapped himself up in his cloak. When he had finally reached the train station and was warm again, he removed the cloak and caught a glance of himself in a mirror. He was wearing not his student clothes, but the Rabbi's long black robe.

"What a fool that innkeeper is!" the student cried. "I asked him to wake me. Instead, look, he woke the Rabbi!"

Sources

Serwer-Bernstein, Blanche L. *In the Tradition of Moses and Mohammed: Jewish and Arab Folktales*. Northvale, NJ, and London: Jason Aronson, 1994.

Sherman, Josepha. *A Sampler of Jewish-American Folklore*. Little Rock, AR: August House, 1992.

Am I Myself?: A Folktale from County Cork, Ireland

What with the flurry of activity that surrounds North American politics, the humor in this folktale is doubled in both the casual way the election is settled and the fact that a foolish fellow has been arbitrarily named mayor.

Once, there was a fellow named Sean who made a meager living for himself and his wife by making brushes and selling them in the town of Cork.

As it happened, the mayor of Cork had died, and there were three candidates vying for the job. Each time the people voted, there was a three-way tie. At last, everyone grew tired of the problem. They agreed that the first man they met would become mayor.

That man was Sean. Before he knew what was what, he was invested with the mayoral robes and chain of office. When it was time to go home, he rode in a great carriage drawn by two gray horses.

When Sean's wife heard the horses outside, she came running out to see what was going on and saw her husband step down from the great carriage in his new regalia.

"Stay back," he called to her.

"Are you not my husband, Sean?"

"I think I am. But stay back from me and pretend you do not know me. I do not even know myself!"

Source

O'Sullivan, Sean, ed. and trans. *Folktales of Ireland.* Chicago and London: University of Chicago Press, 1966. Recorded on December 23, 1932, by Sean O'Suilleabhain from Michael O'Suilleabhain, County Kerry.

Where Is the Jar?: A Folktale from Afghanistan

The Mullah—a.k.a. Nasser-E-Din, a.k.a. Nasreddin, a.k.a. the Effendi, and many other aliases—is a very popular character in Arab lands, Israel, Turkey, and western China. There are hundreds of tales about him. He often is portrayed as a wise trickster, someone who cuts the grand and pompous down to size. But he also can be seen as a fool in other tales, such as this one.

One day, Mullah Nasser-E-Din went to the public baths.

After washing, he saw that all the other bathers were lying on their backs, sound asleep, splitting the air with their snores.

"How good a sweet sleep would be," he said to himself.

But suppose he fell asleep and, while he slept, someone else took his identity?

Aha! There was the answer. He took a jar and a piece of string, tied one end to the jar handle and the other to his waist. Then, he fell asleep, secure in the knowledge that he was himself.

Unfortunately, one of the other bathers woke up and saw the jar. He wanted it. So he untied the string and tied the jar to his own waist.

Now Nasser-E-Din woke up. The jar was not there. He looked frantically around—there it was, tied to someone else's waist. He woke the man up.

"If I am I, where is the jar? But if you are me, then—who am I?"

Source

Noy, Dov. *Folktales of Israel*. Trans. Gene Baharav. Chicago: University of Chicago Press, 1963. Recorded from Zvulun Kort, a Jewish immigrant from Afghanistan.

Where Is the Pumpkin?: A Folktale from Iran

This folktale is similar to the previous one, which was collected from an Afghani immigrant. Which is the older version of the two folktales is open to question, but folklore has traveled up and down the Central Asian trade routes for thousands of years.

Once, there was a poor man, a wrestler, who was, perhaps, not precisely a clever man.

The wrestler had lived all his life in the country. Now, he decided to try his fortune in a great city. But as he entered it, he was awestruck at the number of people traveling its crowded streets.

"I shall certainly not be able to know myself from all the others if I do not have something about me that the others have not."

So he tied a pumpkin to his right leg. He spent the night in an inn, where a witty young man saw the pumpkin and quickly learned the truth about it from the wrestler.

That night, while the wrestler was asleep, the young man untied the pumpkin from the wrestler's leg, and tied it to his own. And then he lay down again.

In the morning, when the wrestler woke up and found the pumpkin tied to the other man's leg, he called to him, "Hey! Who am I, and who are you? If I am myself, why is the pumpkin on your leg? And if you are yourself, why is the pumpkin not on my leg?"

Sources

Clouston, W.A. *The Book of Noodles: Stories of Simpletons; or, Fools and Their Follies*. London: Elliot Stock, 1888; Detroit, MI: Gale Research, Book Tower, 1969.

Sholey, Arthur. *The Discontented Dervishes and Other Persian Tales*. London: Watkins, 2002.

Which Leg Is Mine?: A Folktale from Mexico

This is a folktale type found around the world, although this version comes from Mexico. Lagos, Mexico—like Chelm, Poland, and Gotham, England—is a real place. As is the case with those other towns, no one knows why stories of foolish people became attached to Lagos.

There were five drovers from Lagos who had been traveling down the long, dusty road to market for some time. The day was hot, and they were tired.

So they lay down in the shade of a tree to rest, and soon they were asleep. But when they woke up—oh, what a problem! Their legs were tangled up, one with another.

"How can we get up?" the drovers cried.

"We do not know what legs belong to which man!"

"We will have to stay here forever!"

Just then, another man came along. He saw the drovers and asked, "What is the matter?"

"We cannot get up! We do not know whose legs belong to whom."

"I see." The man drew a long needle from his pack. "I believe I can solve your problem."

He began sticking their legs with the needle. As each man cried, "Ouch!" the man said to him, "That is your leg."

Soon, he had all of them untangled and on their feet. Shaking his head, the man went on his way.

Sources

Campos, Anthony John. *Mexican Folktales*. Tucson: University of Arizona Press, 1978.

Paredes, Americo, ed. *Folktales of Mexico*. Chicago: University of Chicago Press, 1970. Collected by Stanley L. Robe from Maria de Jesus Navarro, no date.

How Many Are We?

Here is a worldwide folktale type that often delights small children just learning to count. In it, despite regional variants, a group of foolish people cannot tell if they are all there, because each time one of them counts, he forgets to include himself in the count.

How the Kadambawa Men Counted Themselves: A Folktale from Sri Lanka

In Sri Lanka, those from Kadambawa often are seen as more foolish than others, even though there is no truth to that perception.

Twelve Kadambawa men were busy cutting sticks for fences. They tied the sticks into twelve bundles, then set the bundles upright and leaned them together.

Then, one of the men said, "Are our men all here? We must count and see."

So one of the men counted them, but he counted only eleven men. "There are only eleven men, but there are twelve bundles of fence sticks," he said.

Then, another man said, "Maybe you have made a mistake," and he counted them again. "There are eleven men and twelve bundles of fence sticks. There is a man missing."

So off they went into the jungle to look for the missing man.

While they were in the jungle looking, a man from another village heard them shouting. He hurried over to them and asked why they were shouting.

The men said, "Twelve of our men came to cut fence sticks. There are twelve bundles of sticks, but only eleven men. One man is missing."

This man saw the problem at once and said, "Each of you pick up your own bundle of fence sticks."

So each of the twelve men picked up his own bundle of sticks. And when they had, all the bundles were picked up. Thus, they all returned to their village.

Never once did they realize that each man who had counted them had forgotten to add himself into the count.

Sources
Parker, H. *Village Folk-Tales of Ceylon.* London: Luzac, 1910–1914.
Premaratne, Geetha. *Andare: Folktales from Sri Lanka.* Linton, Australia: Papyrus, 1999.

The Six Silly Boys: A Folktale from Finland

In a variant of this next silly story, the traveler tells the boys to stick their noses not in mud, but in dung. The variant chosen is up to the storyteller.

Once, six silly boys went for a swim. The stalks of rye seed were swaying in the wind, and it looked like water to them. So, the six silly boys jumped into the field of rye.

That was strange. They did not seem to get wet. So they climbed out of the rye again.

"Are we all here?" one silly boy asked.

"How many of us were there?" asked another.

"Six," they all decided. "There were six of us. Let us make sure we are all still here."

So each silly boy counted. "One, two, three, four, five—oh no, only five! One of us is missing!"

A traveler came by and saw the boys weeping and wailing. "What is wrong?" he asked.

"We just went swimming, over there, and there were six of us. But now there are only five! One of us must have drowned!"

"Let me see you count," the traveler said.

He watched, and saw that each silly boy counted five—because each silly boy forgot to count himself.

"I see the problem," the traveler said. "Do you see that mud?"

They did.

"I want each of you to stick his nose in the mud. Then, count the dents in the mud."

He went on his way, shaking his head.

The silly boys stuck their noses in the mud. They counted the dents. Six! There were six!

"Oh, how wonderful!" they cried. "No one drowned after all!"

Source

Henderson, Helena. *The Maiden Who Rose from the Sea and Other Finnish Folktales.* Enfield Lock, United Kingdom: Hisarlik, 1992. Originally recorded from Albert Wikstedt, 56, Mantala, Finland, 1913, by K.F. Andersson.

The Foolish Peasants: A Folktale from Kashmir, India

Kashmir may be known as the site of much fighting between India and Pakistan, but despite ongoing strife, folklore still survives.

Ten peasants were standing on the side of the road weeping.

"Hey, you!" a passing townsman called. "What is the matter?"

"Oh, sir," said the peasants, "it is terrible. We were ten men when we left the village, but now we are only nine."

"Is that so? Let me see how you count."

The townsman quickly saw that they thought that one of their number had been lost on the way because each man had counted the company without remembering to include himself in the count.

"Take off your *topis*," he told them, the topis being their skull caps. "Place them on the ground. Now count them. See? Ten. You are all there, all ten of you."

"A miracle!" they cried.

The townsman gave up. Shaking his head, he walked away.

Sources

Beck, Brenda E.F., Peter J. Claus, Praphulladatta Goswami, and Jawaharlal Handoo, eds. *Folktales of India.* Chicago: University of Chicago Press, 1987.

Knowles, H.J. *Folk-Tales of Kashmir.* London: Trübner, 1893.

The Seven Fools: A Yugur Folktale from Western China

The Yugur are a Buddhist minority. This version of the "fools fail to count themselves" theme is a bit different, since it includes Buddhism in the solution.

Once upon a time, there were seven fools. They set off to pay their respects to the Dalai Panchen, the wise man known as the Living Buddha.

While they were walking, they came to the Black River. They could not figure out how to cross the water. But while they were looking and talking, talking and looking, a cat came to the other side and calmly swam across.

"Oh, in this way one crosses this Black River!" one man said.

"Let us, too, wade across!" said another.

So they waded across to the other side. But when the seven people decided to count one another: one, two, three, four, five, six, that was all, one of the people was lost.

"You count!" one man said to another.

"One, two, three, four, five, six! One of us really is lost!"

"The water must have dragged him away."

"You count!" they said to one another. But whoever counted, there still were only six!

"Then let us take our hats, and count these!"

"One, two, three, four, five, six, seven!" they counted. "Oh, this means the water has dragged away the one person. This is the hat of the person the water has dragged away."

Then, they decided to hurry on together to the Dalai Panchen, the Living Buddha. They placed an offering of silver before him, bowed low before him, and presented the Living Buddha with a question.

"We have come to bow to you. But did one of us people get dragged away by the water?"

The Living Buddha asked, "How many of you people set off?"

"We set off with seven people."

"Well, in that case, just you count one another for me!"

"One, two, three, four, five, six!"

"You also must count your own body for me!"

"One, two, three, four, five, six . . . seven! We are seven! We are all here!"

Oh, how amazing, they all thought. They had just seen the Dalai Panchen's power. He had revived a person who had died!

Source

Jazyk zheltyx ujgurov (Folktales of the Western Yugur). Moscow, Russia: n.p., 1967. *The Seven Fools* was recorded by Qasqaji, a storyteller from the village Donghaizi (present-day Mínghai), in November 1910.

What Should I Have Said/Done?

In this world folktale type, a foolish man or boy always is one step behind what is happening. For instance, told he must weep at a funeral, he mistakes a wedding for a funeral and weeps. The fool never learns what he has done wrong, but the audience certainly does and usually is highly appreciative of his misadventures.

Jack the Fool: A Folktale from Donegal, Ireland

In this folktale, the mother of foolish Jack learns to appreciate that he is as he is—especially if he brings back gold.

Once, there was a widow woman with one son, a foolish fellow named Jack. One day, the woman sent her son Jack into town to buy a needle. He got the needle, but then, seeing a cart of hay that would be going to his mother's house, stuck the needle into the hay. That way, he thought, he would not lose the needle.

"Where is my needle?" his mother asked.

"Safe and sound in that load of hay," Jack said.

Well, his mother gave him a good thrashing for that. "Who else but a fool would carry a needle in a load of hay?" she cried.

"How should I have carried it?" Jack asked.

"Safely stuck into the breast of your jacket," she said.

Soon after, they ran out of butter, and Jack's mother sent him into town to buy a pound of butter. Jack bought it, then remembered what his mother had said. He put the butter safe inside the breast of his jacket and headed home.

Alas, it was a hot day. By the time Jack got home, well, there was nothing left of the butter but a greasy stain on his clothes.

"What happened to the butter?" his mother cried.

"I did as you told me," Jack said. "I carried it safe inside the breast of my jacket."

His mother thrashed him for that. Jack cried, "How should I have carried it?"

"You should have put it on a cabbage leaf and carried it home on the cabbage leaf."

The next morning, they ran out of milk. Off Jack went to town to buy a pint of milk. He took a cabbage leaf, poured the milk onto it, and set out for home. Of course, by the time he got home, there was nothing more than a damp cabbage leaf.

His mother thrashed him for that. "But how should I have carried it?" asked Jack.

"In a can!" she cried. "You should have carried it in a can!"

Now, they kept some sheep, so Jack's mother sent him off to bring back a sheep-dog. Jack could not figure out how to get a live dog into a can, so he found a dead one and stuffed that into the can.

His mother thrashed him for that. "How should I have brought it?" Jack asked.

"On a string!"

Next, Jack was sent to town to buy a leg of mutton. He tied it to a string and dragged it home. There was little left of it by the time he got home.

His mother thrashed him. "You are a fool!" she cried. "You will always be a fool! And I will not have you in my house any longer!"

So off went Jack without a penny to his name. He came to a graveyard. It began to rain, and it ran down the face of a statue. Jack thought it was weeping and threw his jacket over the statue to help it. But instead, he pulled the statue over.

There beneath the statue was a horde of gold coins! Jack picked the coins up and took them back to his mother.

When Jack's mother saw the gold coins, she sighed. "You are a fool, and you will always be a fool, but I guess that you are my fool. Welcome home, son."

Source
MacManus, Seamus. *The Well o' the World's End*. New York: Macmillan, 1939.

The Foolish Boy: A Folktale from the Lahu People of Southeast Asia and China

This folktale warns about the perils of being foolish. It has a startling and rather final ending.

Once, there was a woman with a very foolish son who just stayed home all day.

One day, the boy smelled a neighbor's curry. It smelled so good that he said, "Mother, I want to eat a delicious curry."

"How can I make a curry at all if you do not bring back any food from the jungle? If you want curry, go look for some food to put in it."

So the boy made a fish trap. But he did not have the patience to wait long. Giving up, sure that the trap was empty, he threw it up into the trees. But there had been a small fish caught in the trap, and an egret landed on the trap and had a nice snack. The boy caught the egret and said to it, "Fly to my home and tell my mother that I said to kill you and make a curry out of you." Then, he let the egret go and watched it fly away.

He went home. "Mother, did you get the egret? I told it to fly home so you could make a curry out of it."

"Son, if you want food, you have to first kill it, then bring it back."

The next day, the foolish boy found a clump of edible mushrooms. He remembered what his mother had said. He beat the mushrooms to a pulp to make sure they were dead, and then he brought the mess home.

"Son," his mother said, "this type of food needs to be picked one at a time, then carried home in your shoulder bag."

Off the son went. He found a hive of bees. Even though they stung him very badly, he managed to put them one by one into his shoulder bag and carry them home.

"Son," his mother said after she, too, had been stung and had chased the bees away with smoke, "for this kind of thing, you must first burn out the hive, then bring it home."

The next day, the foolish boy found a barking deer, which is a small deer that makes doglike noises. "I must burn it," the boy said. He set fire to the deer. It barked, leaped into a river, and swam away.

When the boy told his mother what had happened, she sighed.

"Son, you must first strike it and kill it, bring it home."

So the boy went off into the jungle. He found a Buddhist monk there, struck him over the head, and dragged him home.

His mother, setting about reviving the stunned monk, said, "Son, this is a holy man. You do not strike him. You bow to him."

So the boy went off into the jungle again. He found a tiger. Remembering what his mother had said, he bowed to it. The tiger ate him.

And that is why there is a Lahu proverb: Stupid never survives.

Source
Pun, Angela, and Paul W. Lewis. *49 Lahu Stories*. Bangkok, Thailand: White Lotus, 2002.
    Stories collected from the Lahu people by the Reverend Ai Pun, c. 1939.

Ivan the Fool: A Folktale from Ukraine

In this folktale, the fool never does find out what it is he has said wrong, or why everyone is so angry at him.

Once, there was a man so foolish that he was known as Ivan the Fool.
One day, his wife sent him to the mill to grind a sack of rye, telling him to come back if the weather was neither fair nor cloudy.

Ivan thought that meant he should grind the rye, then wait for it to be neither fair nor cloudy. As he waited, he saw the miller take for himself a measure of flour for every sack he ground.

"That is right," said the miller, "May you get a measure for every sack!"

Ivan started for home. He saw some farmers reaping their wheat and called out, "May you get a measure for every sack!"

The farmers thought Ivan was mocking them and were furious. "Do not say that any more!" they yelled. "Say, 'May you always have more than you can carry!'"

Ivan went on and came across some men carrying a coffin. "May you always have more than you can carry!" he cried.

The furious men nearly dropped the coffin, wanting to beat Ivan up for what he had said. They yelled, "Next time say 'May you never know the like again!'"

Ivan hurried on and soon found himself facing a bridal procession with happy, joyous people. He cried, "May you never know the like again!"

They nearly beat Ivan black and blue, then yelled at him, "Next time say, 'Let the groom kiss the bride and be happy!'"

Ivan went on and saw a man leading a sow. He said, "Let the groom kiss the bride and be happy!"

The man hit Ivan with his walking stick. "Next time say 'Sink in muck and fill your belly!'"

Ivan went on, and saw a man carting dung to the dung heap. He said, "Sink in muck and fill your belly!"

The furious man jumped down from his cart. Ivan, who had no idea why all these people were so angry at him, took to his heels and ran home.

Source
Zheleznova, Irina. *Ukrainian Folk Tales*. Kiev, Ukraine: Dnipro, 1986.

Following Instructions: A Folktale from Japan

In this folktale, the mother of the foolish son learns to face facts and not send the poor boy on errands he cannot understand.

Once, there was a woman with a very foolish son.

One day, the boy was sent to a relative to borrow an iron kettle. He tied a rope to it and dragged it home. But the kettle hit several rocks along the way, and it was badly dented. The boy burst into tears.

"The iron kettle broke when I dragged it home on a rope."

His mother comforted him. She told him that he should have tied the kettle to his back and carried it home that way.

The next day, the boy was sent to borrow an earthenware pot. He tied it to his back, but it fell off and broke. The boy burst into tears.

"I tied the earthenware pot to my back, but it fell off and broke."

His mother comforted him and told him that he should have wrapped up the pot in a *furoshiki,* a cloth that is used to protect items being moved.

The next day, the boy was sent to get the old woman who tended fires. He wrapped her up in a furoshiki, but she got angry and hit him over the head. The boy burst into tears.

"I wrapped up the old woman who tends fires in a furoshiki, but she hit me over the head."

His mother comforted him and said, "It was a hot day today, and she did not want to be wrapped up. A furoshiki is for things, not people. You should have led her home with a smile."

The next day, the boy passed a house on fire. He smiled at the fireman and said, "It is a hot day, today."

The hot, tired fireman hit him on the head. The boy burst into tears.

"I smiled at the fireman who was putting out a house on fire, and I told him it was a hot day. And he hit me."

His mother comforted him and said, "You should have helped put water on the fire."

The next day, the boy passed the blacksmith's shop. He saw the fire in the forge and quickly poured water on it. The angry blacksmith hit him. The boy burst into tears.

"I put water on the fire in the blacksmith's shop, and he hit me."

His mother comforted him and said, "You should have taken a hammer, and helped him pound."

The next day, the boy saw a traveler, and hit him with a hammer. The traveler hit the boy with his staff so hard that the boy saw stars. The boy burst into tears.

After that, his mother gave up trying to explain, and she kept her boy at home.

Source
Mayer, Fanny Hagin, trans. *Ancient Tales in Modern Japan: An Anthology of Japanese Folk Tales.* Bloomington: Indiana University Press, 1984. Transcribed from Ogasawara Kenkichi, Shiwa-gun, Iwate, Japan, no date.

Bajun and Jhore: A Folktale from the Santal Parganas of India

This folktale of two brothers, one ordinary, one a fool, can be told as is or with a darker side. In the darker version, the fool kills his sister-in-law by accident (he has

not fed her) and is then chased by his older brother, who wants to kill him. Both variants are legitimate.

The Santal Parganas live in eastern central India, overlapping into Bangladesh.

Once upon a time, there were two brothers named Bajun and Jhore. Now, Bajun was an ordinary man. But Jhore, he was a fool.

Bajun was married, and one day his wife fell ill. So, as he was going ploughing, Bajun told Jhore to stay at home and cook the dinner.

"Put into the pot three measures of rice," he told Jhore.

Jhore stayed at home, filled the pot with water, and put it on to boil. Then, he
went to look for rice measures. There was only one wooden measure in the house.

"My brother told me to put in three measures. If I only put in one, I shall get
into trouble."

So off Jhore went to a neighbor's house, where he borrowed two more wooden
measures. When he got home, Jhore put all three measures into the pot and left
them to boil.

At noon, Bajun came back from ploughing and found Jhore stirring the pot.

"Is the rice ready?" Bajun asked. Jhore only shook his head, so Bajun took the
spoon from him. "Let me feel how it is getting on," he said.

But when he stirred with the spoon, he heard a rattling noise. And when he
looked into the pot, he found no rice. Instead, there were three wooden measures
floating about.

"Jhore! What have you done?"

Jhore said, "You yourself told me to put in three measures, and I have done
so."

The next day, Bajun said to Jhore, "You do not know how to cook the dinner. I
will stay home today. You go to plough. Take a hatchet with you. If the plough
catches in a root or anything, give a cut with the hatchet."

So Jhore went ploughing. The plough did catch, and he gave a cut with his
hatchet and hit the legs of the oxen. They came limping back.

"What is the matter with them?" Bajun asked.

"I cut at them as you told me," said Jhore.

"No, no, no!" Bajun cried. "I meant that you should give a cut at the roots in
which the plough got caught, not at the legs of the bullocks. You cannot live here
any more if you do such silly things."

"All right," said Jhore, and he ran off into the jungle.

Bajun followed his brother, but all he found was the stomach of a dead goat a
tiger had killed. He thought it must surely mean that Jhore had been killed. So he
went home and performed the funeral ceremonies to the memory of his brother.

Jhore, meanwhile, had come back. He climbed up onto the roof so he could
see what his brother was doing.

Bajun had sacrificed some goats and sheep. He cooked a great basket of rice
and stewed the flesh of the animals he had sacrificed, then offered the food to the
spirit of the dead.

"Jhore, my brother, I offer this rice, this food, for your purification."

Jhore called out from the roof "Well, as you offer it to me, I will take it."

Bajun had hardly expected an answer. He rushed away from there to ask the other villagers if they had ever heard a spirit speak.

While Bajun was away, Jhore took up the unguarded basket of rice and ran away with it, back into the jungle. After going some way, he sat down and ate as much as he wanted. Then, he called out, "Is there anyone who wants a feast?"

A gang of thieves heard him and agreed to let him join them in exchange for the meal. They broke into a rich man's house, and the thieves began to collect the riches.

But Jhore found a drum and began to beat on it. This woke up the people of the house, and they drove away the thieves.

The furious thieves told Jhore that he could not stay with them. So off he went to be his own thief.

Jhore came to a herd of horses and decided to steal one. But he did not jump onto the back of a horse, he jumped onto the back of a tiger that had come to try to eat a horse.

What an odd striped horse this was! Jhore hung on as the startled tiger ran off with him into the jungle.

"Hey, striped horse," Jhore called out, "keep to the road, keep to the road!"

But the tiger ran into the jungle. Jhore fell off, the tiger turned to him—and that was the end of Jhore.

Source

Bompas, Cecil Henry. *Folklore of the Santal Parganas*. Salem, NH: Ayer, 1977.

The Donkey with the Unlucky Name: A Folktale from Morocco

This variant on the "What should I have said?" theme introduces a mischievous donkey into the mix. But there is a happy ending.

A foolish fellow owned a donkey named Fritla. Now, that is a bad name, since it means that every time it is said, the creature bearing that name will slip away. So did the donkey named Fritla.

The foolish fellow went searching for Fritla. He came to a group of hunters. "Have you seen Fritla?" he asked.

The hunters were furious. "You just cursed us! You told us that any game we try to hunt will slip away!"

"But what should I have said?"

"Say, 'I hope that every day you will bring fifty.'"

Off the foolish fellow went, repeating the sentence to himself as he searched for his donkey. He met some mourners carrying a woman's coffin to the graveyard and called out, "I hope that every day you will bring fifty!"

The mourners attacked him in their anger.

"But—but what should I have said?" he asked.

"You should say, 'May God have mercy on her soul and commiserate with her relatives.'"

The foolish fellow went off again, turning this sentence over and over in his mind as he searched for his donkey. Now, he came to a bride being brought to the groom's house. He shouted, "May God have mercy on her soul and commiserate with her relatives!"

The furious bridal party gave him a beating, too.

"But what should I have said?" he asked.

"You should say, 'May God make her feel at home and never want to leave.'"

So off he went with this new sentence in his mind. He came across peasants fighting off a swarm of locusts. "May God make her feel at home," he cried, "and never want to leave!"

Once again, he was beaten.

"Enough!" he cried. "Enough! I never know what to say! I do not even want my donkey any more!"

Just then, he felt a warm muzzle bump his back. Fritla had been following him all along.

Source

El Koudia, Jilali, ed. *Moroccan Folktales.* Trans. Jilali El Koudia and Roger Allen. Syracuse, NY: Syracuse University Press, 2003.

Split-His-Own-Head: A Folktale from the Nehalem Tillamook of the Pacific Northwest

In this folktale, the foolish fellow actually finds himself a very patient wife at the end.

Split-His-Own-Head was not the brightest of men. He lived with his sister and tried to do everything right. But somehow, he never quite understood anything.

One day, his sister, tired of walking everywhere when they had a nice river nearby, said, "I wish you would make a canoe for me. Even one of rotten wood would be better than all this walking I do."

So Split-His-Own-Head made her a canoe. But when the sister tossed her root digger into it, the root digger went right through. "You made the canoe out of rotten wood!" she cried.

"But that is just what you told me to do!" he insisted.

She sighed, then told him very carefully how to make a canoe out of good cedar wood. That, he could do.

Then, one day the sister said, "My digging stick is wearing out. Go split your head end." She was pointing at a spruce limb, but Split-His-Own-Head did not get the point. He went off but came back with his head bandaged.

"What happened?" the sister cried.

"Well, you told me to go split my head!"

"No, no, I was pointing at that spruce limb by you! I wanted you to split that for me!"

That, he could do.

Then came the day when Split-His-Own-Head's sister told him, "Some people are going to buy whale meat. Take these money beads and go with them." (Money beads were dentilia shells that everyone in the area used as coinage.)

But the sister did not want to make her instructions too complicated for Split-His-Own-Head. "Remember, throw your money beads on any old woman." That was a slang saying that meant, get the meat from anyone who gives you a good price.

So off they went to where the whale meat was. Everyone was busily buying meat, but Split-His-Own-Head just wandered about. At last, he saw an old woman who was going apart from everyone else to relieve herself. He followed, and tossed the beads at her.

"Hey, can't an old woman have any privacy?" she yelped.

"I came to buy whale meat. And my sister told me to throw my money beads on any old woman."

The old woman sighed and kindly led him to where he actually could buy some whale meat. Split-His-Own-Head bought the meat and made it home again.

The next problem was that he and his sister were running low on salmon. She gave him a dried salmon, and made the mistake of using slang again. "Today, you will throw rocks at the sun all day." That meant, "Today you will not spend all your time eating; save something for supper."

Off Split-His-Own-Head went. He returned that evening, tired and sore. "What is wrong?" his sister asked.

"I am all worn out from throwing rocks at the sun all day," he told her.

She just sighed. She really had to get him off her hands somehow!

"You are nearly grown now," the sister said. "You need a woman for yourself." But who would want such a foolish fellow? Impatiently, the sister added, "Even a dead woman would be better than no wife at all."

Then she thought, "I should not have said that."

No, she should not. That next morning, Split-His-Own-Head complained that his new wife was all bony.

"Oh no," said the sister. She looked in the bed. "That is a dead woman!"

"You told me to get one."

"No, no, I meant a live wife! A live wife! Now, go put that back where you found it, and get yourself a *young* wife!"

So, he brought back a baby.

"No, no, no!" the sister cried. "You go and give that baby back to her mother right now!"

As it happened, the mother of the baby had a sister who was an amazingly patient woman. She did not mind tending a foolish husband.

And so Split-His-Own-Head found a wife. And Split-His-Own-Head's sister got some peace and quiet.

That is ended.

Source

Jacobs, Melville, ed. *Nehalem Tillamook Tales*. 1956. Corvallis: Oregon State University Press, 1990. Told by Clara Peterson of the Nehalem Tillamook, recorded by Elizabeth Derr Jacobs.

Do Not Count Your Chickens

This is both a wise saying (do not count your chickens until they are hatched) and a tale type known throughout the world in different forms. All teach the same lesson: Do not get lost in dreams, but focus on what is real.

The Broken Pot: A Folktale from Ancient India

This is a tale from the Panchatantra, an Indian collection of fables written in Sanskrit and dating to the fourth to sixth centuries C.E. It consists of five books of over eighty animal fables and magic tales. The author or compiler is unknown, and scholars think that many of the stories predate the book.

In a certain place, there once lived a Brahman named Svabhâvakripana, which means "luckless by his very nature."

By begging, the Brahman had acquired a good amount of rice gruel. After he had eaten what he wanted, there was still a full pot left. He hung this pot on a nail in the wall above his bed, where he could see it.

As the night wore on, he could not take his eyes from the pot. And he began thinking.

"This pot is filled to overflowing with rice gruel. If a famine should come to the land, then I could sell it for 100 pieces of silver."

"Then, I could buy a pair of goats. They have kids every six months, so I would soon have a herd of goats."

"Then, I would trade the goats for cattle. As soon as the cows had calved, I would sell the calves."

"Then, I would trade the cattle for buffalo."

"Then, I would trade the buffalo for horses. And when the horses foaled, I would own many horses."

"From their sale, I would gain a large amount of gold. With this gold, I would buy a fine, large house."

"Then, I would gain a very beautiful girl with a large dowry for my wife."

"My wife will give birth to a son, and I will name him Somasarman. When he is old enough to be bounced on my knee, I will take a book, sit in the horse stall, and read."

"Somasarman will see me sitting there in the horse stall, and he will want to be bounced on my knee. He will climb down from his mother's lap and walk toward me, coming close to the horses' hooves."

"Then, filled with anger at my wife's carelessness, I will shout at her, 'Take the child! Take the child!'"

"But she, busy with her housework, will not hear me. So I will jump up and give her a kick!"

Lost in his thoughts, he kicked—breaking the pot and painting himself white with the rice gruel that had been in it.

Sources

Olivelle, Patrick, trans. *The Panchatantra: The Book of India's Folk Wisdom*. New York: Oxford University Press, 2002.

Ryder, Arthur, trans. *The Panchatantra Translated from the Sanskrit*. Chicago: University of Chicago Press, 1958.

The Boy and the Fox: A Folktale from Sweden

In this variant, the boy loses out because he is greedy about the rye he has not even planted.

Once, there was a boy who was on his way to church, when he saw a fox lying fast asleep on a rock.

The boy quickly picked up a heavy stone. "If I kill that fox," he thought, "I can sell the skin. With the money I get for it, I shall buy some rye, and sow it in my father's field."

"When people on their way to church see my field of rye they will say, 'Oh, what splendid rye that lad has grown!'"

"Then, I shall say to them, 'Keep away from my rye!'"

"But they will not listen to me."

"Then, I shall shout to them, 'Keep away from my rye!'"

"But they still will not listen."

"Then, I shall scream with all my might, 'KEEP AWAY FROM MY RYE!'"

"And then they will listen to me."

But the boy had just screamed so loudly that the fox woke up. It raced off into the forest, leaving the boy without even a fistful of its fur.

> Always take what you can reach,
> For undone deeds you must never screech!

Sources

Djurklou, Gabriel. *Fairy Tales from the Swedish*. Trans. H.L. Brækstad. New York: Frederick A. Stokes, 1901.

Lawson, Polly, ed. *Swedish Folktales*. Edinburgh, United Kingdom: Floris, 2004.

"I Will Grow Rich!": A Folktale from Somalia

This is possibly the shortest "do not count your chickens" folktale ever recorded.

Once, there was a man who wanted to be rich.

He saw a leopard lying by the side of the road and said, "It must be dead. I will take its hide, and sell it for sheep, then sell the sheep for camels, and I will grow rich!"

But he had forgotten in his daydreaming to check that the leopard really was dead.

The leopard was alive.
And soon the man was not.

Sources

Hanghe, Ahmed Artan. *Folktales from Somalia.* Uppsala, Sweden: Somalia Academy of Arts and Sciences, in cooperation with the Scandinavian Institute of African Studies, 1988.

Kapchits, G.L., ed. and trans. *Faaliyihii la Bilkeyday: A Soothsayer Tested: Somali Folktales.* Moscow, Russia: By the Way, 2006.

The Three Sillies: A Folktale from England

This is a well-known folktale, though there are several variants. In all cases, the family of silly people sits wailing over a tragedy that *might* happen in the future, yet they make no move to prevent it. In most variants, the protagonist sets out to find three sillier people, which he does, before returning to marry the silly family's daughter.

Once upon a time, there was a farmer and his wife who had one daughter who was being courted by a gentleman. Every evening, he came to visit her and stop for supper at the farmhouse. And the daughter would go down into the cellar to draw the beer for supper.

One evening, she went down to draw the beer, and she happened to look up at the ceiling while she was drawing. There, she saw a mallet stuck in one of the beams. She had never noticed it before, and that got her to thinking. It was very dangerous to have that mallet there.

"Suppose him and me was to be married, and we was to have a son, and he was to grow up to be a man, and he was to come down into the cellar to draw the beer, like as I am doing now, and the mallet was to fall on his head and kill him. What a dreadful thing it would be!"

With that, she put down the candle and the jug, sat herself down, and began crying.

They began to wonder upstairs why it was taking her so long to draw the beer. Her mother went down to see after her, and found her sitting and crying, with the beer running all over the floor.

"Why, whatever is the matter?" the mother asked.

"Oh, mother," the girl sobbed, "look at that horrid mallet! Suppose my sweetheart and me was to be married, and we was to have a son, and he was to grow up to be a man, and he was to come down to the cellar to draw the beer, and the mallet was to fall on his head and kill him. What a dreadful thing it would be!"

"Dear, dear, what a dreadful thing it would be!" the mother said. She sat down next to her daughter and started crying, too.

Now, the father began to wonder what was happening, and he went down into the cellar to find them. There, the two of them sat crying, with the beer running all over the floor.

"What is the matter?" he asked.

"Oh dear," the mother sobbed, "look at that horrid mallet. Just suppose, if our daughter and her sweetheart was to be married, and they was to have a son, and he was to grow up to be a man, and he was to come down into the cellar to draw the beer, and the mallet was to fall on his head and kill him. What a dreadful thing it would be!"

"Dear, dear, dear, so it would!" said the father, and he sat himself down next to the other two, and started crying.

Meanwhile, the gentleman grew weary of being left in the kitchen by himself. At last, he went down into the cellar, too, to see what was going on.

And there the three sat, crying side by side, with the beer running all over the floor. He ran straight to the tap and turned it off. Then, he asked, "What are you three doing sitting there crying and letting the beer run all over the floor?"

"Oh!" the father sobbed, "look at that horrid mallet! Suppose you and our daughter was to be married, and you was to have a son, and he was to grow up, and he was to come down into the cellar to draw the beer, and the mallet was to fall on his head and kill him!"

And then the three started a-crying worse than before. But the gentleman burst out laughing, and he reached up and pulled out the mallet.

Then, he said, "I have traveled many miles, but I never met three such big sillies as you before. Now, I shall start out on my travels again, and when I can find three bigger sillies than you three, I will come back and marry your daughter."

So he wished them goodbye, and started off on his travels, and he left them all crying anew—this time, because the girl had lost her sweetheart.

Well, the gentleman traveled a long way. At last, he came to a woman's cottage that had some grass growing on the roof. The woman was trying to get her cow to go up a ladder to the grass, but the cow would not go.

"What are you doing?" the gentleman asked.

"Why, look at all that beautiful grass on the roof," she said. "I am going to get the cow on to the roof to eat it."

"That does not sound safe."

"She will be quite safe, for I shall tie a string round her neck and pass it down the chimney, and tie it to my wrist as I go about the house, so she cannot fall off without my knowing it."

"Oh, you poor silly!" said the gentleman. "You should just cut the grass and throw it down to the cow!"

But the woman insisted that it would be easier to get the cow up the ladder than to get the grass down. So she pushed her and coaxed her and got her up there. Then, she tied a string round the cow's neck, passed it down the chimney, and fastened it to her own wrist.

The gentleman went on his way, but he had not gone far when the cow tumbled off the roof and hung by the string tied round her neck. If the gentleman had not hurried back and cut the string, she would have strangled. And the woman, who had been pulled halfway up the chimney by the cow's weight, would have suffocated. Instead, she fell into the ashes with a thump.

Well, that was one big silly.

The gentleman went on to an inn to stop the night. They were so full at the inn that they had to put him in a room with another traveler. The other man was a very pleasant fellow, and that night was no problem for either of them.

But in the morning, when they were both getting up, the gentleman was surprised to see the other man hang his trousers on the knobs of the chest of drawers, then run across the room and try to jump into them. The man tried over and over again and could not manage it, and the gentleman stood wondering why he was doing this. At last, the man stopped and wiped his face with his handkerchief.

"Oh dear," he said. "I do think trousers are the most awkward clothes that ever were. I cannot think who could have invented such things. It takes me the best part of an hour to get into mine every morning! How do you manage yours?"

The gentleman burst out laughing, and showed him how to put them on. The man was very much obliged to him, and said he never should have thought of doing it that way.

So that was another big silly.

The gentleman went on his travels again. He came to a village. Just outside the village was a pond, and round the pond was a crowd of people. They had rakes, brooms, and pitchforks reaching into the pond.

The gentleman asked, "What is the matter?"

"It is the moon! The moon has tumbled into the pond, and we cannot rake her out anyhow!"

The gentleman burst out laughing, and he told them to just look up into the sky, that it was only the shadow in the water. But they would not listen to him and shouted insults at him until he hurried away.

So there were a whole lot of sillies bigger than them three sillies at home.

The gentleman turned back home and married the farmer's daughter. And if they did not live happy for ever after, that is nothing to do with you or me.

Sources
Jacobs, Joseph. *English Fairy Tales*. London: David Nutt, 1890.
Steel, Flora Annie. *English Fairy Tales*. London: Macmillan, 1918.

The Wisest of the Fools

There is a naive innocence in some of folklore's fools that reveals a simple wisdom denied to the more sophisticated people.

The Simpleton's Wisdom: A Folktale from the Sioux People

In this Sioux folktale, the apparently foolish behavior of a kindhearted simpleton saves a grieving mother. An orphan himself, he shares with her the wisdom that while we should honor the dead, we must live on for the living.

There was a man and his wife who had one daughter. When the daughter died, the mother could not be comforted. She did the rituals of mourning, cutting off her hair and gashing her cheek. But she was so deep in despair that she did nothing but sit before the corpse with her robe drawn over her head, and she would let no one take away the body. In one hand, she held a knife.

"I am weary of life," she warned anyone who tried to approach. "I will stab myself and join my daughter in the spirit land."

Her husband and relatives could not get the knife from her, because she pointed it at her chest if they took even a step toward her. "We must get that knife away from her," they said. But they saw no safe way to do it.

There was a boy in the village, a kindhearted simpleton with a good deal of natural shrewdness. He was a poor orphan. His moccasins were worn out at the soles and he was dressed in *wei-zi,* the coarsest of buffalo skin.

The boy came to the tepee where the woman sat mourning, and he said, "I will make her laugh and forget her grief. And I will take the knife from her."

The boy sat down in the tent as if waiting to be given something. He saw the corpse lying where the dead girl had slept in life. The body was wrapped in a rich robe, and friends had covered it with rich offerings out of respect for the dead.

As the mother was sitting with her head covered, she did not at first see the boy, who sat silent. But he began, at first lightly, then more heavily, to drum on the floor with his hands.

After a while, the boy began to sing a comic song. Louder and louder he sang until, carried away with his own singing, he sprang up and began to dance, contorting his body into funny shapes, still singing the comic song. As he approached the corpse, he waved his hands over it in blessing.

The mother uncovered her head. When she saw the poor simpleton with his strange grimaces, trying to do honor to the corpse by his solemn waving and, at the same time, keeping up his comic song, she burst out laughing. Then, she reached over and handed her knife to the simpleton.

"Take this knife," she said. "You have taught me to forget my grief. If, while I mourn for the dead, I can still be mirthful, there is no reason for me to despair. I no longer care to die. I will live for my husband."

When the old men of the village heard the story, they pondered it for some time. Then, one old man spoke up.

"The lad was simple and of no training, and we cannot expect him to know how to do as well as one with good home and parents to teach him. Besides, he did the best that he knew. He danced to make the mother forget her grief, and he tried to honor the corpse by waving over it with his hands."

"The mother did right to laugh, for when one does try to do us good, even if what he does causes us discomfort, we should always remember rather the motive than the deed. And besides, the simpleton's dancing saved the woman's life, for she gave up her knife. In this, too, she did well, for it is always better to live for the living than to die for the dead."

Source
McLaughlin, Marie L. *Myths and Legends of the Sioux.* Lincoln and London: University of Nebraska Press, 1990.

Plate 25.
This 1832 illustration is of Kay-a-gis-gis, a young Plains Ojibwa woman.
This could be the kind, beautiful younger sister in the story "The
Kindhearted Girl."

*Illustration by George Catlin (1796-1872). Courtesy of Smithsonian American Art Museum,
Washington, DC/Art Resource, NY.*

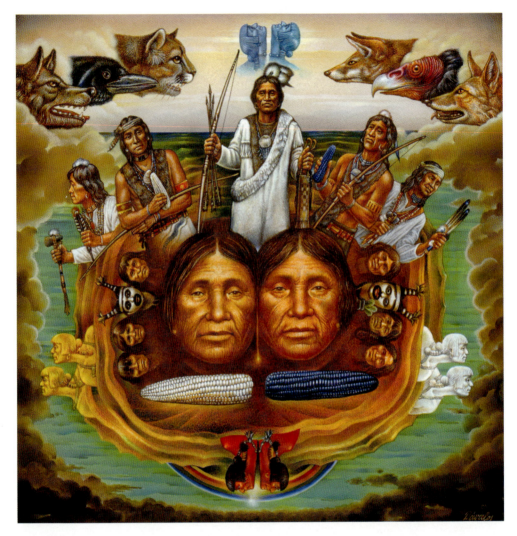

Plate 26.

The vivid oral tradition of the Tewa Indians is illustrated in this imaginative painting.

Illustration by Felipe Davalos. Courtesy of National Geographic/Getty Images.

Plate 27.
Upset and lonely, the man who became a fox lay down under a tree to rest, only to wake up and realize that it may all have been a dream.
Courtesy of Private Collection/The Bridgeman Art Library.

Plate 28.
The water man joyfully plays his fiddle.

Courtesy of Meg Takamura/IZA Stock/Getty Images.

Plate 29.
As in many tales of fools and wise people, this family is made up of both
kinds. Surely, the foolish one eventually will learn his lesson.

Illustration, dated 1934, by Minnie Kyle. © Bolton Museum and Art Gallery, Lancashire, UK/
The Bridgeman Art Library.

Plate 30.
The foolish boy in this 1840 illustration is not afraid of the tiger.

Illustration by Utagawa Kuniyoshi (1798–1861). Courtesy of Private Collection/The Bridgeman Art Library.

Plate 31.
The rich man shows no mercy to the poor man, who is more honest and eventually will be rewarded.

Illustration, dated 1568, by Jos Amman. Courtesy of The Granger Collection, New York.

Plate 32.

The merchant's wise daughter has won herself a prince.

Illustration, dated 1995, by Frances Broomfield. Courtesy of Private Collection/
© Frances Broomfield/Portal Gallery, London/The Bridgeman Art Library.

TALES OF WISE PEOPLE

These folktales are about wise people, clever people, and those who can see through trickery or counter it with tricks of their own. These often are tales of survivors who use wisdom to save themselves or their people.

Wise Judgments

Sometimes, it is the judge, not the accuser, who is the wisest and who can see through an attempted scam or con to reveal true justice.

Wise Judge, Foolish Miser: A Folktale from Mongolia

The *tugrik* is the Mongolian currency. Today, 1 million tugrik might equal approximately $2,000.

Once, there lived a very wise and good-hearted judge. There also lived a greedy fool of a miser. The miser owned rich herds of camels, horses, cattle, sheep, and goats. He dressed in the finest robes and put his wife in so much jewelry that she could barely walk.

But the miser still wanted more. And he still was a fool. One day, as he was returning from the local market, he happened to drop his wallet. There was 1 million *tugrik* within it.

Two poor farmers found the wallet. Being honest men, they went straight to the wise judge with it, without even looking inside or taking any tugrik.

Meanwhile, the miser discovered his loss and was nearly ill over it. No, he could not lose that wallet! He could not lose those tugrik!

So off the miser ran to the wise judge for help. There, to his great relief, he saw his wallet and tried to grab it right off the judge's desk.

"One moment!" the judge said. "You cannot just snatch something off my desk."

"That is my wallet!" the miser cried.

"If it is truly your wallet," the judge said, "then you really should give a reward to the two honest men who turned it in."

"Of course, of course," the miser lied.

The wise judge frowned. "Before I can give this wallet over to you, you must tell me what it contains to prove it belongs to you."

Now, the miser had no intention of giving up any reward money. He lied, "There were 2 million tugrik in it."

"Really? Please count the money."

The miser did, and then looked up in false horror. "But there is only 1 million tugrik in here! Your so-called honest men already must have helped themselves to half. They already have been rewarded."

The wise judge said, "Ah, I see. You planned to reward the finders with 1 million tugrik."

"Of course, of course!"

"Well then," the wise judge said, "I fear this cannot be your wallet. It has only 1 million tugrik in it, the amount that was in it when it was found. I wish you luck in finding your wallet."

The foolish miser quickly said, "Dear, kind, wise judge, I lied just now, I admit it. I forgot that there was only 1 million tugrik in it. I wrongly accused the finders of already having taken the reward."

The wise judge nodded. He knew exactly how to teach this foolish miser a lesson. "Since you were going to give the finders of your wallet 1 million tugrik as a reward, do it now. You may have your empty wallet back. And I trust that you have now learned at least a little wisdom."

The foolish miser grabbed his empty wallet, stuffed it into his sleeve, and hurried off. He never bothered the wise judge again.

Sources

Hangin, John Gombojab, ed. *Mongolian Folklore: A Representative Collection from the Oral Literary Tradition.* Bloomington, IN: The Mongolia Society, 1998.

Metternich, Hilary Roe. *Mongolian Folktales.* Boulder, CO: Avery, in association with the University of Washington Press, 1996.

Too Clever Is Not Clever: A Folktale from the Jews of Eastern Europe

This Jewish folktale features a miser, too. But it also adds the moral point of the poor man who is honest about returning the bag of coins and is rewarded for his honesty.

Once, there was a poor man who did his best but never earned much and had almost nothing in the way of luck.

But one day, the poor man found a small bag. To his amazement, he realized that it held 100 gold coins. That very day, he heard it announced in the synagogue that the richest man in town had lost that bag and was promising a reward to the finder.

Now, the poor man was an honest one. He did not try to keep 100 coins for himself but went straight to the house of the wealthy man.

"I have found your bag of coins," he said to the rich man.

The rich man also was a miser who fancied himself as being very clever. He thought, "I will not give him a single coin."

The poor man said, "You offered a reward to the finder."

"Reward for what?" the rich man roared. "There were 200 gold coins in this bag, and here you have returned only 100 coins to me! You stole 100 coins from me, and you have the nerve to ask for a reward as well?"

The poor man refused to be intimidated. "Let us go to the rabbi," he said.

Unlike the rich man, the rabbi was a truly wise man and a kind one as well. He knew both men, and he knew their reputations. He also knew in a moment the whole story, but he let both men tell their versions in full.

At last, they were done. The rabbi asked the rich man, "How many coins did you say were in your bag?"

"There were 200!" the rich man insisted.

"I see." The rabbi turned to the poor man. "And how many coins were in the bag you found?"

"There were 100," the poor man replied

"In that case," the rabbi told the rich man, "the bag he found is not yours. He gets to keep it and the 100 coins."

The poor man was joyful. The rich man was shamefaced. The rabbi was satisfied.

Sources
Ausubel, Nathan. *A Treasury of Jewish Folklore*. New York: Crown, 1948.
Sherman, Josepha. *A Sampler of Jewish-American Folklore*. Little Rock, AR: August House, 1992.

Two Clever Peasants

Following are two versions of the clever peasant folktale type. The first tale, from Sicily, is about an anonymous king and a peasant. The second tale, from Russia, shows the folk process in action. Not only does it have an additional element, a continuation of the story, but the folktale has become attached to an historical figure, Tzar Peter the Great (1675–1725).

The Clever Peasant: A Folktale from Sicily, Italy

In this version, no historical details are added to make the tale seem more real. It is a simpler version than the next tale from Russia (see page 340), but it has the same coin motif.

Once, a king went riding out into the countryside. He stopped to watch a peasant farming his fields.

"How much do you earn a day?" the king asked.

"Oh, on a good day, I earn four carlini." That was a small coin. "One goes to feed us, one goes for insurance, one goes to repay a debt, and one is thrown away."

The king thought about this, but he finally had to ask, "What is the answer to your riddle?"

"One coin buys food for me and my family. One goes toward the raising of my son, who will someday support me. One goes to my father, who I am supporting. And one goes for taxes."

The king was pleased with this clever answer. "I am the king," he said. "Tell no one the answer until after you have seen my face 100 times."

The peasant promised.

The king went back to his ministers and told them the riddle. None of them could guess the answer. But one minister, more cunning than the others, went to the peasant and asked for the answer.

The peasant said, "I promised the king not to tell anyone the answer until after I had seen his face 100 times."

The minister pulled out a gold coin. The king's face was stamped on it. He pulled out 100 coins, put them in a bag, and gave them to the peasant.

The peasant gave him the answer. The minister went to the king with the answer. The king was furious and had the peasant brought before him.

"You promised not to give anyone the answer until after you had seen my face 100 times."

"But I did," said the peasant, and showed the king the bag of 100 gold coins. "I saw your face 100 times on these coins."

The king was so pleased with this clever answer that he sent the peasant home a wealthy man.

Sources

Calvino, Italo. *Italian Folktales*. New York: Harcourt Brace Jovanovich, 1980.

Crane, Thomas Frederick. *Italian Popular Tales*. New York and Oxford, United Kingdom: Oxford University Press, 2003.

The Peasant and the Tzar: A Folktale from Russia

When Peter the Great was tzar of all the Russias, he often dressed as a commoner and rode out to see how his people were doing. The disguise was not particularly effective as Peter was nearly seven feet tall, so people usually knew who they were facing.

So it was that Tzar Peter, dressed as a commoner, rode out and met a peasant farming his fields.

"Good day, peasant," said Peter.

"Good day, stranger," said the peasant, pretending he did not know who this was.

"Does your farm prosper?" asked Peter.

"God willing, it does," the peasant replied.

"And how much does it earn you a day?"

"On a good day, perhaps four rubles. One ruble goes to feed us. One goes for insurance. One goes to repay a debt. And one flies out the window."

Peter was clever at riddles, but this one puzzled him. "What is the answer to your riddle?" he asked.

"One ruble buys our food. One ruble helps me raise my son, who will someday help support us. One ruble goes to help my father, who supported me. And one goes for taxes, so—out the window."

"I like that!" Peter said. At the time, he was feuding with the boyars, the Russian nobles, and he saw an opportunity to make them look foolish. So Peter said, "Tell no one the answer unless you tell it to my face."

The peasant agreed.

So Peter went back to court and told the boyars the riddle. Sure enough, none of them could answer it. But one boyar rode out to see the peasant.

"Tell me the answer to your riddle," he said.

The peasant refused. "I promised not to tell anyone the answer, unless I told it to the tzar's face."

The boyar held out some golden coins as a bribe. The peasant looked at them, then laughed and told the boyar the answer.

The boyar promptly rode back to court and told Peter the answer.

Peter was furious and had the peasant brought before him. "You swore not to tell anyone the answer unless you told it to my face."

"But I did!" said the peasant, holding out one of the golden coins. "Your boyar gave me this."

There, plainly stamped on the coin, was the tzar's portrait.

Peter laughed. "You are a clever man. And you shall dine beside me tonight."

The boyars were shocked. What, a common peasant in the place of honor? "We must be rid of him," they said. And they chose a simple peasant's game to do the job.

At dinner, the boyar farthest from the tzar slapped his neighbor and said, "Pass it on."

That boyar slapped his neighbor and said, "Pass it on."

Down the line of nobles it went, getting ever closer to the peasant sitting next to the tzar.

Now, there was only one man to go. He slapped the peasant and said, "Pass it on."

Would the peasant dare to slap the tzar? If he did, he would surely be executed. But the peasant saw the trap. "Oh tzar, may I ask a question of you?"

"Of course," said Peter.

"If one is standing on the edge of a cliff, is one obliged to jump?"

"Why, certainly not!"

"The tzar has said it!" cried the peasant. He turned away from the tzar and slapped the boyar back. "Pass *that* on!"

Tzar Peter was so pleased with that cleverness that he sent the peasant home a wealthy man.

Source
Afanas'ev, Aleksander. *Russian Fairy Tales*. New York: Pantheon, 1945.

Impossible Tasks

In this folktale type, an impossible claim is made, such as boiled eggs hatching into chickens or a wagon giving birth to a foal. The claim is proven false by the wise witness who makes an equally impossible claim, such as sowing boiled wheat.

Nasreddin Khoja as Court Witness: A Folktale from Turkey

Here is Nasreddin Khoja once again. (We met him before in the "Tales of Fools" section.) This time, though, he is a wise and clever man, not a foolish one.

Once, two young men came to town to find work.
They had no money. So they ordered two boiled eggs apiece from a restaurant, ate the eggs, and then snuck out without paying.

Later, when they both had found good jobs, the two young men returned to the restaurant and said to the manager, "We wish to pay for the food we ate without paying."

"What did you eat?" he asked.

"Two boiled eggs apiece." And they tried to hand him the right price for two boiled eggs, twenty kurus, or small coins, apiece.

"Oh no, that is not enough," said the manager. "You had that meal when?"

"Ten months ago," they replied.

"So! Those four eggs would have had time to hatch into four chickens, and those four chickens would have laid enough eggs to hatch out twenty to thirty more chickens. So you owe me for all those chickens!"

The two young men refused to pay for so many chickens. The manager took the case to court.

Now, it happened that Nasreddin Khoja heard the story. "I will testify for you," he told the two young men.

But on the day of the trial—there was no sign of Nasreddin Khoja. The cadi, or judge, sent his bailiffs to the Khoja's house. They brought him by force to the court.

"Why were you so late?" asked the cadi.

"I was too busy," Nasreddin Khoja answered.

"What business could possibly be more urgent than appearing in court on time?" asked the cadi.

"Oh, you see, tomorrow, I shall begin to sow my wheat. So today, I had to boil enough water to boil all the wheat before sowing it."

"How do you expect boiled wheat to grow?" asked the cadi.

"As easily as boiled eggs could hatch into chickens," said Nasreddin Khoja.

"Case dismissed," said the cadi.

Source
Walker, Warren S., and Ahmet E. Uysal. *Tales Alive in Turkey.* Cambridge, MA: Harvard University Press, 1966. Collected from Ahmet Uyar, village of Zir, a suburb of Ankara, 1962.

The Wise Girl: A Folktale from Serbia

In this tale of the wise and clever daughter, there is the world theme of the exchanged and answered "impossible" riddles, and the indication that cleverness as well as love conquers all.

Once, there was a poor man who had no riches save his daughter, who was both wise and charming.

One day, the king heard of this poor man's wise daughter, and he had the man brought before him. "Is it true that your daughter is so wise?"

"Yes, it is, sire," the poor man answered.

"Indeed? And who taught her such wisdom? Not you, surely!"

"God and our poverty have made her wise," the poor man replied.

So the king gave him thirty eggs. "Take these eggs to your daughter. If she can bring forth chickens from them, you will be rewarded. If she fails, you will suffer."

The poor man went home in fear. But his wise daughter said, "Do not worry, father. I will solve this puzzle."

She had seen right away that the eggs were hard boiled and could never hatch. That night, she boiled up a pot of beans. Then, she told her father what to do.

The next morning, when the king came to see what had happened, there was the poor man, sowing the boiled beans and shouting, "God grant that these boiled beans give me a good harvest!"

The king stopped. "How can boiled beans bear a crop?"

"As well as boiled eggs can hatch out chickens," the poor man replied.

"That is your daughter's answer. Very well, then."

The king gave the poor man a small bunch of flax. "Tell her to make from this all the sails a ship needs. If she fails, you will suffer."

But once again, the wise daughter never worried. In the morning, she gave her father a small piece of wood and told him what to do.

The poor man went to the king and said, "My daughter asks you to make all the tools needed for spinning and weaving out of this little piece of wood. Then, she will make the sails."

The king was impressed. But he was not ready to give up.

"Take this small glass to your daughter, and tell her that she must empty the sea with it."

But the wise daughter replied by giving her father a small plug. She told him to say to the king, "With this plug, you must stop up all the sources of all the rivers and lakes, and then I will dry up the sea." And so the poor man did.

Now, the king was intrigued. He had the wise daughter brought before him and said, "What can be heard at the greatest distance?"

"Your Majesty, it is a tie: Thunder and a lie can both be heard at the greatest distance," she replied.

"You are a wise young woman, indeed," said the king. "Will you marry me?"

"I will, majesty. But first write this promise on a scrap of paper: If ever you are displeased with me, I shall be allowed to take with me from the palace the thing I like the best."

"Done," said the king.

And so they were wed. They lived happily for several years. But one day, the king grew so angry at his wife's wisdom that he cried, "Leave this palace!"

"Of course. But remember that I may take with me the thing I like the best," his wife replied.

She waited until the king fell asleep. Then, she carried him off in a carriage to her old home.

The king awoke with a shock. "Who brought me here?"

"I did," she said. "See? You promised that I might take with me the thing I like best. And that, my love, is you."

The king kissed her, and they returned together to the palace.

Sources

Mijatovies, Madam Csedomille. *Serbian Folk-Lore.* New York and London: Benjamin Blom, 1874.

Petrovitch, Woislav M. *Hero Tales and Legends of the Serbians.* London: George G. Harrap, 1914.

The Wise and Beautiful Daughter: A Folktale from Ethiopia

In this folktale of the clever daughter and the "impossible" riddles, there is no wedding. But the daughter wins a legal victory over the judge.

Once, long ago, there lived a poor man with a beautiful daughter. But she was as clever as she was beautiful.

One day, while the poor man was begging by the roadside, with his daughter at his side, an important judge of the region rode by on his donkey and saw them. And the judge thought the beggar's daughter was the most wonderful woman he had ever seen. From the way she was stealing sly glances at him, she liked what she saw, too.

But she was a beggar's daughter, the judge reminded himself. He must see if she was wise.

So the judge said to the beggar, "I wish to marry your daughter. But before she comes to me as my wife, I must test her. I will send her a large sack of millet grains, and she must count the grains exactly."

The daughter smiled. "Tell him, father, that I can do this." And she whispered a secret in his ear.

In the morning, there was the beggar at the roadside, and here was the judge. "Well? Was she able to count all the grains?"

"She was," the poor man answered. "And she said to tell you this: The number of grains is exactly equal to the number of hairs on your donkey."

The judge laughed at that clever answer. But he was not quite finished. "Tell your daughter that she must give birth to a son the very day we marry."

So the beggar went home to his daughter, and he was very troubled. She, however, laughed.

"So he does want to marry me, does he? So be it. And I have the answer for him."

The daughter came to the judge's estate. A wonderful wedding feast was prepared. But first the judge said to her, "Give me a son right away."

"Of course," she replied, "but only if you first plough today, gather the harvest today, and give me the first fruit of the harvest you began today. Then I shall, indeed, bear you a son today."

That was too much for the judge. "You win the challenge," he said. And he married her.

Sources

Leslau, Wolf. *Gurage Folklore: Ethiopian Folktales, Proverbs, Beliefs, and Riddles.* Wiesbaden,
      Germany: Franz Steiner Verlag, 1982.

Shack, William A. *The Gurage: A People of the Ensete Culture.* London: Oxford University Press,
      1966.

The Wise Answer: A Folktale from the Gurian People
of the Georgian Republic

Here is an "impossible" riddle tale in which a clever lord who has committed only
some minor offense gets himself out of trouble by outwitting the king.

A king was angry with one of his lords for some minor offence, and he put the
lord in prison.

Because he was so angry, the king decided to keep the lord there. The king
said he would set the man free only if he could bring to the court a horse.

"But it must be a horse that is not gray, black, brown, bay, white, roan, dun,
chestnut, piebald . . ." In short, the king listed every possible color that a horse
could be.

But the imprisoned lord was a wise man. He instantly promised to get such a
horse if the king would set him free at once.

As soon as he was free, the lord went before the king and asked him to send
a groom for the horse. "But," the lord said, "the groom must not come on Monday,
Tuesday, Wednesday, Thursday, Friday, Saturday, or Sunday, but on any other day
of the week that suits Your Majesty."

The king stared. Then, he laughed, and forgave the lord.

"Such a clever man," the king told the lord, "does not belong in prison!"

Sources

Papashvily, George, and Helen Papashvily. *Yes and No Stories: A Book of Georgian Folk Tales.*
      New York: Harper and Brothers, 1946.

Wardrop, Marjory. *Georgian Folk Tales.* London: David Nutt, 1894.

The Wise Thief: A Folktale from the Jews of the Near East

Here, a clever thief who steals only to survive outwits the king with a witty twist on
"Let he who is without sin cast the first stone."

One day, a clever but poor thief was caught and ordered to be hanged. But, being clever, he was not afraid.

The thief announced to the king that he knew a wonderful secret. "What a
shame it would be if it died with me!"

Of course, everyone from the hangman to the king was curious. The thief was
taken from the gallows and brought before the king in his palace.

"What is your secret?" the king asked.

"I could put a pomegranate seed in the ground, and it would grow overnight into a fruit-bearing tree."

He was given a pomegranate seed.

"I said 'could,'" the thief said. "You see, the seed only may be put into the ground by someone who has never stolen or taken anything that was not his. As a thief, of course, I cannot do it."

He handed the seed to the king's vizier. But the vizier remembered that as a youth, he had once taken something that was not his.

The vizier passed the seed to the king's treasurer. But the treasurer remembered that he had once taken a few coins that were not his.

Even the king was forced to admit that once, as a boy, he had taken a necklace belonging to his father.

The thief shook his head. "You are all powerful men who have everything you could possibly desire, yet none of you can plant the seed. Whereas I, who have nothing and was stealing only so I might not starve, I am to be hanged."

The king was so pleased by the thief's clever ruse that he pardoned him and gave him a place at court.

Sources

Ausubel, Nathan. *A Treasury of Jewish Folklore.* New York: Crown, 1948.
Gastner, Moses. *The Exempla of the Rabbis.* London and Leipzig, Germany: Asia Publishing, 1924.

The Merchant's Wise Daughter: A Folktale from Syria

Here is another clever daughter, this one a child of ten who not only saves her father's livelihood but wins herself a princely groom.

Once upon a time, there was a king who decided to ban all peddlers from the streets of his city. Any who disobeyed would be arrested.

One poor peddler of fruit had no other choice. If he and his daughter were to eat, he had to sell his fruit on the streets. So it was that one dark day, he was arrested and thrown into prison.

Now, the peddler's daughter, who was only ten, was as beautiful as she was kind and as kind as she was beautiful. She also was quite intelligent. And she was furious that her father had been arrested just for trying to make an honest living. She swore that she would rescue her father.

So the little girl disguised herself as a fine young woman in a pretty gown and veil, and she went off to the palace. The guards tried to stop her, since she could do nothing to disguise the fact that she was still only as tall as a child of ten.

"You are too little!" they sneered.

"Watch what this little pebble can do," she retorted.

With that, she threw the pebble away from the palace with all of her might. The guards, curious, watched it go—and the little girl slipped past them, and into the palace she went.

That day, the king was to see all the marriageable young women of the city so that he could find a bride for his son—even though the son was not much older than the girl of ten. The little girl slipped into the crowd of lovely maidens. When it came her turn to dance, she danced so charmingly that the little boy prince was delighted.

"Talk to her, Father! Talk to her!"

The little girl bowed low to the king. "Promise me, oh king, that I shall not be harmed."

He touched her shoulder, a sign of agreement. "You shall not be harmed. You are safe here."

"Then, oh king, may I ask you a question?"

"You may."

"What is the purpose of dancing?"

"Why, it is to draw attention to the beauty of the dancers."

"So, you call upon dancers to perform."

"I do."

"Then if you call upon dancers to draw attention to their beauty, why do you arrest peddlers who are calling attention to the beauty of their wares? Do they not have the right, the same as the dancers, to make an honest living? Kings should make laws that help their people, not hurt them."

The king was impressed by the little girl's courage and wisdom. He revoked the law banning peddlers. He had her father released from prison, and he gave them both a lovely suite in the palace.

The little girl and the little boy prince grew up together, and when they were old enough, they married. And they lived with happiness and wisdom all their days.

Sources

Serwer-Bernstein, Blanche L. *In the Tradition of Moses and Mohammed: Jewish and Arab Folktales.* Northvale, NJ, and London: Jason Aronson, 1994.

Tahhan, Samir. *Folktales from Syria.* Austin: University of Texas, 2004.

A Wise Minister: A Folktale from Karnataka, India

Clever ministers are more common in Asiatic tales than in Western ones. While such ministers range from truly wise men to tricksters who win through cunning, they always strive to show themselves in the best light.

Once, there was a king with a wise and witty minister named Appaji. Appaji's fame spread even to neighboring lands.

A nearby king heard about this clever man and decided to test him. He sent a message to the minister to send him some cabbages and radishes. When Appaji saw this, he simply smiled. Both his king and the challenging king were sure that the cabbages and radishes would be shriveled up and dead by the time they ended the journey.

But Appaji had the servants bring a cart filled with rich soil. He planted cabbage and radish seeds in it, and sent off the cart to the other kingdom, with orders to the servants that they water the soil frequently.

Sure enough, when the cart arrived, there were nice, fresh cabbages and radishes for the other king.

The other king was impressed. But now, he sent three small bronze idols to Appaji with the message that he pick the finest and say why it was chosen. The images seemed exactly alike.

But Appaji knew there was a trick, and he found it. He took a long, thin piece of wire and pushed it into the ear of the first figure. It did not go in very far. With the second figure, the wire went in one ear and out the other. With the third figure, the wire went in one ear and out the mouth.

"There we have it," said Appaji, and this was his reply to both kings:

"The first figure is the best, since it tells us that if we hear gossip, we should not spread it without proof. The second figure is of medium worth, since it tells us that whatever gossip comes in one ear should just go out the other. The third figure is the worst. It tells us that it picks up gossip and promptly talks about it. It is a gossip monger."

Both kings agreed after that cleverness that Appaji was, indeed, a wise and witty minister.

Source
Chandran, Praphulla Satish. *Folk Tales of Karnataka*. New Delhi, India: Sterling, 1985.

The Three Questions

Following are clear examples of how a folktale stays basically the same, with the same "punch line," yet can vary in details. The first version is from the island of North Uist, Scotland, and it was collected in 1859. The second is from Galway, on the mainland of Ireland, and it dates to the turn of the twentieth century.

The Three Questions: A Folktale from North Uist, Scotland

In this version of the folktale, it is a scholar who runs into trouble with a harsh master. He is saved from losing his head by a common miller, displaying the cleverness of the common folk.

Once, long ago, there lived a scholar. When he had done learning, his master, who was a harsh man, said that the scholar must now answer three questions or have his head taken off.

The scholar, in a great fright, went to a miller who was the master's brother and asked for his help.

"An easy thing," said the miller.

The miller disguised himself as the scholar, and off he went to the master.

"Very well," said the master. "Here is the first question. How many ladders would it take to reach the sky?

"One," the miller answered, "if it were long enough."

"That is right," the master said grudgingly. "Now, here is the second question. Where is the middle of the world?"

The miller laid down a rod and said, "Here, set a hoop about the world, and thou will find the middle here."

"That is right," said the master. "Now for the third question: What is my thought?"

The miller answered with a grin, removing his disguise, "I can tell. You think that I am the scholar. But I am your brother, the miller."

Source

Campbell, J.F. *Popular Tales of the West Highlands*. Vol. 2. Edinburgh, United Kingdom: Edmonton and Douglas, 1860. Collected from the Brothers MacCraw, North Uist, 1859.

The Farmer's Answers: A Folktale from Galway, Ireland

In this Irish version of the folktale, it is two poor farmers who are the stars of the story and who take advantage of the fact that the landlord never really looks at the common people. Here, the reward is free rent.

There was a poor farmer named Jack Murphy, and when the rent came due, he could not pay it.

The landlord fancied himself a clever man and said, "If you can answer these three questions, you can have the farm free of rent. If you cannot, you are out on the road tomorrow. Here are the three questions: How much does the moon weigh? How many stars are in the sky? And what am I thinking?"

With that, the landlord laughed, sure he would have the farmer out on the road the next day.

Jack was walking home, very sad, when up came a neighboring farmer, Tim Daly, who asked him what was wrong. Jack told him the three riddles, and Tim laughed.

"I will answer them for you," he said. "The landlord never really looks at us ordinary folks, so let me take your place, and he will never notice the difference."

Jack agreed. And the next day, it was Tim who went before the landlord. "I have come to answer your three riddles," he said.

The landlord asked, "How much does the moon weigh?"

Tim answered, "It weighs four quarters."

Then, the landlord asked, "How many stars are in the sky?"

"Why, 9,000,039," Tim answered.

"How could you know that?" the landlord cried.

"Well, if you do not believe me, go count the stars yourself!"

Then, the landlord, frowning, asked the third question, "What am I thinking?"

"Oh, that is an easy one. You are thinking it is Jack Murphy you are asking, but it is not. I am Tim Daly."

The landlord gave up. From that day on, Jack Murphy had his farm rent-free.

Sources
Glassie, Henry. *Irish Folk Tales.* New York: Pantheon, 1985.
Gregory, Lady Augusta. *Poets and Dreamers: Studies and Translations from the Irish.* Dublin,
    Ireland: Hodges, Figgis, 1903.

The Two Lots

This folklore tale type turns up around the world in various forms. It can be a simple story of a girl outwitting a king, or a more complex one of a rabbi defending his Jewish congregation from royal anti-Semitism.

Wise Ma Sabe: A Folktale from Burma

In this version of the basic two lots folktale type, a wise young woman outwits a king, so that she may marry the man she loves. The lots to be chosen here are pebbles.

In the long-ago days, in the royal city of Ava, there lived a wise and beautiful girl named Ma Sabe. She lived with her old blind mother and was being courted by a young blacksmith whom she loved.

Ava, though, was ruled over by a lustful king who already had a harem of 300 beautiful women but still wanted more. One day, the king rode out on his white elephant and saw Ma Sabe. Ah, what a lovely young woman! She must join his harem!

But he could not simply seize her. That was wrong for even a king to do, since in those days, parents could not be forced to give up their children. The king first found out where Ma Sabe lived, then he sent a minister to her mother to ask for her daughter.

But Ma Sabe did not want to live as a prisoner in even a golden prison. She wanted to marry her fine young blacksmith. So Ma Sabe's mother refused to give her permission.

Now, the king wanted Ma Sabe more than ever. So he rode out from his palace dressed in golden armor, with a helmet gleaming with rubies on his head. Following him was a fine procession of soldiers. As the king arrived at Ma Sabe's home, everyone in the village came running to see what was happening.

The king raised a red-embroidered silk bag. "In this bag there are two stones. One is black, the other white. Ma Sabe must choose one. If she picks the white stone, I will leave her in peace. But if she picks the black stone, she will join my harem in the royal palace."

Ma Sabe strongly suspected that the king was cheating. There were surely two black stones and no white one in the bag.

But Ma Sabe thought quickly, then reached into the bag and seized a stone. She held it so closely that no one else could see, but she peeked at it and gave a wild cry of joy. She started to sing and dance and, as if by accident, threw the stone into the river behind her house.

Ma Sabe froze, then bowed deeply before the king. "Please forgive me. I was so overjoyed about not having to leave my mother alone that I did not know what I was doing. But there is still the other stone in the bag. If it is black, then everyone can tell that it was the white stone I accidentally threw away."

What could the king do? Ma Sabe had been wiser than he. He turned his grand procession and returned to his palace.

Ma Sabe married her fine blacksmith, and lived happily ever after.

Sources

Abbott, Gerry, and Khin Thant Han. *The Folk-Tales of Burma: An Introduction*. Boston, Köln, Germany, and Leiden, The Netherlands: Brill, 2000.

Moe, Saw Wai Lwin. *Golden Boy and Other Stories from Burma*. Bangkok, Thailand: White Lotus, 2001.

The Rabbi and the Inquisitor: A Folktale from the Sephardic Jews

This is a much more serious version of the folktale than the previous Burmese tale. Here is mention of the "blood libel," the slander that claimed Jews murdered Christian children for their blood, and the peril of the Inquisition that sought to slay any nonbeliever. That the rabbi keeps calm says a great deal about his wisdom.

A Christian child had been murdered in Seville, and the cry went up that the Jews had killed him. The rabbi of the Jewish community was brought before the Grand Inquisitor to stand trial for his congregation.

The Grand Inquisitor hated the Jews and did his best to prove them guilty, but the rabbi outwitted him at every turn and disproved the charge. The Grand Inquisitor was not about to give up so easily.

"We shall leave the matter to Heaven," the Grand Inquisitor claimed to the rabbi. "There shall be a drawing of lots. I shall place two pieces of paper within a box. On one shall be written 'Guilty,' and on the other, 'Innocent.' If you draw the 'Guilty' lot, you shall be burned at the stake. And if you draw the 'Innocent' lot, I shall accept the will of Heaven and let you go."

Now, the rabbi knew he could never trust the Grand Inquisitor. And so it was, because on both pieces of paper the Inquisitor had written "Guilty." The rabbi suspected such a trick.

When the time came for the rabbi to choose a lot, he picked a piece of paper— and popped it into his mouth and ate it.

"What nonsense is this?" roared the Grand Inquisitor.

"No nonsense at all," said the rabbi with a smile. "You have but to look at the remaining lot."

Of course, it read, "Guilty."

The rabbi's smile broadened. "Then, by the rules you have set, the lot I ate could only have been the one marked 'Innocent.' I am free, and my people are, too."

Fuming, the Grand Inquisitor had to obey.

Sources
Ausubel, Nathan. *A Treasury of Jewish Folklore*. New York: Crown, 1948.
Sherman, Josepha. *A Sampler of Jewish-American Folklore*. Little Rock, AR: August House, 1992.

Wise Heroes

These are the heroes who use brains, not brawn, to overcome evil. They are comparatively rare in the world's folklore, but they do exist.

The Three Clever Men and the Demons: A Folktale from Southern India

In this folktale of three clever men, the main focus is on the archer. He learns that he really is not the smartest of the three and stops, to his wife's great relief, shooting the pearls out of her nose ring. The duel of the three men against the demons provides both excitement and a touch of comic relief.

Once, there lived a man and his lovely wife.

Now, the man thought himself very clever, indeed. He was an excellent archer, and every morning he would shoot through one of the pearls in his wife's nose ring without hurting her at all. That was fine for him, but nerve-wracking for his wife.

One day, she mentioned what was happening to her brother, who was wondering why she looked so nervous. "He is a fine, kind, loving husband," she told him. "And I do love him, too. My only grief is that every morning he amuses himself by shooting one of the pearls from my nose ring, and I think perhaps some day he may miss and kill me. So I am in constant terror. Yet I do not like to ask him not to do it, because it gives him so much pleasure."

"What does he say to you about it?" asked the brother.

"Every day," she replied, "when he has shot the pearl, he says to me, quite happy and proud, 'Was there ever a man as clever as I am?' And I answer him, 'No, I do not think there ever was any as clever as you.'"

"The next time he asks you the question," the brother advised, "answer, 'Yes, there are many men in the world cleverer than you.'"

The pearl shooter's wife agreed. The next time her husband shot the pearl from her nose ring and said to her, "Was there ever a man as clever as I am?" she answered, "Yes, there are many men in the world cleverer than you."

Insulted, he said, "If there are, I will not rest until I have found them."

He journeyed a long way until he came to a large river. On the riverbank sat a traveler eating his dinner. The pearl shooter sat down beside him, and the two began talking cheerfully together.

At last, the pearl shooter said to his new friend, "What is the reason of your journey, and where are you going?"

The stranger answered, "I am a wrestler and the strongest man in all this country. I can do many wonderful things in the way of wrestling and carrying heavy weights, and I began to think that in all this world there was no one as clever as I. But I have lately heard of a more wonderful man who is so clever that every morning he shoots one of the pearls from his wife's nose ring without hurting her."

The pearl shooter laughed. "I am that man."

"Then why are you traveling?" the wrestler asked. "And where are you going?"

"I also am trying to find a cleverer man than myself. Since we have the same idea, let us go together. Perhaps there is still in the world a better man than we."

The wrestler agreed, and so they started on their way together.

They had not gone very far before they came to a place where three roads met. There sat another man. He asked the wrestler and the pearl shooter, "Who are you, friends, and where are you going?"

They answered, "We are two clever men trying to find a cleverer man than us. Now, who are you, and where are you going?"

"I am a pundit renowned for my good head, a great thinker. For some time, I thought there was not in the world a more wonderful man than I. But then I heard of two men of great cleverness, the one of whom is a wrestler and the other a shooter of pearls from his wife's nose ring. I go to find them and learn if the things I heard are true."

"They are," said the wrestler; "for we are the men of whom you speak."

"Excellent!" cried the pundit. "Then, since my house is near here, come rest awhile. Then, each of us can put his powers to the test."

In the pundit's kitchen was an enormous iron cauldron, so heavy that it would take a team of men to move it. That night, the wrestler quietly lifted the cauldron onto his shoulder, carried it down to the river, and buried it in the sand under the water. Then, he returned to the pundit's house and went back to sleep.

But though the wrestler had been very quiet, the pundit's wife had heard him. She woke her husband and whispered, "Someone's creeping about. Maybe we have thieves!"

They tiptoed through the house, finding nothing missing—except for the great iron cauldron. They discovered deep footprints in the sand close to the kitchen door, like those of someone carrying a very heavy weight, and traced them down to the riverside.

Then, the pundit said, "There are the footprints of one man only; and he must have buried the cauldron in the water. For, see, there is no continuation of footprints on the other side. Perhaps the wrestler played us this trick to prove his great strength."

The pearl shooter and the wrestler lay rolled up in their blankets, fast asleep. First, the pundit and his wife looked at the pearl shooter; but the pundit shook his head, saying, "No, he certainly has not done this thing."

They then looked at the wrestler. The cunning pundit licked the skin of the sleeping man and whispered to his wife, "This is the man who stole the cauldron and put it in the river. For he has lately been up to his neck in fresh water, since there is no taste of salt on his skin. In the morning, I will surprise him by showing him I know this."

The next morning, as soon as it was light, the pearl shooter and the wrestler were met by their host, who said to them, "Let us go down to the river to bathe. For

I cannot offer you a bath, since the great cauldron, in which we generally wash, has been mysteriously carried away this very night."

"Where can it have gone?" asked the wrestler.

"Ah, where indeed?" answered the pundit, and he led them down to where the cauldron had been put into the river by the wrestler the night before. Wading about in the water until he found the cauldron, the pundit said, "See, friend, how far this cauldron traveled?"

The wrestler was surprised to find that the pundit knew where the cauldron was hidden, and he said, "Who can have put it there?"

"You," answered the pundit and told how he had discovered it.

The wrestler and the pearl shooter were surprised at the pundit's wisdom. The three clever men returned to the house and amused themselves, laughing and talking all the rest of the day. When evening came, the pundit said to the wrestler, "Friend strongman, pray go and catch the fattest of goats on the hills, and we will cook it for our dinner."

"Of course." And off the wrestler went to the flock of goats browsing on the hillside.

Now, just at that moment a wicked little demon saw the wrestler looking at the goats. The demon thought, "If I can make him choose me, and take me home for his dinner, I shall be able to play him and his friends some fine tricks."

So, quick as thought, the demon changed himself into a fat, handsome goat. When the wrestler saw this one goat so much taller, and finer, and fatter than all the rest, he caught him, tucked him under his arm, and carried him home for dinner.

The pundit heard the wrestler coming and ran out to meet him. But when he saw the goat, he started back in terror, for the goat's eyes were evil looking and burning like two living coals.

"That is a demon!" the pundit thought. "But if I show fear, it will get into the house and devour us all."

So, in a bold voice, he cried, "Oh, wrestler, wrestler, foolish friend, what have you done? We asked you to fetch a fat goat for our dinner, and here you have only brought one wretched little demon. If you could not find goats, while you were about it, you might as well have brought more demons, for we are hungry people. My children are each accustomed to eating one demon a day, and my wife eats three, and I, myself, eat twelve. And here you have brought only one between us all! What are we to do?"

The wrestler was so surprised that he dropped the demon goat. The demon was so frightened at the pundit's words that he came crawling along humbly on his knees.

"Oh sir, do not eat me, do not eat me, and I will give you anything you like in the world. Only let me go, and I will fetch you mountains of treasure—rubies and diamonds and gold and precious stones beyond all count. Do not eat me. Only let me go!"

"No, no," said the pundit; "I know what you will do. You will just go away and never return. We are very hungry. We do not want gold and precious stones, but we want a good dinner. We certainly must eat you."

The demon believed the pundit. Earnestly, he cried, "Let me go, and I promise you to return and bring you all the riches that you could desire."

The pundit was too wise to seem glad. He said sternly, "Very well, you may go. But unless you return quickly and bring the treasure you promise, no matter where you hide, we will find you and eat you. For we are more powerful than you and all your fellows."

The demon already knew the strength of the wrestler and he had heard the pundit express his love for eating demons. He fled, thinking himself lucky to be alive, and took a vast amount of treasure to pay his debt. Then, several other demons caught him and asked where he was going with so much treasure.

The demon answered, "I take it to save my life, because I was caught by terrible sons of men. And they threaten to eat me unless I bring the treasure."

"We should like to see these dreadful creatures," the demons said. "For we never heard of mortals who devoured demons."

"I tell you, these are not ordinary mortals. They are the fiercest creatures I ever saw and would devour our rajah himself, if they got the chance."

They let him go, but the demon rajah ordered him to return the next day.

When, after three days' absence, the demon returned to the pundit's house with the treasure, the pundit asked angrily, "Why have you been so long away? You promised to return as soon as possible."

"My fellow demons detained me. Though I told them how great and powerful you are, they would not believe me. But they will, as soon as I return, judge me in solemn council for serving you."

"Where is your solemn council held?" asked the pundit.

"Oh, very far, far away, in the depths of the jungle, where our rajah daily holds his court," said the demon.

"I and my friends should like to see the place, and your rajah, and all his court," the pundit said. "You must take us with you when you go, for we have absolute mastery over all demons, even over your rajah himself."

"Very well," the demon said. "Mount on my back, and I will take you there."

So the demon flew away with the pundit, the wrestler, and the pearl shooter as fast as wings could cut the air, until they reached the great jungle where the council was to be held. He let them off on the top of a high tree just over the demon rajah's throne.

In a few minutes the pearl shooter, the wrestler, and the pundit heard a rushing noise. Thousands and thousands of demons filled the place, thronging around the rajah's throne.

Then, the rajah ordered, "Let the demon who took some of our treasure to give to mortals be brought to judgment!"

The other demons dragged the guilty one forward. But he said, "Noble rajah, those who forced me to fetch them treasure were no ordinary mortals, but great and terrible. They said they ate many demons. The man who commanded me eats twelve a day, his wife eats three, and each of his children eats one. He also said that he and his friends were more powerful than us all, and that he ruled, Your Majesty, as absolutely as we are ruled by you."

The demon rajah roared, "Let us see these great people of whom you speak!"

The tree upon which the pundit, the pearl shooter, and the wrestler were hiding broke, and down they all tumbled onto the demon rajah. So suddenly did they appear that they seemed to have fallen from the sky.

The three men were alarmed at their awkward landing, and they decided as one to attack. So the wrestler kicked and hugged and beat the rajah with all his might and main, as did the pearl shooter, while the pundit, who was perched up a little higher than either of the others, cried, "So be it! So be it! We will eat him first for dinner, and afterwards we will eat all the other demons!"

The thousands and thousands of demons panicked at hearing this, and they fled away from the confusion, leaving their rajah to his fate.

"Oh, spare me!" the rajah cried. "Spare me! I see it is all true. Let me go, and I will give you as much treasure as you like."

"No, no," said the pundit, "do not listen to him, friends. We will eat him for dinner."

The wrestler and the pearl shooter kicked and beat the rajah harder than before. Then, the demon cried again, "Let me go! Let me go!"

"No, no!" they answered and continued to kick and beat him until they feared they were growing dangerously tired.

Then, the pundit said, "The treasure would be no use to us here in the jungle, but if you brought us a great deal to our house, we might give up eating you for dinner today. You must, however, give us great compensation, for we are all very hungry."

To this, the demon rajah gladly agreed. Calling together his scattered subjects, he ordered them to take the three valiant men home again and convey the treasure to the pundit's house. The demons obeyed his orders with fear and trembling, for they were eager to get the pundit, the pearl shooter, and the wrestler out of Demonland.

When they got home, the pundit said to the demons, "You shall not leave until the engagement is fulfilled." Instantly, demons without number filled the house with riches and then flew away in terror.

So, by never showing that he was afraid, this brave pundit saved his family from being eaten by these evil spirits and also got a vast amount of treasure. He divided the spoil into three equal portions—a third to the wrestler, a third to the pearl shooter, and a third he kept himself—after which he sent his friends with many kind words back to their own homes.

So the pearl shooter returned to his house laden with gold and jewels of priceless worth. When he got there, he called his wife and gave them to her, saying, "I have been on a long journey, and brought back all these treasures for you. And I have learnt that your words were true, since in the world there are cleverer men than I. For mine is a cleverness that profits not, and if it had not been for a pundit and a wrestler, I should not have gained these riches. I will shoot the pearl from your nose ring no more."

And he never did.

Sources

Beck, Brenda E.F., Peter J. Claus, Praphulladatta Goswami, and Jawaharlal Handoo, eds. *Folktales of India*. Chicago: University of Chicago Press, 1987.

Frere, Mary. *Old Deccan Days, or, Hindoo Fairy Legends Current in Southern India, Collected from Oral Tradition*. London: J. Murray, 1868.

O'ouk'en and O'okemp'an: A Folktale from the Tehuelche of Argentina

The Tehuelche today are no longer considered a separate people, having been almost completely assimilated into the Argentinian Spanish culture. But their stories were collected and saved by folklorists before the assimilation was complete.

An O'ouk'en, in Tehuelche tradition, is a man who always tells the truth. He also is often a heroic man of wisdom who can overcome obstacles by thinking them through.

O'okemp'an was a terrible being, a monster who lured children away from their homes and then ate them. He walked on all fours and looked like a horrible cross between a huge pig and a turtle.

One day, O'okemp'an began to feed on children from a certain village. The village's warriors tried to fight, but their spears simply bounced off the terrible being's heavy shell, and he took no notice of them.

The village shaman knew no magic that would stop so strange a being. So he went instead to an O'ouk'en, a truth teller he knew. "Can you do anything to rid us of this O'okemp'an?"

"Of course," the O'ouk'en said, and that was the truth. "Tell this O'okemp'an that I am coming to see him. Tell him I really do wish to speak with him, and tell him to meet me at noon on the mountainside above the high cliff."

So the shaman told the O'okemp'an that there was someone who really wanted to speak with the being, and he told the O'okemp'an where to meet the man.

The O'okemp'an was glad for the chance to boast. Here came the man, all alone and unarmed.

"You wish to speak with me," the O'okemp'an said.

"Yes. I always have wanted to do so. I wanted to meet you and see that you were real," the O'ouk'en replied.

"I am very real!"

"Would you tell me about yourself?" the O'ouk'en asked.

The O'okemp'an began to talk. He talked and talked about all the children he had lured to their deaths. He talked and talked, and he did not notice that the O'ouk'en had moved behind him.

The O'ouk'en gave a mighty shove. The O'okemp'an went flying off the cliff and crashed to his death at the bottom.

"No more children will be stolen," the O'ok'en said.

Source

Wilbert, Johannes, and Karin Simoneau, eds. *Folk Literature of the Tehuelche Indians.* Los Angeles: UCLA Latin American Center Publications, 1984. Collected from Feliciana Velazquez de Martinez, ca. 1963. A similar version was collected from Ana Montenegro de Yebes, also ca. 1963.

Bibliography

Aarne, Antii, and Stith Thompson. *The Types of the Folktale: A Classification and Bibliography.* Helsinki, Finland: Academia Scientifarum Pennica, 1987.

Abbott, Gerry, and Khin Thant Han. *The Folk-Tales of Burma: An Introduction.* Boston, Köln, Germany, and Leiden, The Netherlands: Brill, 2000.

Addy, Sidney Oldall. *Household Tales with Other Traditional Remains.* London: David Nutt, 1895.

Afanas'ev, Aleksander. *Russian Fairy Tales.* New York: Pantheon, 1945.

Aghajanian, Alfred, ed. *Armenian Literature: Comprising Poetry, Drama, Folklore, and Classic Traditions.* IndoEuropeanPublishing.com, 2007.

Andrade, Manuel J. *Folklore from the Dominican Republic.* Memoirs of the American Folklore Society. Vol. 23. New York: American Folk-Lore Society, 1930.

Anonymous. *Folk Tales from China.* 3rd series. Peking, China: Foreign Languages, 1958.

Armitage, Simon, trans. *Sir Gawain and the Green Knight.* New York: W.W. Norton, 2007.

Asbjornsen, Peter Christen, and Jorgen Engebretsen Moe. *East o' the Sun and West o' the Moon.* Trans. George Webbe Dasent. New York: Dover, 1970.

———. *Popular Tales from the Norse.* Trans. George Webbe Dasent. New York: G.P. Putnam, 1896.

Ashliman, D.L. *Fairy Lore: A Handbook.* Westport, CT, and London: Greenwood, 2006.

———. *A Guide to Folktales in the English Language.* New York, Westport, CT, and London: Greenwood, 1987.

Asihene, Emmanuel. *Traditional Folk-Tales of Ghana.* Lampeter, United Kingdom: Edwin Mellen, 1997.

Aung, Maung Htin. *Burmese Folk-Tales.* Calcutta, India: Oxford University Press, 1948.

Ausubel, Nathan. *A Treasury of Jewish Folklore.* New York: Crown, 1948.

Barbier, Jean. *Legendes Basques.* Baiona, France: Elkar, 1991.

Baring-Gould, Sabine. *Curious Myths of the Middle Ages.* New Hyde Park, NY: University Books, 1967; New York: Oxford University Press, 1978.

Barnouw, Victor. *Wisconsin Chippewa Myths & Tales and Their Relation to Chippewa Life.* Madison: University of Wisconsin Press, 1977.

Baudis, Josef. *The Key of Gold: 23 Czech Folk Tales.* London: Allen & Unwin, 1917; Iowa City, IA: Penfield, 1992.

Beath, Paul R. *Febold Feboldson: Tall Tales from the Great Plains.* Lincoln: University of Nebraska Press, 1948.

Beck, Brenda E.F., Peter J. Claus, Praphulladatta Goswami, and Jawaharlal Handoo, eds. *Folktales of India.* Chicago: University of Chicago Press, 1987.

Bellamy, John. *Robin Hood: An Historical Enquiry.* Bloomington, IN: Indiana University Press, 1985.

Benedict, Ruth. *Tales of the Cochiti Indians.* Bureau of American Ethnology Bulletin no. 98. Washington, DC: Smithsonian, 1931.

Berry, Jack, collector and trans., and Richard Spears, ed. *West African Folk Tales.* Evanston, IL: Northwestern University Press, 1991.

Bierhorst, John. *Latin American Folktales: Stories from Hispanic and Indian Traditions.* New York: Pantheon, 2002.

Birkhauser-Oeri, Sibylle. *The Mother: Archetypical Image in Fairy Tales.* Trans. Michael Mitchell. Toronto, Ontario, Canada: Inner City Books, 1988.

Blamires, David. *Robin Hood: A Hero for All Times.* Manchester, United Kingdom: The John Rylands University Library of Manchester, 1998.

Boas, Franz. *Folk-Tales of Salishan and Sahaptin Tribes.* Memoirs of the American Folk-Lore Society. Vol. 11. Lancaster, PA, and New York: American Folk-Lore Society, 1917.

Bogoras, Waldemar. *Tales of Yukaghir, Lamut, and Russianized Natives of Eastern Siberia.* Anthropological Papers of the American Museum of Natural History. Vol. 20, part 1. New York: Trustees of the American Museum of Natural History, 1918.

Bompas, Cecil Henry. *Folklore of the Santal Parganas.* Salem, NH: Ayer, 1977.

Booss, Claire, ed. *Scandinavian Folk and Fairy Tales: Tales from Norway, Sweden, Denmark, Finland, Iceland.* New York: Avenel, 1984.

Botkin, B.A. *A Treasury of American Folklore.* New York: Crown, 1944.

Bowman, James Cloyd, and Margery Bianco, eds. *Tales from a Finnish Tupa.* Trans. Aili Kolehmainen. Chicago: A. Whitman, 1936.

Brean, Herbert, et al., eds. *The Life Treasury of American Folklore.* New York: Time, 1961.

Briggs, Katherine M. *British Folk-Tales.* New York: Pantheon, 1970.

———. *A Dictionary of British Folk-Tales in the English Language.* 4 vols. London: Routledge and Kegan Paul, 1970–1971.

Briggs, Katherine M., and Ruth L. Tongue. *Folktales of England.* Chicago and London: University of Chicago Press, 1965.

Bruford, Alan, and Donald A. MacDonald. *Scottish Traditional Tales.* Edinburgh, United Kingdom: Polygon, 1994.

Bueno, Salvador. *Cuban Legends.* Trans. Christine Ayorinde. Kingston, Jamaica:

Ian Randle, 2003; Princeton, NJ: Markus Wiener, 2003.

Bunanta, Murti, and Margaret Read MacDonald. *Indonesian Folktales.* Westport, CT: Libraries Unlimited, 2003.

Butler, Bill. *The Myth of the Hero.* London: Rider, 1979.

Calvino, Italo. *Italian Folktales.* New York: Harcourt Brace Jovanovich, 1980.

Campbell, C.G. *Tales from the Arab Tribes: The Oral Traditions Among the Great Arab Tribes of Southern Iraq.* London, New York, and Bahrain: Kegan Paul, 2007.

Campbell, J.F. *Popular Tales of the West Highlands.* Vol. 2. Edinburgh, United Kingdom: Edmonton and Douglas, 1860.

Campos, Anthony John. *Mexican Folktales.* Tucson: University of Arizona Press, 1978.

Carrison, Muriel Paskin, and the Venerable Kong Chhean. *Cambodian Folk Stories from the Gatiloke.* Rutland, VT, and Tokyo, Japan: Charles E. Tuttle, 1987.

Chamberlain, Basil Hall. *Aino Folk-Tales.* London, 1888.

Chandran, Praphulla Satish. *Folk Tales of Karnataka.* New Delhi, India: Sterling, 1985.

Chappell, Louis W. *John Henry: A Folk-Lore Study.* Port Washington, NY: Kennikat, 1983.

Child, Francis J. *The English and Scottish Ballads.* Vol. 2. Mineola, NY: Dover, 1962.

Chin, Yin-lien. *Traditional Chinese Folktales.* Armonk, NY: M.E. Sharpe, 1989.

Clouston, W.A. *The Book of Noodles: Stories of Simpletons; or, Fools and Their Follies.* London: Elliot Stock, 1888; Detroit, MI: Gale Research, Book Tower, 1969.

Coffin, Tristram Potter. *Indian Tales of North America: An Anthology for the Adult Reader.* Philadelphia: American Folklore Society, 1961.

Coffin, Tristram Potter, and Hennig Cohen. *The Parade of Heroes: Legendary Figures in American Lore.* Garden City, NY: Anchor/Doubleday, 1978.

Cortes, L., trans. *Byelorussian Folk Tales.* Minsk, Byelorussia: Vysheishaya Shkola, 1983.

Courtlander, Harold. *The Drum and the Hoe: Life and Lore of the Haitian People.* Berkeley and Los Angeles: University of California Press, 1960.

Courtlander, Harold, and Ousmane Sako. *The Heart of the Ngoni: Heroes of the African Kingdom of Segu.* Amherst: University of Massachusetts Press, 1994.

Cowan, James. *Fairy Folk Tales of the Maori.* Wellington, New Zealand: n.p., 1930.

Cox, Marian Roalfe. *Cinderella: Three Hundred and Forty-Five Variants of Cinderella, Catskin, and Cap O' Rushes, Abstracted and Tabulated, with a Discussion of Mediaeval Analogues, and Notes.* London: David Nutt for the Folk-lore Society, 1893.

Crane, Thomas Frederick. *Italian Popular Tales.* New York and Oxford, United Kingdom: Oxford University Press, 2003.

Crockett, Davy. *Davy Crockett's Almanac.* New York: Cozans, 1854.

Croker, Thomas Crofton. *Fairy Legends and Traditions of the South of Ireland.* Vol. 2. London: Murray, 1828.

Crossley-Howard, Kevin, ed. *The Faber Book of Northern Folk-Tales.* London and Boston: Faber and Faber, 1980.

Curtin, Jeremiah. *Irish Folk-Tales.* Dublin: Educational Company of Ireland, 1943.

———. *Tales of the Fairies and of the Ghost World Collected from Oral Tradition in South-West Munster.* Boston: Little, Brown, 1895; New York: B. Blom, 1971.

Damant, M. "Ashey Pelt." *Folk-Lore* 6 (1895): 305–306.

Davidson, H.R.E. *The Hero in Tradition and Folklore.* Mistletoe Series. Vol. 19. London: The Folklore Society, 1984.

Davidson, Hilda Ellis, and Anna Chaudhri, eds. *Supernatural Enemies.* Durham, NC: Carolina Academic Press, 2001.

Davis, Jonathan Ceredig. *Folk-Lore of West and Mid-Wales.* Norwood, PA: Norwood Editions, 1974.

Dawkins, R.M. *More Greek Folktales.* London: Oxford University Press, 1955.

Dayrell, Elphinstone. *Folk Stories from Southern Nigeria, West Africa.* London: Longmans, Green, 1910; New York: Negro Universities Press, 1969.

De Blumenthal, Verra Xenophontovna Kalamatiano. *Folk Tales from the Russian.* 1903. Great Neck, NY: Core Collection, 1979.

de Souza, Eunice. *101 Folktales from India.* New Delhi, India: Puffin, 2004.

Degh, Linda, ed. *Folktales from Hungary.* Chicago and London: University of Chicago Press, 1969.

Dixon-Kennedy, Mike. *The Robin Hood Handbook: The Outlaw in History, Myth and Legend.* Gloucestershire, United Kingdom: Sutton, 2006.

Djurklou, Gabriel. *Fairy Tales from the Swedish.* Trans. H.L. Brækstad. New York: Frederick A. Stokes, 1901.

Dolitsky, Alexander. *Tales and Legends of the Yupik Eskimos of Siberia.* Trans. Henry N. Michael. Juneau: Alaska-Siberia Research Center, 2000.

Dorsey, George A. *Traditions of the Osage.* Publication no. 88, Anthropological Series. Vol. 7, no. 1. Chicago: Field Columbian Museum, 1904.

Dorson, Richard M. *America in Legend: Folklore from the Colonial Period to the Present.* New York: Pantheon, 1973.

———. *Bloodstoppers and Bearwalkers: Folk Tradition of the Upper Peninsula.* Cambridge, MA: Harvard University Press, 1952.

———. *Folk Legends of Japan.* Rutland, VT, and Tokyo, Japan: Charles E. Tuttle, 1962.

Douglas, George. *Scottish Fairy and Folk Tales.* London: Walter Scott, 1901.

Downing, Charles. *Armenian Folk-Tales and Legends.* Oxford, United Kingdom: Oxford University Press, 1993.

Dundas, Alan. *Cinderella: A Folklore Casebook.* New York and London: Garland, 1982.

Duvoisin, Roger. *The Three Sneezes and Other Swiss Tales.* New York: Alfred A. Knopf, 1951.

Eastman, Charles A. *Wigwam Evenings: Sioux Tales Retold.* Lincoln: University of Nebraska Press, 1990.

Eastman, Max. "Davy Crockett as Demigod." *Scribners Magazine* (July 1936): 10.

Ebbutt, M.I. *The British: Myths and Legends.* 1910. London: Senate, 1994.

Eberhard, Wolfram. *Folktales of China*. Chicago and London: University of Chicago Press, 1965.

Edwards, Gillian. *Hobgoblin and Sweet Puck: Fairy Names and Natures*. London: Geoffrey Bles, 1974.

Edwards, L.C. "Antoine Barada." In *History of Richardson County, Nebraska: Its People, Industries and Institutions*. Indianapolis, IN: B.F. Bowen, 1917.

Egan, Joseph B. *New Found Tales from Many Lands*. Philadelphia: John C. Winston, 1929.

El Koudia, Jilali, ed. *Moroccan Folktales*. Trans. Jilali El Koudia and Roger Allen. Syracuse, NY: Syracuse University Press, 2003.

Emrich, Duncan. *Folklore on the American Land*. Boston and Toronto, Ontario, Canada: Little, Brown, 1972.

Erdoes, Richard, and Alfonso Ortiz, eds. *American Indian Myths and Legends*. New York: Pantheon, 1984.

Felton, Harold W., ed. *Legends of Paul Bunyan*. New York: Alfred A. Knopf, 1948.

Fielde, A.M. *Chinese Fairy Stories*. New York: G.P. Putnam Sons, 1893.

Fillmore, Parker. *The Laughing Prince: Jugoslav Folk and Fairy Tales*. New York: Harcourt, Brace, 1921.

Fourie, Coral. *Living Legends of a Dying Culture: Bushmen Myths, Legends, and Fables*. Pretoria, South Africa: Ekoglide, 1994.

Fowke, Edith. *Folklore of Canada*. Toronto, Ontario, Canada: McClelland and Stewart, 1976.

Frachtenberg, Leo J. *Coos Texts. Columbia University Contributions to Anthropology*. Vol 1. New York: Columbia University Press, 1913.

Frachtenberg, Leo J., and Henry H. St. Clair. "Traditions of the Coos Indians of Oregon." *Journal of American Folklore* 22 (1909).

Frere, Mary. *Old Deccan Days, or, Hindoo Fairy Legends Current in Southern India, Collected from Oral Tradition*. London: J. Murray, 1868.

Furness, William H. *Folklore in Borneo: A Sketch*. 1899. Whitefish, MT: Kessinger, 2003.

Fyleman, Rose. *Folk-Tales from Many Lands*. Toronto, Ontario, Canada: Methuen, 1954.

Garry, Jane, and Hasan El-Shamy, eds. *Archetypes and Motifs in Folklore and Literature: A Handbook*. Armonk, NY: M.E. Sharpe, 2005.

Gastner, Moses. *The Exempla of the Rabbis*. London and Leipzig, Germany: Asia Publishing, 1924.

Gerould, Gordon Hall. *The Grateful Dead: The History of a Folk Story*. London: David Nutt, 1908.

Giddings, Ruth Warner. *Yaqui Myths and Legends*. Anthropological Paper no. 2, University of Arizona, 1959. Tucson: University of Arizona Press, 1959.

Giskin, Howard. *Chinese Folktales*. Lincolnwood, IL: NTC, 1997.

Glassie, Henry. *Irish Folk Tales*. New York: Pantheon, 1985.

Golovnev, Andrei V., and Gail Osherenko. *Siberian Survival: The Nenets and Their Story*. Ithaca, NY: Cornell University Press, 1999.

Grayson, James H. *Myths and Legends from Korea: An Annotated Compendium of Ancient and Modern Materials*. London: Routledge, 2000; Richmond, United Kingdom: Curzon, 2001.

Greenway, John. *Folklore of the Great West*. Palo Alto, CA: American West, 1969.

Gregory, Lady Augusta. *Poets and Dreamers: Studies and Translations from the Irish*. Dublin, Ireland: Hodges, Figgis, 1903.

Grimm, Jacob, and Wilhelm Grimm. *The Complete Fairy Tales of the Brothers Grimm*. Trans. Jack Zipes. New York: Bantam, 1987.

———. *Household Tales*. Trans. Margaret Hunt. London: George Bell, 1884; Detroit, MI: Singing Tree, 1968.

Griswold, Jerry. *The Meanings of Beauty and the Beast: A Handbook*. Toronto, Ontario, Canada: Broadview, 2004.

Groome, Francis Hindes. *Gypsy Folk Tales*. 1899. Whitefish, MT: Kessinger, 2004.

Halliday, William Reginald. *Greek and Roman Folklore*. New York: Cooper Square, 1963.

Han, Suzanne Crowder. *Korean Folk and Fairy Tales*. Elizabeth, NJ: Hollym, 1991.

Haney, Jack V. *The Complete Russian Folktale*. Armonk, NY: M.E. Sharpe, 1999.

Hanghe, Ahmed Artan. *Folktales from Somalia*. Uppsala, Sweden: Somalia Academy of Arts and Sciences, in cooperation with the Scandinavian Institute of African Studies, 1988.

Hangin, John Gombojab, ed. *Mongolian Folklore: A Representative Collection from the Oral Literary Tradition*. Bloomington, IN: The Mongolia Society, 1998.

Hansen, Harry. *New England Legends and Folklore*. New York: Hastings House, 1967.

Hansen, William F., ed. *Anthology of Ancient Greek Popular Literature*. Bloomington: Indiana University Press, 1998.

Hardin, Terri. *A Treasury of American Folklore: Our Customs, Beliefs, and Traditions*. New York: Barnes & Noble, 1994.

Hartland, Edwin Sidney. *English Fairy and Other Folk Tales*. London: Walter Scott, 1890.

———. *The Science of Fairy Tales: An Inquiry into Fairy Mythology*. London: Walter Scott, 1891.

Hayes, Joe. *Cuentos de Cuanto Hay: Tales from Spanish New Mexico*. Albuquerque: University of New Mexico Press, 1998.

Henderson, Helena. *The Maiden Who Rose from the Sea and Other Finnish Folktales*. Enfield Lock, United Kingdom: Hisarlik, 1992.

Hla, Ludu U. *Folktales of Burma*. Mandalay, Burma: Letsaigan, Gondanwin, 1972.

Hofberg, Herman. *Swedish Fairy Tales*. Trans. W.H. Myers. Chicago: W.B. Conkey, 1893.

Hole, Christina. *Saints in Folklore*. New York: William Morrow, 1965.

Hoskin, John, and Geoffrey Walton. *Folk Tales and Legends of the Dai People: The Thai Lue in Yunnan, China*. Trans. Ying Yi. Bangkok, Thailand: D.D., 1992.

Hulpach, Vladimir, Emanuel Frynta, and Vaclav Cibula. *Heroes of Folk Tale and Legend*. Trans. George Theiner. London, New York, Sydney, Australia, and Toronto, Ontario, Canada: Hamlyn, 1970.

Hunt, Robert. *Cornish Legends*. Truro, Cornwall, United Kingdom: Tor Mark, 1969.

———. *Popular Romances of the West of England*. London: John Camden Hotten, 1871.

Jackson, Guida M. *Traditional Epics*. New York and Oxford, United Kingdom: Oxford University Press, 1994.

Jacobs, Joseph. *English Fairy Tales*. London: David Nutt, 1890.

———. *More English Fairy Tales*. London: David Nutt, 1894.

Jacobs, Melville, ed. *Nehalem Tillamook Tales*. 1956. Corvallis: Oregon State University Press, 1990.

Jagendorf, M. *New England Bean Pot: American Folk Stories to Read and to Tell*. New York: Vanguard, 1948.

Jazyk zheltyx ujgurov (Folktales of the Western Yugur). Moscow, Russia: n.p., 1967. *The Seven Fools* was recorded by Qasqaji, a storyteller from the village Donghaizi (present-day Mínghai), in November 1910.

Jenness, Diamond. *Eskimo Folklore: Myths and Traditions from Northern Alaska, the McKenzie Delta and Coronation Gulf*. Honolulu, HI: University Press of the Pacific, 2002.

Johns, Andrea. *Baba Yaga: The Ambiguous Mother and Witch of the Russian Folktale*. International Folkloristics. Vol. 3. New York: Peter Lang, 2004.

Johnson, Charles, and Se Yang, eds. *Myths, Legends and Folk Tales from the Hmong of Laos*. St. Paul, MN: Linguistics Department, Macalester College, 1985.

Johnston, Basil H. *Tales the Elders Told: Ojibway Legends*. Toronto, Ontario, Canada: University of Toronto Press, 1993.

Kapchits, G.L., ed. and trans. *Faaliyihii la Bilkeyday: A Soothsayer Tested: Somali Folktales*. Moscow, Russia: By the Way, 2006.

Karajich, Vuk. *Serbian Folk-Tales*. Trans. Wilhelmine Karajich. Berlin, Germany, 1854.

Kavcic, Vladimir. *The Golden Bird: Folk Tales from Slovenia*. Trans. Jan Dekker. Cleveland, OH, and New York: World, 1969.

Keightley, Thomas. *The Fairy Mythology*. London: Bohn, 1850.

Kingsley, Charles. *Hereward the Wake*. London: Macmillan, 1895.

Kirby, W.F. *The Hero of Esthonia and Other Studies in the Romantic Literature of that Country*. London: John C. Ninmo, 1895.

Klipple, May Augusta. *African Folktales with Foreign Analogues*. The Garland Folklore Library. New York and London: Garland, 1992.

Knappert, Jan. *Myths and Legends of Botswana, Lesotho and Swaziland*. Leiden, The Netherlands: E.J. Brill, 1985.

Knowles, H.J. *Folk-Tales of Kashmir*. London: Trübner, 1893.

Kroeber, Alfred L. "Tales of the Smith Sound Eskimo." *Journal of American Folk-Lore* 12:7 (1899): 166–182.

Kunos, Ignácz. *Forty-four Turkish Fairy Tales*. London: George G. Harrap, 1913.

Kvideland, Reimund, and Henning K. Sehmsdorf, eds. *Scandinavian Folk Belief and Legend*. Minneapolis: University of Minnesota Press, 1988.

Lang, Andrew. *The Brown Fairy Book*. London and New York: Longmans, Green, 1904.

Lawson, Polly, ed. *Swedish Folktales*. Edinburgh, United Kingdom: Floris, 2004.

Leavy, Barbara F. *In Search of the Swan Maiden: A Narrative on Folklore and Gender*. New York: New York University Press, 1994.

Lee, Edward. *Haunted House: And Other Presidential Horrors*. Hiram, GA: Overlook Connection, 2007.

Leeming, David, and Jake Page. *Myths, Legends and Folktales of America: An Anthology*. New York and Oxford, United Kingdom: Oxford University Press, 1999.

Leland, Charles G. *The Algonquin Legends of New England, or, Myths and Folk Lore of the Micmac, Passamaquoddy, and Penobscot Tribes*. Boston: Houghton Mifflin, 1884.

Leslau, Wolf. *Gurage Folklore: Ethiopian Folktales, Proverbs, Beliefs, and Riddles*. Wiesbaden, Germany: Franz Steiner Verlag, 1982.

Lewis, Paul W. *Akha Oral Literature*. Bangkok, Thailand: White Lotus, 2002.

Li, Shujiang, and Karl W. Luckert, eds. *Mythology and Folklore of the Hui, a Muslim Chinese People*. Albany: State University of New York Press, 1994.

Li, Xuewei, trans. *Ada and the Greedy King and Other Chinese Minorities Folktales*. Singapore, Kuala Lampur, and Hong Kong, China: Federal Publications, 1991.

Lindahl, Carl, John McNamara, and John Lindahl, eds. *Medieval Folklore: A Guide to Myths, Legends, Tales, Beliefs, and Customs*. New York: Oxford University Press, 2002.

Louis, Liliane Nerette. *When Night Falls, KRIC! KRAC!: Haitian Folktales*. Englewood, CO: Libraries Unlimited, 1999.

Macdougall, A.K., ed. *Australian Folklore. Two Centuries of Tales, Epics, Ballads, Myths and Legends*. Sydney, Australia: Reed, 1990.

MacManus, Seamus. *The Well o' the World's End*. New York: Macmillan, 1939.

Marshall, Bonnie C. *Tales from the Heart of the Balkans*. Englewood, CO: Libraries Unlimited, 2001.

Massignon, Genevieve. *Folktales of France*. Chicago: University of Chicago Press, 1968.

Mathers, Powys, trans. *The Book of the Thousand Nights and One Night, Rendered into English from the Literal and Complete French Translation of J.C. Mardrus*. London: Routledge and Kegan Paul, 1964.

Mayer, Fanny Hagin, trans. *Ancient Tales in Modern Japan: An Anthology of Japanese Folk Tales*. Bloomington: Indiana University Press, 1984.

Mbiti, John, ed. *Akamba Stories*. The Oxford Library of African Literature. London: Oxford University Press, 1966.

McCall Smith, Alexander. *The Girl Who Married a Lion and Other Tales*. New York: Random House, 2005.

McLaughlin, Marie L. *Myths and Legends of the Sioux*. Lincoln and London: University of Nebraska Press, 1990.

Megas, Georgios A. *Folktales of Greece*. Chicago and London: University of Chicago Press, 1970.

Melancon, Claude. *Indian Legends of Canada*. Trans. David Ellis. Toronto, Ontario, Canada: Gage, 1974.

Menon, T. Madhava, Deepak Tyagi, and B. Francis Kulirani, eds. *People of India: Kerala*. Vol. 27. New Delhi, India: Affiliated East-West Press for Anthropological Survey of India, 2002.

Metternich, Hilary Roe. *Mongolian Folktales*. Boulder, CO: Avery, in association with University of Washington Press, 1996.

Metzger, Fritz. *The Hyena's Laughter: Bushmen Fables*. Windhock, Namibia: Kuiseb-Verlag, 1995.

Mijatovies, Madam Csedomille. *Serbian Folk-Lore*. New York and London: Benjamin Blom, 1874.

Moe, Saw Wai Lwin. *Golden Boy and Other Stories from Burma*. Bangkok, Thailand: White Lotus, 2001.

Mooney, James. *James Mooney's History, Myths, and Sacred Formulas of the Cherokees*. 1900. Asheville, NC: Bright Mountain, 1982.

Muir, Tom. *The Mermaid Bride and Other Orkney Folk Tales*. Kirkwall, United Kingdom: Orcadian, 1998.

Muller-Guggenbuhl, Fritz. *Swiss Alpine Folk Tales*. London: Oxford University Press, 1958.

Narvaez, Peter, ed. *The Good People: New Fairylore Essays*. New York and London: Garland, 1991.

Negi, Dev Singh. *A Tryst with the Mishmi Hills*. New Delhi, India: Tushar, 1997.

Noy, Dov. *Folktales of Israel*. Trans. Gene Baharav. Chicago: University of Chicago Press, 1963.

Nozaki, Kiyoshi. *Kitsune: Japan's Fox of Mystery, Romance and Humor*. Tokyo, Japan: Hokuseido, 1961.

Oates, Stephen B. *Abraham Lincoln: The Man Behind the Myth*. New York: Harper & Row, 1984.

Olivelle, Patrick, trans. *The Panchatantra: The Book of India's Folk Wisdom*. New York: Oxford University Press, 2002.

Opler, Morris Edward. *Myths and Legends of the Lipan Apache Indians*. New York: American Folk-Lore Society, 1940.

Orbell, Margaret. *The Illustrated Encyclopedia of Maori Myth and Legend*. Christchurch, New Zealand: Canterbury University Press, 1995.

———. ed. and trans. *Traditional Maori Stories*. Aukland, New Zealand: Reed, 1992.

Orkneyjar: The Heritage of the Orkney Islands. http://www.orkneyjar.com.

Osborne, Mary Pope. *American Tall Tales*. New York: Scholastic, 1992.

O'Sullivan, Sean, ed. and trans. *Folktales of Ireland*. Chicago and London: University of Chicago Press, 1966.

Papashvily, George, and Helen Papashvily. *Yes and No Stories: A Book of Georgian Folk Tales*. New York: Harper and Brothers, 1946.

Paredes, Americo, ed. *Folktales of Mexico*. Chicago: University of Chicago Press, 1970.

Parker, H. *Village Folk-Tales of Ceylon*. London: Luzac, 1910–1914.

Parker, K. Langloh. *Australian Legendary Tales*. London: Senate, 1998.

Parmasad, Kenneth Vidia. *Salt and Roti: Indian Folk Tales of the Caribbean, a First Collection*. Trinidad and Tobago: Sankh Productions, 1984.

Parsons, Elsie Clews. *Micmac Folklore*. Whitefish, MT: Kessinger, 2007.

———. *Tewa Tales*. New York: American Folk-Lore Society, 1926.

Pedroso, Consiglieri. *Portuguese Folk-Tales*. Folk Lore Society Publications. Vol. 9. Trans. Henriqueta Monteiro. New York: Folk Lore Society Publications, 1882.

Perrault, Charles. *Old-Time Stories Told by Master Charles Perrault*. Trans. A.E. Johnson. New York: Dodd Mead, 1921.

Petrovitch, Woislav M. *Hero Tales and Legends of the Serbians*. London: George G. Harrap, 1914.

Philip, Neil. *The Cinderella Story: The Origins and Variations of the Story Known as "Cinderella."* London and New York: Penguin, 1989.

Pigorini-Beri, Caterina. "*La Cenerentola a Parma e a Camerino*" (Cinderella in Parma and in Camerio). *Archivio per la Studio delle Tadizioni Popolari* (Archive for the Study of Popular Culture), Palermo, Italy, 1883.

Pottinger, J.A. "The Selkie Wife." In *Old-Lore Miscellany of Orkney, Shetland, Caithness and Sutherland*. Vol. 1. 1908. Leicester, United Kingdom: The Viking Society for Northern Research, 1992.

Pourrat, Henri. *French Folktales from the Collection of Henri Pourrat*. Trans. Royall Tyler. New York: Pantheon, 1989.

———. *Le tresor de contes*. 7 vols. Paris: Gallimard, 1977–1986.

Premaratne, Geetha. *Andare: Folktales from Sri Lanka*. Linton, Australia: Papyrus, 1999.

Proust, Pierre-Yves. *Legendes, Contes et Recits des Pays Bretons*. Marseilles, France: Editions Autre Temps, 1995.

Pun, Angela, and Paul W. Lewis. *49 Lahu Stories*. Bangkok, Thailand: White Lotus, 2002.

Quang, Mai Ly. *Vietnamese Legends and Folk Tales*. Hanoi, Vietnam: Thé Gioi, 2001.

Radin, Paul. *Culture of the Winnebago: As Described by Themselves*. Baltimore: Waverly, 1949.

Ragan, Kathleen. *Fearless Girls, Wise Women, and Beloved Sisters: Heroines in Folktales from Around the World*. New York and London: W.W. Norton, 1998.

Ralston, W.R.S. *Russian Folk-Tales*. London: Smith, Elder and Son, 1873.

———. *Tibetan Tales*. Delhi, India: Sri Satguru, 1988.

Ramanujan, A.K. *A Flowering Tree and Other Oral Tales from India*. Berkeley and London: University of California Press, 1997.

———. *Folktales from India*. New York: Pantheon, 1991.

Ramos, Maximo D. *The Creatures of Philippine Lower Mythology*. Quezon City, Philippines: Phoenix, 1971.

———. *Legends of the Lower Gods*. Quezon City, Philippines: Phoenix, 1990.

Ranke, Kurt. *Folktales of Germany*. Trans. Lotte Baumann. Chicago: University of Chicago Press, 1966.

Rasmussen, Knud. *Eskimo Folk-Tales*. Trans. W. Worster. London: Gylglendal, 1921.

Ratcliff, Ruth. *German Tales and Legends*. London: Century Hutchinson, 1982.

Reader, H.J. *Newfoundland Wit, Humour and Folklore*. St. John's, Newfoundland, Canada: Macy's, 1982.

Rhys, John. *Celtic Folklore*. Vol. 1. Oxford, United Kingdom: Oxford University Press, 1901.

Riordan, James. *The Sun Maiden and the Crescent Moon: Siberian Folk Tales*. Edinburgh, United Kingdom: Cannongate, 1989.

Rooth, Anna Birgitta. *The Cinderella Cycle*. Lund, Norway: Skanska Centraltryckeriet, 1911.

Ross, Anne. *Folklore of Wales*. Stroud, United Kingdom, and Charleston, SC: Tempus, 2001.

Roth, John E. *American Elves: An Encyclopedia of Little People from the Lore of 380 Ethnic Groups of the Western Hemisphere*. Jefferson, NC, and London: McFarland, 1997.

Rutter, Owen. *The Dragon of Kinabalu and Other Borneo Stories*. Sabah, Malaysia: Natural History Publications, 1999.

Ryder, Arthur, trans. *The Panchatantra Translated from the Sanskrit*. Chicago: University of Chicago Press, 1958.

Sabar, Yona. *The Folk Literature of the Kurdistani Jews: An Anthology*. London and New Haven, CT: Yale University Press, 1982.

Sanders, Tao Tao Liu. *Dragons, Gods and Spirits from Chinese Mythology*. New York: Schocken, 1983.

Saul, G.B. *The Wedding of Sir Gawain and Dame Ragnell*. New York: Prentice Hall, 1934.

Savory, Phyllis. *Bantu Folk Tales from Southern Africa*. Cape Town, South Africa: Howard Timmins, 1974.

Schultz, George F. *Vietnamese Legends*. Rutland, VT, and Tokyo, Japan: Charles E. Tuttle, 1965.

Seal, Graham. *The Outlaw Legend: A Cultural Tradition in Britain, America and Australia*. Cambridge, United Kingdom, and New York: Cambridge University Press, 1996.

Seki, Keigo, ed. *Folktales of Japan*. Trans. Robert J. Adams. Chicago: University of Chicago Press, 1969.

Serwer-Bernstein, Blanche L. *In the Tradition of Moses and Mohammed: Jewish and Arab*

Folktales. Northvale, NJ, and London: Jason Aronson, 1994.

Severo, Emoke de Papp. *Hungarian and Transylvanian Folktales*. Nepean, Ontario, Canada: Borealis, 1997.

Shack, William A. *The Gurage: A People of the Ensete Culture*. London: Oxford University Press, 1966.

Sherman, Josepha. *Mythology for Storytellers: Themes and Tales from Around the World*. Armonk, NY: M.E. Sharpe, 2003.

———. *Rachel the Clever and Other Jewish Folktales*. Little Rock, AR: August House, 1993.

———. *A Sampler of Jewish-American Folklore*. Little Rock, AR: August House, 1992.

———. *Storytelling: An Encyclopedia of Mythology and Folklore*. Armonk, NY: M.E. Sharpe, 2008.

Shigeru, Kayano. *The Ainu: History, Culture and Folktales*. Rutland, VT, and Tokyo, Japan: Charles E. Tuttle, 2004.

Sholey, Arthur. *The Discontented Dervishes and Other Persian Tales*. London: Watkins, 2002.

Shujiang, Li, and Karl W. Luckert, eds. *Mythology and Folklore of the Hui, a Muslim Chinese People*. Albany: State University of New York Press, 1994.

Sikes, Wirt. *British Goblins: Welsh Folk-Lore, Fairy Mythology, Legends, and Traditions*. Boston: Osgood, 1881.

Simpson, Jacqueline. *European Mythology*. New York: Peter Bedrick, 1987; London: Hamlyn, 1987.

———. *Icelandic Folk Tales and Legends*. Berkeley: University of California Press, 1979.

Skinner, Charles M. *Myths & Legends of Our Own Land*. Vol. 1. Philadelphia and London: J.B. Lippincott, 1896.

Smith, David Lee. *Folklore of the Winnebago Tribe*. London and Norman: University of Oklahoma Press, 1997.

Soebiantoro, Afwani, and Manel Ratnatunga. *Folk Tales of Indonesia*. New Delhi, India: Sterling, 1983.

Soupault, Ré, ed. *Breton Folktales*. Trans. Ruth E.K. Meuss. London: G. Bell & Sons, 1971.

Spears, Richard, ed. *West African Folk Tales*. Collected and trans. Jack Berry. Evanston, IL: Northwestern University Press, 1991.

Steckmesser, Kent L. "Robin Hood and the American Outlaw: A Note on History and Folklore." *Journal of American Folklore* 79 (1966): 348–355.

Steel, Flora Annie. *English Fairy Tales*. London: Macmillan, 1918.

Sumner, Laura, ed. *The Weddynge of Sir Gawen and Dame Ragnell*. Northhampton, MA: Smith College Department of Modern Languages, 1924.

Swahn, Jan-Ojvind. *The Tale of Cupid and Psyche*. Lund, Norway: Hakan Ohlssons Boktryckeri, 1955.

Swanton, John R. *Myths and Tales of the Southeastern Indians*. Bureau of American Ethnology Bulletin no. 88. Washington, DC: Smithsonian Institution, 1929.

Tahhan, Samir. *Folktales from Syria*. Austin: University of Texas, 2004.

Tayeng, Obang. *Mishmi Folk Tales of Lohit Valley*. New Delhi, India: Mittal, 2007.

Teit, James A. "The Man Who Married a Branch." *Journal of American Folklore* (1912): 309.

Terada, Alice M. *The Magic Crocodile and Other Folktales from Indonesia*. Honolulu: University of Hawaii Press, 1994.

Thompson, Stith. *Folk Tales of the North American Indians*. 1929. North Dighton, MA: J.G., 1995.

———. *The Folktale*. Berkeley, Los Angeles, and London: University of California Press, 1977.

———. *One Hundred Favorite Folktales*. Bloomington and Indianapolis: Indiana University Press, 1968.

Thundy, Zacharias P. *South Indian Folktales of Kadar*. Sadar, India: Archana, 1994.

Tolkien, J.R.R. *Sir Gawain and the Green Knight, Pearl, Sir Orfeo*. New York: Del Rey, 1979.

Tong, Diane. *Gypsy Folktales*. New York: Harvest, 1989.

Tremearne, Arthur John Newman. *Hausa Superstitions and Customs: An Introduction to the Folk-Lore and the Folk*. 1913. London: Frank Cass, 1970.

Turner, Lucien M. "Ethnology of the Ungava District, Hudson Bay Territory." In *Report of the Bureau of American Ethnology*. Vol. 11. Washington, DC: Smithsonian Institution, 1894.

Walker, Barbara. *The Art of the Turkish Tale*. Vol. 1. Lubbock: Texas Tech University Press, 1990.

———. *The Art of the Turkish Tale*. Vol. 2. Lubbock: Texas Tech University Press, 1993.

Walker, Warren S., and Ahmet E. Uysal. *Tales Alive in Turkey*. Cambridge, MA: Harvard University Press, 1966.

Walton, Geoffrey, ed. *A Northern Miscellany: Essays from the North of Thailand*. Bangkok, Thailand: Silkworm, 1989.

Wardrop, Marjory. *Georgian Folk Tales*. London: David Nutt, 1894.

Warner, Marina. *From the Beast to the Blonde: On Fairy Tales and Their Tellers*. New York: Farrar, Straus and Giroux, 1994.

Webster, Wentworth. *Basque Legends*. London: Griffith and Farran, 1877.

Wei, Cuiyi, and Karl W. Luckert. *Uighur Stories from Along the Silk Road*. Lanham, MD, and New York: University Press of America, 1998.

Welsch, Roger J. *A Treasury of Nebraska Pioneer Folklore*. Lincoln: University of Nebraska Press, 1984.

Wheeler, Howard T. *Tales from Jalisco, Mexico*. Philadelphia: American Folklore Society, 1943.

Wilbert, Johannes, ed. *Folk Literature of the Selknam Indians: Martin Guisinde's Collection of Selknam Narratives*. Los Angeles: UCLA Latin American Center Publications, 1975.

Wilbert, Johannes, and Karin Simoneau, eds. *Folk Literature of the Tehuelche Indians*. Los Angeles: UCLA Latin American Center Publications, 1984.

Wonderly, Anthony. *Oneida Iroquois Folklore, Myth, and History: New York Oral Narrative from the Notes of H.E. Allen and Others*. Syracuse, NY: Syracuse University Press, 2004.

Wratislaw, A.H. *Sixty Folk-Tales from Exclusively Slavonic Sources*. Boston: Houghton Mifflin, 1890.

Wrigglesworth, Hazel J. *The Maiden of Many Nations: The Skymaiden Who Married a Man from Earth*. Manila: Linguistic Society of the Philippines, 1991.

Yolen, Jane. *Favorite Folktales from Around the World*. New York: Pantheon, 1986.

Zhang, Song Nam. *Ballad of Mulan*. Union City, CA: Pan Asian Publications, 1998.

Zheleznova, Irina, ed. and trans. *Estonian Fairy Tales*. Tallinn: Perioodika, 1981.

———. *Ukrainian Folk Tales*. Kiev, Ukraine: Dnipro, 1986.

Zipes, Jack, trans. and ed. *Beautiful Angiola: The Great Treasury of Sicilian Folk and Fairy Tales Collected by Laura Gonzenbach*. London and New York: Routledge, 2004.

———. *The Robber with a Witch's Head: More Stories from the Great Treasury of Sicilian Folk and Fairy Tales Collected by Laura Gonzenbach*. London and New York: Routledge, 2004.

Zitkala-Sa. *Old Indian Legends*. Boston, New York, and London: Ginn, 1901; Lincoln: University of Nebraska Press, 1985.

Index